D0712114

PAOLO SPRIANO teaches the history of political parties at the University of Rome. He is the author of a five-volume *History of the Italian Communist Party*, and of numerous studies of Gramsci, Gobetti, Togliatti, socialism in Turin, and other subjects.

Paolo Spriano

Verso

Stalin and The European Communists

Translated by Jon Rothschild

British Library
Cataloguing in Publication Data

Spriano, Paolo
  Stalin and the European Communists.
  1. Communism — Europe — History — 20th century
  I. Title II. I comunisti europei e Stalin.
  English
  335.43'094   HX238

First published as *I comunisti europei e Stalin*
by Giulio Einaudi editore
© 1983 Giulio Einaudi editore s.p.a., Torino

Verso edition first published 1985
© Verso 1985

Verso
15 Greek Street London W1V 5LF

Filmset in Garamond
by PRG Graphics Ltd
Redhill, Surrey

Printed in Great Britain by
The Thetford Press Ltd
Thetford, Norfolk

ISBN 0 86091 103 9

Contents

Foreword

The title of this book should give sufficient indication of its scope and subject matter. It presents a historical investigation of the relation between Stalin and that portion of the international Communist movement which operated in Europe from the eve of the Second World War to the immediate post-war period. These limits in time and space, however, are not rigidly observed, for considerable reference will be made to preceding and subsequent periods and to events in other centres of the Communist movement, from Asia to the Americas.

In substance, the relation in question was hierarchical, and the hierarchy was accepted by all the Communist parties in fair weather and foul. Its distinctive feature, perhaps, was that Stalin was at once leader and acknowledged master of the movement, and absolute ruler of a country, a state that was drawn into the war and emerged from it with a victory that profoundly altered the foundations of international relations, turning the USSR into a great world power.

Although the book never loses sight of this narrative, it also seeks to present a synthetic view of the history of the Communist movement, through the often tragic vicissitudes, the many unexpected turns, of one of its most turbulent and least-studied periods: from the last Congress of the Third International (1935) to the dissolution of that organization in 1943, from the years of wartime Resistance to the establishment of a new organ, the so-called Cominform, which opened a new historical phase (1947–48). The common characteristics and experiences of the various Communist parties prior to the Cold War's division of Europe into two camps are examined, while due note is taken of the particular national features that emerged during and after the war, which helped make for a stormy evolution of the general situation and contained the seeds of future schisms.

Within the indicated chronological limits, each chapter has been conceived as a sort of dialogue with the conclusions and hypotheses of the abundant available literature. No deeper understanding of the epoch and of the evolution of the Communist movement is possible without engaging with the quite diverse historical writings about the various episodes relating to our central theme, and without critical scrutiny of the lively memoirs and numerous press sources.

Materials such as this may well constitute the starting point of any investigation of contemporary history, but in this case contingent factors make them especially decisive. On the one hand, conjectures and deductions are unavoidable, since many essential archives remain inaccessible (those of the Kremlin, for example, as well as those of the Soviet and most other Communist parties). On the other hand, when dealing with such controversial matters, one must strive to place them in their actual historical context, resisting the temptation to view the past with the benefit of hindsight. At the same time, much contemporary debate about socialism, and in particular about the involution of the systems of rule typical of what has come to be called 'actually existing socialism', would undoubtedly be enriched by the background of historical knowledge that may be gleaned from the dramatic decade examined here. The results we draw today will in turn influence the way we view the past.

Many different issues are dealt with in this book. Some relate to the general history of the great events of the period, to classic disputes that have been debated repeatedly over the past forty years (the significance of the Munich pact of 1938; the nature of the German-Soviet treaty of 1939; the prospects offered by the international conferences of Tehran and Yalta; the causes of the Cold War). Others concern the dialectic of the workers movement more directly: the demise of the Comintern; Trotskyism and the birth of the Fourth International; the time of the Popular Fronts in France and Spain; the decline and laborious new rise of the Socialist International.

Other questions are examined because of their own intrinsic interest, beyond the temporal limits of this book. An example is the famous history of the Soviet Communist Party known as the 'Short Course', which was a sort of *summa* of Marxism-Leninism for entire generations; I propose that it should be read partly as indicative of the immediate orientations of Soviet foreign policy and partly as a durable doctrinal 'model' of party and state. Another example is the 1939–41 period of Soviet neutrality (up to the Nazi invasion), which is itself no less disconcerting than Stalin's well-known 'astonishment' at the invasion. A third example is a great problem that emerged again in subsequent decades, albeit in different terms: the attempts to reunify the workers movement, to heal the rift between its Socialist and Communist components. Here we will follow the uncertain course and ultimate failure of those attempts — during 1935–37 and immediately after the war — in those countries in which 'organic unity' seemed closest to success.

The final question of this kind is the demand for national autonomy, the call for 'polycentrism' in European (and non-European) Communism, the rise and concrete manifestations of which became evident during the Resistance, in Yugoslavia as in Italy and France, in Greece as in Bulgaria and Czechoslovakia. The various theorizations of this concept, expressed in 1946–47 in the formulas 'new roads to socialism' and 'democracy of a new type' are considered, along with how and why this impetus was crushed from above, as the Communist movement congealed anew, partly as a result of the mounting conflict between the two major victorious powers, the United States and the Soviet Union. The book ends here, on the threshold of the Cold War, although we will take note of the episode that heralded a historic schism destined to provoke new incidents of post-war crisis: the 'excommunication' of Tito in June 1948.

Through it all looms the figure of Stalin: his political and ideological personality, his methods of rule, the repression with which his name is sullied, his use of theory as an instrument to justify momentary tactical zigzags. The book is therefore a contribution to the analysis of Stalinism and its characteristics and consequences, and also seeks to provide a vantage point from which to observe broader tendencies and contradictions of the Communist movement, both when it was mired in adversity (the book opens with a sort of group portrait of the movement in the spring of 1939) and when it enjoyed extraordinary numerical, political, and intellectual expansion, as in 1945–47.

Acknowledgements

I would have liked to have thanked all those who gave me useful advice and information, but they are far too numerous to list. I would at least like to mention those who contributed directly to the work: above all Corrado Vivanti, who encouraged me to undertake the research. Special thanks are due to the members of the Gramsci Institute of Rome, where the research was done, including the director, Aldo Schiavone, and my many friends in the Institute's library and archives, who very kindly facilitated my access to books, maps, and journals. The courtesy of Mr Stephen Bird of the Labour Party archives in London and of the personnel of the Bibliothèque de Documentation Contemporaine of the University of Nanterre (Paris) was also invaluable. Thanks also to Giorgio Caredda for having supplied me with documents he tracked down in French archives of the period of Nazi occupation. Finally, warm thanks to Antonietta Sciancalepore for her distinguished work in typing the manuscript and in improving the text and notes.

1

A Million or More

The Eighteenth Congress of the Communist Party of the Soviet Union opened in the 'great hall' of the Kremlin on the afternoon of 10 March 1939. A marble statue of Lenin 'looked out over the table of the Presidium', according to the official minutes of the session.[1] The next day, Dimitri Manuilski mounted the podium to deliver his report on 'the activity of the Soviet delegation to the Executive Committee of the Communist International'. When he concluded with the customary encomium to Stalin, the 'genius of toiling humanity' who 'tirelessly watches over the interests of the working class of the entire world', he was greeted, according to the notation in the minutes, with 'thunderous applause'. The entire assembly rose to its feet and cried: 'Hurrah! Long live the great leader of world Communism!'

Manuilski's speech, however, like those of Stalin, Molotov, and Zhdanov, reflected not so much enthusiasm as a tense concern on the part of the Soviet party and people about an international situation of mounting gravity. The Spanish Republic was living out its final, tragic days. Catalonia had already fallen, and Madrid was on the point of defeat. On 15 March Hitler's motorized troops occupied Prague. Not by chance was the prevalent theme of the Congress the 'new imperialist war', which, Stalin said, was 'already a reality', albeit still only a 'strange and one-sided reality', since it had not yet become 'a general war, a world war.'[2]

Manuilski ran dutifully through the usual outline of analysis and predictions, which I will come to in a moment. But his report is of special interest because it offered a rare listing of the forces of international Communism during one of the bleakest and most difficult moments of its history. Nearly four years had passed since the Seventh Congress of the International, which turned out to be its last. The internal life of that organization, conceived and founded by

Lenin twenty years before, had become increasingly stifled and bureaucratized. Plenary sessions of the Executive (the famous 'plenums' held so frequently in the twenties and early thirties) were no longer even convened, nor would they ever be again. The years 1936 to 1939 had seen both glorious battles and internal tragedies. Thousands of Communist cadres had lost their lives fighting in the International Brigades in Spain. The policy of the Popular Front had been a fundamental historical stage for the movement in France, Spain, and elsewhere, but it, too, was over now. Only in China, where Communists and Nationalists were fighting the Japanese invaders, had unity in struggle with other political and social forces been preserved, and even there it was unsteady enough, already under attack.

Dimitri Manuilski had much to say, and more than a little to withhold, for Stalinist repression had also wreaked havoc among the many members and leaders of the Comintern who had taken refuge in the USSR, and the Polish party had even been secretly dissolved. Manuilski himself was Ukrainian. While undoubtedly of less political and intellectual personal force than Dimitrov or Togliatti — who were generally considered the number one and two men of the Comintern — he was no mediocrity: a man of spirit, of vigorous character and acute intelligence, according to various contemporaries.[3] Although he was an old Bolshevik (born in 1883) who had been close to Trotsky in 1917, Manuilski later won Stalin's confidence during the struggle against the various opposition currents. For some time he had been posted to the Secretariat of the International, dealing mostly with the parties of Western Europe, and he was by no means stingy in his often bitter criticism of them. His authority rested on the fact that he was the Soviet party's representative to the Presidium and the Executive, and the CPSU was incomparably superior to the other parties not only in prestige, but also in numbers: alone it had more members than all the Communist parties of the five continents put together. The Soviet party was the model, the beacon, the very essence of an internationalism whose first language was Russian.

In a pamphlet published in 1939 to accompany a book which we will later consider as a political-ideological phenomenon in its own right (the 'compendium' of the history of the Bolshevik Party), Manuilski affirmed that 'the country of victorious socialism is implementing the proletarian internationalism of Lenin and Stalin.[4] But the absolute, unchallengeable supremacy of the CPSU rested not so much on the proportion (or rather disproportion) of forces as on the general and constantly reiterated identification of the cause of the USSR with the cause of international Communism, both in principle and in fact.

What was the general picture presented in Manuilski's report? He said that there were a total of one million and two hundred thousand Communists 'in the capitalist countries'. The reporter did not give the number of party members in the 'land of socialism', but according to Malenkov's report at the same congress, there were 1,589,000 'active members'[5] (and this was a party vastly pruned by the purges and arrests of 1936–38). The figure for 'foreign' Communists was highly approximate. Manuilski himself noted that his count did not include 'tens of thousands' of militants fighting underground or languishing in the prisons and concentration camps of the fascist countries or under reactionary dictatorships. Tens of thousands of German Communists, for example, had been interned in Hitler's camps since 1933 (in the space of six years regular German courts sentenced some 225,000 people for political offences; the arrest level remained high even after the initial wave of terror had subsided: 11,687 people were arrested for Communist activities in 1936, and 8,068 in 1937).[6] The Italian Communists had been underground for twelve years; several thousands of them, old and young alike, remained in Italy scattered in small groups with little contact either among themselves or with their exile centre in Paris, while about eight hundred were in internal exile. The older Communists sentenced by the Special Tribunal were now joined in prison by two or three hundred newly arrested and sentenced comrades.[7]

Manuilski was particularly critical of the failings of the Italian Communist Party (PCI), whereas he had only praise for the Spanish Communists. He reckoned that there were three hundred thousand of them at the time of his report (including the forty-five thousand members of the United Socialist Party of Catalonia, the PSUC), but at that very moment they were threatened by the ferocious manhunt of the victorious Francoists: there were summary executions, arrests, and prison sentences, while the harsh Vernet camp had been opened for those who managed to escape over the French border. Tens of thousands of veterans of the Republican Army had been herded into internment camps in North Africa.[8]

The only European Communist party that was still a genuine mass party was the French, with its two hundred and seventy thousand members, and it received due praise from Manuilski. The other parties, in order of membership, were those of Czechoslovakia, with 60,000 members (underground since the Munich conference, and about to face German occupation); Sweden, with 19,000; Britain, with 18,000; Holland, with 10,000; Denmark, with 8,000; and Belgium, with 7,000. The reporter gave no figures for party membership in east-central Europe or the Balkans. We will return to the case of Poland shortly. As for the rest, other sources suggest that the Yugoslav Communist Party — also underground, and now under its soon-to-be-legendary general secretary Josip Broz Tito — had 3,000 members (plus another 17,800 members in the Communist Youth, or Skoj).[9] The Romanian and Hungarian parties consisted of a few hundred persecuted members, as did the Bulgarian, which, however, had more sturdy roots. The Communist Party of Albania (another country that was about to be invaded, by fascist Italy in April 1939) did not yet exist. The Greek Communist Party, on the other hand, had already proven itself a combative force, although it was racked by factional divisions. When the struggle against the Metaxas dictatorship began in 1936, the party had 17,500 members; now, in the spring of 1939, with its main leader, Nikos Zachariades, in prison (the young leader Maltezos had been murdered during a police interrogation) and despite its dramatic internal conflict, it remained a militant grouping prepared for long resistance to the fascist aggressors.[10]

Such, more or less, was the organizational state of European Communism on the eve of the Second World War. These forces did not exhaust the international movement, although the Kremlin's viewpoint had been rather 'Eurocentric' for at least a decade. Manuilski also mentioned the Chinese Communists (saying that they had 148,000 members),[11] the Communist Party of the United States (claiming that it numbered some 90,000),[12] and two significant-sized parties in Latin America, in Mexico (30,000 members) and Cuba (23,000). But exactly what was the purpose of international Communism? What was it meant to be, and how successful was it? Manuilski was reticent on a number of essential points, not even commenting on the extent of the clandestinity that was becoming nearly universal for the various parties affiliated to the Third International. Yet the list of those sections 'mired' in the most complete illegality was impressive: the German, Austrian, Spanish, Portuguese, and Czechoslovakian parties had now been joined by the Greek, Bulgarian, Romanian, Hungarian, Turkish, and Tunisian. Most of the Communist parties of the Middle East were illegal (that is, where they existed at all), and in the Far East the Japanese (60,000 of whose members had been arrested in the space of ten years, according to Manuilski) and Indonesian parties were illegal, while the Indo-Chinese party, already barely legal, was outlawed by the French authorities (along with the PCF itself) when the war broke out. In Latin America the Brazilian, Argentinian, Peruvian, and several other parties were illegal.

The historical and psychological fact of this illegality must on no account be overlooked. Communists — members of a political formation representing a small minority and considered partners of the Kremlin, against which Japan, Italy, and Germany had already formed a pact — were persecuted nearly everywhere even before world war broke out. Prison was often the tomb of Communists, but also their school of doctrine and character. A few legendary figures were already part of the Communists' new moral and sentimental patrimony: Georgi Dimitrov, the 'hero of Lipsia', who in 1933 had placed his Nazi judges in the dock; Dolores Ibarruri, 'La Pasionaria', symbol of the resistance of the Spanish Republic; Carlos Prestes, the Brazilian 'horseman of hope' who had been serving ten years in solitary confinement since 1936. Then there were the martyr-leaders of their respective parties: the Italian Antonio Gramsci, who died in 1937 after ten years of torment; the Hungarian Mátyás Rákosi, imprisoned since 1925; the German Ernst Thälmann, interned in a concentration camp from which he would never emerge alive. Spain was the crucible in which new military commanders of the people were being forged: Modesto, Lister, Carlos (Vittorio Vidali), to all of whom the Eighteenth Congress of the Communist Party of the Soviet Union paid great homage.

Manuilski's report was not without its epic moment, for he hazarded this admittedly one-sided historic judgement: for the first time since the October Revolution and the immediate post-war conflagrations of 1919–21, great masses were in motion; Communists stood at the head of struggles that had turned into armed clashes in Spain and China. In the former country, the Republic had resisted for nearly three years, and Manuilski assured his audience that the fight was not over yet; in the latter, a new page of inestimable value was being written with the Long March of 1934–35 and the creation of a people's army that was now battling the Japanese aggressors (although Soviet praise was by no means limited to the Communist component of the anti-Japanese forces). In both cases it was and remained an anti-fascist struggle. That was the distinctive feature of the epoch of the Popular Fronts, which would be the bridge to the epoch of national resistance.

It was a phase of transition, and from this point of view Manuilski's report exhibits various shifts, instances of uncertainty, and patches of obscurity. The interpretative schema was more or less the following, a construction we shall encounter again when discussing the international crisis of 1939 and the foreign policy of the USSR . The cause of both the war that has already begun and the war soon to erupt is the inescapable crisis of the capitalist and imperialist world. That world is divided into aggressive states on the one hand (Germany, Italy, and Japan) and states satisfied with the existing order on the other. Just because they are satisfied, these latter states want peace, although they remain imperialist and colonialist by nature. But despite their superior economic and military resources, the so-called 'democracies' have been and still are unable to mount effective resistance to the bloc of fascist countries. The reason for this is that they do not want to resist effectively, because they are led by reactionary and fiercely anti-communist ruling groups. For Manuilski, as for the Soviet government, the black day of Munich, the surrender to the Nazis in September 1938 by the British government of Chamberlain and the French government of Daladier, was not caused by illusions or pacifistic cowardice. If the immediate result of Munich had been the end of Czechoslovakian independence and a fatal blow to the Spanish Republic, it also revealed an overt design on the part of 'world reaction': to encourage the Nazis to unleash their aggression in the East, against the Soviet Union. In this regard, Manuilski was even more explicit than Stalin. He said:

> The bloc of fascist aggressors has been and still is supported by the forces of world reaction, by the reactionary elements of the French and especially the English bourgeoisie. These elements dream of using German fascism as a battering-ram of reaction against the USSR, of employing it as a gendarme against the international working class, against the Popular Front and the liberation movement of the oppressed peoples. The plan of the reactionary English bourgeoisie is to sacrifice the small states of south-east Europe to German fascism in order to direct Germany to the East, against the USSR, and to try, through this counter-revolutionary war, to halt the advance of socialism and the victory of communism in the USSR, and thus to divert Germany's imperialistic claims on British colonies. Moreover, English reaction would like to use the USSR to break the back of German imperialism, to weaken Germany for many years to come, to maintain the supremacy of English imperialism in Europe. A secondary aim of English reaction is to divide Spain and the Mediterranean sphere of influence with Italy, to the detriment of France, in order to bring about an imperialist equilibrium in Europe, and obtain an agreement with Italy, luring her away from Germany. In the third place, in the Far East the English reactionaries dream of dividing up China. Today they allow Japan to ravage and weaken China, while at the same time they

fail to oppose the military and economic expansion of Japan, so that they can later act as arbiters and establish a 'Munich peace' in the Far East. In the fourth place, English reaction has no wish to see the collapse of the fascist regimes in Germany, Italy, and Japan, and intends to help the governments of these countries save themselves from bankruptcy by offering them credit, thus also making the fascist states dependent on English imperialism to some extent.[13]

For the moment, what is of interest to us in Manuilski's indictment of English imperialism and its global plans is the light it sheds on his general view of the world. It confirms that Munich was indeed a watershed: not only the USSR, but the entire Communist movement felt that the accord represented the betrayal of the policy of collective security against Hitlerite aggression. Was the Popular Front policy therefore condemned as a failure? Manuilski did not say that it had failed, and even formally continued to advocate it. But the tone had changed completely, and the failure was thereby registered implicitly, indirectly. The Comintern leader now spoke to the Socialist International as though reading a bill of indictment rather than a call to re-establish anti-facist unity. Although Communist polemics against 'Social Democracy' had not ceased completely during the previous four years, there had been no further talk of unmasking the reactionary leaders of the Second International as agents of imperialism. But now the tone tended to shift back to that of 1923–33, the decade of deepest division between Socialism and Communism. Manuilski now held that the task of the working class was to exert pressure from below against the 'capitulators', against the 'Munichites', against the Social Democratic leaders, who had now been exposed as 'implacable enemies' of the Popular Front.

This was not a mere propagandist shift. The Socialist International was deeply divided. Munich had sharpened the internal conflicts, and the fissures now opening were not so much between left and right, as they had clearly been in 1934–37, but between national sections. The French Socialists, for example, maintained that the September 1938 surrender to Hitler had been necessary, while the British Labour Party criticized it bitterly (as did prestigious conservatives like Churchill and Lloyd George); the Scandinavian, Belgian, Dutch, and Swiss Socialist parties had taken agnostic positions. It has been noted quite correctly that 'for the second time since its foundation, the Socialist International was heading into a world war that would demonstrate the substantially illusory character of Social Democratic internationalism when faced with a decisive conflict of national interests.'[14]

For the moment, there were no such fissures in the Communist International. But the whole context of Manuilski's report suggests a situation that allows little room for any alliances or mass movements in Western Europe. His call for the defence of peace is also more than a little hazy in view of his basic assessment that conflict, already initiated among contending imperialists, is now inevitable. Another traditional theme was also resurrected: this conflict would entail an armed attack on the 'bastion of peace', the USSR, whose defence was therefore once again the fundamental task of the 'international working class'.

That stormy spring of 1939, which saw the fall of Spain and Czechoslovakia, two of the last democratic states of Europe, was a season of defeat for the entire workers movement and saw the impotence of its international organizations, which had virtually disappeared from the scene. The gun would soon have the floor, after the palaver in the chancelleries had continued for another few months. And yet the decline of the Popular Fronts, the exhaustion and collapse of various national coalitions and experiments, was not yet completely definitive. Echoes were still heard, effects still felt. Although the Popular Front experience was now virtually drowned in polemic and division, it is at least appropriate to note the factors that made the 'Fronts' more than a mere episode or tactical formula, but a milestone in the long history of the Communist movement. At the same time if we keep in mind the condition and attitude of the movement at the beginning of 1939, we will more clearly grasp just how exceptional the previous five years had been.

Notes

1. *La Correspondance Internationale*, vol. 18, no. 11, 13 March 1939, p. 232.

2. Ibid., no. 14, p. 283.

3. See, in particular, Ernst Fischer, *An Opposing Man*, London 1974, pp. 296-98.

4. D. Manuilski, *Lenin e il movimento operaio internazionale*, Edizione italiane di cultura, Paris 1939, p. 15.

5. See Leonard Schapiro, *The Communist Party of the Soviet Union*, London 1960.

6. Giorgio Vaccarino, *Storia della Resistenza in Europa: 1938–45 (I paesi dell' Europa centrale)*, Milan 1981, p.59.

7. Paolo Spriano, *Storia del Partito comunista italiano*, Turin 1970–73, vol. 3, pp. 336-48, vol. 4, pp. 36-39. For the figures given by the fascist police authorities for those sentenced by the Special Tribunal and those sentenced to internal exile, see Renzo de Felice, *Mussolini: il duce*, II, *Lo Stato totalitario*, Turin 1981, pp. 45-48.

8. Cesare Colombo, *Storia del Partito comunista spagnolo*, Milan 1972, pp. 144 and 149-53.

9. Phyllis Auty, *Tito*, Harmondsworth 1974, p. 162. The number increased between 1939 and 1941. 'By April 1941, the number of CPY members had grown to 8,000, of whom about 3,000 were in prison.' (Josip Broz Tito, *The Struggle and Development of the CPY Between the Two Wars*, Belgrade 1979, p. 68.

10. Antonio Solaro, *Storia del Partito comunista greco*, Milan 1973, pp. 57 and 77-96.

11. The membership of the Chinese Communist Party soared from year to year: from 40,000 in 1937 it rose to 800,000 in 1940. The great mass base for this recruitment was the peasantry. See Jacques Guillermaz, *Storia del Partito comunista cinese 1921–1949*, Milano 1970, p. 404.

12. The figure corresponds to the one given by Joseph Starobin, *American Communism in Crisis, 1943–1957*, Cambridge, Mass. 1972, p. 21.

13. From the text of Manuilski's report, published 'in extenso' in *La Correspondance Internationale*, vol. 19, no. 22, 24 April 1939, p. 450.

14. The quotation is from Werner Röder, cited in Rolf Steininger, 'L'Internazionale socialista dopo la seconda guerra mondiale', report published in *La sinistra europea nel secondo dopoguerra 1943–1949*, Florence 1981, p. 139.

2
The Movement's Advance Guard

In Communist terminology, 'the turn' *par excellence* was the shift in policy of 1929–30. But the real turn, the point at which the sharpest break with the past occurred, came in 1934–38, during the time of the Popular Fronts, anti-fascist unity, and the left 'united front'. Was this a genuine change in strategy? This remains a matter of historical and political controversy, and doubts and fine distinctions between tactical and strategic turns proliferated as the long-term effects of the contradictory features of that period, with its extraordinary innovations and its underpinning not merely of continuity but of dogmatic rigidification, emerged and took root in 'historic memory'. It seems clear that the greatest contradiction was between a courageous policy of unity on the one hand and an aggravation of Stalinist repression on the other, which became a full-blown terror against Soviet Communists and those of other 'fraternal' parties. But to ask the question is to probe the value of the new orientation, to strive to define its scope, to cast doubt on its sincerity or to challenge its coherence.

One thing now seems beyond doubt. Although the policy inaugurated by the Seventh Congress of the Communist International in the summer of 1935 was most closely associated with the names of two of the International's most prestigious leaders, Dimitrov and Togliatti, who had recently risen to positions of great responsibility within the organization, its real architect was Stalin himself. The date at which the new international course was initiated seems equally certain: June 1934 (some have suggested that the first concrete sign of it appeared in an article published in *Pravda* on 30 May).[1] It was then that a belated but salutary lesson was drawn from Hitler's accession to power: the aggressive and destructive dynamic of Nazism was declared the *main enemy* of the workers movement and of peace, as well as a most serious danger to the security of the Soviet Union itself. This was the origin of a shift in perspectives that was further developed in subsequent years. It marked a 180-degree turn from the orientation and slogans of 1930 and 1931–33. In those years, Communist activity was based on total opposition to the Socialist International, which was regarded as just as bad as fascism. The inflammatory term 'social-fascism' was coined to suggest that Social Democracy was an even more dangerous enemy than fascism, since it acted as the bourgeoisie's emissary within the movement and therefore had to be opposed even more strongly the further left it pretended to be. Social Democracy, Stalin warned, was the twin of fascism.

But beyond the formulas, the entire outlook of the Communist leadership condemned the movement to immobile isolation. The Communist view was that capitalism would inevitably give rise to fascism; democratic rights were held to be a mystification. New trade unions had to be set up to counter those led by the Socialists. This 'class against class' line was based on the assumption of a social radicalization, an immediate revolutionary opportunity created by the great economic crisis of the early thirties. On the basis of this view, the French Communists had to deny, against all evidence, that there was a reactionary and subversive right-wing danger in their country. In the 1932 elections they suffered a setback. The German Communists, defeated in their electoral clashes with the Socialists between 1930 and 1932, proved incapable of committing the mass forces they commanded to an effective opposition to Nazism. The lesson of Hitler's victory and of the rapid transformation of the state into a dictatorship was slow to dispel the illusion that the disintegration of the Weimar Republic might lead directly to proletarian revolution, although as early as February 1934 powerful anti-fascist pressure for workers' unity was creating the basis for a reversal of direction and perspectives in France.

The schema of counterposition to Social Democracy finally collapsed under the combined weight of Stalin's concern about the early initiatives of Hitler's foreign policy (which exhibited a 'dynamism' that could well target the East) and the yearning for unity on the part of the French working class, a mood that was now sweeping through the Social Democratic parties and trade unions. Although both the Second and Third Internationals had been weakened by their complete loss of influence (or indeed of any presence at all) in Germany, where triumphant Nazism dissolved all the organizations of the Marxist workers movement, a new political line was being applied further west in Europe, in France and Spain: the policy which considered Popular Fronts urgent and indispensable defensive weapons against the spread of fascism in those countries. In the summer of 1934 an agreement for united action was reached between the PCF and the SFIO, the French Section of the Second International. Reunification of the trade unions was begun, and preparations were made to contest the spring 1936 legislative elections with joint Popular Front lists in both France and Spain. An alliance was sought with Republican, Radical, and Liberal forces in an effort to broaden the workers alignment beyond the bounds of the 'united front' to include non-proletarian, petty-bourgeois, peasant social groups.

The Fronts scored stunning successes at the polls. In both countries the left groupings won the majority of the seats in parliament and the defensive united bloc soon spawned an offensive drive for social change far more sweeping than the initial limits of the Popular Front. In France working class agitation for social demands soared in June 1936, leading to the historic conquest of the forty-hour working week as well as other victories on the wage front. Pressure was mounting, and it could not be easily contained within the framework of gradualist reformism. Masses of peasants, proletarians, and semi-proletarians were in motion in Spain, demanding an agrarian reform that would destroy the semi-feudal structures of the countryside and the abusive power of the large landowners, supported by the Church and the financial oligarchy. Aspirations for complete collectivism, for Communist-libertarian revolution, were extremely powerful throughout the Spanish mobilizations, not only in the unions led by the anarchists (CNT) and the Socialists (UGT), but also among the political forces that had brought the Popular Front its electoral victory.

The Communists were suddenly and unexpectedly thrust into the limelight, assuming responsibilities and attracting forces they could never have hoped for. Even the bare figures are sensational. According to official sources, the PCF had 30,000 members in 1934; by January 1936 the membership had risen to 74,000, and the following year it hit 341,000 as the party registered 254,000 new members between its eighth and ninth congresses. The party's vote doubled between 1932 and 1936, and because of the joint lists presented by the Popular Front, the number of Communist deputies in parliament rose from 10 to 72 (while the Socialists won 149 deputies, and the Radicals 109).[2] In 1930 the Spanish Communists had been a small sect, with about a thousand members. By 1934 they numbered 24,000, and by January 1937 the party claimed no less than a quarter of a million members, to which we must add the 50,000 or so members of the United Socialist Party of Catalonia and the 20,000 militants of the Basque Communist Party. In the February 1936 elections the Communist Party of Spain (PCE) elected 14 of its candidates, while the Frente Popular held 267 seats in all.[3] It is true that the tumultuous growth of the party in Spain was partly the result of the increasingly prominent role played by Communists in the armed defence of the Republic. And Togliatti, who went to Spain as an adviser of the PCE, considered the recruitment figures inflated (he believed that there were slightly more than 200,000 members).[4] But the fact remains that there had been a qualitative leap forward: mass Communist parties now existed in Western Europe for the first time, and they had achieved their status essentially because of a great political turn which was welcomed, supported, and driven forward by masses of workers, peasants, and members of the middle class.

It is the scope and character of this metamorphosis that is of most interest to us here. The French and Spanish Communist parties became the advance guard of the entire movement, although the fundamental decisions, political direction, and major choices all emanated from the International, and therefore directly from Stalin. It was just this fact — that the turn was being led from the centre — that gave it a more general allure. Communism had acquired a new countenance; it spoke with a different voice — not just for a few days or weeks, but for years on end, even though the Popular Front itself did not last long.

In France the party draped itself in the tricolour, speaking in almost querulous patriotic tones and accents. Maurice Thorez, the young secretary of the PCF who now became a symbol of the party's working-class character (he came from the mining district of Pas-de-Calais and liked to be called a 'son of the people'), fought for a united front with the Socialists while calling for broad national unity to include not only Radicals but even Catholics and war veterans. The idea was to isolate a handful of exploiters, the notorious 'two hundred families' of big manufacturers and finance capital. Thorez hailed the 'mission' of France in a manner that was no less sincere for its simultaneous eulogy of the USSR, land of socialism. This excerpt from his report to the Ninth Congress of the PCF, held in December 1937, was typical of his style:

> On the whole, it is legitimate to affirm that life is happier, freer, and more beautiful in France, our country. Apart from the Soviet Union, France now occupies first place in the world; once again it has become a land of progress and liberty.[5]

A literary and artistic Popular Front rhetoric extolled the new dignity and 'beauty' of the workers movement. But there was a very real confluence of intellectual forces, moral values, and democratic spirit that made these years — especially 1934–36 — the first in which the Communist world merged with the humanistic and libertarian tradition of Western Socialism. There was a real sense that a choice had been made, an antithesis posed: anti-fascism became the order of the day. The struggle against fascism was the struggle for civilization, for liberty. It was this spirit that attracted many artists and scientists to the Front, and especially to the Communist parties, as 'fellow travellers'; it was this that enabled the Communists to win over the young vanguard that went to fight in Spain.

As we have seen, the retreat of 1939 saw a retrenchment on both sides, and polemical reprisals rekindled traditional diatribes and ritual accusations. Nor should it be forgotten that even between 1935 and 1937 charges of tactical manoeuvring and deliberate prevarication were levelled at the patriotic and pro-unity Communist movement, which had astonished everyone with its speed in extending its hand to other political forces and its moderation in the heat of the social tension that had brought the left electoral victory. In June 1936 Thorez told workers barricaded in their occupied factories that one had to know how to end strikes as well as start them. The Communist International had even advised its French comrades not to join the Léon Blum government but to support it from outside, in order not to frighten the Radicals on the right wing of the Front coalition.

Programmatically, too, in discussions of social 'projects' of economic planning (if not nationalization), the PCF sought to curb the enthusiasm and impatience of the more intransigent Socialist wing, using the doctrinaire argument that the transition to socialism depended upon the seizure of power, which was not on the agenda.[6] Thorez told the Socialists that the Communists, too, supported socialization, that they desired the 'pure and simple expropriation of the capitalist exploiters'. But, he said, they hold that 'there is a precondition, just one minor precondition, for socialization: to hold power, to take power. Now, there is only one method of taking power . . .and that is the method of the Bolsheviks: the victorious insurrection of the proletariat, the exercise of the dictatorship of the proletariat and soviet power.' It has been pointed out that this response is marred by a 'fissure between tactics and strategy' that 'can render the effectiveness of political action somewhat problematic'.[7]

These are sensitive, even painful, points about Communism's 'ideological state of mind'. They are relevant not only to the years of the Popular Front, but to any period in which there is a popular movement of significant scope. Thus we find, on distinct and non-intersecting levels, an unchanging schematic model for the revolutionary seizure of power and a cautious policy imbued with a 'spirit of compromise'. The dichotomy itself is an obstacle to a proper understanding of the new features of the situation. The relation between politics and economics, and the more general theme of 'transition to socialism', thus remain unexamined and untested.

The PCF of the Popular Front period was wide open to this sort of historical-theoretical criticism, and was frequently subjected to it. It is perfectly true that the 'principles' of Leninism, while part and parcel of the party's intellectual baggage, never impeded its actions in the slightest. The party was 'Bolshevized'. Although Thorez had passed successfully through the Leninist school of Moscow years before, he was nevertheless provided with a Comintern adviser, the mysterious and celebrated Clément (his real name was Eugene Fried, a Czechoslovak citizen, of the minority Hungarian nationality), who proved to be a flexible and intelligent proponent of the new line.[8] Indoctrination — always particularly obstinate in the PCFM took the form of an act of faith that was never modified by the 'new' philosophers the party had absorbed, like Georges Politzer, Henri Lefebvre, and Paul Nizan, the most interesting of these figures intellectually.[9]

Critics alleged that the PCF was more Bolshevik than Leninist, that it was essentially imbued with a strain of 'French ideology' which, in the 'workers' Jacobinism' of Jules Guesde, had laid special emphasis on the Great Revolution of 1789.[10] Historical features like these, traceable over long periods, may well have existed, but the real problem was what to do in practice, how to extend the policy of the Popular Front throughout the country.

Given the political and social realities, the claim that the Communists impeded a revolutionary-socialist development of the situation seems unconvincing.[11] As always, retrospective disputes about what might have happened if the leaders had acted differently are often reflections of current controversies; they are more political than historiographical. And no history of the French Popular Front has seriously doubted that the PCF fought unreservedly and powerfully for the unity and stability of the victorious coalition of spring 1936. The Front's enemies were on the right, where robust class opposition to the left parties was virtually complete. Curiously, Blum himself resorted to an argument little different from Thorez's claim that power had not been seized, partly in order to justify his own weakness and hesitation. At the Riom trial in 1942, as Blum stood in the dock of the Vichy collaborators, he said:

> Even when the elected chamber seemed to have a popular majority, the bourgeoisie retained weapons of resistance which they were temporarily too afraid to use but which were effective once calm had returned. . . . The French bourgeoisie held power: it did not intend to cede or share it. It preserved it completely.[12]

The Front never had a moment's peace. Italian and German fascism were on the offensive in Europe and had more than one card to play in France and Spain. In France, the employers sought to sabotage the accords that had been won by the unions: they launched a 'strike' of their own in the form of the export of capital, stimulated inflationary pressure, and inaugurated an alarmist campaign that had considerable effect on many modest savers. The capitalists sought to take advantage of the social radicalization that the government, for its part, was trying to avert. In Spain the revolt of the generals led by Franco broke out on 17 July and spread rapidly, endangering the very existence of the democratic republic. The 'rebel' troops conquered whole provinces and regions, especially in the south, and soon threatened Madrid and Barcelona.

The internationalization of the Spanish conflict threw the entire left alignment into crisis. Popular resistance in Spain succeeded in preventing a sudden collapse, but Blum lacked the courage to commit France to supply the massive quantities of arms to the Spanish republic that would have been decisive in the summer of 1936. Pressured and blackmailed by the Conservative British government and hindered by the indecision of his own general staff, Blum opted for the fatal policy of 'non-intervention', while Nazi Germany and fascist Italy — the former having managed to remilitarize the Rhine in February 1936 without encountering any resistance, the latter victorious in Ethiopia — prepared to intervene resolutely on the side of the Spanish nationalist rebellion, sending arms, armoured detachments, and finally a full-fledged expeditionary corps numbering seventy to eighty thousand troops.

It was paradoxical. The Popular Front had been formed to defend France and Spain against fascism, but in the weaker of these countries the most violent reactionary forces were now taking their revenge. Popular Front France was unable to come to the aid of democratic Spain at the crucial moment. The Communists — the PCF, the Comintern, and the USSR —grasped the contradiction quite clearly. The whole message of the Seventh Congress of the International had been to sound the alarm about the gravity of the assault throughout Europe (even throughout the world, for Japan had invaded China). But the French Communists went unheeded even when they fought to rouse the majority of the Front itself. The USSR decided to take action from the very outset, in July–August. In September it intervened.

It was at this point that Stalin decided to extend concrete and urgent aid to the Spanish republic. By the early autumn of 1936, Soviet military support was already arriving: planes, armoured vehicles, machine-guns, rifles, ammunition, food. The Comintern began organizing the International Brigades, sending first thousands and then tens of thousands of its most determined militants to Spain (up to thirty-five or forty thousand in all), on the most nationalist basis possible: there was the German-Austrian Edgard André Brigade, the Polish brigade named after the communard Dombrowski, the Franco-Belgian brigade, also named after the Paris Commune, and the Italian Garibaldi Brigade. Prestigious Communist leaders such as André Marty and Luigi Longo took charge of training, under the auspices of the Spanish army. The 'Stalinists' were joined in the International Brigades by members of other parties: Socialists, democrats, and young people of no party affiliation. They came from Britain, the United States, Yugoslavia, Canada — up to fifty nationalities were represented.

Stalin's intervention must of course be seen within the context of the Soviet foreign policy of 'collective security', which sought an agreement primarily with France. But it was expressed in a wide range of mass political initiatives, a historical novelty for the USSR. For years the Soviet Union had been turned in on itself, engaged in the colossal effort of industrialization and collectivization of agriculture. Now it was turning outward.

There is no doubt whatever that Soviet military aid saved Madrid and the Republic in October–December 1936,[13] but the intervention was also expressed in sensational political and 'intellectual' terms, as Stalin resorted to an internationalist language that seemed to echo the words of the Bolsheviks in 1917 and during the civil war of 1918–20. On 16 October 1936, he sent a 'historic telegram'[14] to José Díaz, the secretary of the PCE:

In aiding the revolutionary masses of Spain, the toilers of the Soviet Union are only doing their duty. They know that to rid Spain of the reactionary fascists is not the task of Spaniards alone, but is the common cause of all progressive humanity.

It was evident that here Stalin was not speaking solely, or even mainly, as the head of the Soviet state, but as a Communist leader addressing comrades engaged in an implacable struggle. Even more significant was a letter sent by Stalin (signed by Molotov and Voroshilov as well) to Largo Caballero, the Socialist President of the Council, on 21 December 1936. It advised the Spanish rulers to undertake a policy of broad social alliances that would include peasants and the petty- and middle-sized bourgeoisie, implicitly warning them against any collectivist extremism, which would narrow the front and alienate the middle layers of society. But Stalin went further. He told 'comrade' Largo Caballero:

> The Spanish revolution is opening paths that differ in many respects from the road taken by Russia. This is determined by the historical, social, and geographical differences and by the exigencies of the international situation, which differ from those faced by the revolution in Russia. It is possible that the 'parliamentary road' will lead to a process of revolutionary development more effective in Spain than it was in Russia.[15]

Stalin made no secret of the fact that there was an immediate political motivation for his advice, for he added that if the Spanish Republic pursued a policy that encouraged the small peasant proprietors, avoided confiscation of property, guaranteed freedom of trade, and curried favour with the most moderate of anti-fascist groups, then the 'enemies of Spain' would be unable to portray the state as 'a communist republic'. This would forestall 'any open intervention, which is the greatest danger for Republican Spain'. None the less, for the first time — in a situation offering a possible revolutionary outcome (in the course of what Gramsci would have called 'mobile warfare') — he raised the possibility of a road to socialism different from that taken in Russia. Such language was used again just after the war, between 1945 and 1947, and yet again in 1956, at the Twentieth Congress of the Soviet Communist Party, when Khrushchev too spoke of a 'parliamentary road'. In any event, the question of 'differences' was posed.

Stalin's allusion — which did not even draw a distinction between democratic and socialist revolution — had its pendant in the analysis of Spanish Communists and in Palmiro Togliatti's assessment of 'Spanish affairs'. Both the Spanish Communists (especially José Díaz[16]) and Togliatti emphasized that Spain was going through a phase of *democratic revolution*; but they also introduced a new concept which served as the foundation of the idea of *anti-fascist*

revolution which later became common in the Communist movement during the Resistance.

In brief, the concept was this: by waging an armed struggle against
the big landowners and finance capitalists, who were the pillars of
fascism, the Spanish popular masses were not merely carrying out a
classic bourgeois-democratic revolution, but were leading a renovation of society as a whole which would produce new forms of
democracy — or rather, a *democracy of a new type* that would
overstep the bounds and limits of bourgeois democracy. The value
and practice of political democracy were lauded, but in Spain the
important thing was not so much parliament — for Togliatti was by
no means convinced that it would be possible to rely on parliament,
even if new elections were held, although far be it from him to
contradict Stalin — as the democratic life of the republic. The
question that was now being asked, and would be much pondered
and variously answered in another period of 'mobile warfare', during
the Resistance, was this: in what forms could this *new democracy* be
embodied? There were many possibilities: Popular Front committees in the workplaces and elected assemblies; rank-and-file trade
unionism; effective structures of local and regional self-government;
cooperatives.

Discussion of these matters — sometimes in barely a whisper —
had only just begun when it was simply buried by the mounting
difficulties of the situation, in France and Spain alike. What is most
striking about the confusion of events —the details of which obviously cannot be described here — is the steady deterioration of the
internal situation. In Spain everything was subordinated to the war
raging on the fronts, where despite the tenacious and heroic resistance of the Republic, the Nationalists gained ground inexorably
throughout 1937 and early 1938: half, then two-thirds, of the
country was soon in the hands of Franco's armies; Catalonia was
besieged; the 'central front' between Valencia and Madrid was barely
holding out. Yet there were other 'negative' features besides the
unhappy outcome of these unequal battles. The most striking
passages in Togliatti's confidential reports to the Kremlin were those
that depicted a Popular Front in the process of political collapse, a
working class that remained deeply divided. The anarchists were
increasingly hostile, relations among the various Socialist currents
and between Socialists and Communists got steadily worse, and
genuine democracy was lacking:

The most striking thing is the absence of any forms of democracy that would enable the broad masses to participate in the life of the country and in politics. The parliament hardly represents anyone at all in Spain today, and in the present situation there is no point in contemplating fresh elections. The municipal councils — *ayuntamientos* — and provincial councils were formed from the top down, by governors who distributed the posts among the various parties, in consultation with their leading bodies. The Popular Front committees, which at one time sprang up everywhere and acted as ruling organs, subsequently had to hand responsibility for these activities over to the municipal councils. Since then the Popular Front committees have effectively ceased to exist, except in certain areas in which they survive even though they are not elected by the masses. There are factory committees, but it is difficult to say whether they have been elected or appointed from above. . . . There is very little democracy in the trade unions, which have become powerful economic organizations. The political parties, except for our own, conduct scant political activity among their own members. The country's political life unfolds outside the control of the masses. Political questions are decided in meetings, discussions, machinations, and struggles among the various committees of the parties and unions, etc.[17]

It is a tragic portrait, and it is particularly significant that in it one of the major leaders of the Communist International demonstrates that for him political democracy means mass democracy — or rank-and-file democracy, participatory democracy, the exact term matters little. Moreover he cites its absence as one of the causes of defeat. This, too, is a novelty worthy of note: at the very least it marks a reprise by the Italian Communist leader of earlier conceptions, partly Leninist, partly Gramscian, of the relation between workers democracy and the construction of a socialist system.

Similar problems existed in France, in less distressing but also less open terms. The Front lacked any active base. It was increasingly besieged by external enemies, by a pervasive climate of anxiety and disintegration, by a spirit of indolent pacifism that sapped the will of broad layers of the petty and middle bourgeoisie, and of popular strata as well — the spirit that lay at the root of the Munich surrender. The decline of the Popular Front was rapid. The first Blum government fell in June 1937, and the Committee of the Popular Front seemed to have closed down already. The subsequent cabinets of Chautemps and Blum were no more than pale shadows of the coalition that had triumphed in June 1936. The Daladier government, formed in April 1938 and composed of Radicals and supporters of the centre-right, with the parliamentary backing of Socialists and Communists, was the Front's grave-digger, prepared to pursue a foreign policy so docile as to yield to Nazism and even to recognise Franco: it was, in short, the government of the Munichites. The change in atmosphere between 1936 and 1938 was stunning. Even the French working class now seemed turned in on itself. It has been said that this was partly because 'the ideological basis of the French workers movement, both Socialist and Communist, was pacifism, . . . the dominant sentiment until the 1939 war'.[18] In June 1936 this working class seemed poised for revolutionary action. It was a time when 'everything was possible'. But in subsequent years it sank into isolation. Part of the problem was lack of political unity, a legacy of the abortive attempt to reunify Socialists and Communists.

Notes

1. See Jacques Fauvet, Histoire du Parti communiste français, Paris 1964, pp. 143-45; and Fernando Claudín, The Communist Movement: From Comintern to Cominform, Harmondsworth 1975, pp 171-77. For confirmation of the import of the 'turn', see Giorgio Amendola, Storia del Partito comunista italiano, Rome 1978, pp. 228-34.

2. Histoire du PCF Parti communiste français (manuel), Paris 1964, pp. 307, 310, 343.

3. See also Historia del Partido comunista de España, Havana 1964, and Guy Hermet, Les communistes en Espagne, Paris 1971.

4. See the report to Dimitrov and Manuilski, 28 January 1938, in Palmiro Togliatti, Opere, Rome 1979, vol. 4, I, p. 300.

5. 'La France du Front populaire et sa mission dans le monde', in Maurice Thorez, Oeuvres, Paris 1954, vol. 14, p. 221.

6. On these points, see Giorgio Caredda, Il Fronte popolare in Francia 1934–1938, Turin 1977, pp. 64-87 and 208-28. See also Umberto Coldagelli, 'Sinistra e società blocata. I. Il sistema politico della Terza Repubblica', Laboratorio Politico, vol. 1, no. 3, May-June 1981, pp. 32-68.

7. Franco de Felice, 'I fronti popolari: perché ieri e non oggi', Rinascita, vol. 33, no. 24, 11 June 1976.

8. On his long mission to France and his activity alongside Thorez, see Giulio Cerreti, Con Togliatti e Thorez, Milan 1973, pp 198-203.

9. Many of his articles and previously unpublished correspondence may be found in Paul Nizan, Intellettuale comunista: 1926–1940, edited by Jean-Jacques Brochier, Florence 1974.

10. Note the interesting observations and analyses in Daniel Lindenberg, Il marxismo introvabile. Filosofia e ideologia in Francia dal 1880 a oggi, Turin 1978.

11. Classic in this regard is Daniel Guérin's indictment in the form of personal testimony and historical reconstruction, in his Front populaire, révolution manquée, Paris 1963. Many authors have followed the Trotskyist militant's lead, from Claudín, The Communist Movement, to Colette Audry, Léon Blum, ou la politique du juste, Paris 1955. For a discussion of these positions, see Jean Lacouture, Léon Blum, Paris 1977, pp. 299-301. For all available studies of the Popular Front and the role of the PCF and the SFIO within it, see the bibliography appended to the essay by Georges Lefranc, 'Il socialismo in Francia', in Storia del socialismo, edited by Jacques Droz, Rome 1978,

vol. 3, pp. 499-502. Also fundamental is Lefranc's *Histoire du Front populaire*, Paris 1965.

12. 'Devant la cour de Riom', in Léon Blum, *À l'échelle humaine*, Paris 1945, pp. 86-87.

13. See David Cattell, *I comunisti e la guerra di Spagna*, Milan 1962, pp. 88-105. For other testimony, see Gabriel Jackson, *Aproximación a la España contemporánea, 1898–1975*, Barcelona 1981, p. 111.

14. See José Díaz, *Por la unidad, hacia la Victoria*, report to the Central Committee of the PCE, 5 March 1937, Barcelona 1937.

15. The Spanish text is in *Guerra y revolución en España 1936–39*, Moscow 1966, vol. 2, pp. 101-2.

16. For his report to the PCE, see *Por la unidad*, and more generally, *Tres años de lucha*, Barcelona 1939.

17. From the report dated 30 August 1937, in Togliatti, *Opere*, vol. 4, I, pp. 264-65.

18. Leo Valliani, *Fronti popolari e politica sovietica* (report delivered to the seminar organized in April 1972 by the Luigi Einaudi Foundation), in *Problemi di storia dell' Internazionale comunista*, edited by Aldo Agosti, Turin 1974, p. 211.

3

The Failure of 'Organic Unity'

The history of a failure is not the history of 'ifs'. The failure of the attempts during the period of the Popular Fronts to heal the great schism of 1920–21 and to achieve an 'organic' political reunification of Socialists and Communists must be analysed with the greatest care, for it affords us an opportunity to gauge the gap separating the two components both nationally and internationally. Moreover, the attempt at reunification was repeated ten years later, between 1944 and 1946–47, and the second failure, while it exhibits new and more general features, also mirrors some earlier ones and therefore provides a more accurate sense of the fissure that has divided the European workers movement for decades.

Today we inevitably view the attempt in the light of its ultimate frustration, but this may lead us to underestimate the genuine thirst for unity in the workplaces, the factories, and the streets. The ferment penetrated the leadership bodies, and was stimulated by the excitement of the Front's electoral victory, seen as the prelude to more sweeping social conquests, to the creation of people's power. There is little point in rehearsing the general limitations of the left coalitions in France and Spain, the only countries in which there was substantial talk of organic unity between 1935 and 1937. The initial impetus of these proposals, which began to circulate around the end of 1934, however, should be properly located. The slogan of organic unity was first raised in the ranks of the SFIO, among Zyromski's Socialist left, the supporters of Marcel Pivert's 'gauche révolution-naire', and others. They saw unity as part of a 'maximalist' task: to forge a single party that would fight for, and be able to achieve, the dictatorship of the proletariat in France. Its programme would call for the socialization of the means of production, above all the banks and some large manufacturing industries. The PCF replied that the 'united front' had to be consolidated first, and that organic unity had to emerge from unity in action.[1] This was the line of the Communist International. In any event, here we have the first paradox: two parties that seemed to rival each other in their pursuit of 'sovietist' perspectives were affiliated to international organizations that were not even able to find ground for common action in defence of peace and in the struggle against Nazism. Despite this, in 1935 they apparently felt obliged to take steps to describe in some detail the design, or the architecture, of a model for a workers state. A joint unification commission was formed, drafts were exchanged. But the most delicate questions were barely mentioned: the PCF's relation to Moscow, Trotskyist penetration of the SFIO, the internal structure of the prospective united party, relations with the Socialist International.

When Dimitrov delivered his report to the Seventh Congress of the Communist International in July 1935, citing the PCF as an example for all, he did not avoid the subject of organic unity. But he prescribed the 'principled' conditions for this most ambitious objective. Read with hindsight, the platform presented by the Comintern general secretary seems so rigid as to preclude any real progress. The relevant passage of Dimitrov's report ran as follows:

> This unification is possible only:
> *First,* on condition of *complete independence of the bourgeoisie and complete rupture of the bloc between Social Democracy and the bourgeoisie;*
> Second, on condition that *unity in action* is first achieved;
> *Third,* on condition that the necessity for the *revolutionary overthrow of the rule of the bourgeoisie* and for the establishment of the *dictatorship of the proletariat in the form of soviets* is recognized;
> *Fourth,* on condition that the parties renounce support of their own bourgeoisie in *imperialist war;*
> *Fifth,* on condition that the party is organized on the basis of *democratic centralism,* which guarantees unity of will and action and has been proven sound by the *experience of the Russian Bolsheviks.*[2]

In substance, then, unification would amount to the absorption of the Socialists into a Bolshevik Party that viewed the Russian experience and the Russian model as definitive. Dimitrov said nothing about the possible dissolution of the Third International. He was careful, however, to warn against the manoeuvres of those who would work for a united party of the working class only in order to resurrect a new Socialist party, to breathe life into a 'new International which, directed against the Communist movement, would deepen the split in the working class'. The spectre of Trotskyism was haunting the Communist movement — and it would continue to do so, as we shall see. But quite apart from that concern, the rigidity of the Comintern's stance would seem to suggest that the only sort of unity Moscow wanted was unity in action. If desire for unity is really more intense than that, Dimitrov suggests, then let us weld our forces into a disciplined united party, governed by democratic centralism and capable of implementing the anti-fascist policy of broad democratic unity of which Stalin was so enamoured — in France and Spain in the first place.

At the Seventh Congress there was keen concern not to displace the ideological axis, not to shift the horizons of the revolutionary forces. Glorification of Stalin had already become a ritual, performed in the tone we have noted for 1939. Reporters and speakers at the Seventh Congress took special care to insist that there would be no tampering with the theoretical and strategic assumptions of 'Marxism-Leninism'. Dimitrov explained that the search for transitional forms was not meant to inaugurate an 'intermediary democratic stage' but to promote proletarian revolution, to bring about the proletarian dictatorship, as in the Soviet Union. On this solemn occasion Thorez parroted Dimitrov virtually word for word. He told the Congress delegates that the PCF sought organic unity based on the following principles: 'Preparation for armed insurrection, for the dictatorship of the proletariat, for soviet power as the form of workers government; consistent internationalism; membership of a single world party of the working class; democratic centralism.'[3]

Were these insuperable obstacles to the process of political unification? At bottom they were, and they would be again in 1944-46. The course of the negotiations, which continued in 1936 and 1937, suggests that when mass pressure for unity was strongest, as the Popular Front wave crested, the Socialists were determined not to allow the Communists to have a monopoly on calls for organic unity. When matters became more complicated, however, they stalled, raising the most diverse reservations.

If we turn from France to Spain, we find a similar picture, with only apparent differences. The PCE made unity proposals to the Spanish Socialists. Unification was achieved in Catalonia, but the PSUC brought together only minority groupings of Catalan Socialists and even Communists. In the summer of 1936 the PSUC, headed by the ex-Socialist Juan Comorera,[4] affiliated to the Third International. In the meantime, however, heterodox currents had founded a number of groupings that merged in the Workers Party of Marxist Unification (POUM), which would be a constant target of Stalinist attack (sadly, not merely political) until the physical liquidation of Andrés Nin, the party's dominant personality, a friend, but not an orthodox follower, of Trotsky.[5] The fusion of the Socialist Youth led by Santiago Carrillo with the Communist Youth of Fernando Claudín in April 1936 likewise amounted in practice to the absorption of the Socialists by the Communists. All the fundamental groupings of Spanish socialism — from Prieto's 'centre' to Caballero's left — flatly rejected the PCE's propositions. And not only the PCE's. According to reliable Socialist and anarchist testimony, in February 1937 Caballero sharply rejected a detailed proposal from Stalin himself, who offered to supervise a fusion of Socialists and Communists. Caballero is reported to have replied that the PCE was pursuing a policy of proselytism designed simply to absorb the other party.[6] Just one month later in March José Díaz publicly admitted that conditions for organic unity did not exist.[7]

Even trade-union unification was unsuccessful in Spain. In fact, the original division of the Spanish proletariat into three formations — Socialist, anarchist, and Communist —actually deepened. But the unhappy fate of the attempt at political unification was only a reflection of the more general crisis of the Popular Front, of the schism between the Socialist and Communist Internationals. The former was about to be ripped apart by centrifugal forces. De Brouckère and Adler, the president and secretary of the Socialist International respectively, spent most of their time in exhausting internal mediation.[8] In July 1937, after an inconclusive meeting with Comintern delegates in Annemasse, the Social Democratic leaders rejected all further Communist proposals for united action in support of republican Spain.

The great foreign-policy issues that divided the European Socialists nation by nation in 1938–1939 were already causing impotence and schism. As G.D.H. Cole has written: 'The Labour and Socialist International, from 1933 onwards, was in effect little more than a loose federation of the British and French parties with those of certain small states of Western Europe.'[9] The sole common denominator was aversion to the Communist International. The case of the British Labour Party is indicative. Here a left tendency favoured collaborating with the Communists, who would have liked to join the Labour Party. But the most open and far-sighted groups of intellectuals, such as that of Harold J. Laski and John Strachey, which had created the Left Book Club, were brushed aside: the Labour Party executive responded to the 'unity manifesto' issued by Laski, Cripps, and several leading trade unionists in January 1937 by expelling the 'Socialist League', which had promoted it, from the Labour Party.

Such was the general climate. It should therefore come as no surprise that from autumn 1936 to autumn 1937, as the first real Popular Front government deteriorated, meetings and contacts were wearily arranged to prepare a fusion that was never to be. Cole has admirably summed up the story this way:

> The unity negotiations between Socialists and Communists that went on intermittently, to the accompaniment of much mutual recrimination, during these years were conducted largely at cross-purposes. The Communists wanted the Socialist Party to amalgamate with them, confident that they would be able, with their concentrated energy and determination, to establish their control over a united party; whereas the Socialists, who rejected the whole notion of 'democratic centralism' and party dictatorship but understood the strength of popular feeling in favour of united action, favoured a form of collaboration between the two parties that would leave both of the intact.[10]

There is no doubt, then, that the SFIO of Léon Blum and Paul Faure had no desire for organic unity. The structural differences between the two parties also remained enormous. The PCF was highly centralized and penetrated the workplaces through its effective organization into factory cells, while the SFIO was divided into various currents. Its leading body, the Permanent Administrative Committee, had no real decision-making power over the organizations in the field or over the parliamentary group.[11] As Jacques Fauvet has remarked, the Socialists were well aware that 'unity would sound the death-knell of the SFIO'.[12] Why, then, when the SFIO drew back the hand it had first extended, did the PCF offer its own with an insistence that somehow seems almost pathetic? Was it simply to win a propaganda victory? To unmask the 'enemies of unity' in the tried-and-true manner? To salvage what could still be saved, namely united action? To be able to resist conservative pressures from the Kremlin more effectively? We can only speculate. The atmosphere in Moscow, where the great trials were now under way, was hardly conducive to any dialogue about organic unity. The fact that the French Trotskyists, tiny minority though they were, had joined the SFIO aggravated the PCF's irritation.

In June 1937, when the Socialists were insisting most forcefully that international links would have to be severed if there was to be any unification and that the prospective new party would have to have a 'democratic character', Georges Cogniot wrote an article in the Comintern's official organ in which he repeated the call for unification but flatly rejected any notion of abandoning democratic centralism and any concession to a 'system of currents and factions'. [13] In November 1937 Dimitrov wrote an article that the SFIO took as its cue, or pretext, to bury the Communist proposal definitively. In this article, Dimitrov, who had fought for united action as hard as anyone, vehemently attacked 'Social Democratism' and its historic tradition in terms reminiscent of the language of 1930 and not unlike Manuilski's speech of 1939. Dimitrov quoted the Stalin who had affirmed in 1934 that 'it is impossible to eliminate capitalism without first liquidating Social Democracy in the workers movement.'

It is true that Dimitrov also commented favourably on the steps towards unity that had been taken in recent years in France, Spain, and even Italy; and he sought to distinguish the 'reactionary chiefs' of the Socialist International from those of its leaders who favoured unity. But the general tone marked a return to hardened traditions: unification would have to be inspired by the Bolshevik model, and attitude to the USSR was a historic line of demarcation. The existence of the land of socialism was 'the greatest factor contributing to liquidating the split in the world workers movement'. [14] Around the same time, Maurice Thorez wrote that the new united party would have to 'accept democratic centralism as a guarantee of the party's unshakeable steadfastness.' [15]

And yet in late December 1937, at the Ninth Congress of the PCF, Jacques Duclos gave a speech wholly devoted to the subject of organic unity in which he reiterated the Communists' offer to the SFIO in the warmest possible terms, despite the Socialists' definitive rejection of it. The Tours split, he said, which had occurred exactly seventeen years before, had to be healed; fusion was needed, the sooner the better.

> We Communists, whose aim is to free humanity from the shackles of capitalism, we who have always sought to unite the people under the banner of Marx, Engels, Lenin, and Stalin, we pledge to struggle with all our might to create as soon as possible the united party of the working class of France, token of our future victories, of the cohesion and unity of the Popular Front for bread, freedom, and peace.' [16]

A single working class, a single trade union, a single party — that was the slogan of the PCF, reintroduced at the Congress. Duclos then added, invoking unity in the name of the German comrades languishing in Nazi camps, of the soldiers of the Spanish Republic, of the

Italians deported to the bleak islands to which they were confined by Mussolini, of the mothers who did not want their sons massacred in a new war: 'Think of the power a new party would represent in France, with 450,000 Communists and 300,000 Socialists fraternally united!' In this lengthy report, which was free of polemics and even mentioned Dimitrov's indictment of Social Democracy only to attenuate and minimize it, Duclos seemed not to assume that negotiations with the SFIO were over. The Socialist rejection, however, was definitive. The SFIO's Permanent Administrative Committee had decided unanimously to have nothing further to do with the matter.

Discussion then turned to more general considerations, to the mounting obstacles encountered by the Popular Front, which was now but a shadow of its former self and, even in Spain, held together as a façade more than as a real united coalition, despite its agonizing fight for survival. Nevertheless, Communist policy, including the efforts to achieve a new unity, was not a mere tactical ploy. Both Thorez and Togliatti, to take two examples, genuinely believed in unity. Although both were as disciplined as could be, the former had waged a tenacious struggle against sectarianism in his own party, while the latter commented from Moscow as late as May 1939 (in other words, after Manuilski's report) that on several occasions in Spain he had had to oppose a tendency to believe 'that all the various problems could be solved if and when the party gained control of all the levers of power.'[17] Even in the days of its defeat, Togliatti repeated that the policy of the Popular Front had been the only correct one. But he and the other Communist leaders who had been active in France and Spain also felt, no less sincerely, that they had been left to fight for that policy on their own, that they had increasingly been surrounded by a jumble of disparate forces, inside and outside the Front, that were determined to see it fail.

During and after the Resistance, however, everyone had this first historic experiment in mind. In France in particular there was widespread awareness in the working class that unity was the left's weapon of victory. This theme of the united left has run through French history ever since, through success and failure alike. The Popular Front was also seen as a fundamental experience for the Italian workers movement, which at the time of the Front was composed of emigrés who followed every event with baited breath. Fusion was not achieved between the PSI and PCI either, but the renewal of the pact for united action between the two parties in 1937[18] was a step toward forging a unity — primarily in the fight against the fascists — that was deeper and more intense than it had been, or ever would be, in France or Spain.

Another implication of the unity policy came to be understood more clearly in the following decade. It was the Popular Front experience, the persistent search for unity at both rank-and-file and leadership levels, the education of cadres and masses in the practice of 'doing politics' in the thick of events and in the harsh light of day, of dealing with the great issues of national life, that finally created mass Communist parties in Western Europe. Leo Valiani has correctly remarked:

> It was precisely in the period of the defeat of the Popular Front that the Communist parties, hitherto small sects, became the great mass parties that they have remained ever since. The Italian Communist Party was a small party before it sought to establish the United Front and the Popular Front in exile and then to implant them within the country as well. By 1939 the party in exile was already a mass party in embryo. The French Communist Party was not exactly tiny, but its trade-union federation, the CGTU, had more or less 250,000 members in 1934, while the Socialist trade-union federation, the CGT, had 900,000. The French Communist Party had 10 or 12 deputies in parliament, while the Socialist Party had ten times as many. By the end of the Popular Front period, despite the defeat of the Front and the collapse of unity in action, the PCF had the great majority of the French working class on its side.[19]

It is true that this was not the declared objective of organic unity, the goal of which was more immediately political: to create, if not a new instrument for socialist revolution, at least an impregnable workers' bulwark against fascism. That objective was not attained, and as we have seen, by 1939 the situation for Communism was tragic, and no less disastrous for European Socialism, which was drifting down the perilous slope of docility and impotence in the face of Hitler. But the Comintern still saw unity primarily as the absorption of the Socialists into a united party of the 'Bolshevik' type. Why? To answer this question we must consider the nature of the Communist International, in particular its relation to Soviet foreign policy and its 'internal regime', which was one of the factors that frustrated sincere attempts at unification.

Notes

1. J. Berlioz, 'La marche au parti unique du prolétariat français', *La Correspondance Internationale*, vol. 14, no. 113-14, 30 November 1935.

2 Georgi Dimitrov, *La classe operaia contro il fascismo* (report to the Seventh

Congress of the Communist International), Brussels 1935, p. 94.

3. From Maurice Thorez's speech to the Congress of the Communist International, 3 August 1935, *La Correspondance Internationale*, vol. 15, no. 106, 12 November 1935.

4. See Manuel Tuñon de Lara, *Storia del movimento operaio spagnolo*, Rome 1976, pp. 661-64. On the PSUC during the civil war, see Togliatti's very severe assessment in *Opere*, vol. 4, I, pp. 272-75.

5. On Nin see F. Bonamusa, *Andrés Nin y el movimiento comunista en España*, Barcelona 1977.

6. Luís de Araquistain, *El comunismo y la guerra de España*, quoted in José Peirats, *La Cnt nella rivoluzione spagnola*, Milan 1978, vol. 3, p. 172. The episode is confirmed by Claudín, *The Communist Movement*.

7. See his report to the Central Committee of the PCE, *Por la unidad*.

8. See Leonardo Rapone, 'L'età dei fronti popolari e la guerra', in *Storia del socialismo italiano*, directed by Giovanni Sabbatucci, vol. 4, 1926–43, Rome 1981, pp. 270-71.

9. G.D.H. Cole, *A History of Socialist Thought*, vol. 5, *Socialism and Fascism 1931–39*, London 1960, p. 71.

10. Ibid., pp. 106-7.

11. On the structure of the SFIO, see Lefranc, *Il socialismo in Francia*, pp. 462-64.

12. Fauvet, *Histoire du PCF*, p. 215.

13. G. Cogniot, 'Le Front populaire de France et l'unité de la classe ouvrière', *L'Internationale Communiste*, vol. 19, no. 6, June 1937, pp. 551-63.

14. G. Dimitrov, 'L'Union soviétique et la classe ouvrière des pays capitalistes', ibid., nos. 10-11-12, October-December 1937, pp. 947-54.

15. Maurice Thorez, 'La grande Révolution d'Octobre et la France', ibid., pp. 110-13.

16. Jacques Duclos, *Faire l'unité* (report on the 'liquidation of the split and the reconstitution of unity' to the Ninth Congress of the PCF, Arles, 25-29 December 1937), Paris 1938, p. 46.

17. Togliatti, *Opere*, vol. 4, I, p. 271.

18. The 'new charter' signed by representatives of the PSI and the PCI on 26 July 1937 stated: 'The two parties see unity in action as a first step towards the united party of the working class, which will be the most powerful weapon of the proletariat in its struggle against fascism and capitalism.' For the text, see 'Trenta anni di vita e di lotte del Pci', *Quaderno di 'Rinascita'*, no. 2, Rome 1952, pp. 147-48.

19. Leo Valiani, 'Fronti popolari e politica sovietica', in *Problemi di storia dell 'Internazionale comunista*, p. 212.

4
The Great Terror

There has never been a secret report like the one Nikita Khrushchev delivered to the Twentieth Congress of the Communist Party of the Soviet Union (CPSU). It was devoted to the repression suffered during the 'great terror' between 1936 and 1939 by 'foreign' militants and leaders of the Third International, political refugees, workers who had emigrated to the USSR, and even veterans of the International Brigades returning from the battlefields of Spain.

The sinister story can be reconstructed from the many disclosures and eyewitness accounts that have been published since (and even before) the Khrushchev report. But no exhaustive account has yet been presented by the leading bodies of those Communist parties — almost all of them illegal in their own countries at the time — against which the repression raged most fiercely: primarily the Polish, German, Hungarian, and Yugoslav parties, but also the Bulgarian, Romanian, Italian, Finnish, Estonian, and Austrian.

The only parties spared by the wave of arrests, trials, summary executions, and deportations were those which were actively engaged in the Popular Front policy. Above all, these were all legal parties functioning in democratic countries in which the disappearance of a Communist leader could not have been hushed up: France, Britain, the United States, Belgium, Sweden, Czechoslovakia. The acidly ironic comment of Humbert-Droz, one of the most seasoned and best known Comintern cadres and a leader of one of the smallest parties, the Swiss, could have applied to them all. He said that he constantly feared arrest in Moscow in 1938, but felt that he was perhaps protected by the fact that in the event of his disappearance half the Communist delegation to the Swiss parliament would be absent.[1] Yet even the Swiss party had its victim, Fritz Platten, sentenced to five years' hard labour. He died in the camp.

No rule or distinction can be regarded as absolute in a domain governed by pure whim. Madness abounded and any person's fate could be decided by chance. Humbert-Droz himself, for instance, speculated that 'perhaps Stalin just happened to be in a good mood or a little drunk on vodka the day he gave the order to allow me to return to Switzerland.' In 1961 Khrushchev affirmed: 'Stalin was capable of looking at a comrade seated at his own table and saying, "Your eyes are evasive today." You could be sure that the comrade whose eyes were thought to look evasive had fallen under suspicion.'[2]

'Stalin is a very suspicious man', Togliatti confided to Ernst Fischer.[3] The anecdote serves to remind us that no analysis based solely on rational motivations for the terror, no hypothesis built on economic and political factors or founded on investigation of the specific mechanism of power capable of producing such 'perverse' results, can be considered exhaustive. There will always be a shadowy area that can be illuminated only by psychological inquiry or the diagnosis of pathology. The obsessive aspect must always be taken into account, both as regards the mind and spirit of a man who could sentence anyone to death with a mere gesture or the stroke of a pen and as regards the dynamic of the repression itself. The use of anonymous informers, the widespread summoning of accomplices by the inquisitors, the confessions of guilt sought and obtained from nearly all the major defendants, even when it entailed public self-flagellation and heaped discredit on their own revolutionary past — all these factors aggravated the repression.

Not by chance are the accounts of historians and the reflections of surviving victims frequently evocative of the atmosphere and character motivations of Dostoevsky's novels. The strange complicity between victim and executioner is also a common theme. Otto Bauer, the most authoritative theorist of Austro-Marxism, who nevertheless remained a supporter of the Soviet Union, was the first to explain the stunning confessions of the major prisoners in the dock, all of them old Bolsheviks. 'A sort of horrible complicity in defence of the socialist regime arose between the accused and the accusers, a complicity between those whose only role now was to serve, through their confessions, the social order that they had nonetheless contributed to building and those who, trapped in the machinery of the dictatorial regime itself, were using the instruments of terrorist despotism to defend that same order.'[4]

This interpretation found a literary expression in Arthur Koestler's famous novel *Darkness at Noon*, written in 1940. In reality, however, the confessions (the only 'proof' of guilt, in the absence of any documentary evidence) were generally extracted under torture and through threats against the families of arrested persons who failed to collaborate during interrogation, especially during the great trials of 1936–38.[5] On the other hand, it is true that many of the 'minor' defendants adopted a tactic widely recommended among the prisoners: to implicate the greatest possible number of innocent people in their accusations, so that Stalin, who was thought to be unaware of the wave of repression, would realize that the repression itself was the only genuine plot that had been hatched against the Soviet Union and its regime. As Yevgeny Yevtushenko, a poet who was a child at the time, has written, the cult of Stalin already ran deep among party militants and the people.

> Many genuine Bolsheviks who were arrested at that time utterly refused to believe that this had happened with his knowledge, still less on his personal instructions. They wrote to him. Some of them, after being tortured, inscribed 'Long live Stalin' in their blood on the walls of their prison.[6]

Many of the 'deep' recesses of the world of the concentration camps have been excavated in memoirs and in literature. They may also be seen in the ideological fury, the residues and grudges left by earlier struggles, both in the Bolshevik Party and in the various Communist parties. The 'demonization' of Trotskyism, for example, which was often the leitmotif of the repression, has itself become a subject of historiographical debate: was the figure of the 'hideous' Trotsky, supreme architect of all the conspiracies and acts of sabotage, deliberately created to justify the repression? According to Robert McNeal:

> Trotsky had to be universally seen as a dark impersonal force, even more evil than the capitalist in the top hat, the Nazi warmonger, and the various other political figures regularly pilloried in cartoons and manifestos. Trotsky thus finally took on an important role in Stalinism. Far from being obliterated, his name on the contrary continued to circulate in the USSR in counterposition to Stalin's, and with nearly the same frequency. Trotsky was the symbol of evil in the world, regardless of economic systems. He was not even a capitalist: he wanted to destroy socialism purely to satisfy his own lust for power, to gratify 'his own handsome face', as Radek put it. An entity of this kind was necessary if Stalin was to justify the continuing struggle against any form of deviation and the need for unflagging vigilance. If there had been no Trotsky, Stalin would have had to invent him. And so he did.[7]

But here again we encounter an image, a paradox, which also fails to exhaust the problem of the causes and effects of the struggle against

Trotskyism. During the meeting of the party Central Committee held in February–March 1937 (the session that would later be called the meeting of the 'doomed', the last that Bukharin would ever attend), Stalin set the tone for that struggle by drawing a distinction that later had multifarious consequences, as we shall see. The distinction was this: whereas previously Trotskyism had been a 'political tendency' within the workers movement, however mistaken, now it had become 'a gang of saboteurs, defeatists, spies, and assassins devoid of principles or ideology'. 'Absolute and supernatural' ideological categories were inherent in this axiomatic definition: on the one hand there was Good, on the other the Evil of Trotsky. This carries us into the field of psychology, but also of inheritance, for it may be considered an instance of the 'degeneration' of an ideological 'tradition' that had always been marked by an element of Manichaeanism.

Isaac Deutscher maintains, for example, that the most striking case of terror against the militants of a foreign Communist party, the veritable massacre of Polish Communists, was to some extent a reflection — once again partly obsessional, partly rational — of Stalin's old hostility to Luxemburgism, the tendency from which a part of the leadership cadre of the Polish Communist Party had emerged.

> It seems to me that no single motive or sober calculation can explain Stalin's behaviour in this matter. His irrational impulses were quite as important as his 'rational' calculations; and he was impelled to act as he did by old grudges and ancient phobias, all intensified to the utmost by the persecution mania which gripped him at the time of the great Moscow trials, when he was settling his final accounts with the Leninist old guard. In this frame of mind, Stalin saw the Polish CP as the stronghold of hated Luxemburgism — the Polish 'variety of Trotskyism' — which had defied him as long ago as 1923; the party in which some leaders were close to Bukharin and others to Zinoviev; the party of incurable heresies, proud of its traditions and of its heroism; the party, finally, which might well in certain international situations become an obstacle on his road . . .[8]

We could go on. Was the ferocity against so many Jewish Communists (quite numerous in the leadership bodies of almost all the parties of the Third International) purely a product of Stalin's suspicion of anything 'cosmopolitan', of anything that lacked a country of its own? Or was it also the expression of atavistic anti-Semitism, which ran deep in Stalin as it did in the popular mind in the old society, in Russia and elsewhere?

We may well hesitate among various hypotheses, for there is an exceptional caesura that is not merely historiographical but also historical: Khrushchev's denunciation of Stalin, first aired at the Twentieth Congress in 1956, became a veritable avalanche of accusations at the Twenty-Second Congress in 1961; since then, however, there has been more than twenty years of official Soviet silence about the extent, causes, and course of the Great Terror. Back in 1962, Academician Pospelov affirmed in his official capacity: 'I can state that one need only study the documents of the Twenty-Second Congress of the CPSU to see that of course neither Bukharin nor Rykov was a spy or terrorist.'[9] Nevertheless, the major defendants of the Moscow Trials have never been granted the explicit 'rehabilitation' that minor figures have received. One Communist party after the other has by now done the same, sometimes openly, sometimes surreptitiously, for its own lamented victims. On the whole, 'the most recent Soviet history books simply avoid mentioning the trials, as if they had never taken place.'[10] Voices of varying inspiration and tone, but all equally based on the facts and on direct testimony, have been raised within the Soviet Union, however, from Medvedev's *Let History Judge* or *Question of Stalin* to Solzhenitsyn's *Gulag Archipelago*, not to mention the memoirs of Ehrenburg and many other survivors. They have never been seriously challenged, although many have remained clandestine in their native land.

I shall seek to disentangle the threads that are connected most directly to our undertaking, while keeping in mind that the overall atmosphere was admirably expressed by the Austrian Communist Ernst Fischer (who came out of the ranks of left Socialism and was a Comintern official at the time): the terror burst 'like some primeval dragon intruding into a world which invoked Marx and Lenin, reason and the rights of man, a monster with the power of speech, spouting the jargon of a demented bureaucracy.'[11]

A few summary indications of the scope and targets of Stalin's internal terror, inseparable from the repression against the 'foreigners', will suffice. In 1936 the offensive was directed primarily against the Bolshevik Party, including both its leaders and its entire membership. It spread to the commanders of the Red Army and the state apparatus (even felling the diligent architects of the repressive machine and the secret police itself, including Yagoda, Yezhov and many others), struck at writers, artists, and intellectuals, and finally assumed a mass character in 1937, the year of 'the most massive and devastating offensive of political repression the Soviet Union had ever seen'.[12] It continued through 1938 and died out only in 1939.

In two of the three great public trials of 1936–38 Zinoviev and Bukharin, both of whom had headed the Communist International during its first decade, were sentenced to death. Karl Radek, one of the most popular figures of the Comintern, died in prison. Also shot were Piatakov, Sokolnikov, Serebryakov, Kamenev, Ivan Smyrnov, Rykov, Rakovski, and Piatnitski (while Tomski committed suicide). All the most prestigious leaders of Lenin's party were eliminated, consigned to oblivion under slanderous charges of having been a gang of spies in the pay of foreign secret services. Any distinction between members of the former Left and Right oppositions was obliterated: Trotskyists and 'Right Opportunists' were said to have been united in a single 'bloc'.

But many orthodox cadres trained in the Stalin faction were also shot, without public trials: Russians, Ukrainians, Belorussians, Georgians — there were victims from all the Soviet Republics. According to Khrushchev's report, of the 1,966 delegates to the Seventeenth Congress of the Soviet Communist Party (held in 1934), a total of 1,018 were arrested. Of the members of the Central Committee elected at that congress (71 full members and 68 alternates), 10 were shot in 1936 and 98 arrested, most of whom were killed in 1937 and 1938. The officer corps of the Red Army was decimated. The victims of secret trials and summary executions included the renowned Marshal Tukhachevski, the army commander; Marshal Blyucher, chief of the General Staff; Marshal Egorov; the tank commander Yakir; Admiral Orlov, commander of the Navy; armour commander Uborevich; and many commanders of the armoured divisions and military districts. Repression against Soviet officers seems to have eliminated 35,000 people, a worse decapitation than would have been caused by a war. Entire regional party committees disappeared. The 'activist' core of the Leningrad party organization perished *en bloc*. In Tbilisi, two-thirds (or 425) of the 644 delegates to the May 1937 congress of the Georgian party were arrested, deported, or shot during the months following the congress. The toll was similar in Armenia, the Tatar republic, and Uzbekistan. 'It would be difficult', one author has noted, 'to rank the various republics in order of the number of victims.'[13] The repression against intellectuals was massive: more than 600 writers were arrested; celebrated figures such as Babel, Pilniak, Mandelstam, and Meyerhold disappeared; many committed suicide.

Administrators, technicians, and functionaries of Soviet industry were also hit. A small example: 117 out of 161 directors of the steel companies were eliminated. Famous scientists like Vavilov and Tulaykov were killed.

What was the total number of victims? There are no definite figures, and estimates vary. According to Roy Medvedev, 'at least' four to five hundred thousand were killed and four or five million arrested.[14] According to the Yugoslav leader Moša Pijade, 'in 1936, 1937, and 1938, in the Soviet Union over three million people were killed.'[15] The British scholar Robert Conquest believes that about eight and a half million people were arrested and that about 10 per cent of those were executed. The number of dead 'was probably around a million', although 'no exact numbers can yet be given.'[16] Not every one of them was sent to the slaughterhouse by Stalin personally, of course, but he does seem to have 'reviewed' most of the lists of condemned prisoners.

The scope of the carnage was so great that there must have been elements of irrationality in it. Historians have produced a virtual flood-tide of speculation about the causes of the Great Terror. Some have concentrated on the bloodthirsty character of the tyrant, a new Ivan the Terrible, others on the maelstrom in which the repressive machinery itself became trapped. There can be no reasonable doubt that neither the old Bolsheviks (whether former oppositionists or not), nor the minor leaders of the party, nor the commanders of the Red Army had hatched any plots or were in any way guilty of the offences to which they confessed (in any case, the entire edifice of charges that the major defendants of the public trials had maintained links with the exile Trotsky was demolished at the time of the trials themselves in a counter-trial over which John Dewey presided[17]). The general interpretation of Isaac Deutscher, shared by Rudolf Schlesinger, has therefore gained considerable credence, although in different variants. It holds that Stalin, facing the prospect of an approaching war, wanted to eliminate from the very outset any potential oppositionist who might some day be able to seize upon military defeats to take power or to form a rival government.[18] The repression was therefore pressed to extreme limits in order to forestall or crush any potential self-defence within the party and the army.[19]

Consideration of the causes of the terror had been abundant and varied in past decades. Some have emphasized the forced collectivization of land, others the 'very close interpenetration of the party and state apparatus'.[20] Yet others have stressed the mentality that saw every failure to achieve a target of the economic plan as evidence of sabotage.[21] The 'theoretical' origin of the police degeneration has been ascribed to Stalin's claim that the more successes were registered in the building of socialism, 'the more ferocious the remnants of the old defeated exploiting classes will become, . . . the more they will resort to the most desperate methods of struggle, as a condemned man does.'

The consolidation and spread of an inquisitional spirit of 'mass vigilance', of a state of siege mentality — particularly in the context of mounting threats of war, while the struggle raged in Spain and fascism was sweeping across Europe — were certainly significant factors both in the international repercussions of the terror and in the connection between Stalin's foreign and domestic policies. All this gave an impetus to the establishment of Stalin's absolute power, to the cult of his personality and function. Medvedev has drawn attention to a factor of this type:

> Paradoxical as it may seem, another important factor explaining the triumph of Stalin's cult was the crimes he committed. He did not commit them by himself. Taking advantage of the people's revolutionary enthusiasm and trustfulness, the enormous power of party and state discipline, and the low educational level of the proletariat and the peasantry, Stalin involved millions of people in his crimes. Not only the punitive organs, but the entire party and government *apparat* participated actively in the campaigns of the 1930s. Thousands of officials were members of the *troiki* that condemned innocent people. Tens of thousands of officials sanctioned the arrest of their subordinates, as required by a Politburo resolution in 1937. Commissars had to sanction the arrest of their deputies, *obkom* secretaries the arrest of party officials in their *oblasti*, while the chairman of the Union of Writers sanctioned the arrest of many writers. Hundreds of thousands of Communists voted for the expulsion of 'enemies of the people'. Millions of ordinary people took part in meetings and demonstrations demanding severe reprisals against 'enemies'. Frequently people demanded such penalties against their former friends. The majority of Soviet people believed in Stalin and the NKVD in those years, and were sincere in their indignation against 'enemies of the people'.[22]

It therefore seems clear that Vyshinski's insistence in the widely publicized sessions of the Moscow trials on the infiltration of spies, the acts of sabotage supposedly organized from abroad by foreign secret services (mainly of Germany and Japan), had a broader significance, designed to convince the masses that the USSR was surrounded by hardened and merciless enemies, that the people had to close ranks and prepare for fresh sacrifices, and that they had to rely more than ever on Stalin's unshakeable determination.

Perhaps a more profound view of the phenomenon is that the real cause of Stalin's mass repression, considered as a 'qualitative change' in the Soviet regime, was Stalin's determination to strike at the entire leading layer of the Bolshevik Party so as to crush any potential alternative definitively. The old Communist Party would always be a danger, an obstacle, to Stalin, for it embodied the 'soul' of Communism, which would continually rise afresh and might yet generate an opposition to Stalin's system of rule and his conception of power. In his dialogue with a generally accommodating Gilles Martinet, for example, Giuseppe Boffa writes:

> The aim was to assault and annihilate organs that had acquired real power in preceding battles. It was therefore necessary to place the police apparatus above the party, so that it could act unfettered against the party itself. The mechanism of terror inevitably became uncontrollable, feeding on grudges and informers, and finally became generalized in 1937–38. It would have been difficult indeed to attack such an extensive political stratum, which led not only the party but society as a whole, without creating an atmosphere of generalized fear, of obsessive fright, such that no one dared to voice any protest.[23]

Stalin thus had to annihilate a resistance which he had not previously managed to stifle completely, and he had to kill the spirit of old Bolshevism in the first place. The repression was therefore an essentially counter-revolutionary phenomenon. Not without reason, it struck at those Soviet and foreign Communists most closely linked to the old Bolshevik leading group.

It seems obvious that the internal regime of the Comintern must have deteriorated as the terror unfolded, given the threatening ambience in Moscow and throughout the country. It should be noted, however, that even at the Seventh Congress of the Communist International in 1935, the apparatus was already in the hands of NKVD functionaries, completely beyond the control of Dimitrov or Togliatti and directly dependent on the chief of police. N.I. Yezhov himself was added to the Comintern Executive at that congress, while a certain Moskvin — pseudonym of Mikhail A. Trilisser, a leader of the NKVD who, incidentally, later fell victim to the repression himself — was added to the Presidium and the Secretariat.[24] The police atmosphere had catastrophic consequences in a situation in which most of the affiliated Communist parties were already financially dependent on the 'Centre' and in which refugees from countries newly conquered by Nazism continued to arrive in the USSR, swelling the population of political émigrés, of party militants persecuted in their home countries who had sought refuge in the Soviet Union.

The dynamic of the Moscow trials also affected the various leadership groups living in Moscow: the axe fell mainly on old cadres, in many cases people who had been members of the Zimmerwald Left during the First World War.[25] The Poles were among the hardest hit: victims included Mieczyslaw Bronski, Adolf Warszawski (pseudonym Warski), Maksimilian Horowitz (Walecki), Wladislaw Stein, and Pawel Lewinson (pseudonym Lapinski). But the Poles were not alone. Also arrested, apart from Platten, the Swiss Communist mentioned earlier, were the Austrian Franz Koritschoner; many Hungarians, including Béla Kun and Jozsef Rabinovicz; the German Hugo Eberlein, who had been one of the founders of the Comintern in 1919; as well as Finns, Letts, and Yugoslavs of the Old Guard gathered around Lenin during the First World War. But the repression against revolutionary refugees in the USSR did not obey any fixed rules. First place in a contest for the number of victims would surely go to the Polish party, whose leading cadre were exterminated and which was secretly dissolved in August 1938.[26] Apart from those already listed, the dead included the party's secretary Julian Leszczyński (pseudonym Leński); Edward Prochniak, a member of the Comintern Executive; Henryk Stein (Domski); Maria Koszutska, better known under the pseudonym Wera Kostrzewa, a high-ranking leader arrested in 1937 (as were most of the others) who died in Lubianka Prison; Jerzy Heryng (pseudonym Ryng), who had been living underground in Poland, was called to Moscow at the end of 1937 and subsequently disappeared. Another leading member of the Political Bureau, Saul Amsterdam (pseudonym Henryk Henrykowski), suffered the same fate.

I have named only major leaders of the Polish party, but the repression also felled rank-and-file militants and even 'non-party' workers who had been resident in the USSR for some time. Tens of thousands of people were affected. 'According to one Polish Communist, 10,000 Poles from Moscow alone were shot at the time of the Bukharin trial, with a total of 50,000 in the country as a whole.'[27] The Polish tragedy was the most grievous, and the decision to dissolve that Communist Party could not be characterized any more accurately than it was by Palmiro Togliatti in 1961 (although he, like the other members of the Secretariat, endorsed the measure at the time): 'a mistaken and catastrophic decision'.[28] Besides the factors mentioned by Deutscher, the division of the Polish party by bitter political struggles also weighed against it, as did the contacts that many party leaders had maintained with members of the Bolshevik oppositions in the twenties. But all the various general observations about this painful chapter of Soviet history also apply to the Polish case. Everyone was under suspicion, and orthodox zeal drove many to implicate their own comrades.

Paolo Robotti, an Italian Communist militant and skilled worker in a Soviet industry (he was Togliatti's brother-in-law as well), was arrested on 9 March 1938 and released on 4 September 1939, after having been tortured in prison. He later testified that his interrogators not only wanted him to 'confess' that some Italian members of the 'club degli emigrati' (of which he was a leader) had hatched a plot, but also sought to implicate higher leaders, including even Togliatti and Giuseppe Di Vittorio, who were then in Spain and France respectively.[29] The episode would suggest that the machine was accumulating 'dossiers' on everyone. Robotti survived because he managed to resist the physical pressures and continued to deny all the charges against him until the repression finally ebbed. But the witch-hunt was systematic for more than two years. Most of the Polish leaders had already been shot when the party was dissolved. In his 1939 report Manuilski said only that the Polish party had proved to be 'the most heavily encumbered with enemy elements'. In the meantime the party had been disencumbered of this burden.

Losses were also heavy in the German Communist Party, as repression deprived that organization of some of its most prestigious members. I have already mentioned Hugo Eberlein, who was in Moscow for the founding congress of the Communist International in 1919. Others killed included Heinz Neumann, member of the Political Bureau (arrested in 1937 with his wife, Margarete); Leo Flieg, member of the Control Commission; Hermann Remmele, who represented the German party in the Comintern Executive until his arrest in 1937; Fritz David, Hermann Schubert, Hans Kippenberg, Werner Hirsch, and many more. We should also note the mysterious death of Willi Münzenberg, a very powerful personality who organized the Comintern's shipment of arms and volunteers to Republican Spain. Münzenberg refused to return to Moscow in 1937. In 1939 he was interned in a French concentration camp and in 1940 he was shot while being transferred to another camp: his body was found in a wood some time later. Margarete Buber, the wife of Hans Neumann, has testified that only the intervention of Togliatti had enabled Münzenberg to get out of the USSR in 1936.[30] Tito has reported that Dimitrov saved him from the charge that he was a disguised Trotskyist, an accusation that would have been fatal; but the Yugoslav Communist Party lost more than a hundred members to Stalin's repression. In 1937, while the police force of the reactionary Yugoslav dictatorship was arresting thousands of underground Communists, the Moscow purges decapitated the exile leadership group. As Tito himself has written:

> Those who were arrested, tried, and liquidated in the course of the purges, or who left no trace after being put in prison included Filip Filipović, Kamilo Horvatin, Kosta Novakovič, Djuka and Stjepan Cvjič, Rade and Grgur Vujović, Mladen Conič, Anton Mavrak, and others. Their tragedy was so much the greater as they were sent to their deaths under monstrous charges for crimes they had never committed. The situation at that time was exceptionally involved. Even our entire party was under accusation. There were rumours in the Comintern that it would be disbanded.[31]

Tito's list should be amended to include another major figure, Milan Gorkič, party secretary and candidate member of the Comintern Executive, who was arrested and shot in 1937, along with his Ukrainian wife, Betty Glane, denounced as a spy for the Intelligence Service. The most significant point of Tito's testimony, however, concerns the threat to dissolve the Yugoslav party.[32] This indicates just how authoritarian the central apparatus of the International became under the influence of the secret services of the Soviet Ministry of the Interior: every leadership group was swept up in what had become a rage of 'purges'.

Although it seems to be true that the moderating influence of Togliatti and Dimitrov saved the Italian and Bulgarian parties, which alone among the illegal groups escaped the purges, it is equally certain that in the atmosphere of witch-hunts against 'Trotskyists' and 'provocateurs', in the welter of charges of insufficient 'revolutionary vigilance', the exile centre of the PCI (operating, to its great good fortune, in Paris) fell under such intense criticism and suspicion that in 1938 Moscow dissolved its Central Committee in a measure similar to those taken or contemplated against the Poles, Letts, and Yugoslavs.[33] About a hundred Italians living in the USSR — Communists, anarchists, and 'non-party' workers, most of them 'in production' but including some officials of political or trade-union groups — perished in the repression. Among them were Edmondo Peluso, a journalist well-known in Gramsci's time; Vincenzo Baccalà, who had been secretary of the Romana federation of the PCI; Giuseppe Rimola, a Novarese factory worker; Natale Premoli, Lino Manservigi, Paolo Baroncini, Giuseppe Guerra, Emilio Guarnaschelli,[34] and many others, almost all of them workers or technicians, and almost all previously sentenced *in absentia* by the fascist Special Tribunal.[35]

A most illuminating detail, reported by Paolo Robotti, concerns the mentality of the inquisitors, who were often very young functionaries recently recruited by the NKVD: they considered their suspects' earlier armed activity against fascism as evidence for the prosecution. Describing an interrogation conducted by one of these people, Robotti writes:

> His ignorance of international affairs was absolutely stunning. He insisted in particular on the accusation of terrorism and found 'evidence' in the fact that while abroad I had organized a few acts of reprisal against fascism.
> 'Is it true or not?' he screamed.
> 'Yes it's true, and I'm proud of it!'
> 'So, you see you *are* a terrorist!'[36]

Behind the 'subversive', the enemy of the Stalin order could always be lurking, especially if he was a foreigner, coming from a little-known world always depicted in bleak colours. Civil-war Spain was no exception. Vladimir Antonov-Ovseenko, the Soviet consul in Barcelona and the man who directed the assault on the Petrograd Winter Palace in 1917, was recalled to Moscow and perished in the repression. Mikhail Kolkov, author of the highly popular 'letters from the front' published in *Pravda,* suffered the same fate.[37] The Yugoslav Vlada Čopić was eliminated the moment he returned from Spain, where he had commanded an International Brigade. Many veterans of the Brigades were also liquidated. This mentality persisted into the post-war period. We need only recall the famous book about the Prague interrogations of 1949 by the Czechoslovak Artur London, who had also fought in Spain.[38] Vittorio Vidali, commissar of the 'Fifth Regiment', who returned from Spain to Paris in 1938, was warned by his friend Elena Stassova, Lenin's former secretary, not to return to the USSR. It would be better, she said, to go to the United States, even if it meant being arrested. The English Communist Tom Bell, who carried her message to Vidali, told him that the international apparatuses in Moscow had been cleaned out 'two or three times already'.[39] The leaders of the illegal parties survived only when they operated in European countries, whether democratic or not. Ambrogio Donini, one of the leaders of the PCI, has said: 'It was a real drama, which only Togliatti's firmness — and the sudden change in the international situation with the outbreak of war and the dispersion of the comrades hit by repression in France, Spain, and

Italy — prevented from degenerating into a tragedy no less bloody and nightmarish than that which engulfed the Soviet Union itself between 1936 and 1939.'[40]

Of the Bulgarian Communists, some of those arrested were released after Dimitrov's intervention, while others disappeared, among them Blagoi Popov and Vasil Tanev, who had been co-defendants with the secretary of the Communist International at the Lipsia trial. Among the Romanian victims were Marcel Pauker, general secretary and representative of the RCP in the Comintern Executive (his wife, Ana Pauker, was arrested by the fascists in Romania at the same time as her husband's arrest in the USSR, where he was liquidated).[41] Pauker was accused of belonging to the Zinoviev-Kamenev group and was shot in 1937. Some Hungarian Communist leaders were arrested on similar charges of collusion with Trotskyist or Zinovievist opposition groups, among them the famous Béla Kun, leader of the ephemeral but glorious soviet republic of 1919. Béla Kun no longer held any position of political responsibility, although he had been a member of the Comintern Executive. Arrested in June 1937, he seems to have died in November 1939. His wife, also interned and confined in a camp from 1938 to 1946, was officially informed of his death only in 1955.[42] It was left to Eugene Varga to 'rehabilitate' the good name of Hungary's greatest revolutionary, at the time of the Twentieth Congress of the CPSU (*Pravda*, 21 February 1956). Thousands of Finnish exiles, by no means all Communists, were reported to have been deported.

It is not difficult to see that given a holocaust of such proportions, the Communist International could not survive as a political organization with the slightest vitality or internal life. Giorgio Amendola commented in lapidary terms: 'The Communist International never recovered from the blows inflicted by the repression.'[43]

Notes

1. Jules Humbert-Droz, *Dix ans de lutte antifasciste, 1931–1941*, Neuchâtel 1972, p. 349.

2. From the 'Conclusions' of N.S. Khrushchev, *XXII Congresso del PCUS, atti e risoluzioni*, Rome 1962, p. 680.

3. Ernst Fischer, *An Opposing Man*, p. 17.

4. Massimo L. Salvadori, 'La critica marxista allo stalinismo', in *Storia del marxismo*, Turin 1981, vol. 3, II, p. 101.

5. On this point, see in particular Stephen Cohen, *Bukharin and the Russian Revolution*, London 1974, p. 375.

6. Yevgeny Yevtushenko, *A Precocious Autobiography*, London 1963, p. 13.

7. *Stalin,* edited by Robert McNeal, consultant Stephen Cohen, Milan 1980, p. 866.

8. 'The Tragedy of the Polish Communist Party', in Isaac Deutscher, *Marxism in Our Time,* Tamara Deutscher, ed., Berkeley, California 1971, pp. 156-57. [Reprinted in *Marxism, Wars and Revolutions,* Tamara Deutscher, ed., Verso, London 1984.]

9. Giuseppe Boffa, *Storia dell'Unione Sovietica,* Milan 1976, vol. 1, p. 593.

10. Ibid.

11. Fischer, *An Opposing Man,* p.305.

12. Boffa, *Storia dell'Unione Sovietica,* vol. 1, p. 575.

13. Ibid., p. 584.

14. Roy Medvedev, *Let History Judge, The Origins and Consequences of Stalinism,* New York 1971, p.239.

15. See Vladimir Dedijer, *Tito Speaks,* London 1953, p. 101.

16. Robert Conquest, *The Great Terror,* London 1968, pp. 525 ff.

17. See Isaac Deutscher, *The Prophet Outcast: Leon Trotsky 1929–1940,* New York 1965, pp. 371-74.

18. Isaac Deutscher, *Stalin,* Harmondsworth 1966, pp. 372-75.

19. Rudolf Schlesinger, *Il Partito comunista dell'URSS,* Milan 1962, p. 261.

20. Giuliano Procacci, *Il partito nell'Unione Sovietica,* Bari 1974, p. 154.

21. Pietro Ingrao, 'L'origine degli errori', *Rinascita,* vol. 18. no. 12, December 1961.

22. Medvedev, *Let History Judge,* p. 365.

23. Giuseppe Boffa and Gilles Martinet, *Dialogo sullo stalinismo,* Bari 1976, p. 103.

24. See M.M. Drachkovitch and B. Lazich, *The Comintern: Historical Highlights,* New York 1966, p. 140. See also Giuseppe Berti, 'Problemi di storia del Pci e dell'Internazionale comunista', *Rivista Storica Italiana,* vol. 82, no. 1, March 1970, pp. 190 ff.

25. See Drachkovitch and Lazich, *The Comintern: Historical Highlights,* pp. 142 ff.

26. See *Storia dell'Internazionale comunista,* Progress Publishers, Moscow 1974, p. 455. This is a 'brief essay' on the history of the Comintern edited by the Marxism-Leninism Institute of the Central Committee of the CPSU, drafted in collaboration with leading figures of the Communist International; it therefore has an official character. It is noted in the essay that charges that the Polish party was 'in the hands of class enemies' in 1937–38 were unfounded.

27. Conquest, *The Great Terror,* p. 434.

28. Palmiro Togliatti, 'Diversità e unità nel movimento comunista internazionale', *Rinascita,* vol. 18, no. 12, December 1961, p. 909. On Togliatti's personal participation in the decision to dissolve the Polish party, see Paolo Spriano, *Il compagno Ercoli,* Rome 1981, pp. 147-51.

29. The most complete testimony was presented by Robotti in 1980, in an interview with Italian television. For his account of his trials, see Paolo Robotti, *La prova,* Bari 1965; for autobiographical notes, see Paolo Robotti, *Scelto dalla vita,* Rome 1980.

30. Margarete Buber-Neumann, *La révolution mondiale,* Tournai 1971, p. 386.

31. Josip Broz Tito, *The Struggle and Development of the CPY Between the Two Wars,* Belgrade 1979, p. 54.

32. According to evidence gathered by Conquest (*The Great Terror,* p. 428), the Latvian Communist Party was also virtually dissolved in 1937–38.

33. See Paolo Spriano, *Storia del Partito comunista italiano,* Milan 1982.

34. See Emilio Guarnaschelli, *Una piccola pietra,* Milan 1982.

35. An unofficial calculation by a Soviet source in 1942 says that 104 of those killed or imprisoned were supposed to have been 'rehabilitated' after the reviews of the cases

of victims of the repression (Spriano, *Storia del PCI*, vol. 3, p. 242). On the tragedy that befell the Italians resident in the USSR, see also Guelfo Zaccaria, *200 comunisti italiani tra le vittime dello stalinismo*, Milan 1964; Renato Mieli, *Togliatti 1937*, Milan 1964, pp. 90-97; and, most of all, the personal testimony of a survivor, Dante Corneli, *Il redivivo tiburtino*, Milan 1977.

36. *La prova*, p. 202.

37. The letters are available in Mikhail Kolkov, *Diario della guerra di Spagna*, Milan 1966.

38. Artur London, *On Trial*, London 1970.

39. Vittorio Vidali, *La caduta della Repubblica*, Milan 1979, pp. 116-18.

40. Ambrogio Donini, 'I comunisti e la Chiesa di fronte alla guerra', in *I comunisti raccontano*, edited by Massimo Masara, Milan 1972, vol. 1, p. 267.

41. Drachkovitch and Lazich, *The Comintern: Historical Highlights*, pp. 163-64.

42. Iren Gal, *Béla Kun*, preface by Enzo Santarelli, Rome 1969, p. xxv.

43. Amendola, *Storia del Pci*, p. 344.

5

Trotsky and the Fourth International

The image of the USSR within the organized workers movement and among progressive intellectuals and democratic public opinion was not substantially tarnished by Stalin's raging repression, at least until the Russo-German Pact of August 1939. That image remained broadly positive. The reason was essentially political, related to the dividing line between fascism and anti-fascism that had already emerged and became ever sharper during the Second World War. But there were other factors, too. The scope of the terror was not widely known, even among Communist militants. Only the three great Moscow Trials were held in public. And it is striking that noted cultural figures of the left were reluctant to display any solidarity with Trotsky or Zinoviev. Romain Rolland, Barbusse, Theodore Dreiser, Max Lerner, Anna Louise Strong, and Paul Sweezy all refused to do so. Many others, from Bertolt Brecht to George Bernard Shaw, exhibited concern not to attack the Soviet Union, while American newspapers printed letters from Louis Fischer and Leon Feuchtwanger endorsing the credibility both of the charges against the defendants in the great trials and of their confessions.[1]

For those who were somewhat puzzled by the trials, there was a 'historicist' argument based on the great precedent of the French Revolution: if Danton and Mirabeau had betrayed the revolution, Bukharin and Trotsky might have done so as well.[2] Others, who did not think that the defendants had become agents of the German or Japanese secret services, believed that Bolshevism's tradition of bitter factional struggles could well have turned the oppositionists into conspirators. Any doubts party militants may have had were countered by their spirit of discipline and trust.[3] Times were hard, and with fascism on the offensive it was impermissible to sow divisions, for no European state had proven so decisively anti-fascist as the USSR. Eric Hobsbawm has written:

It is impossible to understand either the reluctance of men and women of the left to criticize, or often even to admit to themselves, what was happening in the USSR in those years, or the isolation of left critics of the USSR, without taking account of the conviction that in the struggle against fascism communism and liberalism were fighting for the same cause, in the deepest sense of the word. Not to mention the most obvious fact, that each needed the other and that in the conditions of the thirties what Stalin was doing, however chilling, was of Russian concern, whereas what Hitler was doing was a threat to everyone.[4]

Symptomatic was the rule strictly followed by the French Socialist press, which published nothing about the Moscow trials except official Soviet accounts. Blum long kept silent.[5] There were some who openly denounced the wave of repression, especially Social Democrats, like De Brouckère and Adler, as well as the most authoritative and prestigious German and Austrian theorists of the Second International: Karl Kautsky, Rudolf Hilferding, and Otto Bauer. Social Democratic criticism of the Soviet Union was not new, but it grew sharper in the wake of the trials. Its themes were by no means uniform although they all charged that the Soviet Union was afflicted by a regime of personal despotism and a 'bureaucracy' that subordinated the whole of society to itself. Whereas Kautsky held that the course of the Bolshevik revolution from Lenin to Stalin made it inevitable that the minority dictatorship, the party dictatorship, would be transformed into the dictatorship of an individual over the party and state, Hilferding emphasized the 'uncontrolled political absolutism' that had overridden the economy and bestowed upon politics a 'primacy unprecedented'[6] even for a totalitarian regime.

But even harsh analyses did not necessarily draw the negative conclusions of a Kautsky, Hilferding, or an exile like Victor Serge.[7] Otto Bauer, for instance, brought the discussion back to the general crisis of capitalism that was spawning fascism, and he affirmed that the building of socialism in the USSR had been more successful than he himself had thought just a few years before. Bauer argued that the 1936 terrorist repression would be no more than a brief passing phase and would be followed by a democratic transformation of the Stalin regime. The illustrious Austro-Marxist held that one major cause had to be defended and built upon: the common purpose and efforts of the Socialist International and Russian Bolshevism in the preservation of peace.[8] Stalin was becoming a symbol of steadfastness, the guarantor of intransigence, even for non-Communist anti-fascists. Even André Malraux—a man of undisguised sympathy for Trotskyism, who had been among the first to go to Spain, where he commanded an air squadron, and who travelled to the United States in 1937 to raise money for the Republic—refused to give a deposition before the Dewey Commission, explaining his attitude in these terms: 'Trotsky is a great moral force in the world, but Stalin has lent dignity to mankind; and just as the Inquisition did not detract from the fundamental dignity of Christianity, so the Moscow trials do not detract from the fundamental dignity of Communism.'[9]

Throughout the period of the Popular Fronts, Communist propaganda continued to place heavy emphasis on the theme of democratic rights. The promulgation of the new Soviet constitution was seen as part and parcel of this concern, as evidence of fresh evolution towards socialist democracy. This document did not challenge the leading role of the single ruling party. Nevertheless, its articles generally encouraged an interpretation that focused attention on two elements: its assertion that 'Soviet society has already, in the main, succeeded in achieving socialism,'[10] and its emphasis on the guarantees of political and civil rights accorded Soviet citizens. The first postulate was said to be the most striking manifestation yet of Stalin's 'theoretical decisiveness'. In this case Stalin undoubtedly fashioned a theory to suit his political design. The classics of Marxism described socialism as a classless society, and since Stalin could not possibly effect such a transformation of Soviet society in 1936, 'why not resort to a theory that would proclaim what did not exist as socialist?' 'The decision was made not by achieving the object but by modifying it.'[11]

But it was the second aspect that was most enthusiastically hailed in the West: the Soviet Union now had a fully democratic constitution, even more democratic than the bourgeois constitutions, because it sanctioned freedom based on justice. The noted American journalist and author Louis Fischer, for example, held that 'the rule of law is now definitively established in the Soviet Union'.[12] The left Labour intellectual Harold Laski wrote that 'great steps have been taken to pass from the dictatorship of the proletariat to democratic socialism.'[13] The British poet Stephen Spender said that the 1936 constitution 'already satisfies the most ambitious hopes and promises of liberalism'.[14] The famous English Fabian couple Sidney and Beatrice Webb went even further. 'It is clear', they wrote, 'that based on the revised constitution of 1936, the Soviet Union is the broadest and most egalitarian democracy in the world.'[15]

Apologies for the Stalin constitution by progressive cultural figures served another purpose too. Attempts to theorize new forms of democracy, in republican Spain for instance, were encouraged and supported by reference to the 1936 constitution, which was frequent and ritualistic, among both Communists and 'fellow travellers', throughout the years of the Popular Fronts. Trotsky's acerbic polemical comments also encouraged sympathy for the USSR among Socialists and Liberals, for his claim that Stalin and the Communist International were acting as grave-diggers of the revolution in France and Spain seemed unconvincing. Trotsky did not argue that it was wrong to join forces to win the war in Spain, but he held that the Republic would gain ground against Franco only if it took revolutionary steps internally. [16] In May 1937, however, the anarchist and POUM revolt in Barcelona was condemned by anti-fascists as an unconscious diversion, if not a deliberate provocation. This, for example, was the view of Carlo Rosselli[17] and Pietro Nenni. [18] Trotskyism was considered a divisive force. Embarrassment and antagonism were expressed no more clearly than by the Italian anti-fascists of the Giustizia e Libertà group, who protested against the Moscow trials, but in these terms:

> Even if we were not the defenders of the Soviet Union that we are, we still would not have any sympathy for Trotsky or Trotskyism. Trotsky is less politically serious than Stalin, and his magniloquent culture is highly reminiscent of the ostentatious wealth displayed by some extremely intelligent profiteers made famous by the war in Europe. Trotskyism is among the most muddled and demagogic products of post-war political struggle. But to allow innocent revolutionaries to be shot without protest would be a form of complicity unworthy of anti-fascists who are also fighting for the cause of justice. [19]

To understand the struggle of the 'Stalinists' against Trotskyism, then being waged with unprecedented violence, we must distinguish the various features of Trotsky's polemic and situate Trotskyism itself. Trotsky held that the revolution had been 'betrayed' under Stalin's rule: power was now in the hands of a despotic bureaucracy, and the USSR had lost its internationalist purpose. But the book entitled *The Revolution Betrayed*, published in 1936, is by no means a mere display of invective or abstraction. On the contrary, it presented a penetrating analysis of the development and contradictions of Soviet society. At its heart stood Trotsky's analysis of the contradiction between the bureaucracy, personified by Stalin, and the toiling masses. Trotsky, like Hilferding, observed that politics had become the decisive factor in social life, in the sense that there 'is no other government in the world in whose hands the fate of the whole country is concentrated to such a degree'. [20] He also invoked the precedent of the French revolution, arguing that the USSR was going through a phase of 'Thermidor' that would inevitably give way to fresh crises. But what sort? Trotsky emphasized the provisional character of the bureaucratic victory, defining 'the present Soviet regime, in all its contradictoriness, not [as] a socialist regime, but [as] a *preparatory* regime *transitional* from capitalism to socialism'.[21] In substance, he maintained, it was still possible for the masses to rid themselves of the counter-revolutionary bureaucracy. The gains of the October Revolution had not been definitively lost.

Trotsky's entire analysis was inspired by his faith in a new revolutionary upsurge and by his call for a return to the original 'liberating' spirit of the Russian revolution. He warned that Stalin's 'pedagogic' dictatorship weighed oppressively on Russian culture.

Spiritual creativeness demands freedom. The very purpose of communism is to subject nature to technique and technique to plan, and compel the raw material to give unstintingly everything to man that he needs. Far more than that, its highest goal is to free finally and once and for all the creative forces of mankind from all pressure, limitation, and humiliating dependence. Personal relations, science and art will not know any externally imposed 'plan', nor even any shadow of compulsion.[22]

While Trotsky defined the bureaucracy as a privileged social stratum, he polemicized vigorously against the theory that the USSR was 'state capitalist', and he equally vehemently denied that the distortions and degeneration had fundamentally altered the social character of the USSR. For him the Soviet Union was still a 'workers state', albeit a degenerated workers state. The bureaucracy had not become a class.

The bureaucracy has not yet created social supports for its dominion in the form of special types of property. It is compelled to defend state property as the source of its power and its income. In this aspect of its activity it still remains a weapon of proletarian dictatorship. The attempt to represent the Soviet bureaucracy as a class of 'state capitalists' will obviously not withstand criticism. The bureaucracy has neither stocks nor bonds. It is recruited, supplemented and renewed in the manner of an administrative hierarchy, independently of any special property relations of its own. The individual bureaucrat cannot transmit to his heirs his rights in the exploitation of the state apparatus. The bureaucracy enjoys its privileges under the form of an abuse of power.[23]

For Trotsky, then, the USSR was a transitional society between capitalism and socialism. The general framework of Trotsky's analysis, at least between 1935 and 1937, can be summarized in one phrase: it was a time of revolution on a world scale, but especially in

Europe. The proletarian revolution was on the agenda in France and Spain, and the Western working class would act as a transmission belt infusing the Russian proletariat, now imprisoned by the Stalin bureaucracy, with fresh consciousness and vigour. Hence his bitter polemic against the 'moderate' line of the Popular Fronts, which would curb and impede the revolutionary advance of the French and Spanish workers, blocking their 'road to power'.

In 1939 and 1940 Trotsky's anxious analysis faced more urgent dilemmas. But two additional points should be made about the preceding phase. The first is that whereas Trotsky was quite lucid in denouncing the mistaken Comintern formula about 'social fascism' in the early thirties, accurately pinpointing the divergent class bases and state forms of Social Democracy and Nazism-fascism, he was less far-sighted about the crisis that gripped Europe in 1936–38. His tone was voluntaristic, his assessment one-sided, stressing only the revolutionary potential of the situation, both in France in 1935 and 1936 and in Spain from the time of the Asturias rising to the outbreak of the civil war. As we have seen, this has been a subject of historiographical controversy. As for the more general Trotskyist worldview — if we may so describe the personal opinion of the 'prophet outcast' — its most characteristic limitation was its assumption that 'the problems of the USSR will be solved in the Iberian peninsula, France, and Belgium'. In other words, a proletarian revolution in the West would be *required* if the masses of Soviet workers were to awake. The final paragraph of *The Revolution Betrayed* is illuminating in this regard:

> If the Soviet bureaucracy succeeds, with its treacherous policy of 'people's fronts', in ensuring the victory of reaction in Spain and France — and the Communist International is doing all it can in that direction — the Soviet Union will find itself on the edge of ruin. A bourgeois counter-revolution rather than an insurrection of the workers against the bureaucracy will be on the order of the day. If, in spite of the united sabotage of reformists and 'Communist' leaders, the proletariat of Western Europe finds the road to power, a new chapter will open in the history of the Soviet Union. The first victory of a revolution in Europe would pass like an electric shock through the Soviet masses, straighten them up, raise their spirit of independence, awaken the traditions of 1905 and 1917, undermine the position of the Bonapartist bureaucracy, and acquire for the Fourth International no less significance than the October revolution possessed for the Third. Only in that way can the first workers state be saved for the socialist future. [24]

As we know, things worked out differently. It therefore seems legitimate to consider Trotsky's schematic alternative a typical case of wishful thinking. Trotsky did not regard the real alternative — fascism or democracy, for the Western working class too — as decisive, and in this he dissented from a broad alignment which, at least at the time of the Popular Fronts, included Communists, Socialists, and those 'liberals' to whom Hobsbawm referred. It would not be correct to claim that Trotsky was completely insensitive to this theme. The transformation of the proletarian dictatorship in the USSR into Stalinist 'caesarism' had already led him to wonder whether political democracy was not after all an indispensable precondition for the development of socialism, but he tended to set aside that option: the world revolution would smash both the 'plebiscitary Bonapartism' sanctioned by the 1936 Soviet constitution and reactionary fascism in Europe.

This was the function ascribed to the Fourth International then in process of formation. But what was the strength of the Trotskyist current in 1935, or even in 1937–38? Isaac Deutscher — Trotsky's great biographer and an active follower as well, though his work shuns hagiographical temptations — presented a brutally revealing panorama of the forces of international Trotskyism. Objective conditions, he noted, were among the factors limiting their ability to act. During all the years of his ardent confidence in the new revolutionary upsurge and his efforts to stimulate and direct it, the Leader was buffeted from country to country. He was deported from France in 1935 and allowed to move to Norway, but pressure from the Soviet government soon led to his expulsion. He finally had to abandon the European continent entirely, seeking exile in Mexico in January 1937.[25] Trotsky's last genuine supporters were being exterminated in the USSR, along with former and alleged new Trotskyists, while groups explicitly claiming allegiance to him were rare even in those European countries in which it was still legally possible for them to organize, albeit under the constant threat of provocation.

The project of building a Fourth International around the 'Bolshevik-Leninist opposition' dates back to 1933 at least. But it was not until 1938 that the first real step was taken to implement it. Despite the scepticism of some 'sections' — in particular of two leading Polish militants (both in exile, of course) — Trotsky decided to proceed to a founding congress, mindful of an event which he held to be imminent and in which he hoped and expected that his new organization would play an irreplaceable role: the outbreak of the second world war. Here, at least, he and Stalin were of one mind: war was inevitable, and was fast approaching. In August 1937 Trotsky wrote:

> Thus war may break out toward the end of the next three to four years, that is, precisely at the time when the fulfilment of the armament programmes should 'assure peace'. Naturally, we indicate this date only for purposes of general orientation. Political events may hasten or defer the moment of the explosion. But its inevitability is rooted in the dynamics of economy, in the dynamics of social antagonisms, as well as in the dynamics of armaments. [26]

In 1937 and 1938, in the midst of the crisis of the Popular Fronts, the ebb of the 'offensive' upsurge of the masses of workers, and the increasingly tortured course of the struggle in Spain, Trotsky had no illusion that the West European workers would be able to halt the drift to war. But he held that this made it even more necessary to replace the 'morally defunct' Second and Third Internationals with a new body that would be able to confront the tasks that would be posed by the war. Trotsky seemed certain that 'the masses who will be driven to exasperation by the war will find no leadership except that offered by the Fourth International'.

Trotsky spent the summer of 1938 in Mexico City preparing the 'draft programme' and resolutions for the 'founding congress' of the new International. In reality, Deutscher tells us, the congress — held in Périgny, a village near Paris, on 3 September 1938 — was no more than 'a small conference of Trotskyists . . . Twenty-one delegates were present, claiming to represent the organizations of eleven countries.'[27] In attendance were veterans like the Frenchman Alfred Rosmer, as well as Pierre Naville, also French, plus the Italian Alfonso Leonetti and the American Max Schachtman, who presided. More obscure personalities were also present, among them agents of Stalin. 'Somewhere outside the conference room' was 'a man calling himself Jacques Mornard', Trotsky's future assassin, Ramón Mercader, who murdered his victim in his Mexico City study on 20 August 1940. Another, no less insidious provocateur was 'Etienne', who was supposed to represent the Russian section but actually represented the NKVD. His real name was Mark Zborowski, and since he had long since won the trust of both Trotsky and his son Lyova, he knew all the 'secrets' of the organization. The congress ran through its agenda rapidly.

> Naville delivered the 'progress report', which was to justify the organizers' decision to proclaim the foundation of the Fourth International.

Unwittingly, however, he revealed that the International was little more than a fiction: none of its so-called Executives and International Bureaus had been able to work in the past few years. The 'sections' of the International consisted of a few dozen, or at most, a few hundred members each — this was true even of the American section, the most numerous of all, which claimed a formal membership of 2,500.[28]

The congress approved the resolution to found the Fourth International by a vote of nineteen in favour and three against (including the two Polish delegates). The representatives of the only 'sympathizing' groups with a modicum of substance and independent political experience — the Catalan POUM, itself now reduced to modest proportions, and the small Workers and Peasants Socialist Party (PSOP), formed in April 1938 by a left split from the French Socialists and led by Marceau Pivert — were not admitted to the discussion.

Although the numerical size of the Fourth International was minimal and its ability to influence the political situation negligible, the fact remains that Trotsky's ideas — bolstered by his prestige and the force of his personality as a man and a writer — still had an influence, especially among intellectuals, that went well beyond the organizational and numerical confines of the followers of the persecuted and much-slandered exile. As far as the evolution of international Communism is concerned, however, the principal problem arises precisely from this crying disproportion: why were the 'national sections' of the Comintern called upon so peremptorily to vent such rage, to 'mobilize' so 'vigilantly' against tiny Trotskyist groups, to ostracize them so completely?

Part of the answer has to do with the psychological dimensions to which I alluded earlier in discussing Stalin's crimes, but that is not enough. Neither can it be reduced to the observation, reasonable though it may be, that the 'monstrous' Trotsky (and the danger he was supposed to represent) was *invented* in an effort to justify the repression and to create a climate of intimidation, suspicion, and rigid orthodoxy. The struggle against Trotskyism was also quite prominent abroad; it was prosecuted with particular bitterness in France and Spain.[29] Its immediate negative political effects, already tangible, became even worse because of the way they poisoned the movement. In France the anti-Trotskyist campaign was one of the factors (albeit secondary) that generated friction between Socialists and Communists. In Spain, where the struggle against Trotskyist 'bandits' was conducted by means of physical liquidation, (particularly of the POUM, whose leader Andrés Nin was shot in Barcelona on 16 June 1937),[30] the consequences were even more serious. They helped to weaken the Front, and caused deep fissures in the Negrin government. This has been confirmed by observers who cannot be suspected of any sympathy for Trotskyism (or for anarchism). Tuñon de Lara, for example, has written:

> On the one hand, the Communists were carrying out the Popular Front policy, seeking change within the framework of republican legality, while the Soviet Union was helping Spain, opposing non-interference, and pursuing a foreign policy that sought the unity of the democratic countries against fascism. On the other hand, Stalinism was entering its first virulent phase, violating socialist legality itself and in practice aiding international fascism through its persecution of Communists. In the case of Spain, polemical weapons were being handed to those who were trying to fight the Negrin government and whose demagogy contributed to weakening or dividing the struggle front of the Spanish people and their government.[31]

There is also the sad testimony of Fernando Claudín, based on first-hand experience:

> For our part, let us add that the repression against the POUM and the heinous assassination of Andrés Nin was the blackest page in the history of the Spanish Communist Party, which was guilty of complicity in the crime, committed by Stalin's secret services. We Spanish Communists were certainly alienated — as were all the world's Communists, at that time and for many years to come — by the monstrous lies fabricated in Moscow. But this does not absolve us from our historic responsibility.[32]

The most serious contradiction of the general struggle against Trotskyism was the identification of Trotskyism with fascism, so untenable as to appear grotesque. But this identification — upheld by José Díaz and Maurice Thorez, by Togliatti and Dimitrov — obviously undermined the line of unity analytically, quite apart from its military and political effects in Spain. It was perhaps Palmiro Togliatti, the leader who worked hardest for unity and had the clearest grasp of its novelty, who exhibited this contradiction most graphically. During his mission in Spain, Togliatti tirelessly emphasized the necessity of attracting even the anarchists to support the government and the Front; he warned the Communists against any tendency to try to settle political difficulties by simply increasing their weight in the army and in the organizations and administrative apparatuses of the state; he understood that the internal divisions of the Spanish working class were deeply rooted in diverse traditions and living conditions, that 'subversion' and even 'ultra-leftism' had nothing whatever in common with fascism. But despite all this, he too upheld the equation 'Trotskyism equals fascism' and maintained that anti-fascist unity could be strengthened only if the Trotskyists were eliminated,[33] almost as though such a purge was actually a precondition for unity. He argued that to describe the Spanish war as a fight between the proletariat and capitalism was to open the road to provocation and betrayal.[34] Not that both had not occurred. Pietro Nenni, the Italian Socialist who had been in Spain, noted in his diary that 'there were times when the attitude of the anarchists bordered on provocation, and they fell into it with the Barcelona uprising of May 1937'.[35] Fernando Claudín is of the same view.[36] But in 1938, when anti-fascist unity was further weakened and a kind of anti-Communist coalition arose among Spanish political forces within the Republic, it was partly, if not mainly, the result of the discriminatory violence and authoritarian police methods exported by Stalin.

The struggle against Trotskyism also brought about a campaign of intimidation within the various Communist parties, for anti-Trotskyism became a tool for demanding the most complete obedience from every leader, as everyone was called upon to endorse the repression. Not for nothing did Togliatti offer this advice to a leader of the PCI who arrived in Moscow in February 1937: 'It would be a mistake to think that only or primarily the comrades here in Moscow should write against Trotskyism and in defence of Stalin's policy. Due note is taken of what is written by all the party leaders.'[37] This explains the chorus of the entire international Communist press in 1936–38, as the various parties rivalled one another in denouncing the Trotskyist danger. It was a deafening chorus intended to make it clear that Trotsky was not only morally comparable to Hitler or Franco, but just as threatening an enemy as the fascist dictators. The verbal attacks were so intense and the struggle against Trotskyism so merciless that the hypothesis of one historian, that Stalin was genuinely frightened of Trotsky, cannot be ruled out. Adam Ulam argued that Stalin feared Trotskyist contagion in Spain, and also feared Trotsky's potential influence in a USSR threatened by war or invasion:

> When the [Spanish] war was moving to its bloodiest phase in 1937, another worry entered the Soviet mind. Among the fantastic profusion of Spanish radical parties, one bearing the initials POUM had a clear Trotskyite colouring. It was not out of the range of possibility that the POUM and the anarchists, especially strong in Catalonia, might coalesce to create a semi-Trotskyite regional regime, thus creating even if temporarily, a

political focus for the heresy. Hence the systematic campaign of assassination conducted by agents of the Soviet secret police and the Spanish Communists against Trotskyites and declared anti-Communists among the anarchists, a campaign that led to incidents of civil war *within* the Republican camp.[38]

And he added that Stalin seriously considered Trotsky to be just as dangerous as Hitler:

> Superfluous to say, not a shred of evidence has ever been uncovered linking any of the Trotskyites to German or Italian agents. But Stalin and his colleagues were haunted by history. Barely twenty years before, another exile had returned to Russia to lead a handful of supporters, and within six months they were in power.

Notes

1. See Deutscher, *The Prophet Outcast*, pp. 367-68.
2. This sort of interpretation was common among French Communists. See Philippe Robrieux, *Histoire intérieure du Parti communiste français*, Paris 1980, vol. 1, p. 471.
3. Typical in this respect was the reaction of Italian Communist leaders in the fascist prisons, with a few exceptions, like Altiero Spinelli, who broke with the party. See Pietro Secchia, 'L'azione svolta dal Partito comunista in Italia durante il fascismo: 1926–1932', in *Annali Feltrinelli 1971*, Milan 1973, p. xxiv.
4. 'Gli intellettuali e l'antifascismo', in *Storia del marxismo*, vol. 3, II, p. 449.
5. Lilly Marcou, ed., *L'Urss vue de gauche*, Paris 1982, pp. 141-42.
6. Salvadori, *La critica marxista allo stalinismo*, pp. 83-128.
7. It was his view in 1937, expressed in *Destin d'une révolution*, that Soviet society was 'a society of unequals in the making'. For his political evolution, see *Memoirs of a Revolutionary 1901-1941*, London 1963, an autobiography justly described by Salvadori (La critica marxista allo stalinismo, p. 115) as 'one of the masterpieces of political memoirs'.
8. Otto Bauer, *Tra due guerre mondiali?*, introduction by Enzo Collotti, Turin 1979, pp. 289-90.
9. See Deutscher, *The Prophet Outcast*, p. 370.
10. From the report 'On the Draft Constitution of the USSR', in Joseph Stalin, *Leninism. Selected Writings*, New York 1942, p. 386.
11. Valentino Gerratana, 'Stalin, Lenin e il marxismo-leninismo', in *Storia del marxismo*, vol. 3, II, p. 191.
12. *New Statesman and Nation*, 1 August 1936.
13. Ibid., 20 June 1936.
14. Stephen Spender, *Forward From Liberalism*, London 1937. p. 275.
15. Sidney and Beatrice Webb, *The Truth About Soviet Russia*, London 1942, p. 51. In 1936 the Webbs had published an apology for the USSR, *Soviet Communism, a New Civilization*, which had wide success.
16. 'Interview With Havas', 19 February 1937, in Leon Trotsky, *The Spanish*

Revolution (1931–39, New York 1973, pp. 242-44.

17. Carlo Rosselli, 'Guerra e politica in Spagna', *Giustizia e Libertà*, 7 May 1937.

18. Pietro Nenni, 'Stringiamoci attorno alla Spagna, al suo esercito, al suo governo', *La Voce degli Italiani*, Paris, 5 August 1937.

19. Fen, 'Il nuovo processo di Mosca', *Giustizia e Libertà*, 29 January 1937.

20. Trotsky, *The Revolution Betrayed*, New York 1965, p. 43.

21. Ibid., p. 47

22. Ibid., p. 180.

23. Ibid., pp. 249-50.

24. Ibid., p. 290.

25. On Trotsky's peregrinations, see, apart from the work of Deutscher, Jean Van Heijenoort, *With Trotsky In Exile*, Cambridge, Mass. 1978.

26. Trotsky, 'On the Threshold of a New World War', in *Writings of Leon Trotsky (1936–37)*, New York 1970, p. 388.

27. Deutscher, *The Prophet Outcast*, p. 419.

28. Ibid., p. 420.

29. See Claudín, *The Communist Movement*.

30. See Julian Gorkin, *Les communistes contre la révolution espagnole*, Paris 1978, pp. 139–50; Pierre Broué and Emile Témime, *The Revolution and the Civil War in Spain*, London 1970, pp. 302–5. On Togliatti's alienation, see Spriano, *Il compagno Ercoli*, pp. 110–12.

31. Manuel Tuñon de Lara, *Storia della repubblica e della guerra civile in Spagna*, Rome 1966, p. 590.

32. See Claudín, *The Communist Movement*.

33. 'Gli insegnamenti del processo di Mosca' (December 1936), in Togliatti, *Opere*, vol. 4, I, pp. 155-77.

34. From a confidential letter to a leader of the exile centre of the PCI 20 March 1937, cited in Spriano, *Storia del Pci*, vol. 3, p. 174.

35. Pietro Nenni, *Spagna*, Milan 1958, p. 53.

36. Claudín, *La crisi del movimento comunista*, Italian edition, p. 182.

37. See Spriano, *Il compagno Ercoli*, pp. 107-08.

38. Adam B. Ulam, *Expansion and Coexistence. The History of Soviet Foreign Policy 1917–67*, London 1968, p. 244.

6

The Munich Capitulation

Munich is one of those words of the political lexicon, one of those geographical symbols, that has never lost its significance. Ever since that twenty-ninth day of September 1938, when Chamberlain and Daladier scurried to the Bavarian city and accepted Hitler's ultimatum, Munich has been synonymous with surrender. The two statesmen's exact motivations may be marginally controversial, but the results of their conduct are not. Six months later, the Nazis rolled into Prague, and less than a year later into Danzig. If the Western democracies were under the illusion that they had preserved peace (for an entire generation, according to the British prime minister upon his return to London), reality's verdict on their defeat brooks no appeal. It has since become obvious that the abandonment of Beneš's Czechoslovakia, the West's compliance with that initial partition of its territory through the Third Reich's annexation of the Sudetenland, was a fatal error for both France, which had a military assistance pact with Czechoslovakia, and Britain. That this surrender not only failed to avert the war but actually made it inevitable is no less certain.

Winston Churchill himself, a tenacious defender of the British empire and an anti-Communist of impeccable credentials, highlighted the essential facts of the matter. On 21 September in Paris, where he had gone to visit the French ministers Reynaud and Mandel, Churchill noted:

> The partition of Czechoslovakia under pressure from England and France amounts to the complete surrender of the Western Democracies to the Nazi threat of force. Such a collapse will bring peace or security neither to England nor to France. On the contrary, it will place these two nations in an even weaker and more dangerous situation. The mere neutralization of Czechoslovakia means the liberation of twenty-five German divisions,

which will threaten the Western front; in addition to which it will open up for the triumphant Nazis the road to the Black Sea. It is not Czechoslovakia alone which is menaced, but also the freedom and democracy of all nations. The belief that security can be obtained by throwing a small state to the wolves is a fatal delusion. The war potential of Germany will increase in a short time more rapidly than it will be possible for France and Great Britain to complete the measures necessary for their defence. [1]

Here Churchill revealed extraordinary foresight. Later, looking back on the events of September 1938, he mentioned two other aspects no less critical for future developments. The first was that by winning the submission of Czechoslovakia without having to resort to force, Hitler gained credence among the German generals, who had been both reluctant and worried, and had opposed embarking on such a perilous challenge. At the Nuremberg Trials, Marshal Keitel said that if the Western powers had supported Czechoslovakia, the Reich would not have attacked. And he added a point of particular interest to us, the second aspect noted by Churchill: 'The object of Munich was to get Russia out of Europe, to gain time, to complete the German armaments.'[2] Maxim Litvinov, the Soviet minister of foreign affairs, had solemnly declared that if France would honour its commitments, the USSR would also have been prepared to intervene, to furnish immediate and effective aid to Czechoslovakia in the event of Nazi aggression. Churchill believed that the isolation and humiliation of the USSR were among the most serious errors. 'Events took their course as if Soviet Russia did not exist. For this we afterwards paid dearly.'[3]

'Particularly sordid and sinister' was one description of the role of Poland, led by the reactionary Colonel Beck.[4] Poland seconded Hitler in the destruction of Czechoslovakia, fomenting irredentist demonstrations by the Polish minority of the Czechoslovakian territory of Teschen. The isolation of the USSR was aggravated. While Stalin threatened to abrogate the Russo-Polish non-aggression pact of 1932 if Poland attacked Czechoslovakia, the French advised the Czechoslovaks to cede to Warsaw's claims.[5] It may be disputed whether the USSR really would have rushed to Czechoslovakia's aid alongside the French in September 1938,[6] and it had also been argued that Czechoslovakia would have been well-advised to resist alone (since militarily it was capable of doing so),[7] but the fundamental point remains the surrender of Daladier and Chamberlain, who thereby demonstrated that they had no intention of availing themselves of Soviet aid.

Was there a conscious plan to drive Nazi Germany eastwards? Was the conspiracy outlined by Manuilski at the Seventeenth Congress of the Soviet Communist Party in March 1939 in operation? It would be a mistake to underestimate the fear, panic, and faint-hearted pacifistic illusions that lay behind Chamberlain's unseemly dash to Munich at Daladier's side. These were sentiments shared by broad masses of Europeans in September 1938. The Munich participants were greeted by genuine ovations upon their return home; there was a wave of deep relief in Paris and London as in Italy. Mussolini had gone to Munich ostensibly as a mediator but actually to support the German proposals.[8] On his return he was jubilantly hailed as the 'saviour of peace'. Galeazzo Ciano, Mussolini's minister of foreign affairs, related that 'In Italy, along his route from Brennero to Rome, the Duce enjoyed receptions such as I have never seen, from everyone from the king to the peasants. He himself told me that he had seen such warmth only on the evening of the proclamation of the empire.'[9]

In Britain 250 Labour MPs voted against Chamberlain's conduct (while Churchill and a small minority of Conservatives abstained), but the French Socialists made their satisfaction clear to Daladier. Even Blum spoke in the 1 October *Le Populaire* of 'joy', of a sense of liberation. The Communists denounced the capitulation and betrayal in terms that left no doubt that they no longer entertained any possibility of common action with the Socialist International.[10] There were already signs of a return to the line of 'unity from below' against the traitorous leaders of the Second International.

But let us return to the effects of Munich and the intentions of Chamberlain and Daladier. Was it purely a matter of illusions and mistakes, of misconceived confidence that Hitler would demonstrate moderation? It seems doubtful. Although British imperialism had not concocted the diabolical plot claimed by Manuilski, the policy of 'appeasement' of Nazi Germany did reflect more than mere disorientation. At least one reason for it was lack of military preparation, which motivated a desire to avert any threat of war, to seek peace 'at any price'. But there was also a clear political propensity, which may be interpreted in one of two ways: either as an attempt to reach agreement with Germany on a division of spheres of influence that would turn Germany against the USSR and thereby encourage Berlin to abandon any claims on British colonies; or as a simple means of allowing Hitler a free hand in the East, even if not directly fostering aggression against the Soviet borders. The former interpretation is shared by many historians who have emphasized that Conservative circles in Britain planned to make Germany the major bulwark against Bolshevism, the threat of which they regarded as the main danger in Spain even back in 1936. Enzo Collotti, for instance, has written

> The very attempt to divert the impending storm eastwards confirms that Chamberlain was not unaware of the expansionist designs of National Socialism. The Soviet Union was excluded from the Munich conference as a natural result of the policy of the Western powers, which although they had been free with their blandishments against Nazism and fascism, had deliberately ignored the existence of Soviet power in Europe.[11]

This point is essential. Much evidence, including their diplomatic and political conduct itself, indicates that Britain and France had scant respect for Soviet military capacities, which had been further undermined by the purges in the army; they too were concerned about the internal state of the Soviet armed forces. The British historian A.J.P. Taylor, who has argued that Chamberlain gave in at Munich partly because he was convinced of the justice of the aspiration of more than 3 million Sudeten Germans to rejoin their motherland, has written:

> The British and French governments acknowledged Soviet Russia only to emphasize her military weakness; and this view, though it rested no doubt on their information, represented also their desire. They wanted Soviet Russia to be excluded from Europe; and therefore readily assumed that she was so by circumstances. Did their wishes go further? Did they plan to settle Europe not only without Soviet Russia, but also against her? Was it their intention that Nazi Germany should destroy the 'Bolshevik menace'? This was the Soviet suspicion, both at the time and later. There is little evidence of it in the official record, or even outside it. British and French statesmen were far too distracted by the German problem to consider what would happen when Germany had become the dominant power in Eastern Europe. Of course, they preferred that Germany should march east, not west, if she marched at all. But their object was to prevent war, not to prepare one; and they sincerely believed — or at any rate Chamberlain believed — that Hitler would be content and pacific if his claims were met.[12]

In any event, the Munich pact dramatically altered the situation in Eastern Europe. The French policy of collective security collapsed, and Germany, now supported by Poland, became the leading power in the region. After Munich, both France and Britain helped to encourage Hitler's adventure in the Ukraine, supporting an irredentist movement of Ukrainian exiles based in Germany. It is difficult to conceive of a policy more blind and morally contemptible than the attempt in the autumn of 1938 to preserve peace in the West by fomenting subversion in the Ukraine. According to André Scherer, Paris considered an 'indirect' attack by Hitler probable:

> It was well known that he was holding some good cards, and that he was a master at fomenting internal disorder among his neighbours. It was thought that the most immediate German objective would be to establish an independent state in the Ukraine. This conviction was based on the activities in Germany of the Ukrainian nationalist movement of Colonel Evhen Konovaletz and the subversive broadcasts of Radio Vienna. Bonnet said that he had information that there had been some turmoil in the Ukraine following the many recent executions in' Russia. He considered it likely that there were separatist movements in the Ukraine. Finally, he thought that the food situation was so catastrophic in Germany that expansion to the Ukraine would be vitally necessary for Berlin. [13]

Paris was determined to point Hitler eastwards and was under the illusion that France could effectively hide behind the Maginot Line. Prime Minister Daladier and his minister of foreign affairs, Bonnet, may well have considered Munich humiliating but not threatening. 'They assumed that a stalemate had been established in Western Europe. They could not impede the advance of German power in Eastern Europe; equally Germany could not invade France.' [14] The conviction proved ill-founded, but in 1938–39 few convictions were as widely shared as that of French military invincibility.

France was in turmoil, permeated with reactionary and pro-fascist currents, divided, hostile to any prospect of a real anti-Nazi security alliance with the USSR and under the illusion that Mussolini could be lured away from Hitler. All this drew Paris close to British policy. People were afraid of war; they did not wish to die for the Sudetenland. Even the argument that national honour had been tarnished by failure to aid Czechoslovakia aroused little response. The employers were on the offensive: a bill introduced by the Daladier government proposed to roll back the historic conquest of the forty-hour week. Giorgio Amendola, an Italian Communist then in exile in Paris, graphically described the atmosphere in Paris in the autumn of 1938:

> Among the French people, diplomatic and military calculations were overshadowed by the general desire to maintain the rhythm of daily life at all costs, to prolong tranquillity as much as possible. True, there was

inflation, prices were going up; but unemployment was down, the more highly skilled workers were making good money, and in the butcher shops women of the popular classes could afford to compete with society ladies for the best cuts of meat. In the summer workers had rivalled petty-bourgeois vacationers for rooms in the more modest *pensions*. The middle class was scandalized! The bourgeoisie was gripped by blind and selfish hatred of Léon Blum and the Jews, of the working class, and naturally of the Communists. The reds were losing in Spain, and what they needed was another lesson in France, even at the price of an agreement with Hitler. The divided and embittered workers did not respond consistently to the bourgeoisie's attack, but instead dug in to defend the gains they had already won.[15]

At a large public meeting in the 'Vel' d'Hiv' on 7 October Maurice Thorez strikingly reflected the atmosphere described by Amendola. He issued ringing protests, reiterated solidarity with the Spanish Republic (which had been stabbed in the back by the Munich pact), and lamented national humiliation ('How shameful! We should blush before all the world! Who can have any confidence in France's word?'). There was an anxious sense of isolation, but also pride in intransigent defence. The Communists, Thorez said, like the USSR, had but one watchword: it was not a matter of choosing between guns and butter, 'we will not rummage in the garbage for our food.'[16] The CGT called a strike against the Daladier bill for 30 November. But the government and the employers won the test of strength. The PCF now faced victorious reaction. The entire 'Communist world' had a palpable sense of being on the defensive. It is essential to recall this state of mind when considering Communist reaction to the trauma of the German-Soviet pact. Who was the first to sell out? That was the response of many Communist militants. An irresistible wave of sectarianism was mounting. When the aged Karl Kautsky died in exile in Amsterdam in October 1938, the official organ of the Communist International vented its rage on the tomb of the 'renegade': 'The anti-Bolshevik seeds sown by Kautsky have sprouted. Fascism defeated the divided working class first in Germany and then in Austria. Now it has won a great victory over the Czechoslovak Democratic Republic.'[17]

For the USSR, defensive retrenchment brought a return to 'traditional suspicion of the capitalist world as a whole, whether fascist or democratic, and therefore to the previous tendency to regard clashes within it as mere rivalries and conflicts between imperialist blocs. It was further assumed that the Soviet Union should seek to take advantage of these divisions, returning to the traditional doctrine that any participation in armed conflict should be avoided for as long as possible.'[18] Did this attitude arise only in September 1938, after Munich? Was it a turn? Perhaps the best way to disentangle the complicated skein is to consider it on two planes: the general level of what might be called a simultaneously historical and ideological attitude and the particular one of day-to-day Soviet foreign policy, based on the changing circumstances of those years.

At certain points, of course, these two levels intersect (as in the summer of 1939), but the distinction is none the less indispensable. Metaphors aside, even in 1934–38 Stalin never really believed that there was a qualitative difference between the German fascist 'gangsters' and the Anglo-American imperialist 'gangsters'. As far as their basic attitude to the land of socialism was concerned, they were just the same: enemies of the USSR one and all. Nor had his assessment of Western Social Democracy ever changed. Much has been made of the 'restrictive' interpretation of the line of the Seventh Congress that was always upheld by Stalin and the other leaders of the Communist International. Only the tactics were new.[19] This interpretation, this reserve, was encouraged by the crisis of the Popular Fronts, by British aversion to republican Spain, by the French general staff's reluctance to agree to a military convention that would give the 1935 Franco-Soviet pact any teeth, and by the general conduct of the Socialist International which baulked at united action with the Comintern.

On the other hand, it is undeniable that Stalin did pursue, both within the League of Nations and in bilateral relations (albeit with some scepticism), a policy of collective security with France and Britain to confront the Nazi danger, which was increasingly pressing and aggressive from the spring of 1936 onwards: intervention in Spain, intensive rearmament, the annexation of Austria, and the attack on Czechoslovakian sovereignty. Not for nothing was the line of the Popular Fronts inaugurated just after the alarm signal of the Polish-German rapprochement of 1934; not for nothing had Stalin tried to sponsor an agreement on Spain with the Blum government (this was one of the reasons for the moderation he urged upon the Spanish Socialists and French Communists).

Admittedly, Stalin did not believe that a socialist revolution was possible in the West in 1935–37, and did not favour it in any event. Nor did he expect that the theory of the 'main enemy' so cautiously elaborated at the Seventh Congress of the International would turn anti-fascist unity into a weapon that could ward off the threat of war indefinitely. He believed that war was inevitable, and also felt that it could be turned directly against the USSR at any moment. What would prevent the two groups of 'gangsters' from coming to some agreement at the expense of socialism?

The Spanish Communist Santiago Carrillo has observed that Stalin's foreign policy was always a kind of 'game' on the 'international chessboard, permitting all kinds of zigzags and feints, depending on chance circumstances, advancing and retreating, avoiding the resolute road of radical confrontation with the axis forces.'[20]

More than ever after Munich, it could well be added. But before? Trotsky wrote in September 1939:

> The collapse of Czechoslovakia is the collapse of Stalin's international policy of the last five years. Moscow's idea of 'an alliance of democracies' for a struggle against fascism is a lifeless fiction. No one wants to fight for an abstract principle of democracy: all are fighting for material interests. England and France prefer to satisfy the appetites of Hitler at the expense of Austria and Czechoslovakia rather than at the expense of their colonies.[21]

Trotsky's idea of the Western democracies was not very different from Stalin's. But the old oppositionist added: 'We must now surely expect an attempt by Soviet diplomacy to draw closer to Hitler at the cost of fresh retreats and capitulations that in turn will inevitably bring nearer the fall of the Stalin oligarchy.'

Ultimately, then, rapprochement with Hitler would be the result of the docile and hypocritical policy of the French and British governments. Some have gone even further. George F. Kennan has put forward a complex hypothesis linked to Soviet 'domestic policy'. While agreeing with those who argue that the Great Terror was related to Stalin's conviction that war was inevitable and imminent, Kennan also sees a connection with two possible options. From 1936, he says, Stalin contemplated a twofold eventuality: he might find himself embroiled in a conflict against Hitler or he might come to some agreement with him. In either case, he had to protect his rear as far as the internal situation was concerned. In 1937, before Munich, he became convinced that France and Britain would not genuinely oppose Hitlerite expansionism. His decision to seek an agreement with the German dictator therefore dates from that year: hence the purges, so that no potential internal opponent could impede his manoeuvre.[22]

This conjecture is too mechanical, for it fails to take account of the dynamic of the repression itself (which was not so coldly calculated)

and the lack of security that threatened Soviet policy after the great
wave of terror, for the 'decapitation' of the armed forces seriously
weakened the defensive capacities of the USSR. Nor does it give
proper weight to the bitter lesson of Munich: it was then that Stalin
finally realized just how far the spirit of surrender had spread in the
Western democracies and genuinely came to fear that there was a
conscious plot to direct Hitler's fury against the Soviet Union,
beginning with a penetration of the Ukraine. Many historians, for
instance, have noted Litvinov's comment immediately after the
Munich pact. On 4 October 1938, receiving the French ambassador
at the Soviet Ministry of Foreign Affairs, he told him: 'I merely note
that the Western powers deliberately kept the USSR out of the negotiations. My poor friend, what have you done? As for us, I do not see
any other outcome than a fourth partition of Poland.'[23] Joseph
Davies, an attentive observer of Soviet policy and American ambassador to Moscow until June 1938, wrote to Harry Hopkins on 18
January 1939:

> Specifically, there is one thing that can be done now in my opinion and
> that is to give some encouragement to Russia to remain staunch for
> collective security and peace. The reactionaries of England and France
> have quarantined her . . . The Chamberlain policy of throwing Italy,
> Poland, and Hungary into the arms of Hitler may be completed by so
> disgusting the Soviets that it will drive Russia into an economic agreement
> and an ideological truce with Hitler. That is not beyond the bounds of
> possibility or even probability . . .[24]

The Germans made no great secret of their desire to expand eastwards. As Keitel recalled, the objective of Munich was to keep Russia
out of Europe, and in December 1938 General Franz Halder, head of
the German General Staff, told Raymond Geist, American consul in
Berlin: 'You should take careful note of the National Socialist
programme for the East. If you Western powers oppose this programme, we will have to go to war.'[25] The programme included not
only the occupation of Czechoslovakia, but also the invasion of
Poland, Yugoslavia, Romania, and the USSR. In fact, Nazi aggression
was so generalized that for Hitler there was no 'main enemy': all
European countries had either to fall under his rule or to act as
vassals. In fact, this may well mark the limit of Stalin's behaviour,
once due allowance is made for the myopia and dangerous
manoeuvres of Franco-British diplomacy: leaving all options open,
as Stalin sought to do, could only retard, but not prevent, a settling of
accounts with Nazism.

As we shall see when we consider the dramatic circumstances that preceded, accompanied, and followed the German-Soviet pact of 23 August 1939, the USSR's conduct during the Second World War was determined by a variety of calculations, urgent necessities, and fears. But there is yet another hypothesis that cannot be ruled out: Stalin may have really thought that he could ward off Hitler's attack so consistently as to make it virtually impossible; in other words, he may have had a long-term compromise in mind. Especially after Munich, one particular historical-ideological component of Soviet tradition increasingly tended to predominate in the USSR: the idea that the capitalist world as a whole was a direct and permanent enemy of the Soviet Union, which therefore should not and could not make any *strategic* decision to foster an anti-fascist coalition of states and peoples, countries and toiling masses. The USSR had to rely on itself alone.

In the meantime, anti-fascism was itself in crisis, and certainly had no part in the motivations of Daladier and Chamberlain. Working-class unity had collapsed in France, while the Spanish Republic was in its death throes. The antithesis between fascism and anti-fascism nevertheless proved decisive during the Second World War in terms that the Soviet leaders seem never to have grasped, facing the onerous choices that they did, both before and after Munich. This does not mean that immediately after the Munich accords Stalin opted for rapprochement with Nazi Germany as the only realistic option of day-to-day policy. At the Eighteenth Congress of the Soviet Communist Party in March 1939, Stalin continued to draw a distinction between the 'aggressor countries' (Germany, Japan, and Italy) and the 'peaceful countries', the 'non-aggressive democratic states' (Britain, France, and the United States). But this distinction had now become purely empirical rather than theoretical. Whereas the 'aggressor' states were so characterized because they had formed a 'military bloc' bent on territorial conquest, the 'peaceful' states were simply satisfied with the status quo, with the colonies they already held, and with their existing economic and military power. Obsession with the prospect of the Soviet Union's being 'offered up' to the aggressors by the 'peaceful' states, even if only in order to let the Germans and Russians or the Japanese and Russians bleed themselves dry, is already noticeable in Stalin's remarks during the discussion at the Eighteenth Congress of the 'non-intervention' policy of the Western democracies:

The policy of non-intervention amounts to an encouragement of aggression, the unleashing of war, and consequently its transformation into world war. The policy of non-intervention reveals a will and desire not to disturb the aggressors in their sinister work, not to prevent, for example, Japan from undertaking its adventurous war against China and above all against the Soviet Union, not to prevent Germany from becoming entangled in European affairs, from launching a war against the Soviet Union, to allow the belligerent countries to sink ever deeper in the muddy swamps of war, to encourage them secretly, to allow them to exhaust one another, and then, when they are weak enough, to enter the scene with fresh forces, to intervene, naturally 'in the interests of peace' and to dictate conditions to the weakened warring countries.[26]

As we have seen, Manuilski advanced the same argument, though in less bitter terms. The USSR, Stalin repeated, must rely on its own strength in the first place — and in the second, third, fourth, and fifth places too: on its own economic power, on its own moral and political unity, on the friendship of the peoples of the Soviet Union, on the Red Army and the Red Navy, and on its peace policy. Only in the sixth place would it rely on 'the moral support of the workers of all countries, who have a vital interest in the preservation of peace' and in the seventh place on 'the wisdom of those countries which, for one reason or another, have no interest in the violation of peace.' The USSR, Stalin said in no uncertain terms, was not prepared to pull anyone else's chestnuts out of the fire; Moscow favoured peace with *all* countries. Adam Ulam writes: 'The possibility of coming to an agreement with Hitler, although contemplated previously, did not enter Stalin's mind as a concrete possibility until March 1939.'[27]

Apart from the overt statements and cautious suggestions made in the Soviet Union in March 1939, we have a document that is rather more important than any diplomatic dispatches or largely inaccessible archive material in affording us a better understanding of the more profound, more deeply rooted inspiration of Stalinist communism. It is a book, a manual of history, that became a sort of 'sacred text' for the entire movement around that time.

Notes

1. Winston Churchill, *The Second World War*, vol. 1, *The Gathering Storm*, London 1948, p. 238.

2. Ibid., p. 250.

3. Ibid., p. 240.

4. L.B. Namier, *Diplomatic Prelude: 1938–39*, London 1948, p. 447.

5. Vaccarino, *Storia della resistenza in Europa*, vol. 1, p. 297.

6. Max Beloff, *La politica estera della Russia sovietica*, Florence 1953, vol. 1, p. 360.

7. This was Churchill's opinion (*The Second World War*, vol. 1, *The Gathering Storm*, p. 237). See also Milos Hájek and J. Novotny, 'La politique et l'armée de la Tchécoslovaquie', *Revue d'Histoire de la Deuxième Guerre Mondiale*, vol. 13, no. 52, October 1963, pp. 7-8.

8. Renzo de Felice, *Mussolini: il Duce*, vol. 2, pp. 513-36.

9. Galeazzo Ciano, *Diario: 1937–38*, Bologna, 1948, p. 254.

10. This is clear in a manifesto issued by the Communist International after Munich, which calls for an international peace conference to be held under the auspices of political organizations and trade unions. The manifesto fell on deaf ears. For the text, see *La Correspondance Internationale*, vol. 17, no. 53, 15 October 1938.

11. Enzo Collotti, 'Sul significato del patto di Monaco', *Il movimento di liberazione in Italia*, no. 58, January-March 1960, p. 69.

12. A.J.P. Taylor, *The Origins of the Second World War*, Harmondsworth 1964, p. 204.

13. André Scherer, 'Le problème des "mains libres" à l'Est', *Revue d'Histoire de la Deuxième Guerre Mondiale*, vol. 8, no. 32, October 1958, pp. 4-5.

14. Taylor, *Origins of the Second World War*, p. 234.

15. Giorgio Amendola, *Un'isola*, Milan 1980, pp. 250-51.

16. 'Après la trahison de Munich' (report by Maurice Thorez, 7 October 1938), *La Correspondance Internationale*, vol. 17, no. 53, 15 October 1938.

17. 'Karl Kautsky (1854–1938)', ibid.

18. Boffa, *Storia dell'Unione Sovietica*, vol. 1, p. 624.

19. See Giuliano Procacci, 'Aspetti e problemi della politica estera sovietica', in *Momenti e problemi della storia dell'Urss*, Rome 1978, pp. 36-48. See also Marta Dassú, 'Fronte unico e fronte popolare: il VII Congresso del Comintern', in *Storia del marxismo*, vol. 3, II, pp. 621-26.

20. Santiago Carrillo, *'Eurocommunism' and the State*, London 1977, p. 114.

21. 'After the Collapse of Czechoslovakia, Stalin Will Seek Accord with Hitler', in Leon Trotsky, *Writings of Leon Trotsky (1938–39)*, New York 1969, p.29.

22. George F. Kennan, *Russia and the West Under Lenin and Stalin*, London 1961, p. 315.

23. Robert Coulondre, *De Moscou à Berlin*, Paris 1959, p. 165. Note that this testimony is confirmed in André Fontaine, *History of the Cold War*, London. 1968, p. 98.

24. Joseph Davies, *Mission to Moscow*, London 1942, p. 277.

25. Ihor Kamenetski, *Hitler's Occupation of Ukraine (1941–44)*, Milwaukee, Wisconsin 1956, p. 64.

26. From 'Stalin's Report on the Activity of the Central Committee and of the Communist Party of the Soviet Union', *La Correspondance Internationale*, vol. 19, no. 11, 13 March 1939.

27. Ulam, *Stalin*, pp. 540-41.

7

The 'Short Course':
Compass of Communism

The scope of the phenomenon was truly exceptional. The 'Short Course' on the *History of the Communist Party (Bolshevik) of the Soviet Union,* published in October 1938, was drafted by a commission composed of top political leaders such as Kalinin, Molotov, Voroshilov, Kaganovich, Mikoyan, Zhdanov, and Beria, under Stalin's direct supervision.[1] It was without doubt the world's most successful historical compendium.

Twelve million copies of the Russian edition were immediately printed, and 2 million in the various languages of the Soviet Union. Between autumn 1938 and spring 1939 translations were published in many foreign languages, the total print-run reaching 673,000.[2] The number of copies distributed over the next twenty years among new generations of militants throughout the world — students, workers, and intellectuals — was astronomical.[3] The ideas of this concise exposition of the history of the 'guiding party' were also disseminated through a network of party schools, and study of it was compulsory in the Soviet education system. By 1948, a decade after its publication, 200 editions had been produced in 62 languages: a total of 34 million copies in all.[4]

The operation was unprecedented in the international workers movement. The distribution of the Short Course dwarfed the circulation of the *Communist Manifesto* among generations of Socialists in the nineteenth and early twentieth centuries,[5] or of Lenin's *State and Revolution* among the Communist levies of the period just after the First World War. Only Mao Zedong's 'Red Book' invites quantitative comparison. This general dimension must not be forgotten. At the Eighteenth Congress of the Communist Party of the Soviet Union, at which nearly all reporters were already pledging their allegiance to the Short Course, Andrei Zhdanov said that 'since the inception of Marxism, no Marxist book has ever had such wide circulation'.[6] Twenty years later, an observer as scrupulous as Schlesinger noted that whatever one might think of the fidelity with which the text presented historical events, it had to be remembered 'that it was in the formulation given in this book that Marxism was received by the political cadres who now lead a third of humanity'.[7] But that is not all. The book can and must be read as a document: as a reflection both of the immediate objectives it was designed to achieve and of the sort of interpretation of history and 'doctrine' it offers, for it was closely linked to the dramatic circumstances of those years.

The unscrupulous use of 'Marxist-Leninist' theory in the interests of immediate policy is undoubtedly one of the constituent features of Stalinism. We shall examine several instances in due course. More generally, György Lukács was correct to note that there was a substantial difference between Lenin's and Stalin's approaches to Communism's intellectual heritage and to the 'scientific method' of testing it. Lukács wrote:

> Stalin, who lacked Lenin's authority — built upon great and important theoretical achievements and now considered to be somehow 'natural' — found a way to offer an immediately evident justification for all his measures by presenting them as direct and necessary consequences of Marxist-Leninist doctrine. To this end he had to eliminate mediations, and theory and practice were inevitably and immediately fused. . . . Stalin's lack of scruples went to the point of altering theory itself if necessary, to justify his claims to authority.[8]

The same observation applies to the nonchalance with which history was altered, primarily the history of the movement and the party. 'Marxism-Leninism' itself was now tailored to an internal historiographic project. As Ernesto Ragionieri has noted, history became 'the source and supreme criterion of the ideological education of militants'.[9] The illustration and simplification of doctrine were brought to bear on the interpretation of historical events, and in turn contributed to simplifying these events themselves, to ascribing a one-sided meaning to them. Not for nothing was a portion of the book's fourth chapter (written by Stalin himself[10]) dedicated to an exposition of the principles of dialectical and historical materialism: about forty pages meant to convince the reader that 'the science of the history of society, despite all the complexity of the phenomena of social life, can become as precise a science as, let us say, biology.'[11] There was a logical corollary as well. Individual investigation was not sufficient to produce real knowledge of history, or to master its laws and lessons: an official interpretation had to be given, the interpretation of the party. A Central Committee resolution stated that the book should be considered 'an irreplaceable guide . . . that furnishes an official interpretation of the fundamental problems of the history of the CP(B) . . . in order to prevent all arbitrary interpretations.'[12]

This preventive effort came at just the right time. As Lukács pointed out, the publication of the Short Course marked the culmination of the tendency to establish an immediate link between raw facts and the most general theoretical positions. If Lenin was to be used to justify contingent political policy, there could be no hesitation in deleting anything in his writings that might seem to contradict that policy (the Marx-Engels Institute was reorganized for this purpose, and a new, suitably edited version of Lenin's works was prepared). The sacramentalization of party history helped to sanctify the canonical line of succession leading from Marx and Engels through Lenin to Stalin, making the latter not only the legitimate successor and legatee of Lenin, but also the individual with whom the party, the cause of socialism, and ultimate doctrinal authority were identified. This process had actually begun before 1937–38. Its beginning can be traced back to the 'clean up' of the field of historical studies initiated with Stalin's famous 1931 letter to the review *Proletarskaya Revolutsia*, in which he accused various scholars of smuggling in Trotskyist ideas and of exhibiting 'rotten liberalism'.[13]

One indication of just how deeply rooted this concept was among Soviet Communist leadership circles was the sort of criticism made of the manual (despite the continuing high esteem in which it was held) by Anastas Mikoyan in his speech to the Twentieth Congress of the Soviet Communist Party in 1956.

> The Central Committee report states clearly that the level of our propaganda work is inadequate. One of the fundamental reasons for this is that in general Marxism-Leninism is studied only in the Short Course. And this, of course, is wrong. The wealth of ideas of Marxism-Leninism cannot be contained in the limited compass of the history of our party, and still less of a short course about it. We must therefore write theoretical manuals for comrades of varying degrees of training. This is the first thing to do. Second, the Short Course is also unsatisfactory because it does not deal with the events of the last twenty years of our party's life. Can there be any justification for the absence of a detailed history of the party over the past twenty years?[14]

Such was the view of one of the consultants — or compilers — of the Short Course twenty years on. Since then new theoretical and historical manuals have been produced, in the USSR and elsewhere. The French Communist Party published an official manual of its own history in 1964,[15] eight years after the Twentieth Congress and three years after the Twenty-Second, during which there was an avalanche of accusations against Stalin, now depicted as a bloody despot. The demiurgic view of the 1938 manual faded during the period of limited de-Stalinization in the USSR, but the methodological criteria, the notion that an official history was the only acceptable kind, did not change. Nor did the structure that underpinned theoretical Stalinism: the famous fourth chapter of the Short Course, masterpiece of so-called *diamat,* or dialectical materialism. This foundation has been characterized as follows:

> Every concept is generated by an axiomatic definition, and every definition gives rise to a sequence of simple deductions leading to the evident conclusion that 'proletarian socialism is a direct deduction from dialectical materialism'. Plainness and deductive simplicity were requisite principles of Stalinist theorizing from the very outset, and they always remained so. Anything that did not lend itself to these requisites had to be set aside. Stalin could safely ignore the complexity of analysis in *Capital,* for all he needed from Marx's thought was to extract simple formulas that could be translated into slogans (for the same reason, he could be satisfied with manual-type expositions). He was unquestionably consistent, since what he needed was a theory that could serve as the foundation for unshakeable faith and could be readily inscribed on a battleflag. It is therefore not surprising that the hammer became the most important instrument of philosophy, as it did in other fields.[16]

Axiomatic simplication, of course, has negative effects in the long run, leads to an ossification of Marxism, and becomes a barrier to free research. But Schlesinger has called attention to other, no less interesting aspects which became characteristic features of the new party *cadres,* part of the education of the typical central, intermediate, and lower-level leaders of all the Communist parties, who thus became far more homogeneous than the first-generation cadres of the Communist International had been. Simplified indoctrination — intended to be accessible to men and women of working-class and peasant origins on an unprecedented mass scale — became a significant feature of reality. The 'cadres decide everything', Stalin said, and these cadres led popular masses effectively and manifested a more stable spirit of discipline just because they were endowed with a *certainty of faith.* They felt that they had mastered the laws of social evolution.

We could easily dwell on this thicket of indoctrination, which also permeated the youth of the various peoples of the Soviet Union and the vanguard fighters of the Communist parties abroad. It continued to operate throughout the war and especially during the first postwar decade — at least until 1956 — as many Communist parties, which had now become mass parties, either came to power (as in Eastern Europe and Asia) or recruited hundreds of thousands of new members (as in Italy and France). The Short Course thus continued its long itinerary, [17] encountering no serious obstacle even among those Western intellectuals who had become Communists (although they did, or at any rate could, also seek sustenance from less arid founts of Marxist culture, from its genuine 'classics').

The quality, utility, and complete legitimacy of the kind of vulgarization offered by the Short Course were never challenged during that decade, primarily because the role of the 'guiding party' was never contested, nor Stalin's theoretical authority within it. Subsequent ideological criticism arose mainly with the crisis of that role and the demolition of that image initiated at the Twentieth Congress and deepened by the dramatic events of 1956. The Short Course had been a powerful ideological instrument for unifying the movement around its centre and Soviet society around the party. The history of the Communist Party was considered *exemplary*, especially its reconstruction through internal struggles, which were always presented as conflicts between the 'correct line' (destined to win out) and various left and right opportunists, from the 'Economists' to the Mensheviks, from the Trotskyists to the 'Bukharin-Rykov' group. It was a history designed to de educate all the other national 'departments', although the other parties were not even mentioned in it.

The supremacy — the almost splendidly exceptional character — of the Bolsheviks was unconcealed in the text. Of the four hundred or more pages of the Short Course no more than a couple were devoted to the founding of the Third International in 1919. Its subsequent congresses were listed fleetingly, but the Seventh Congress did not even get a mention. [18] This omission was deliberate, yet another indication, if any were needed, of the limited and tactical interpretation of that congress that was now prevalent.

The events of the international workers movement — from the defeat of the revolution in the West after the First World War to the extraordinary phenomenon of the volunteers who fought for the Spanish Republic — were passed over in silence, even though they had moved Soviet public opinion and were important elements in the widespread popular anti-fascist sentiment. The Chinese liberation struggle against the Japanese invasion, on the other hand, figured prominently, and was described as essentially a national struggle. And for good reason. The book and the mass campaign to distribute it and to illustrate its theses were by no means unconnected to current events and the exigencies of timely political 'agitation'. These opportunities arose from the book's compact ideological foundation, from the general depiction of a particular society (in which socialism had already been 'essentially' achieved) and a particular state (the Soviet state, whose continuity had been consolidated from Lenin to Stalin, the only two 'positive' personalities treated in the text) as the direct products of the laws of social evolution. In fact, continuity was also exalted through a direct appeal to the Russian past, to the Russian people's effort to unite all the peoples of the Union.[19]

More generally, the task of the Short Course was to create an ideological foundation for official doctrinal truths. But of what sort? They were designed to accentuate the role and continuity of the state, now defined as socialist. Stalin was seeking to establish a theoretical point, which he reiterated at the party's Eighteenth Congress: the socialist state still had critical functions to perform, and the Marxist theoretical analysis 'of the process known under Engels's formula as the withering away of the state' had to be shelved. He remarked that the traditional thesis was correct in certain conditions but incorrect in others.

> Instead of raising the problem of the manner, the *forms*, the *pace of development*, the *difficulties*, and the *contradictions* through which the process of the withering away of the state could occur in the particular conditions of Soviet society, he dispensed with the problem altogether on the grounds that Engels had presented it in 'a general and abstract' manner. The significance of generalization and abstraction in Marxist theory was of course completely distorted, and what Engels had described as a process Stalin recast as a mere scholastic hypothesis.[20]

Stalin was presented as the sole heir and faithful continuator of Lenin's work. He claimed the same status in the domain of theory. His elaboration of a theory of the socialist state was legitimated as the natural complement to Lenin's theory of the state, almost as a kind of second instalment of *State and Revolution* which the author had never had the time to write. Such was the formal premiss. 'In substance,' Valentino Gerratana noted, Lenin's 'analysis was replaced by a completely new theory of the socialist state.'[21] It was a theory that raised the repressive function of the state machine to a position of primacy.

The immediate aims of the editorial initiative seem generally perceptible. One of them appears to have been retrospectively to validate and justify the Moscow trials, which had ended just a few months earlier. Trotsky, Zinoviev, Kamenev, Piatakov, and Bukharin were depicted as 'monsters' intent on conspiring against the revolution and the building of socialism. Their 'anti-Bolshevik positions' and 'imperialist and chauvinist conceptions' were presented as not merely errors but personal defects of a kind that would lead naturally to the alleged conspiracy against Lenin between 1918 and 1924 later renewed against Stalin. The language is obviously clumsy; this was another characteristic that profoundly marked the entire movement, ruling out any possible political motivations for dissent in favour of slanderous epithets that could be applied to all 'oppositionists', real or potential. This would be seen again after the Second World War, and not only in the trials held in the 'People's Democracies'.

But the judicial inspiration and criminal terminology are not the book's most prominent feature. Far more essential is the fact that the party's evolution is portrayed as an autochthonous process with respect to society and external circumstance alike. At the same time, the history of the USSR is presented as the chronicle of a country resisting an uninterrupted assault by foreign imperialists aided by paid saboteurs and spies. The fascist states were so defined, but it was added that the other capitalist countries had been no less ardent in tightening the siege of the Soviet Union in the past.

> The so-called democratic states, of course, do not approve of the 'excesses' of the fascist states and fear any accession of strength to the latter. But they fear even more the working-class movement in Europe and the movement of national emancipation in Asia, and regard fascism as an 'excellent antidote' to these 'dangerous' movements.[22]

In the text, as at the Eighteenth Congress of the CPSU, the 'second imperialist war' is described as inevitable. In fact, in March 1939 Stalin repeated from the Congress podium what had already been written in the last chapter of the Short Course ('. . . the second imperialist war has actually already begun, furtively, without any declaration of war'). It is worth noting that this passage was clearly drafted before the Munich pact and therefore points to the continuity of the ideas that inspired Stalin: mistrust and suspicion of the 'so-called democracies', trust only in the strength, solidity, and internal cohesion of the USSR and in its faithful friends in 'the workers movement in Europe and the liberation movement in Asia'. As for the Western powers, a symptomatic historic parallel was drawn:

> The ruling circles of the 'democratic' states, especially the ruling Conservative circles of Great Britain, confine themselves to a policy of pleading with the overweening fascist rulers 'not to go to extremes', at the same time giving them to understand that they 'fully comprehend' and on the whole sympathize with their reactionary police policy towards the working-class movement and the national emancipation movement. In this respect, the ruling circles of Britain are roughly pursuing the same policy as was pursued under tsardom by the Russian liberal-monarchist bourgeois, who, while fearing the 'excesses' of tsarist policy, feared the people even more, and therefore resorted to a policy of pleading with the tsar and, consequently, of *conspiring* with the tsar against the people.[23]

The book closed on that sombre note. For Soviet citizens, it was a warning of the fresh trials that now awaited them. For foreign readers, the study of this work was further designed to 'firm up the ranks' of the Communist movement. In 1938 and 1939, to read, distribute, and study the Short Course was to absorb the very essence of 'Bolshevism' as an iron, centralized, and self-assured form of organization, and to pay due homage to the 'guiding party' at a time of grave crisis in international affairs.

The various Communist parties responded in exactly those terms, as their leaders pledged themselves to propagandize the Short Course. A few examples will make the point. In April 1939, when the French edition came out, Georges Cogniot held a press conference in which he announced that three hundred thousand copies of the book had been printed in France. He called upon militants to read it paper and pencil in hand — or rather, with a notebook in which the quotations from the classics, the major historical references, and so on could be listed in columns. But the PCF leader also recommended that the book be read for its topical lessons. The international situation, he said, was serious and alarming, but not so serious as to shake the confidence of Communists. It may seem naive, but Cogniot told his audience in the 'Salle Pleyel' that although anti-fascism had suffered defeats in Austria, Czechoslovakia, and Spain, there was no reason to lose hope, for the 1905 revolution in Russia had also been defeated. It was followed, however, by the victorious October of 1917. But Cogniot borrowed the most important point from the general portrait the Short Course sought to present: the entire world, except the USSR, 'is in the grip of chaos'. The Soviet Union is now the lifeline of salvation, the beacon from which the light of Marxism still shines. And its history is 'the compass of communism'.

> For the moment, life is peaceful in [France] ; the organs of leadership and transmission of the workers movement are functioning normally. But you know very well that we are living in times in which things change rapidly. There may be circumstances in which members will be dispersed, in which Communists and even non-party anti-fascists will find that they have to make solitary decisions, to take serious initiatives on their own. In the army, isolated combat groups are given compasses. We too have a compass that we can give to every worker, every toiler, every honest democrat. . . .This compass exists. It is the *History of the Communist Party of the Soviet Union* . . .[24]

A weapon. A compass with which to find one's bearings in the gathering storm. A tribute to the Soviet Union in the form of renewed commitment by Communists. 'We are closely linked to the land of socialism with every fibre of our being,' Cogniot said, 'as members of the world party of Communists of which Stalin is the leader and teacher.' The same message was repeated in the press of all the Communist parties, both legal and underground. The British Communists made great efforts, distributing 127,000 copies of the first English edition. The 1939 Italian edition was printed in the USSR, but the PCI exile centre in Paris, which called the book 'an event of historic importance in the ideological life of all the Communist parties',[25] immediately began to distribute it among the Italian workers in France. The book was to serve every Communist as a guide 'that points to the road of the liberation of our people from the fascist yoke.'

Translations were also used for organizational and propagandistic purposes by the various Communist parties. In China, for instance, Mao Zedong, then engaged in a campaign against sectarianism and schematic thinking among party members, picked out the methodological instructions presented in the fifth 'item' of the book's conclusions.[26] It said: 'A party is invincible if it does not fear criticism and self-criticism, if it does not gloss over the mistakes and defects in its work, if it teaches and educates its cadres by drawing the lessons from the mistakes in Party work, and if it knows how to correct its mistakes in time.'

Mao's warnings recall another canon of the Communist movement at the time: a history book, like a work of theory, must be used for present purposes, for in the one as in the other, a quotation can always be found to support whatever position is being upheld.

88

Notes

1. *Pravda* began serial publication in September 1938, announcing that Stalin himself had presided over 'this immense work'. See 'Un abrégé de l'histoire du Parti communiste de l'Urss', *La Correspondance Internationale*, vol. 17, no. 50, 24 September 1938. The names of the Soviet leaders are listed in an elegant Italian edition published in Naples in March 1944 under the auspices of Riccardo Ricciardi.

2. Boffa, *Storia dell'Unione Sovietica*, vol. 1, pp. 612–13.

3. L. Grunwald, 'Per una storia della "storia del Pcus" ', *L'Est*, vol. 8, no. 1, 31 March 1973, p. 60.

4. See 'Una possente arma ideologica del movimento comunista internazionale', *Per una pace stabile, per una democrazia popolare!*, vol. 2, no. 19, 1-15 October 1948.

5. See Hert Andreas, *Le Manifeste Communiste de Marx et Engels (Historie et Bibliographie: 1848–1918)*, Milan 1963.

7. Schlesinger, *Il partito comunista nell'Urss*, p. 272.

8. From Lukács's written response to '8 Questions about the Twenty-Second Congress of the CPSU', *Nuovi Argomenti*, no. 49-50, March-June 1961, p. 121.

9. Ernesto Ragionieri, *La Terza Internazionale e il Partito comunista italiano*, Turin 1978, p. 234.

10. This section was soon published as a pamphlet and distributed by all Communist parties. It is significant that as soon as it became legal again, the PCI printed an Italian edition, in Naples in 1944, and it was reprinted in Rome the following year. The introduction to the pamphlet notes that the essay 'represents the simplest and most profound statement of the theory of Marxism–Leninism yet written'. See J. Stalin, *Materialismo dialettico e materialismo storico*, published by the 'PCI delegation for southern Italy', Naples (1944). The 1945 Roman edition is listed as the fifth pamphlet of the collection 'nuova biblioteca marxista-leninista'.

11. *Dialectical and Historical Materialism*, London 1941, 'Little Stalin Library', no. 4, pp. 14-15.

12. Schlesinger, *Il partito comunista nell'Urss*, p.271.

13. See Medvedev, *Let History Judge*, p.143; and Boffa, *Storia dell'Unione Sovietica*, vol. 1, p. 456.

14. From Mikoyan's speech, in *XX Congresso del Partito comunista dell'Unione sovietica. Atti e risoluzioni*, Rome 1956, p. 202.

15. *Histoire du Parti communiste français (manuel)*, Paris 1964. The manual was written by a Central Committee commission under the direction of Jacques Duclos and François Billoux.

16. Gerratana, *Lenin e il marxismo-leninismo*, p. 182.

17. Some figures on the print-runs of post-war editions: France, 24,000 copies in 1944–45, another 300,000 between 1945 and 1948; Italy, 350,000 copies in 1944–48; Romania, 300,000 copies in 1945–48; Bulgaria, 95,000 copies in 1944–48; Hungary, 90,000 copies in 1945–48; Britain, 125,000 copies in 1940–48; Poland, 100,000 copies in 1948; Holland, 30,000 copies in 1945–48; Austria, 26,000 copies in 1946 and 10,000 in 1948. (From 'Una possente arma ideologica'.)

18. See V.M. Lejbzon - K.K. Sirinija, *Il VII Congresso dell' Internazionale comunista*, Rome 1975, p. 263.

19. See Jacques Droz, 'Il comunismo sovietico ed europeo', in *Storia del socialismo*, Rome 1981, vol. 4, p. 455.

20. Gerratana, *Ricerca di storia del marxismo*, Rome 1972, p. 178.

21. Ibid., pp. 179-80

22. *History of the Communist Party of the Soviet Union (Bolsheviks): Short Course*,

Moscow 1939, p. 334.

23. Ibid., p. 334.

24. Georges Cogniot, 'Ce que nous enseigne l'*Histoire du parti bolchévik*', *La Brochure Populaire*, no. 9, April 1939.

25. From the resolution of the Central Committee of the PCI published in *Lo Stato Operaio*, vol. 13, no. 9, 15 May 1939.

26. 'Oppose Stereotyped Party Writing', in *Selected Readings From the Works of Mao Tse-tung*, Peking 1967, p. 193.

8
The German-Soviet Pact

Let us return to our starting point: that March 1939 snapshot of the Communist movement. The Eighteenth Congress of the CPSU had not even ended when the ephemeral hope that peace might somehow be preserved, nurtured by the European peoples after Munich, collapsed. Hitler was fomenting fresh crises and arousing new tensions. Czechoslovakia disappeared from the map during the night of 14–15 March 1939. As the Slovakian state was proclaimed independent in the shadow of the swastika, under the puppet government of Monsignor Tiso, Hitler entered Prague, and Bohemia-Moravia became a German protectorate. This was a new challenge to the Western powers that had signed the now violated Munich pact, but it was also another step in Hitler's march to the East. On 23 March Germany also annexed the Lithuanian district Klaipeda (called Memel in German). Poland's time was coming.

The new demand now suddenly placed on the table by the Führer was the annexation of Danzig. The German government also asked Warsaw to cede possession of the highway and rail lines leading to the city: the 'Danzig corridor', a strip of land separating eastern Prussia from the rest of Germany, given to Poland by the Versailles Treaty. On 3 April Hitler issued a secret directive to the commanders of the German armed forces in which he instructed them to annihilate the Polish army in the event of any resistance along the border. 'Preparations must be made in such a way that the operation can be carried out at any time from 1 September 1939 onward.'[1]

In other words, a deadline was set, which turned out to be the actual date of the attack: dawn of 1 September. But in March-April it seemed that Poland was determined to defend itself. There was an important new development in the West as well. On 31 March the British government pledged unilaterally to guarantee the independence and territorial integrity of Poland. This was the first decisive response to Hitler, though it would later be followed by rather less robust initiatives. In fact, the tortured events of subsequent months, leading to that fatal September, involved a sequence of probes, manoeuvres, and talks that were anything but clear. In any case, it was the events themselves that mattered most, and they all pointed to an aggravation of international tension. On 7 April, in an action favoured with particular enthusiasm by Ciano, the minister of foreign affairs, Italy invaded and annexed Albania. The 'hot spots' had now reacted by offering guarantees to Greece and Romania.

On 3 May a piece of news from Moscow set the diplomatic world buzzing, arousing various interpretations. Litvinov, for years the most tenacious exponent of the policy of collective security against Nazi aggression, was removed from his post in the 'People's Commissariat of Foreign Affairs' and was replaced by Molotov, president of the Council. Even if this move did not herald a change of direction, it suggested at least that Stalin wanted to emphasize, by confiding the conduct of foreign policy to one of his closest and most skilled associates, that the USSR would now reserve greater freedom of initiative and manoeuvre.

On 22 May the fascist powers, Germany and Italy, signed the 'pact of steel'. As its dramatic name suggested, this accord committed each signatory to rush to its partner's side 'with its full military power' in the event of 'armed conflict with one or more other powers'. In other words, the pact was to come into force even if one of the signatories launched a war of aggression. Although the pact did not come into effect quite that automatically in September 1939, Italian fascism's decision to link itself so closely to the German enterprise, to form a military bloc of attack rather than defence, was duly noted. On 23 May Hitler assembled his military commanders to inform them that war was inevitable, although its scope could not be predicted.

> There is no question of sparing Poland and we are left with the decision: *To attack Poland at the first suitable opportunity.* We cannot expect a repetition of the Czech affair. There will be war. Our task is to isolate Poland. Success in isolating her will be decisive.[2]

Between May and August, in the heat of the immediate prelude to war, political and diplomatic manoeuvring seemed to unfold within a triangulation of relations as complex as it was murky. Whereas Hitler ought to have had an interest in assuring Soviet neutrality in the event of a British–French intervention on behalf of Poland, British and French interests would seem to have dictated that they seek an alliance with the USSR. This would have been the only way to avert the danger against which Coulondre, the French ambassador to Berlin, was already warning: that this time Hitler and Stalin would manage to reach agreement at Poland's expense.[3]. More generally, the achievement of a binding tripartite Russion–French–British alliance might at least have forced Hitler to fight on two fronts, West and East, if not dissuaded him from igniting the powder-keg. Poland's interest would seem to have been to assure itself of Soviet aid in the event of a German invasion. But such aid could be forthcoming only if the Soviet Union sent its own armed forces into Polish territory. Stalin's interest was seemingly to guarantee his security against the Hitlerite threat to his borders by seeking a military and political pact with the Western powers.

I have put all this in the conditional, and it should be obvious that I speak with hindsight, knowing how things actually worked out, whereas the politicians involved in the tortuous events themselves appear to have acted on the basis of suspicion and guile rather than well-defined strategic options. It is nevertheless of some interest that Winston Churchill was well aware what was at stake in the spring of 1939. Addressing himself to the British government, he said in the House of Commons on 19 May:

> All along the whole of this eastern front you can see that the major interests of Russia are definitely engaged, and therefore it seems you could fairly judge that they would pool their interests with the other countries similarly affected. If you are ready to be an ally of Russia in time of war, which is the supreme test, the great occasion of all, if you are ready to join hands with Russia in the defence of Poland, which you have guaranteed, and of Romania, why should you shrink from becoming the ally of Russia now, when you may by that very fact prevent the breaking out of war?[4]

Chamberlain, however, was not in favour of a real alliance with the USSR, perhaps fearing that it would prejudice his attempts to reach a new compromise with Germany. The low esteem in which he held Soviet military capabilities (an opinion shared by his advisers, as well as by the French) was probably another factor in the equivocation of the British prime minister. But the USSR was not marking time. Economic negotiations with Germany had begun. In May Molotov hinted to Schulenburg, the German ambassador to Moscow, that the talks could be taken up again as soon as the 'necessary political basis' had been laid. In the meantime, he pressed the Western powers for an agreement. On 27 May Chamberlain decided, against his better judgement, to start talks with Moscow (and the French did the same).

There was talk of a mutual assistance pact, a military convention, and a guarantee for the countries threatened by Hitler. But the Soviet government, which had put forward this proposal, wanted a joint commitment, extensive and binding. The British were doubtful and the conversations dragged on sluggishly in June. On 29 June, *Pravda* published an article by Andrei Zhdanov, who expressed a 'personal' but highly authoritative view:

> It seems to me that the British and French Governments are not out for a real agreement acceptable to the USSR but only for talks about an agreement in order to demonstrate before the public opinion of their own countries the alleged unyielding attitude of the USSR and thus facilitate the conclusion of an agreement with the aggressors. The next few days will show whether this is so or not.[5]

Can this article be construed as a warning to London and Paris? Was it another hint to Berlin? There was much conjecture, and contacts continued between Soviets and Germans. But the USSR also made new proposals to the Western powers. Not until 23 July did the latter agree to convene a conference of experts to work out a military convention. There was no hurry to reach agreement. The British instructions were to 'proceed very slowly'.[6] The Anglo-French military missions took a full week — from 5 to 11 August — to reach Moscow, via Leningrad, to which they had come by sea. They did not have full decision-making powers. In the meantime, the political talks were suspended and the military talks encountered insuperable obstacles. The demands of the Soviet delegation, headed by Voroshilov, for a detailed commitment to mutual assistance were evaded.

It is possible that by this time Stalin had made up his mind. He now turned to the Germans. In the early days of August, the repeated probes, initially examining the possibility of economic relations between the two countries, were transformed into negotiations with a more particularly political objective. On 14 August Ribbentrop had the German ambassador in Moscow hand Molotov a long memorandum which stated:

> The crisis which has been produced in Polish–German relations by English policy and the attempts at an alliance which are bound up with that policy make a speedy clarification of German–Russian relations necessary. Otherwise matters . . . might take a turn which would deprive both governments of the possibility of restoring German–Russian friendship and in due course clarifying jointly territorial questions in Eastern

Europe. The leadership of both countries, therefore, should not allow the situation to drift, but should take action at the proper time. It would be fatal if, through mutual ignorance of views and intentions, the two peoples should finally drift apart.[7]

At this point, between 15 and 19 August, Molotov seemed inclined to seek a general political agreement, a genuine non-aggression pact between the Soviet Union and Germany. In the meantime, Hitler, who was busy finalizing the military plans for an attack on Poland any time after 1 September, made no secret of his impatience: he wanted a rapid agreement. Ribbentrop proposed to go to Moscow personally as soon as possible. Molotov's positive response arrived on 19 August. Hitler insisted that his minister of foreign affairs be received, as a plenipotentiary, on 22 or 23 August. Appealing directly to Stalin, the Führer openly acknowledged that his haste was motivated by the 'now intolerable' tension between Germany and Poland. He needed a non-aggression pact with the USSR to avert the danger of a war on two fronts, and he may also have hoped even to ward off British and French entry into the war. Stalin's response arrived on the night of 21 August:

> To the Chancellor of the German Reich
> A. Hitler
> I thank you for your letter. I hope that the German–Soviet non-aggression pact will bring about a decided turn for the better in the political relations between our countries.
> The peoples of our countries need peaceful relations with each other. The assent of the German government to the conclusion of a non-aggression pact provides the foundation for eliminating the political tension and for the establishment of peace and collaboration between our countries.
> The Soviet government have instructed me to inform you that they agree to Herr von Ribbentrop's arriving in Moscow on August 23.
>
> J. Stalin.[8]

That same evening, 21 August, Marshal Voroshilov informed the British and French military delegations that the USSR had waited fruitlessly for a response on the decisive point: the Polish government's agreement to the entry of Soviet troops in the event of a German attack. The talks were therefore stalled. Despite increased Anglo-French pressure, Colonel Beck continued to refuse as late as 19 August. And neither Lord Halifax nor Bonnet would resort to the only threat that could have been effective in overcoming Polish reticence: to rescind the unilateral guarantee they had given Poland. Just a few hours later, the world was stunned by the announcement broadcast by Radio Berlin at midnight on 21 August: 'The government of the Reich and the Soviet government have decided to conclude a non-aggression pact. The Reich minister of foreign affairs will arrive in Moscow on Wednesday, 23 August, to conclude the agreement.'

The next day, 22 August, Hitler, now assured of Soviet neutrality, convoked his leading officers for the nth time: he wanted to move the deadline up, to attack Poland on 16 August. [9] In the meantime, Chamberlain let the German dictator know, through a letter entrusted to the British ambassador to Berlin which he brought to Hitler in Berchtesgaden, that Britain would maintain its commitment to the Poles. [10] The French ambassador, Coulondre, took a similar initiative, while Mussolini warned Hitler that Italy was in no position to fight an immediate war. This bad news merely convinced Hitler to delay the attack: it was set back to 1 September again, the day it was actually launched.

In the next chapter we will consider the consternation provoked by the German-Soviet pact in the ranks of the workers movement, both Socialist and Communist. But let us first note the scope of the accord (the complete terms of which came to light only after the war, when the Third Reich's archives were opened). The agreement was broad: there was a public part, itself important and classic, and an even more exacting secret part. The public non-aggression treaty was straightforward, though laden with consequences. It stipulated that neither of the signatories would enter into agreements directed against the other part nor support hostile actions against it. A 'Secret Additional Protocol' stipulated a partition of Poland between the USSR and Germany. This protocol provided for exceptional new developments ('transformations'):

1. In the event of a territorial and political transformation in the territories belonging to the Baltic States (Finland, Estonia, Latvia, Lithuania), the northern frontier of Lithuania shall represent the frontier of the spheres of interest both of Germany and the USSR.
2. In the event of a territorial and political transformation of the territories belonging to the Polish State, the spheres of interest of both Germany and the USSR shall be bounded approximately by the line of the rivers Narew, Vistula, and San.
The question whether the interests of both parties make the maintenance of an independent Polish State appear desirable and how the frontiers of this State should be drawn can be definitely determined only

in the course of further political development.

In any case both governments will resolve this question by means of a friendly understanding.[11]

Finally, Germany declared its lack of interest in Bessarabia (a region lost by Russia in 1919 and incorporated into Romania). This clearly suggested that the Soviets did have an interest in recovering the region. The substance of the protocol was therefore fairly obvious. Germany and the USSR agreed to partition Poland; Stalin would have a free hand in the eastern Baltic, including Finland. Hitler's concessions seem significant, even though we now know that he had no intention of respecting the pact. The agreement, drafted rapidly during Ribbentrop's stay in Moscow (two meetings on the evening of 23 August were sufficient to finalize both the treaty and the protocol), was fêted in a lengthy and convivial session. Stalin toasted the Führer's health ('I know how the German nation loves him. . .') and reminded Ribbentrop that the USSR took the pact *very seriously* and would not betray its commitments.

Why did Stalin decide on such a weighty move? The explanations advanced by various historians are less diverse than might be expected. For a simple reason: all the conjectures are based on assessments of the state interests of the USSR at that decisive moment. All the USSR'S political positions and ideological values, as well as its *image* (as a socialist country, as an intrinsically anti-fascist force, antithetical to Nazism by its very nature; the country's past, the battles waged during previous years) are left out of account, though they were of enormous importance both in 1939 and after.

Since the past has been evaluated mainly in terms of state relations alone, historians have generally offered more justification than criticism. Deutscher in particular emphasized the negative effects on the Soviets of the way the British and French military missions had been formed, reached Moscow, and acted once they arrived, noting their reluctance to make any definite commitments and Chamberlain's weakness in the face of Polish resistance. Deutscher wrote:

> Stalin could not have had the slightest doubt that the pact at once relieved Hitler of the nightmare of a war on two fronts, and that to that extent it unleashed the Second World War. Yet he, Stalin, had no qualms. To his mind the war was inevitable anyhow: if he had made no deal with Hitler, war would still have broken out either now or somewhat later, under conditions incomparably less favourable to his country. He did not feel an incendiary — it was Hitler who was setting fire to the world. He, Stalin, was merely diverting the conflagration away from Russia. He expected

Poland, as subsequent events demonstrated, to resist longer than she did. But he had no doubt that Poland would succumb and that the Western powers would not be able or willing to give her effective help. [12]

Taylor also tends to justify the pact:

> However one spins the crystal and tries to look into the future from the point of view of 23 August 1939, it is difficult to see what other course Soviet Russia could have followed. The Soviet apprehensions of a European alliance against Russia were exaggerated, though not groundless. [13]

Many commentators have emphasized these concerns and hinted that they were not without foundation, in particular D.F. Fleming, who holds that the exclusion of the USSR from Munich and the Western refusal to conclude an anti-Nazi alliance were of crucial importance. [14] Another American scholar observed that Anglo-French lack of resolution against Hitler aroused 'an almost total estrangement of the USSR from the West'. [15] The Frenchman André Fontaine, who declines to take a firm position on the vexed question of if and when Stalin decisively chose one course or another, analyses Moscow's German option this way:

> People are still debating the Soviet Union's real intentions during this period, although they seem quite clear. The two explanations that have been current for twenty years — that Stalin had tried unsuccessfully to come to an agreement with the Allies, and that he had long since thrown in his lot with Hitler — are equally debatable. Preferring neither side right up to the last minute, he tried to find the best and least dangerous course for himself. Like the Führer, he was sceptical as to the West's will to fight, convinced, not without reason, that they were profoundly hostile to all that he represented, unwilling to engage his country in a war if he could avoid it, or at least postpone it, and he abandoned the West when the time came, without the least scruple. [16]

Fejtö's opinion is not dissimilar:

> The Germans were prepared to offer a higher price for Soviet neutrality than the Anglo-French had proposed for an alliance. The deal therefore seemed quite a bargain to the Soviet leaders. They believed that the consequence of the now-inevitable German–Polish conflict would be either a new Munich, though one in which the USSR would be invited to participate, or war between the Germans and the West. In the latter event, Germany's aggressive might would be deflected westward, and neutrality

would put the USSR in a position to increase its influence and the price of its possible intervention in support of one or the other of the adversaries. [17]

The French historian Pierre Renouvin reasons similarly, arguing that Stalin naturally preferred to see war break out in the West rather than in the East, that he 'had every reason to expect that it would be a long war and to hope that at the opportune time, the USSR would not only be able to impose its own arbitration, but would also enjoy favourable conditions for world revolution.'[18] In this view, the revolutionary lurks behind the shrewd and free-wheeling statesman. A very similar point of view is expressed by Celeste Negarville, an Italian Communist who, discussing what had happened in 1940 and 1941, noted in his diary in 1942:

> It is very likely that the Soviet government was more convinced of the necessity of the pact with Germany than of its reliability, or at least expected far more serious French military resistance than was actually offered. Greater resistance would have prevented Germany from launching an attack on the Soviet Union less than a year later. In that event, Soviet neutrality would have increasingly appeared to the masses as the only correct policy. The unprecedented sacrifices of the war would have enhanced the prestige of the country that had been able to stay out of the conflict, and the tormented peoples would have pinned their hopes on the CPs of the various countries. [19]

It seems unlikely that Stalin made all these complex calculations in August 1939. If he thought that Poland would resist more vigorously, that France and Britain would fail to intervene (as he told Churchill in 1942[20]), or that France would withstand the attack of the German army, then his calculations were certainly belied by reality. William Shirer's observation that the compromise with Nazi Germany 'was the greatest blunder of his life'[21] would then be unchallengeable. Was it a forced error, and therefore not really a mistake at all? Many historians (French and Italian Communist scholars in particular agree on this point[22]) have argued that the USSR had little choice in the anxious situation of that dramatic summer of 1939: it had to avert war on its borders at all costs, even if that meant a shift in policy, for the country was not prepared militarily, faced great economic difficulties, and had to contend with the urgent danger of Japanese attacks along the Manchurian border (very serious incidents had occurred along the Šilka), which seemed to herald an assault on Inner Mongolia simultaneous with the German attack on Ukraine.

Soviet historians have listed the benefits the USSR obtained from the pact of 23 August 1939. Moscow averted the danger of a 'common front' of the capitalist countries against the land of socialism (which had been the nightmare of Soviet foreign policy for twenty years); it put space and time between itself and Nazi Germany; it regained many of the territories inhabited by Russians and Ukrainians that had been taken from it under the Treaty of Versailles; it parried the threat of a joint German–Japanese attack.[23] Nevertheless, even if we grant that urgent necessities and unexpected opportunities were involved, it is undeniable that many of the calculations Stalin may have made in deciding to sign this 'truce' proved fallacious: when Hitler attacked the USSR in June 1941, he was master of the entire European continent and was therefore able to unleash the full fury of his armies against the Soviet Union. Britain was still holding out, but it has been asked with good reason how Stalin used his nearly-two-year respite and why he was so surprised by Hitler's invasion when it finally came.[24] It cannot be ruled out that Stalin had something more in mind than a mere 'truce' with Hitler. (We will return to this point when considering the subsequent extension of the German–Soviet accord.) In any event, the 'spiritual' dimension noted in the reflections of the Soviet writer Konstantin Simonov remains open, and fraught with disturbing questions. Simonov wrote:

> It still seems to me that the pact of 1939 was founded on *raison d'état,* in the almost hopeless situation we were in then, the summer of 1939, when the danger of the Western states pushing fascist Germany against us became immediate and real. And yet, when you look back, you feel that for all the logic of *raison d'état* in this pact, much that accompanied its conclusion took away from us, simply as people, for almost two years, some part of that exceptionally important sense of ourselves, which was and is our precious peculiarity, connected with such a concept as 'the first socialist state in the world.' . . . that is, something happened which was in a moral sense very bad.[25]

Today it would be called an identity crisis.

Notes

1. From 'Case White', reproduced in William L. Shirer, *The Rise and Fall of the Third Reich*, London 1960, p. 468. This is one of the most significant documents taken from the secret archives of the Nazi government by the Allies in 1945. The other materials we will cite come from the same source. Shirer has made more extensive use of these precious documents than any other author.

2. Shirer, *Rise and Fall*, p. 485.

3. Ibid., p. 484.

4. Churchill, *The Second World War*, vol. 1, p. 293.

5. Shirer, *Rise and Fall*, p. 496.

6. This seems to have been the secret instruction of the Chamberlain government to Admiral Drax (who lacked even written credentials), according to research done by Arnold Toynbee and his associates for the work *The Eve of War, 1939*, London 1958.

7. Shirer, *Rise and Fall*, p. 514

8. Ibid., p. 528.

9. Ibid., pp. 528-30.

10. Churchill. *The Second World War*, vol. 1, pp. 308-09.

11. Shirer, *Rise and Fall*, p. 541.

12. Deutscher, *Stalin*, Harmondsworth 1966, pp. 428-29.

13. Taylor, *Origins of the Second World War*, p. 319.

14. D.F. Fleming, *The Cold War and Its Origins, 1917–1960*, London 1961, pp.80-83.

15. P.E. Haley, 'Sur les origines de la deuxième guerre mondiale', *Revue d'Histoire de la Deuxième Guerre Mondiale*, vol. 19, no. 75, July 1969, p. 102.

16. André Fontaine, *History of the Cold War*, p. 116.

17. François Fejtö, *Histoire des Démocraties Populaires*, Paris 1952, p. 36.

18. Pierre Renouvin, *Histoire des relations internationales*, vol. 8, *Les crises du XXe siècle*, Paris 1958, pp. 184-85.

19. The text of the note is in Spriano, *Storia del Partito comunista italiano*, vol. 4, p. 315.

20. Churchill, *The Second World War*, vol. 1, p.308.

21. Shirer, *Rise and Fall*, p. 544.

22. See Jean Elleinstein, *Storia dell'Urss*, Rome 1976, vol. 2, pp. 9-20; Boffa, *Storia dell'Unione Sovietica*, vol. 1, p. 635; Roberto Battaglia, *La seconda guerra mondiale*, Rome 1960, pp. 46-52; Amendola, *Storia del Pci*, pp. 392-93.

23. For an analysis of these contentions, see Boffa, *Storia dell'Unione Sovietica*, vol. 1, pp. 633-35.

24. Adriano Guerra, *Gli anni del Cominform*, Milan 1977, pp. 35-36.

25. Cited in Medvedev, *Let History Judge*, p. 442.

9

'If War Breaks Out . . .'

The international Communist movement has its own traumatic dates, times when the image of the USSR is damaged in the eyes of party militants themselves, like February and November 1956, August 1968, December 1981. At such moments, the contradiction between the Soviet Union's supposedly socialist character and the evidence of events becomes too obvious. Some react by drifting away, others by taking refuge in faith, others by seeking explanations and extenuating circumstances. Whereas Khrushchev's secret report to the Twentieth Congress of the CPSU opened discussion mainly about a particular time period, the subsequent armed intervention in Hungary, the invasion of Czechoslovakia, and the encouragement of military repression in Poland once again raise the question of internationalism, of the manner in which the USSR takes account (or fails to take account) of the interests, experience, and autonomy of the Communist parties and states in its own camp. The doctrine of 'limited sovereignty' was a reality even before it was formulated, and failure to accept it passively brought tragedy to entire peoples.

The twenty-third of August 1939 was undoubtedly the first really traumatic date. On the whole, it is easy to gauge and document the turmoil it aroused in the various 'branches' of the movement that were able to manifest their reactions publicly (and the clandestine parties were no less seriously affected). It is more difficult to look beyond those days and months and to evaluate the historic scope of the crisis that took hold at the time and has had many and recurrent effects since then. Giorgio Amendola, who remarked that the Communist International 'never recovered from the blows dealt it' by the Stalin repression of 1936–38, believed that the consequences 'not so much of the German–Soviet pact itself as of the way in which the international Communist movement fell in line with its official justification, were even more enduring than those of the repression. In 1978 he wrote:

> The price paid by the Communist parties for having approved the line of the Communist International in 1939, in absolute agreement with that of the Soviet government, is high even today. It is a price the Communist parties will continue to have to pay, despite the trials met with heroism in the patriotic struggle against Nazism and fascism, for the independence and freedom of their countries. The problem of the shipwreck of the Communist International and of the autonomy of the Communist parties takes on enormous topicality in the face of the German–Soviet Pact. [1]

Here we are faced with historical and political questions that have been refracted through time: the autonomy of the individual Communist parties; the demise of a centralized organization already mortally wounded by repression and reduced to the status of a mere sounding-board for the Soviet government; the more limited yet illuminating question of the initial signs of differentiation which were immediately covered over by the absolute conformity or 'agreement' to which Amendola refers. Let us bear the complexity of the picture in mind and begin with the stunning announcement of 22 August. The shock was greatest in France, the only country with a mass Communist party that was still legal: it had slightly less than three hundred thousand members, including seventy-two members of parliament; its trade unionists, though they were a minority in their organization, were in the leadership of a confederation and of many of the affiliated unions as well; the party had councillors in three hundred city councils and was active, often alongside the Socialist Party (although the alliance was in crisis), in all areas of the country. When the pact was announced, consternation and dumbfounded amazement preceded indignation. The other political forces took advantage of the latter reaction not only to isolate the Communists, but virtually to outlaw them. On 23 August Léon Blum expressed the state of mind of those who, while astonished, sought not to lose their heads. The USSR and Nazi Germany had concluded a political agreement! How could it have happened?

> Our amazement is redoubled when we remember that horror and hatred of communism are the sentiments by which Hitler has sought to justify all his recent actions, including the destruction of the Spanish and the Czechoslovakian republics; that anti-Communist ideology lies at the very base of Nazism; that the diplomatic instrument which has enabled Germany and Italy to draw allies around them is an anti-Comintern pact. And now Hitler not only accepts, but even, it appears, proposes a

political rapprochement with the Soviets.

For its part, Soviet Russia has ceaselessly supported anti-fascist propaganda everywhere. Communism has unerringly denounced Hitler as the enemy of justice, liberty, and civilization. Now, at the most acute, the most dangerous, moment of the European crisis, Soviet Russia seems to have leaned in Hitler's direction. One could hardly imagine greater lack of restraint, more brazen contempt for public opinion, a greater defiance of morality.[2]

This initial reaction of amazement was accompanied by sorrow, and by an implicit internal polemic. How many French Socialists had justified Munich, how many had genuinely fought to 'incorporate Soviet Russia in a resolute peace front', as Blum had asked, and how many had instead followed Paul Faure in identifying the cause of pacifism with anti-Communism?[3] This division persisted after the fall of France in May-June 1940, and even with the formation of the Pétain government. In French Communist ranks, reaction was varied, and was expressed with varying speed. The initial shock was great among leaders and intellectuals, both members and 'fellow travellers'. It is difficult to evaluate the reaction of the working-class and popular core of the party. Surprise was surely universal. No one in the PCF seems to have had the slightest suspicion of the imminent bombshell, of Moscow's sudden volte-face. All the party leaders were on vacation on 22 August, some in the Alps, some in the Pyrenees (except Gitton, who was later discovered to be a police agent).[4] The line taken by a hastily summoned Central Committee meeting on 25 August was flimsy and shame-faced, but nevertheless significant. The pact was hailed as a contribution to peace, but was also described as an incentive for the French and British governments to seek to conclude the political and military accords with the USSR that had seemed so imminent. It was denied that any people's freedom was endangered by the pact, although this was obviously feared. The meeting took a position that reflected the party's anti-fascism and patriotism. The parliamentary group released a statement whose tone is indicated by this excerpt.

If Hitler unleashes war despite everything, let him be aware that the people of France will stand united against him, with the Communists in the front ranks, defending the country's security, the freedom and independence of all peoples. That is why our Communist Party approves the measures taken by the government to protect our borders, and, if necessary, to speed the required aid to the threatened nation to which we are bound by a treaty of friendship.[5]

The threatened nation was Poland. Although Thorez could not have known that the aggression would come in the space of just one week, he could hardly have had any illusions about its inevitability. The patriotic, anti-Nazi character of the party's statement is therefore particularly significant. Even more interesting, as a reflection of an autonomous orientation, is the fact that Togliatti, who stood rather higher in the Comintern hierarchy than his French comrade, issued a similar declaration in the name of the PCI. Togliatti-Ercoli had been in France for several weeks, following his daring escape from Spain in the last days of the Republic and his subsequent brief stay in Moscow. Exactly why Togliatti returned to Paris in the summer of 1939 has never been clarified. But there is no doubt that he was there as secretary of the International.[6] And it is quite likely that his mission was to try to reestablish links with the Socialist International. In May Togliatti had presented a full report in Moscow on 'Spanish affairs', in which he continued to maintain that the line of the Popular Front was the only correct one — and not only in the past or for Spain. 'The correctness of the Popular Front policy has been fully confirmed by the Spanish experience', he said.[7]

Between April and August 1939, as we have seen, that line was never officially abandoned by the Comintern, despite the reservations and the accusations of the sort levelled against the Socialists in Manuilski's report. In its May Day appeal the Communist International had denounced Italo-German fascism as a 'wild beast roaming across Europe', which 'is throwing a noose around Poland's neck'. The British and French governments, 'supported by the capitulators among the leaders of the Second International', were described as both accomplices and potential victims of Nazism, but the Socialist parties and trade unions were still called upon to support united action:

> Interpreting the will of the working class of all countries, the Communist International calls upon the Executive Committee of the Socialist International and the Socialist trade unions to open negotiations without delay with the aim of bringing about a united front for struggle against the warmongers. It proposes a platform of united action to the Socialist International: defence of peace through an energetic response to the fascist aggressors, through the organization of collective security, and through the struggle — in every capitalist country — against the policy of betrayal practised by the reactionary bourgeoisie, which seeks compromises with the fascist aggressors at the expense of the freedom and independence of their respective peoples.[8]

There was no response from the Executive of the Socialist International. For the very simple reason that as a political force it was already dead, as had been expressly acknowledged by its secretary, Friedrich Adler, in a memorandum presented in June.[9] The Second International was dead, Adler wrote, because it had not succeeded in remaining a collective body. Each Socialist party acted on its own account, none considered the decisions of the Executive binding, and the illegal Socialist parties (in the fascist countries) had practically no voice. They pressed for an international mobilization against imperialist aggression, while the French, British, Dutch, Belgian, and Scandinavian parties were concerned primarily with the tactical exigencies of daily policy in their own countries and were imbued with the same immobility that weakened the Western and Nordic governments against Nazism. The president of the Socialist International, the Belgian De Brouckère, resigned.

When war broke out the European workers movement as a whole was silent and immobile. In this respect it was 1914 all over again. The struggle for peace was already lost, the popular masses had withdrawn from it. How long would this silence last? Friedrich Adler himself anxiously asked this question, on which the socialist revolution among other things depended. At the meeting of the Socialist International Executive held in Brussels 26–28 August 1939, he said:

> The working class now faces the most terrible of wars without its principal weapon, international organization.
>   The war itself poses unprecedented tasks for the workers movement. When the unspeakable misery of the war drives the masses to desperation, when defeat and rebellion, revolt against hunger and mass strikes herald its end, the working class of every country will need men capable of setting goals and giving a direction to their desires. When fascism is beaten, the realization of socialism will once again become a current task rather than a far-off objective in many states. But in the future, as in the past, the reformist parties will not conquer and realize socialism.[10]

The sorrowful prophecy of the old Austrian Socialist (who, in 1916, in the midst of the war, had assaulted Count Sturgkh, the president of his country's council, shocking international public opinion) echoes the programmatic schema of 1914, for the Socialist left had expected mass rebellion just after the war. In the course of the Second World War, however, other similar voices were raised in the ranks of Socialism, even in its reformist wing. In the meantime, during that tragic late August of 1939, the persecuted worker militants in many fascist countries fervently hoped that war would break out, for only war would permit the overthrow of the fascist dictatorships. So it was in Italy and Germany, in Spain and Czechoslovakia. In the latter two countries Communists vainly hoped that with the outbreak of a general war they would be able to unite with the Socialists to fight for freedom with the other peoples. 'International events', affirmed the manifesto of the exile Central Committee of the PCE, 'are unfolding so rapidly that Spain will very soon be in the running once again, side by side with all those struggling for democracy and liberty. This certainty that the struggle will continue . . . unites us with all those alongside whom we have fought for a freer Spain.'[11]

Forty years would pass before Spain regained its freedom. Internationally, war was erupting without the formation of any real anti-fascist front of states or peoples. The workers movement was gripped by isolationism. Its Communist component had closed ranks in a defensive ring around the Moscow centre; in other words, it too was nationally oriented, supporting the isolationism of the USSR.

But let us return to Togliatti in Paris during the last week of August. When he heard the news of the German–Soviet pact, he confided to his Italian comrades that in his view the French Communists ought to be most aggressive in their struggle against Hitler. One of them later wrote:

> I remember what Ercoli told me two days after the pact. He thought that if war broke out the French CP should take an attitude similar to that of Clemenceau before he entered the government during the 1914–18 war. In other words: bitter criticism of all the weaknesses exhibited by the government in the conduct of the war. On the basis of that attitude I was able to affirm two days later at the meeting of the World Youth Council that we Communists would be second to none in a war against Hitlerism. That was the line we would have to pursue.[12]

Togliatti's position, then, was similar to Thorez's. He expressed it in a statement issued in the name of the PCI on 25 August. He began with a rather unconvincing argument intended to defend the German–Soviet pact, which he claimed was a blow against the Rome–Berlin Axis and the pact of steel, 'whose principal participant has now had to bow before the power of the working class, which has curbed its aggressive plans'! The PCF also seized upon this argument. But Blum immediately replied: 'Give up this nonsense! You yourselves cannot possibly believe what you are saying.'[13] Nevertheless, from this most flimsy foundation Togliatti managed to renew his attack on the 'reactionary elements directing the policy of the so-called democratic countries'. But the main feature of the statement was the attitude taken to the predominant question of international relations. Here the PCI's stance was the same as the PCF's:

> If war breaks out despite everything, we repeat that we will fight unremittingly for it to result in the military and political defeat, the collapse, of fascism; this is one of the preconditions for the inauguration of a future of liberty, peace, and social progress for all the peoples of Europe. [14]

In an 'open letter to the Italian Socialist Party' Togliatti was even more explicit. In the event of war, the Italian Communists would fight unconditionally, with all their might: 'To achieve this aim, we will grasp all the possibilities open to us, if necessary entering the French army to fight the fascists and to help to defeat them, just as we fought in Spain, at Guadalajara.' [15]

That was as far as it went. No official organ of the Communist parties condemned the German–Soviet Pact — perhaps because they did not realize that its immediate consequence would be the Second World War. But even if that was the reason, the pact nevertheless marked the traumatic end of any prospect of united action with Socialist forces. Pietro Nenni, the exile secretary of the PSI (who resigned his post exactly because of this failure), denounced this fresh crisis in an article in his party's paper:

> From the pages of this newspaper, in which we have fought against all odds for the unity of the proletariat over the past five years, unhesitatingly denouncing the errors even of the Socialist parties and of men for whom we feel fraternal friendship, we now turn to the Communist comrades with whom we have worked, to the Communist proletarians who are in no way separated from the Socialist proletarians, and we say to them: 'The cause of unity is in your hands. Say the word that your conscience must dictate. All we ask of you is that you acknowledge that the Moscow pact does not fall within the political line for which we have jointly fought, and which we all want to triumph. All we ask of you is that you reestablish harmony of thought and action, even if you have to take some distance from Moscow, just as we have not hesitated to part company with fraternal parties or Socialist governments on certain points. A severe blow has been dealt to the political line of united action, and our common enemies are taking advantage of it.' [16]

The fervour of Nenni's desperate appeal must be measured against the atmosphere and proposals of the preceding days. The Italian political émigrés in France were organized in the Anti-Fascist

Alliance. A mass organization called Unità Popolare (with some seventy thousand members) sought to cement the Alliance. On 7 August Thorez appealed to Johan W. Albarda, the new, Dutch president of the Socialist International, to call an international workers conference, 'in the struggle that unites the forces of the toilers against fascism and war.' Thorez wrote:

> Fascism and reaction are continuing their offensive against the working class, threatening to plunge the world into an abyss of oppression and into the horror of a new war.
> Great peoples have already fallen to fascist slavery, entire nations have been wiped off the map, and any sign of division among the partisans of liberty and peace augments the insolence of the fascist warmongers. [17]

Unity was invoked and conceived essentially in the name of the struggle against Hitler. Could the Socialists now agree to the USSR's 'opting out' of that struggle? How could they possibly believe that this was a victory for peace? On 25 August the PSI declared the unity pact with the PCI null and void. A crisis erupted in Unità Popolare, whose president, the Communist Romano Cocchi, condemned the German–Soviet pact and was expelled from the PCI after a number of stormy meetings. The CGT was divided, but the majority of the Executive voted for a motion condemning the pact. The trade-union leaders of the PCF, on the other hand, supported it.

The Communists were already deeply isolated when armed conflict broke out. Daladier, who planned to raise French troop strength to more than 2 million, [18] shut down the Communist press. On 26 August L'Humanité and the fellow-traveller newspaper Ce Soir ceased publication. Of the two Communist leaders I have quoted, Thorez was drafted into the army and Togliatti was arrested (as were many other Italian Communist exiles, among them Luigi Longo, and some Germans too). But the French Communists did take one important step before the repression became really massive. On 2 September, with the invasion of Poland already under way, the Chamber of Deputies voted to grant the government war credits, and the Communist deputies raised their hands along with everyone else. The next day Coulondre and the British ambassador in Berlin informed Ribbentrop that France and Britain considered themselves at war with Germany.

The events of the week between 23 August and 3 September therefore demonstrate that the German–Soviet pact was the precondition for Hitler's aggression. Thorez and Togliatti's call for continuation of the Anglo–French–Soviet negotiations now seemed futile. Voroshilov dismissed the British and French missions. The very last sign of any PCF autonomy along the lines of its 25 August statement came in an article by an aged and renowned party leader, Gaston Monmousseau. War had already broken out when he wrote:

> The president of the Council has declared that one man alone is responsible: Hitler. We have nothing to add. Hitler alone is responsible for the war. Hitler himself, as the highest representative of the Hitlerite system of destruction of democratic rights, Hitler as head of the greatest totalitarian state, is the number-one enemy of all the toiling classes of all countries. [19]

Looking at the other Communist parties, we find a similar picture, although the positions they took had no real effect and amounted to a catalogue of intentions more than anything else. The Belgian Communist Party (9,000 members) reaffirmed that the anti-Hitler struggle would continue: 'If Hitler attacks Belgium, the Communists will stand in the front ranks defending its independence and the freedom of its populace arms in hand.' [20] Campbell made a similar statement in the name of the British Communist Party (about 18,000 members), then led by Harry Pollitt. Campbell wrote that 'if war breaks out, the British people will fight to assure the crushing defeat of fascism.' William Gallacher, a founder of the British Communist Party and its only member of Parliament, voted for the war credits, and when the war began Campbell again affirmed that the British people would reject Nazi peace offers and would support the war to the end, while Harry Pollitt wrote a pamphlet entitled *How to Win the War*. [21] Even the Central Committee of the German CP, which expressed its 'satisfaction' with the pact as 'a step toward peace', issued a statement on 25 August calling upon the German people to continue the struggle against the dictatorship and against Hitler's plans for aggression. 'If Hitler nevertheless plunges the German people into the catastrophe of war, then every German will realize that National Socialism is responsible for the war.' [22]

This communiqué was issued by the German Communists in Paris. It may thus be concluded that the Communist parties in the Paris–Brussels–London area loyally, even zealously, pledged that they would fight in the event of war. The Western Communist parties saw the conflict as an anti-fascist war even then, whatever the misdeeds and hypocrisy of the Western governments and regardless of the immediate Soviet determination to remain aloof from the fray.

Little is known of the rest of the movement in Europe, which was clandestine or semi-clandestine. The Polish Communists no longer even had a party. Those who remained in Poland fought arms in hand to defend Warsaw in September, and Gomulka seems to have disapproved of the pact.[23] The outlawed Czechoslovak party advised its members to wait for information from Moscow and in the meantime denounced the invasion of Poland.[24] The Communist International drafted a resolution on 7 September, but the text was never made public. We do have some individual testimony about what was going on in the Comintern's Moscow apparatus in those early days of September. One of the most interesting accounts comes from Tito — but it was written forty years after the fact. The secretary of the Yugoslav Communist Party was in Moscow in late August 1939 and went to the Comintern headquarters for an orientation session.

I remember an episode when Manuilski brought together a group of representatives of the Communist sections, or parties, and gave us the assignment to write a proclamation, in the light of the existing situation, each for his own country, determining our directions of activity. I based myself on fairly clear principles. In my opinion, Hitler was wanting to neutralize the USSR during his forthcoming conquests in Europe, and the Soviet Union was hoping to ensure an extra spell of peace for itself. I believed that the pact did not substantially affect the policy of the Communist parties.

In the belief that fascism continued to be the principal danger for progressive mankind, during one night, I quickly wrote a proclamation to this effect. The next day, when we came to Manuilski in the Comintern, I alone had a prepared text. The others either had nothing or had only come with some theses. No one knew how to formulate the text concerning the signing of the pact. Some came highly confused, not knowing what they were expected to do. When I read the prepared proclamation, Manuilski liked it, and he said that I had done a good job. Mainly, people were afraid of making a mistake, and a mistake then meant Lubianka (the main prison of Moscow). I realized that in our proclamations we were no longer to mention the Soviet Union, and this is what Manuilski himself told us: write about the threat to your nation and make preparations for the eventuality of a fascist attack, because your job is to fight and not to concern yourselves with what the Soviet Union may have done.[25]

There is no confirmation of this testimony. It may have been 'reconstructed' to show that the autonomy won so arduously in 1948 had this precedent as well as the others diligently listed by the Yugoslav leaders later on. But one fact is incontrovertible: several weeks, almost a month, passed before the Communist International was told that it was necessary not only to defend the German–Soviet pact, but also to cease calling Hitler an enemy who was primarily responsible for the war. The Communist parties were then compelled to renounce their pledge that they would fight against Nazi Germany in a war. Before that, a distinction between the Soviet Union and the Communist parties was undoubtedly tolerated, perhaps even encouraged, by Dimitrov and Manuilski.

No Communist party, of course, openly contested the Soviet Union's signing of the pact, even in the absence of any directive. Ernst Fischer recalled that it was justified more often than criticized among the leaders of the Comintern apparatus. He himself defended it in discussions with a number of badly shaken German comrades, among them Wilhelm Pieck, Philip Dengel, and Wilhelm Florin. His arguments were probably the same as those circulating through the rank-and-file of the various Communist parties. Because of the pact, the reasoning went, Britain and France instead of the USSR had been forced to absorb the first blows of the German war machine. The Red Army, already infested with traitors, could not afford a conflict. In any case, it served the Western powers right: they had abandoned Czechoslovakia and Spain, and now they declared a war of liberation on behalf of semi-fascist and oppressive Poland! 'Now they had a war, but it was their war, not ours. . . . Maybe in the end the Soviet Union will be a power for peace which, together with the workers of all lands, will dictate the peace.'[26]

It seems certain that arguments of this sort circulated and took root. Not for nothing had the ideological orientation of the Short Course emphasized the duplicity, the bad faith, of the 'so-called democratic countries'. Trust in Stalin was still absolute, perhaps especially so among the thinned-out ranks of those parties already reduced to clandestinity, and if anything, it was reinforced by the news that the Soviet army had entered Poland on 17 September. A report drafted by a PCI emissary in contact with the working-class rank-and-file of Turin is indicative of this attitude. In it he told the exile centre:

> The announcement of the German–Soviet pact was a great surprise to the anti-fascist workers of Turin. At first they thought that it had been signed with Britain's agreement to dupe Hitler. Newspaper photographs of Stalin at the signing ceremony received this comment: 'Look at the expression on Stalin's face. He is really satisfied. He seems to be saying to Ribbentrop: I tricked you well and good. Ribbentrop, on the other hand, looks ill at ease. He doesn't know what's going to happen to him, but he

already feels that something's wrong.' When Russia entered Poland, things became clearer, and people said: 'It is really only a military manoeuvre, you see; there's not even any reason for shots to be fired: if the Poles don't fight against the Russians, it means that they are happy to be liberated. The Germans are advancing too, but they're fighting a real war, whereas the Red Army was hailed when it arrived. You see, Stalin has everything under control. He said to Hitler: You've gone far enough, that's it now, from here on I'm in command; I'm taking the oil, the Romanian border is mine.'[27]

It may well be that in the absence of any 'official' interpretations, Communists formulated varying hypotheses inspired by continuing faith in the USSR and resentment against the Munichites (which remained sharp even after the outbreak of the conflict, during what came to be called the Phoney War in the West). This does not mean that Communists were not disconcerted, especially leaders and intellectuals for whom anti-fascism had been the reason, or one of the main reasons, for their adherence to Communism. Various Italian Communist leaders, whether they were in exile in France or in captivity, were more than perplexed, among them Giuseppe Di Vittorio[28] and Mario Montagnana (while Leo Valiani decided to leave the party). From their place of confinement in Ventotene, Umberto Terracini and Camilla Ravera announced their aversion to the abandonment of the line that Hitler was the 'main enemy'.[29] The shock was far greater in the ranks of the PCF: about a score of members of parliament resigned from the party, as did several cultural figures. Among them was Paul Nizan, who was then serving in the army; he publicly announced his resignation to Jacques Duclos on 25 September and explained its significance in a letter sent to his wife from the front. He commented on the current situation and lucidly anticipated events to come:

I have read the complete text of the Kremlin accord. I think I have understood the game Josip Vissarionovich is playing: the least one can say is that it is a double game held together by a red thread. Just what I was afraid of has happened, and to understand what is now going on we have to recall the story of Charles XII rather than the complete works of Marx. You will therefore understand why I had to make my position public. This is undoubtedly the only way to guarantee the future. In fact, the French leaders have acted like idiots, because they have failed to understand. They should have learned the lessons of opportunism and strategy elsewhere. Just as they were wrong not to read Clausewitz and Ilich. This business has only just started. . . .[30]

Nizan's elusive but significant reference to the behaviour of the Swedish king who attacked the Russians and suffered defeat in 1709, like his allusion to the reasons of state through which the French Communists should have been able to see, was a rare manifestation of foresight. The PCF, however, was not in trouble solely because it was unable or unwilling to express open disapproval of the actions of 'Josip Vissarionovich', namely Stalin. Daladier was trying to extract himself from an embarrassing situation in his own way, by taking more vigorous action. On 26 September he dissolved the PCF; the 300 Communist-controlled municipal councils were suspended; 2,770 councillors were removed from office; 159 periodicals were banned, among them *L'Humanité* (circulation 150,000) and *Ce Soir* (250,000). In addition, 620 Communist-led trade unions were dissolved, 3,400 militants were arrested and interned, and 8,000 Communist state employees were sacked. There were also 11,000 searches.[31]

The repression went further in subsequent months. For the time being, PCF members of parliament were not deprived of their immunity; the Communist group changed its name, now calling itself the 'workers and peasants group'. It is of course difficult to gauge the party loyalty of all three hundred thousand members. But there were no mass resignations in the factories and workplaces during September. In that sense, the outlawing of the party froze its political crisis but did not destroy its structure. For its part, the British government did no more than ban the Communist newspaper, the *Daily Worker* — and that only in 1941. In any event, at the end of September 1939 the British and Swedish were the only legal Communist parties left in Europe. What assessment can we make of the attitude taken by those parties which were able to express their opinion independently before that final wave of repression? François Fejtö has written:

> These positions, repudiated several weeks later, are important because they show the spontaneity and impetus of the Popular Front strategy, as well as the temptation, sharp in some if not all Communist parties, to act according to the exigencies of the national situation. But the course of events revealed that internationalist Muscovite and Stalinist conditioning was more powerful than any other temptation. Given the choice between obedience to Moscow and defence of their own countries and parties, the great majority of Western Communist cadres chose Moscow.[32]

This we shall see when we consider the 'course of events'.

Notes

1. Amendola, *Storia del Pci*, p. 393.
2. From the extract reproduced in Lacouture, *Léon Blum*, p. 439.
3. Richard Gombin, *Les socialistes et la guerre*. *La SFIO et la politique étrangère entre les deux guerres mondiales*. Paris's Gravenhage 1970, pp. 235 and 251.
4. Robrieux, *Histoire intérieure du Parti communiste français*, vol. 1, p. 494.
5. Fauvet, *Histoire du Parti communiste français*, pp. 251-52.
6. From the testimony of Giuseppe Berti, cited in Spriano, *Storia del PCI*, vol. 3, p. 306.
7. Togliatti, *Opere*, vol. 4, I, p. 404.
8. 'Manifesto per il 1o maggio 1939'. The text is in Aldo Agosti, *La Terza Internazionale*, Rome 1979, vol. 3, II, p. 1149.
9. Friedrich Adler, 'La situation de l'Internationale socialiste ouvrière', *Le Mouvement Sociale*, no. 58, January-March 1967, pp. 97-102.
10. Adler, 'Les socialistes autrichiens et l'Internationale socialiste ouvrière', ibid., p. 111.
11. Agosti, *Le Terza Internazionale*, vol. 3, II, p. 1103.
12. From the diary of Celeste Negarville, previously cited.
13. Léon Blum, 'Cessez le feu!', *Le Populaire*, 27 August 1939.
14. 'Dichiarazione del Partito comunista d'Italia', *La Voce degli Italiani*, Paris, 25 August 1939.
15. See *Il compagno Ercoli*, p. 175, n. 13.
16. Pietro Nenni, 'Il voltafaccia della politica sovietica', *Il Nuovo Avanti!*, 31 August 1939.
17. 'Pour l'unité d'action', *L'Humanité*, 7 August 1939, reprinted in Maurice Thorez, *Oeuvres*, Paris 1958, vol. 18, p. 110.
18. William L. Shirer, *The Collapse of the Third Republic*, London 1970, p. 459.
19. Gaston Monmousseau, 'Le peuple de France unanime contre l'aggression', *Vie Ouvrière*, 7 September 1939.
20. Claude Levy, 'Il socialismo nell'Europa di Hitler durante la seconda guerra mondiale', in *Storia del socialismo*, p. 564. See also *Le Parti communiste de Belgique (1921–1944)*, Brussels 1980, pp. 65-69.
21. See Jane Degras, ed., *The Communist International: Documents*, vol. 3, p. 440.
22. Agosti, *La Terza Internazionale*, p. 1163.
23. M.K. Dziewanovski, *The Communist Party of Poland*, Cambridge (Mass.) 1959, p. 340, note 13.
24. P. Osusky, 'Sur la Tchécoslovaquie', *Revue d'Histoire de la Deuxième Guerre Mondiale*, vol. 13, no. 51, p. 37.
25. Josip Broz Tito, *CPY Between the Two Wars*, pp. 62-63.
26. Ernst Fischer, *An Opposing Man*, p. 344.
27. From a report on the work of 'X', March 1940, in Spriano, *Storia del Partito comunista italiano*, vol. 4, p. 18.
28. Michele Pistillo, *Giuseppe Di Vittorio*, Rome 1975, vol. 2, pp. 204-14.
29. Umberto Terracini, *Al bando del partito*, Milan 1976, p. 41; Camilla Ravera, *Diario di trent'anni*, Rome 1973, pp. 633-43.
30. Niazan, *Intellettuale comunista 1926-40*, p. 332.
31. *Histoire du Parti communiste français (manuel)*, pp. 378-79.
32. François Fejtö, *Storia della guerra freda*, Florence 1958, p. 139.

10

The Comintern Conforms

The period beginning in the second half of September 1939 and ending abruptly on 22 June 1941 is a slice of the Stalin epoch during which it is particularly evident that every assertion 'of principle', every appeal to doctrine, was actually designed to bolster some immediate tactical shift. All the speeches, communiqués, and articles of those twenty-one months must be read with a sharp eye to the exigencies, and even the appearances, of Soviet foreign policy.

The texts and 'Marxist-Leninist' positions of the Communist International and the individual parties affiliated to it, as well as the philosophical digressions in which Molotov freely indulged, would otherwise seem strangely anachronistic and well detached from the fray. The traditional Comintern interpretation of the First World War was now presented anew, in a sort of return to origins. But Nazism, the new factor that lay at the root of the Second World War, proved an intractable element of the schema. Its existence and continued vitality remained the dominant concern in Moscow as elsewhere. The more anxious the Kremlin became, the more its fears went unexpressed. Within several weeks the swastika was flying over Warsaw; in the space of a few months the German armies began their westward march, from Copenhagen to Oslo, taking Belgium, Holland and France in May–June 1940.

Did Moscow view this 'new factor' 'without principles'? Maximum broad-mindedness, even anxiety and fear, must be kept to the fore in assessing the various positions that were taken. At the same time, by no means should we discount the practical weight of ideological canons consolidated during Lenin's time and anchored in the 'theoretical Stalinism' of the Short Course. There are also philological complications. In more than one case, the authenticity or representative character of a text from the period of Soviet 'neutrality' has been challenged or doubted. In part this is because certain actions and assertions of individuals or leadership groups seem surprising in view of the fact that after the Nazi invasion of the Soviet Union these same people threw themselves into the resistance struggle with such audacity. Stalin himself later denied the validity of the analysis of the war formulated during the period of Soviet 'neutrality', when the Second World War was defined as an imperialist war just like the First. In 1946 Stalin said that from the outset 'the Second World War assumed the character of an anti-fascist war and a war of liberation, one of the tasks of which was also the re-establishment of democratic rights'.[1] Not only that. On 7 November 1941, with Moscow closely threatened by the invading troops, Stalin said:

> The Hitlerites are the sworn enemies of socialism, the most ferocious reactionaries and brigands, who have deprived the working class and the peoples of Europe of their elementary democratic rights. To hide their reactionary and gangster character, the Hitlerites attack the Anglo-American internal regime as plutocratic. But in Britain and the USA democratic rights exist, there are workers representatives for the toilers, there are labour parties, there is a parliament, while the Hitler regime has abolished these institutions.[2]

The reader may well think that Stalin considered these contrasts between Nazism and the 'democratic countries', now hailed so enthusiastically, as no less fictitious than he had claimed between September 1939 and June 1941. But such statements should be kept in mind as part of the documentary panorama I am trying to present. Some documents, as I noted earlier, are rare as *incunabula*, while others are of dubious authenticity. As the Italian scholar who has used them most systematically has observed, the sources for a history of the Communist International become especially difficult to find and show ever greater gaps with the outbreak of the war.[3] The publications *La Correspondance Internationale* and *Rundschau*, bulletins for the political orientation of the movement, were suspended at the end of 1939, partly replaced by the periodical *World News and Views*, published in London, and by a German edition, *Die Welt*, published in Stockholm. Almost all the Communist parties produced clandestine publications, copies of which are hard to find because of the retrospective censorship imposed by the leaders of these parties themselves. Moreover, it is not easy to get used to the vaguely hallucinatory atmosphere. One American historian has said about the period of Soviet neutrality: 'If we were limited to reading the editorials published in *Communist International* during this phase of the Second World War, it would be difficult to know that there was a state called Germany or that it was the greatest power of one of the two warring coalitions.'⁴

The theoretical organ *Communist International* continued to come out in German until May 1941, and in Russian until the dissolution of the Comintern in May 1943. 'Germany' was not the only forbidden expression up until the invasion of the Soviet Union. Another proscribed word, for which one may search in vain, was 'fascism', which disappeared from the vocabulary of the Communist press. Ilya Ehrenburg says in his memoirs that when he returned from France, the authorities in Moscow told him that if he wanted to publish his book about Paris in the years 1936 to 1938, he would have to avoid that word: 'The text included a description of Paris demonstrations and I was asked to substitute for the slogan 'Down with fascism!' 'Down with the reactionaries!'⁵

Nikita Khrushchev suggested that Soviet leaders themselves found this philo-Germanic zeal embarrassing, and it is not difficult to believe him.

> It was very hard for us — as Communists, as anti-fascists, as people unalterably opposed to the philosophical and political position of the fascists — to accept the idea of joining forces with Germany. It was difficult enough for us to accept this paradox ourselves. It would have been impossible to explain it to the man in the street. Therefore we couldn't admit outright that we had reached an agreement on peaceful coexistence with Hitler. Coexistence would have been possible with the Germans in general, but not with the Hitlerite fascists.⁶

The mystery that remains to be clarified — if indeed it is possible to do so, fully, in view of what happened in June 1941 — is the scope of Stalin's agreement with Hitler and the prospects the former had in mind. On 17 September, when Polish resistance to the German advance had already collapsed, Soviet troops entered the portion of Polish territory stipulated in the secret protocol of 23 August. Stalin, however, preferred to restrict Soviet encampments to the regions in which a clear majority of the population was Ukrainian or Belorussian. In exchange for accepting German occupation of all the predominantly Polish areas, Stalin gained a free hand in Lithuania, as well as in Estonia, Latvia, and Finland, as had already been agreed. The three Baltic countries thus came under Soviet control (though Finland proved a far more irksome problem). The modification of the previous pact was officially sanctioned during another visit to

Moscow by Ribbentrop, which produced a full-fledged 'German–Soviet Boundary and Friendship Treaty' signed on 28 September 1939.

The part of the treaty that was made public states that Germany and Russia would reestablish 'peace and order' in the territories they had absorbed and would also 'assure the people living there a peaceful life in keeping with their national character'. The two secret protocols stipulated the inclusion of Lithuania in the Soviet 'sphere of influence'. As for occupied Poland, the treaty stated: 'Both parties will tolerate in their territories no Polish agitation which affects the territories of the other party. They will suppress in their territories all beginnings of such agitation and inform each other concerning suitable measures for this purpose.'[7]

In the part of Poland under German occupation, this 'suppression' meant Hitlerite terror not only against Jews, but against Poles as well. Molotov claimed that the intervention of the Red Army in the part of Poland under Soviet occupation was justified because 'blood brothers, Ukrainians and Belorussians living in this territory, have been abandoned to their fate and left without protection.' Thirteen million people were thereby 'saved from the yoke of bourgeois Polish domination.' Prisoners were taken among the two hundred to three hundred thousand soldiers of the defeated army and sent to internment camps.[8]

But the German–Soviet friendship treaty went beyond the partition of Poland. The alliance between the two powers was proclaimed in a declaration arguing that after the collapse of Poland — Warsaw had fallen the day before — 'it is in the real interest of all peoples to put an end to the existing state of war between Germany on the one hand and Britain and France on the other.' 'If the efforts of the two governments prove unsuccessful', it was added, 'this will show that France and Britain are actually responsible for the continuation of the war.'

From then on, the official justification of Soviet foreign policy, at least as explained in Molotov's speeches, was pitched insistently in that same key. Ideological-political contrivances and excuses were stretched to absurd lengths. Speaking to the Supreme Soviet on 31 October 1939 for example, Molotov said:

> Certain old formulas are completely out of date. In recent years, the concepts of aggressor and aggression have acquired a new concrete content, another meaning. If we consider the European great powers today, Germany is a state that aspires to a rapid cessation of the war and

desires peace, while Britain and France, which only yesterday were declaiming against the aggressor, favour the continuation of the war and are against the conclusion of peace. The roles, you see, have changed.[9]

The 'old formulas' were none other than the ones employed by the Soviets, by the Comintern after 1935, and by Stalin himself, at the Eighteenth Congress of the CPSU: precisely the distinction between peaceful and aggressive states, between fascist and 'so-called democratic' states. Now Molotov went so far as to say that 'a strong Germany is an essential, even preliminary, condition for lasting peace in Europe'. His polemic against the Treaty of Versailles, though by no means a new theme of Communist propaganda, now heralded Soviet support for possible German 'revanchist' initiatives: 'Relations between Germany and the other bourgeois states of Western Europe over the past twenty years have been determined by the German desire to break the chains of the Treaty of Versailles, whose authors were France and Britain, aided by the USA.'

Support for Hitler's positions did not stop there. Molotov ridiculed the notion of an 'ideological war' and denied the credibility of a 'battle for democracy'. Here is the passage of his speech that brings in the 'philosophical', or at least methodological, dimension:

In Britain, as in France, the partisans of war have declared an ideological war against Germany reminiscent of the religious struggles of old. As we know, the religious wars had the most ruinous consequences for the popular masses: economic collapse and the decline of the culture of the peoples. No war of this kind would be justifiable today for any reason. Hitlerite ideology, like any other, can be accepted or rejected: this is a matter of personal political ideas. But anyone can see that an ideology cannot be destroyed by force. It is therefore not only senseless, but downright criminal, to portray this war as a struggle to destroy Hitlerism, under the false banner of a battle for democracy.

A year after the publication of the Short Course, with Stalin's famous chapter 4, Soviet leaders were producing apologies for ideological agnosticism. But it is useful to look more closely at how insistent the theoretical and political approach that served to justify friendship with the Nazis actually was. We know too much about the structure of the Communist International and its dependence on Moscow's tactical shifts to have to belabour the point that it conformed absolutely to the new line. The French, British, Czechoslovak, and all other Communists received the new directive even before the end of September (and thus before the PCF was outlawed).[10] The change in line included an instruction to Thorez that he go underground. This he did, deserting his regiment on 5 October and seeking refuge in Belgium, whence he went by ship to the USSR,[11] a serious incident that had repercussions during the Resistance and even after. For the British, the new line meant a change in leadership: Harry Pollitt was forced to relinquish his post as secretary and was provisionally replaced by R. Palme Dutt, while party membership declined to twelve thousand.[12] The directive sowed confusion and division in the Czechoslovak, Greek, Romanian, and Yugoslav parties — in fact, in all the underground parties. We will discuss these parties when we consider the Nazi occupation, against which they began fighting in 1941. But the consequences of the Comintern volte-face were naturally greatest in France and Britain. The authoritative historian Eric Hobsbawm has advanced the most passionate apology for the French and British Communists, who were taken by surprise by events:

> There is something heroic about the British and French CPs in September 1939. Nationalism, political calculation, even common sense, pulled one way, yet they unhesitatingly chose to put the interests of the international movement first. As it happens they were tragically and absurdly wrong. But their errors, or rather that of the Soviet line of the moment, and the politically absurd assumption in Moscow that a given international situation implied the same reactions by very differently situated parties, should not lead us to ridicule the spirit of their action. This is how the Socialists of Europe should have acted in 1914 and did not: carrying out the decisions of their International. This is how the Communists did act when another world war broke out. It was not their fault that the International should have told them to do something else.[13]

Georgi Dimitrov, the Comintern general secretary, offered a doctrinal illustration of the 'new course'. He wrote a long article whose contents were summarized in an appeal issued by the Comintern Executive Committee on the occasion of the twenty-second anniversary of the October revolution. These two texts faithfully mirrored Molotov's claim: the British and French were the ones responsible for the continuation of the war. Dimitrov maintained that their aim was to turn Hitler's Germany into 'an armed fist against the USSR'. Germany, he said, faced a dilemma: either bow to the commands of British and French imperialism and wage a potentially fatal war against the USSR, or shift its foreign policy decisively and undertake to establish peaceful relations with the USSR. 'The facts show that the German leaders chose the latter course.'[14] At this point

Britain and France launched the struggle against their major imperialist rival, using the defence of Poland, 'prison-house of peoples', as a pretext. The Comintern Executive's appeal tilted the balance even further in Germany's favour. Denunciation of the Western powers was stronger. The text affirmed that 'the three richest countries — Britain, France, and the United States — dominate the world's major trade routes and markets, and have seized the major sources of raw materials'.[15] They 'hold more than half the human race in subjugation', under the mask of democracy, the better to deceive the masses. 'The other capitalist states' (no longer characterized as fascist or aggressive), which entered 'the road of colonial expansion later', were now challenging this hegemony. This was Dimitrov's advice to the Communist parties:

> The Communist parties must rapidly reorganize themselves in a manner corresponding to wartime conditions; they must purge their ranks of capitulationist elements; they must establish Bolshevik discipline. They must concentrate their fire on opportunism, expressed in a tendency to drift toward positions of 'defence of the fatherland', in acceptance of the myth that the war has an anti-fascist character, and in retreat in the face of the bourgeoisie's acts of repression.

The instructions given the working class of the capitalist countries was consistent with this analysis. Since the workers faced a new imperialist war, they had to struggle against the war in all countries, in full knowledge that the task of putting an end to capitalist exploitation was posed with new sharpness. International Social Democracy had proven to be an agent of Western imperialism and had to be unremittingly exposed as such. 'In the present conditions, unity of the working class can be achieved only *from below*, on the basis of the extension of the movement of the working masses themselves in a resolute struggle against the traitorous leaders of the Social Democratic parties.' The formula of Popular Fronts is no longer acceptable, Dimitrov explained, except in China. There was an obvious political-military reason for this exception: the USSR's interest in a joint fight by Chinese Nationalists and Communists against the Japanese invaders, who were already threatening the Soviet border.

The theoretical framework presented here is eloquent in itself. The jettisoning of the Popular Front policy was complete, though not unexpected (for as we have seen it was in gradual eclipse during the previous months). Nor should it be forgotten that both the Short

Course and the Eighteenth Congress of the Soviet Communist Party had already endorsed the axiom that 'imperialism' was an absolute enemy of the USSR; the distinctions of *substance* within imperialism were already blurred. Now, however, only Western imperialism was denounced, and to the unprecedented extent of justifying German conduct, of crediting Hitlerism with a desire for peace.

Did Moscow really hope for a rapid end to the war, which would allow the USSR to benefit from its new territorial acquisitions? Or did the Kremlin expect a long and bitter struggle, and was it therefore in effect informing the Nazis (attentive readers of the Communist press) that the Comintern too held the Anglo-French imperialists responsible for the continuation of the conflict? Ulam wrote: 'Hitler could not be trifled with. He would not believe that Stalin meant to be loyal if foreign Communists continued to fight and to denigrate the Nazis.'[16] Let us postpone examination of the possible answers until we consider the events of 1940, which will give us more to think about. For the moment, since Dimitrov's article would obviously be read primarily as a document of the Soviet Ministry of Foreign Affairs, it is no less interesting to take note of what it does *not* contain.

What might seem to be its natural corollary was absent. If the second imperialist war was just like the first, then where was the decisive slogan that distinguished Lenin's line in 1914–17: turn the imperialist war into a civil war! Nothing of the kind was argued here. It was obvious that defeatist propaganda, however little effect it might have, was now considered appropriate in democratic Western Europe, where there was still an organized workers movement (albeit fragile, divided, and disconcerted), whereas in the fascist countries the movement no longer existed. But there was no talk of genuine 'revolutionary defeatism'. The Kremlin had no desire to hand Germany (or Italy, whose failure to enter the war so far was appreciated) an excuse to claim that the Communists were calling on the workers to sabotage the country's war effort. Nor did it have any intention of asking the British and French working class to do any such thing. As for the American workers (who were beyond the Comintern sphere of influence in any case), it is interesting to note that Earl Browder, secretary of the Communist Party of the United States, fell into line immediately, arguing that America had to be kept out of the conflict: 'The war was born of the fundamental contradictions of monopoly capital.'[17]

The European CPs, too, soon towed the line. In the vast majority of cases, their agreement was expressed in clandestine documents, for the Communist movement was now underground everywhere in Europe except in Britain and Switzerland (the two countries in which Comintern journals were published, although without official sanction). The painful 'correction' was accompanied by merciless self-criticism: the backsliding and opportunism of the parties' initial anti-fascist reactions, of their proclamations of loyalty to the anti-Hitler coalition on the outbreak of the war, were roundly denounced. As usual, the PCF went furthest:

> Grave errors were made. The parliamentary group made no use whatever of the sole available session of the Chamber of Deputies to protest against the reactionary war policy of Daladier and the Socialist leaders. The Communist deputies instead voted for the war credits. The mistaken orientation persisted into September. The Central Committee failed to understand the significance of the changes that had occurred at the end of August and at the beginning of the war. Once Hitler had willy-nilly renounced war against the USSR, the London and Paris provocateurs took the road of armed conflict with Germany. There was therefore no longer any question of a peace front, nor of collective security, nor of mutual assistance. Reaction had moved openly to an attack on the USSR.[18]

The PCF's self-criticism did not stop there: legalistic and parliamentarist tendencies had arisen within the party, and concessions had been made to the myth of the 'anti-fascist character of the war'. But now the correction had been made. France had entered the war for purely imperialist reasons: 70 million colonial slaves suffered under the yoke of the French empire. The most savage repression of its history, save that which followed the Commune, was now under way in France itself.

> Capitalist reaction is using the war to bolster its domination, to deal the harshest blows to the working class. The basic antagonism between the working class and the bourgeoisie is being aggravated. The war is effacing the secondary distinction between bourgeois democracy and fascism, both of which are forms of the dictatorship of Capital, and is more clearly exposing the reactionary and imperialist class content of the dictatorship of Capital.

This self-criticism, in other words, challenged the very foundation of the Popular Front policy, the distinction between fascism and 'bourgeois democracy', which was now considered secondary. The French case was not unique. The Italian Communists made similar self-criticisms. In the spring of 1940, after Togliatti had been released from prison in Paris and a nucleus of exiled leaders assembled in

France, they also spoke to the Italian workers living in France of opportunism, errors, and disorientation. Togliatti set the tone with this directive:

> It is the task of the French workers to wage the struggle in France against the imperialist war and for peace. Our main enemy is in our own country. But we are internationalists, and whatever country we are living in, we must always have a correct and clear idea of the international situation and the tasks of the working class. Moreover, we cannot wage the struggle against the enemy in our own country by isolating ourselves from the international workers movement and above all from the movement in those countries whose fate is linked most closely with that of our own; we need the closest possible connection with them. [19]

It may be noted that the schema of imperialist war put the Italian Communists — who had no presence whatever in their own country — in a rather less embarrassing position than the French and other Communists. The PCI still told Italian workers that the Italian state was their main enemy, whether it was called fascist or not. But what about the Czechoslovak Communists, for example? As Jiři Pelikan has explained, they found themselves in an absurd position: how could they possibly maintain, in a country occupied by the Nazis, that the exiled President Beneš was primarily responsible for the people's oppression?[20] Yet that was just the line taken by the Central Committee of the Czechoslovak Communist Party.

But the limit was undoubtedly reached by a number of German Communist leaders in Moscow, Ulbricht for example, whose assertions seem even more stunning:

> The revolutionary workers and progressive forces of Germany have no intention of exchanging the present regime for national and social oppression imposed by British imperialism and the pro-British circles of German big capital. Why did Hitler seek a rapprochement with the USSR? Because any support for the British plan of war against the USSR would have made him a satellite of British imperialism and because the strength of the Red Army and the sympathy of the German toiling masses for the USSR would have condemned any anti-Soviet adventure to failure.[21]

Ulbricht therefore called upon the workers, peasants, and intellectuals of Germany, Austria, Czechoslovakia, and Poland to become the 'most resolute guarantors of the Russo–German pact, bulwark of the struggle against British war plans'. But Ulbricht's verbal aberrations count for little when measured against a real episode of unprecedented gravity. In February 1940, the very month in which Ulbricht wrote this article, some five hundred Germans who had been imprisoned in the USSR during the Stalin repression — nearly all of them Communists — were transferred from Sikeria to Brest-Litovsk, along the demarcation line between the territories of the two 'friendly' powers, and there handed over to the Nazis. Their destination was German concentration camps. Among them was Neumann's widow, Margarete Buber, who was interned in Ravensbrück and survived to write a measured but dramatic account of her experience:

After all they had suffered, these Communists no longer had any illusions in the Soviet system, but they never would have believed it possible that things could have come to this. The impossible, however, was now reality. Stalin handed the Communist exiles over to Hitler.[22]

Roy Medvedev reported a tragically ironic flourish: Beria, head of the NKVD, ordered the administrators of Soviet concentration camps to forbid the guards to call political prisoners 'fascists'. 'The order was rescinded only in June 1941.'[23]

Notes

1. 'How We Won', speech delivered in Moscow on 9 February 1946, in *Per conoscere Stalin*, an anthology of his works edited by Giuseppe Boffa, Milan 1970, p. 392.
2. From the text of the speech published in *Lo Stato Operaio*, vol. 1, no. 11-12, New York, November-December 1941, p. 168.
3. Agosti, *La Terza Internazionale*, vol. 3, p. 1161.
4. Kermit MacKenzie, *Comintern e rivoluzione mondiale*, Florence 1969, p. 182.
5. Ilya Ehrenburg, *Men, Years–Life*, vol. 4, *Eve of War*, London 1963, p. 272.
6. *Khrushchev Remembers*, Edward Crankshaw, ed., Harmondsworth 1977, p.151.
7. Shirer, *Rise and Fall*, p. 631.
8. See Vaccarino, *Storia della Resistenza in Europa*, vol. 1, pp. 312-15, and the interesting personal testimony in K.S. Karol, *Visa for Poland*, London 1959, pp. 67-69.
9. The full text is in *Le Monde*, Brussels, 4 November 1939. See also A. Rossi [Angelo Tasca], *Deux ans d'alliance germano-soviétique*, Paris 1949, pp. 111-16.
10. See Courtois, *Le Pcf dans la guerre*, pp. 52-55.
11. Ibid., pp. 111-17.
12. François Bedarida, 'Il socialismo in Gran Bretagna', in *Storia del socialismo*, vol. 3, p. 183.
13. E.J. Hobsbawm, *Revolutionaries*, London 1973, pp. 5-6.
14. G. Dimitrov, 'La guerra e la classe operaia dei paesi capitalistici'. For the full text, see *Cahiers du Bolchévisme*, vol. 17, 2nd semester 1939—January 1940, photostated copy in '*Les Cahiers du Bolchévisme*' *pendant la campagne 1939_40, avant*

propos de A. Rossi [A. Tasca], Paris 1951, pp. 1-15.

15. 'Appello del Ce per il ventiduesimo anniversario della Rivoluzione d'Ottobre (novembre 1939)', in Agosti, *La Terza Internazionale,* vol. 3, II, pp. 1197-1202.

16. Ulam, *Stalin,* p. 517.

17. Earl Browder, 'The Socialist Revolution', *The Communist,* November 1939, collected with other writings in *The Second Imperialist War,* New York 1940, p. 168.

18. 'Le PCF en lutte contre la guerre impérialiste', *Cahiers du Bolchévisme,* vol. 17, 2nd semester 1939—January 1940, p. 11.

19. 'Tentennamenti ed errori opportunistici all'inizio e nel primo periodo della guerra', *Lettere di Spartaco,* no. 11, 1-15 April 1940, reproduced in *Opere,* vol. 4, II, pp. 30-31.

20. J. Pelikan, *S'ils me tuent,* Paris 1977, pp. 28-29.

21. From an article published in *Die Welt,* 9 February 1940, quoted in François Fejtö, *L'heritage de Lénine (Introduction à l'histoire du communisme mondial),* Paris 1973, pp. 138-39.

22. Buber-Neumann, *La révolution mondiale,* p.397. The episode is confirmed in Medvedev, *Let History Judge,* p. 222.

23. Ibid., p. 443.

11
The Soviet Union's
Strange Neutrality

The way the Second World War began seemed to justify the greatest reservations about the anti-fascist commitment of the British and French governments and armed forces. The Phoney War dragged on without battles, as the Germans dug in behind the Siegfried Line, the French behind the Maginot. Historians, authors and journalists have described it lavishly. Some have estimated that if the French had attacked at the very outset, they could have thrown eighty-five divisions against slightly more than forty for Hitler, who was still busy wiping Poland off the map. But another calculation has been made as well: in the spring of 1940, when the German army was preparing its breakthrough on the western front, Hitler left his eastern borders undefended, with barely five divisions stationed there. In other words, had the Red Army invaded, it could have driven all the way to Berlin.

The 'ifs' cannot be avoided, for in the early days of the war the possible 'scenarios' (to use the current term) were infinitely varied, the different hypotheses paradoxical. In late 1939, for example, when the USSR attacked Finland after the Finnish government refused to grant Moscow any military bases in the nearby Finnish Gulf (and rejected territorial changes that would have moved the border further from Leningrad), the potential scenario might well seem completely absurd. While the Finnish army resisted brilliantly for more than three months, the French General Staff (followed, though with some reluctance, by the British) worked out detailed plans for military intervention by an expeditionary corps. Had these plans been implemented, the Western democracies would have been at war with Germany and the USSR simultaneously. Then, in June 1941 the Soviet Union would have been at war with Germany as well: everyone against everyone else.

It is not difficult to imagine that the propensity to surrender, which had contributed so much to Munich, was still palpable between 1939 and 1940, especially in France. General Gamelin's bellicosity seemed reserved for the 'Bolsheviks', both within the country and abroad. In January 1940 William Bullitt, the American ambassador to Paris, heard it said in the French Ministry of Foreign Affairs that the Soviet Union should be destroyed.[1] In the meantime, hardly a shot was being fired against Germany. Anglo-French lack of military action, which continued through September 1939, suggested to Hitler — who, as we have seen, was backed by Molotov — that a high-sounding 'peace campaign' might be useful. The Führer was soon arguing that it would be absurd to let millions of people die in a struggle to reconstruct the defunct Polish state. 'No, war in the West cannot resolve any problem.'

Many people in France agreed. Defeatism was widespread, fuelled by the Phoney War itself. The spectre of a new bloodbath just twenty years after the end of the First World War was rife. More than two million men were mobilized. The French government seemed convinced that Germany, once weakened by economic blockade, would heed more moderate counsel. Ideological enthusiasm was completely lacking: the French bourgeoisie, concerned to preserve its 'empire', wanted the conflict brought to a halt as soon as possible; the working class was silent; the trade unions had lost more than half their membership since 1937, and had been further enfeebled by the purge of Communist cadres. Entreaties for peace took unusual forms. Moderate intellectuals circulated an appeal drafted by Alain which argued that 'the price of peace will never be so ruinous as the price of war.'[2]

Was Communist pacificism indistinguishable from the pacificism of the right? Though it did reflect the mood of masses of workers who were primarily concerned about the rising cost of living and the employers' spirit of revenge, the Communist peace campaign was nevertheless so obviously the product of new directives from Moscow that it inevitably rang false. Hence the greater political isolation in which the Communists found themselves. The schism with the Socialists that had opened in 1939 widened. On 1 October the so-called Worker–Peasant parliamentary group, formed after the dissolution of the PCF in September, sent a letter to Herriot, the Radical president of the Assembly, asking that Paris offer peace proposals to Hitler. The request, which sought to exploit widespread fear of the massacres entailed by a new war, paralleled the Soviet peace campaign, itself conducted in unison with the Nazis. The French Communists were cautious and ambiguous about Germany:

It is absolutely necessary to prevent the peace proposals from being rejected out of hand, which would drive us to worse adventures and catastrophes. With all our heart we want a just and lasting peace, and we think it can be rapidly won, because against the imperialist warmongers and Hitler's Germany, rent by internal contradictions, stands the power of the USSR, which can permit a policy of collective security capable of assuring peace and of safeguarding French independence.[3]

Exactly what was meant by the 'internal contradictions' of Hitler's Germany is not clear. Only about forty of the seventy-three Communist deputies to the Assembly supported the motion presented by the letter, signed by Florimond Bonte and Arthur Ramette. Some of them were arrested. At that time, the Communists who had been drafted into the army were more or less classified as untrustworthy, and the party's semi-clandestine organization was highly fragile. According to Jacques Duclos, there were only about two hundred reliable members in the Paris area.[4] An underground edition of *L'Humanité* began to appear at the end of October. The Communist deputies were first stripped of their immunity and then, in January 1940, were divested of their seats by a vote of 522 to 2. The Soviet–Finnish conflict was increasingly shaking Communist 'public opinion', which was isolated among political circles, though less so in society itself. Léon Blum offered what was probably the best brief description of the state of mind of the workers when he spoke of 'a mistrustful and hostile muteness'. The old Socialist politican warned that the Socialists had to deepen the Communists' embarrassment if they were to gain new recruits:

How exactly should we define the task of our party in the situation created by Communist disintegration?
    First of all, we must encourage and accelerate the detoxification treatment, constantly expose Stalin's crime, the worst sort of crime against humanity, because if Stalin had wanted peace, Europe would not be at war. With all the means at our disposal and without the slightest reticence, we must rebut the Communist propaganda now arising in France again and merging ever more closely with Hitlerite propaganda. On all this we agree. That is our immediate, elementary, and obvious task. But is that all? Shall we abandon to their fate the hundreds of thousands of men and women who have broken the Communist chains?[5]

But there was no visible shift of opinion among the masses. Military inaction, lack of awareness of the looming danger, and the inertia of a pacifism unshaken by the formation on 21 March 1940 of a new government (headed by Reynaud) which received a reduced majority in the Assembly because it proposed a greater war effort — all these things were leading France to catastrophe. Anti-Communism could not take the place of anti-fascism. But muting their own anti-fascism did not pay off for the Communists, and it scandalized others. Denunciation of the Daladier and Reynaud governments for inconsistency and for their reactionary measures was not easily reconciled with propaganda that insisted that anti-Nazism was mystification. The same observation goes for the British Communists, who, despite their small forces, based their line on an even more compromising pacificism, even trying to build a movement around a phantom Peace Council. The British Communist Party asserted in a Central Committee resolution passed on 7 October, with only Pollitt and Campbell dissenting:

> Nazi aggression has been checked and limited by the power of the Soviet Union, and today the Nazi leader is suing for peace. It is the ruling classes of Britain and France who demand the continuation of the war. . . . The struggle of the British people against the Chamberlains and Churchills is the best help to the struggle of the German people against Hitler. We demand that negotiations be immediately opened for the establishment of peace in Europe.[6]

This fantastic peace offensive failed, while anti-communism and anti-Sovietism were fuelled by the war between the USSR and Finland. The contradictions of this paradoxical period, when war was liable to break out among all parties simultaneously, were also noted by Mussolini, who sought to remind Hitler of his unremittingly anti-Bolshevik historical mission. The Duce admonished Hitler in the following terms on 5 January 1940:

> I feel that you cannot abandon the anti-Semitic and anti-Bolshevik banner that you have held aloft for twenty years and for which so many comrades have died. You cannot disavow your gospel, in which the German people have blindly believed. It is my duty to add that any further step in your relations with Moscow would have catastrophic repercussions in Italy, where anti-Bolshevik unanimity, especially among the fascist masses, is absolute, granite-hard, and irreversible. Allow me to believe that this will not come to pass. The solution to your problem of *Lebensraum* lies in Russia and nowhere else. . . . Germany's task is to defend Europe from Asia. This is not only Spengler's theory. Until four months ago, Russia was enemy number one: it is not, nor can it become, friend number one. This has deeply disturbed the fascists in Italy, and perhaps many National Socialists in Germany too. The day we demolish Bolshevism will be the

day we keep faith with our two revolutions.[7]

As for the number-one friend, month after month, Stalin scrupulously respected the accords signed with Hitler on 23 August and 28 September. In the meantime, the USSR moved swiftly to complete the outright annexation of the Baltic countries and Bessarabia.[8] In the occupied Polish territories, Moscow hastened to nationalize industries and land: in other words, to establish the Soviet economic and political system. Isaac Deutscher noted the paradox of Stalin's expropriation of the big landlords, his division of their estates among the peasants, and his nationalization of industry and banking in Poland's eastern marches:

> Thus an act of revolution resulted from Stalin's co-operation and rivalry with the most counter-revolutionary power in the world. At a stroke, Stalin fulfilled the main desiderata which had always figured in every programme of Polish and Ukrainian socialists and communists, the desiderata they themselves had not been able to realize. The social upheaval in the annexed lands was, of course, the work of the Soviet occupation forces, not of the Polish and Ukrainian toilers — it was the first of the long series of revolutions from above which Stalin was to impose upon Eastern Europe. And while he was expropriating the possessing classes economically, he expropriated the workers and peasants politically, depriving them of freedom of expression and association.[9]

In Finland, things did not go as planned. The most conspicuous feature of the Russo–Finnish war was the miserable performance of the Soviet armed forces. A great country had attacked a small people jealous of their independence and sovereignty, and succeeded in winning only after three months of bitter fighting and at great human cost (fifty thousand dead). The Finnish 'issue' alienated many who had been sympathetic to the USSR and had enormous negative repercussions for its image abroad. The USSR suddenly seemed weaker than other states had believed. And among the people themselves, estimates of strength, including military strength, were among the basic factors of mass psychology. The Italian Communist source I quoted earlier, for instance, noted:

> When Red Army units entered Finland, it was a great surprise. There were many comments, especially since the fascists, who up to then had their backs to the wall in most discussions, took the offensive again, saying that Stalin was a liar and a traitor who promised peace and then invaded small states, sending fifty men against one. . . . . What had even greater effect

and aroused lack of confidence was the depreciation of the Red Army, of
its officers and cadres. . . . The workers wondered why the Red Army
was not advancing. Partisans of the USSR became less frequent in the café
discussions.[10]

Soviet use of the clandestine Finnish Communist Party, many of
whose leaders had emigrated to the USSR (Kuusinen, the founder, had
been a major Comintern leader for years), was also less than brilliant.
The USSR cobbled together a Finnish 'people's government' headed
by Kuusinen himself, and then signed a treaty of friendship with it.
But this initiative automatically 'changed the whole character of the
war, transforming it from a limited territorial conflict into a confrontation over Finland's internal regime and international policy.'[11]
Then, when the real Finnish government, headed by Marshal
Mannerheim, signed a peace treaty with the USSR on 11 March 1940
(ceding more territory than Moscow had demanded in November
1939), no further mention was made of the Kuusinen government.
The Central Committee of the Finnish Communist Party had gone
so far as to claim, in an appeal dated 30 November 1939, that 'the
Mannerheim ruling clique did not accept the Soviet demands so that
they, along with the other agents of foreign imperialism, could
prosecute their plans to conquer Leningrad'! The Red Army was
hailed as the 'liberator of our people': 'The Red Army is an invincible
army behind which stands the power of a gigantic people 183 million
strong. It is therefore ridiculous to suppose that the generals of the
Finnish army could oppose the Red Army, which is better trained
and equipped than any of the world's armies.'[12]
But that army — whose defence of Leningrad alongside the population of the city, martyr to freedom, would win glory just two years
later — certainly failed to score impressive results in a war that soon
looked like a war of aggression even though it was not Stalin's
intention to annex Finland. Once the unfortunate Finnish–Soviet
episode was over, Molotov again restated the general description of
the world conflict that he had advanced in October 1939. Speaking to
the Supreme Soviet on 29 March 1940, he emphasized the aggressive
character of the 'Anglo-French imperialists', who on the one hand
wanted 'to crush and dismember Germany', which desired peace,
and on the other hand manifested equally bitter hostility to the USSR.
'In the chorus of enraged howls against the Soviet Union', Molotov
added, 'the loudest of all have always been the strident voices of the
corrupt Socialists of the Second International — the Attlees and the
Blums, the Citrines and the Jouhaux, the Tranmaels and the

Hoeglunds — all those servants of capital who have sold themselves to the warmongers body and soul.'[13] Beyond the verbal pyrotechnics, Molotov confirmed that 'we must maintain a position of neutrality and abstain from taking part in the war among the European great powers.'

Molotov's schema, re-echoed by Dimitrov's article of November 1939, remained in force in the Communist International throughout 1940: the war was an imperialist war, and the task of the international working class was to struggle to end it. 'In every single country a workers united front must be formed, a people's front of toilers established by the masses from below.' References to the Social Democrats once again featured the epithets of the period of 'Social Fascism': lackeys of imperialism', 'servants of the bourgeoisie', 'traitors', 'rabid anti-Soviet dogs'. These all figured in the 1940 May Day manifesto issued by the Comintern.[14]

Meanwhile, the ill-famed Second International was truly outstanding in its reticence. It was motionless, silent, internally divided. At its last meeting, held in Brussels on 3 April 1940, the Executive decided to put aside its quarrels and issued an insignificant May Day manifesto of its own — 'in which Hitler and Stalin were not even mentioned'[15] — pledging to appoint a commission to work out a programme for the post-war reconstruction of Europe. Social Democratic internationalism was completely exhausted. The national divisions among the British, French, Belgians, Dutch, and Scandinavians had paralysed the Socialist International for years now, and in July 1940, after the fall of France, the British Labour Party, the only section of the International that still really existed, rejected even a proposal of the new president, Camille Huysmans, that the Executive meet in London.

In May the Labour Party had joined the Churchill national unity government, with Attlee as deputy prime minister, and the Labour leaders had no intention of subjecting their conduct to the scrutiny of their foreign comrades, even on the subject of common war objectives. Hostility to the German Social Democratic exiles — who were now joined by Danish, Belgian, Dutch, Czech, Polish, and French newcomers — was deep and ill-concealed, although England's most irritating wartime guest was a non-Socialist Frenchman, Charles De Gaulle, the man who came to personify 'La Résistance'.

In view of the decomposition of the political organizations of the European workers movement during the bleak two-year period of Soviet neutrality, there is good reason to wonder what the Communist International demanded of its own affiliated parties apart from discipline and study of the Short Course. Did Dimitrov, Togliatti, and Stalin really intend to use this enfeebled lever to launch and sustain a mass peace movement? Did they really expect that Britain would yield and that peace would mean the European victory of the Nazi-fascist regimes, primarily Germany? Or did they actually fear this possibility? Did they perhaps believe that if the imperialist war ended, the European working class would take the initiative again?

Let us try once again to sort out this labyrinth, relying on the few facts we possess. We shall begin with the overt expressions of Soviet foreign policy, since the Comintern's propaganda in 1940, fragmented into various national 'adaptations', was but a pale reflection of the Kremlin's real intentions, concerns, and hopes, and may sometimes even conceal them. Very little is directly observable: primarily the surprise, even panic, aroused by the sudden French defeat in June 1940, which came on the heels of the Nazi occupation of Denmark, Norway, Belgium, and Holland. When Paris fell into German hands, the myth of the invincibility of the French army fell with it, although London continued to hold out, and by the end of the summer Hitler had given up trying to invade Britain. On 1 August 1940 Molotov made a speech to the Supreme Soviet in which he ruled out a rapid end to the conflict. This was a most important point: 'The first year of the war in Europe is now drawing to a close, but the war's end is not yet in sight. It is more likely that we stand on the eve of a new stage in the intensification of the war between Germany and Italy on the one side and Britain, aided by the United States, on the other.'[16]

Molotov nevertheless continued to hail the German–Soviet accord, saying that he was convinced that the latest events of the war had not only not undermined its value, but confirmed 'the importance of its existence and of its further development'. Molotov affirmed: 'The basis of that accord, and of the neighbourly and friendly relations established between the Soviet Union and Germany, rests not on accidental and transitory considerations, but on fundamental state interests of both the USSR and Germany.' The president of the Soviet Council also noted that relations had improved with Mussolini's Italy, which had entered the war on 10 June 1940 to share in the spoils of defeated France. Molotov said: 'An exchange of views with Italy has shown that there is every possibility of our two countries' achieving a mutual understanding in the field of foreign policy. The prospects for more extensive commercial relations are therefore well-founded.'

One important fact emerges from German documents: Hitler began preparations for the attack on the USSR even before he abandoned the invasion of Britain. In late July 1940 the German dictator told his leading officers that he intended to invade Russia in the spring of 1941:

> Russia needs only to hint to England that she does not wish to see Germany too strong and the English, like a drowning man, will regain hope that the situation in six to eight months will have completely changed.
>   *But if Russia is smashed, Britain's last hope will be shattered.* Then Germany will be master of Europe and the Balkans.
>   *Decision: In view of these considerations Russia must be liquidated. Spring 1941.*
>   *The sooner Russia is smashed, the better.*[17]

The German general staff set to work at the beginning of August 1940. At the time, of course, the USSR could not have known of this decision, partly because there was more than a little madness in Hitler's plan to 'liquidate' Russia in a few months, or even weeks, as Poland had been liquidated. Stalin, who was so cautious and wary in foreign policy, would not have thought Hitler so insane. From the little we know, there is no reason to believe that Stalin expected a German attack in the short run — quite the opposite. Perhaps he assumed that the conflict would drag on; he still feared a Japanese attack, and was seeking to keep the USSR out of the war for as long as possible in any case. Perhaps he contemplated a broader agreement with Hitler. As we shall see, Stalin remained deeply hostile to Britain, and concerned not to provoke Germany. But this concern was not accompanied by adequate efforts to reorganize the Soviet armed forces. Caution would not have prevented the USSR from seeking to fortify all the strong points along the borders delineated by the treaty with Germany, for there was unquestionable tension in various hot spots along the borders of the German and Soviet zones, from Finland to the Balkans. In June and July 1940, the USSR completed the occupation and annexation of the Baltic countries, Bessarabia, and northern Bukovina. Germany, for its part, had consolidated its domination of Romania (and thus its control of the Romanian oil fields). In August 1940 Hitler forced the Romanian leaders to cede a large part of Transylvania to Hungary, thus bringing the entire bank of the Danube under his own aegis. In September the Tripartite Pact between Germany, Japan, and Italy was signed. Although Article 5 of the pact explicitly stipulated that the alliance was not directed against the USSR Stalin's concern mounted.

Controversy was apparent when Molotov visited Berlin in November, as disputes and disagreements about Eastern Europe emerged. The USSR was sufficiently worried about this region not to let itself be gulled by German chatter about a proposed division of the world into spheres of influence. Britain was by no means conquered, and Molotov therefore considered discussion of possible Soviet penetration of India and the Persian Gulf to be a fatuous or even dangerous exercise. But he did not seem averse to contemplating the German offer to join the Tripartite Pact if this could bring an increase in Soviet influence in the Balkans. Throughout 1940 and early 1941, there was no palpable shift in the orientation of Stalin's foreign policy. Ulam, a historian who has made a special study of Soviet foreign policy, wrote that it was then 'an amazing mixture of occasional defiance and utter blindness'. [18] The USSR, he observed, already faced an insoluble dilemma: Moscow had to avoid excessive accommodation yet avoid giving Hitler any pretext for aggression. Changes in Soviet foreign policy were barely perceptible and may have denoted no more than increasingly urgent defensive moves from month to month. The fall of France changed the strategic situation dramatically, since Hitler no longer had to contend with two fronts on the European continent (and was already transferring division after division to the east). Italy's entry into the war on 10 June 1940 further broadened the conflict and made peace impossible unless Britain collapsed, an eventuality Stalin was inclined to rule out.

In such circumstances, was it still possible to believe that the two sides would wear each other down, to the advantage of the USSR? Did Stalin expect American intervention? With good reason Ulam has written:

> We may never know the exact balance of fears and calculations that inspired the Kremlin in its new policy. The interpretation put upon it at the time — that Stalin genuinely associated himself with Hitler in his plans for conquests — is obviously absurd. He could have had no doubts about Germany's long-range plans. The policy formally proclaimed on September 28 had to be the product of fear. [19]

Fear of being unable to withstand a German attack and of being forced to subject the regime to the arduous test of surviving the inevitable initial defeats. Perhaps this fear was mitigated by some hope that a settling of accounts could be postponed to 'the long term'. It would then be understandable why the Comintern was used throughout this period to suggest to Hitler that the USSR endorsed his propaganda campaigns. From month to month the offices and corridors of the Moscow headquarters were packed with newly arrived leaders and functionaries who had often had lucky escapes from their occupied countries, or from the countries in which they had earlier sought refuge and which they now had to abandon to escape the invading German troops. There were the Spaniards Dolores Ibarruri and Jesús Hernández (José Díaz was very ill in hospital and died of tuberculosis in Georgia in 1942); the Frenchmen Maurice Thorez (still 'underground' for the moment), André Marty, and Raymond Guyot; the Austrians Koplernig and Fischer; the Germans Pieck, Ulbricht, and Florin; the Czechs Gottwald and Rudolf Slánský; the Hungarians Rákosi (one of the Communist leaders released after the German–Soviet pact in 1939; he seems to have been exchanged for old Hungarian banners of the 1848 revolution which the Soviets surrendered to the Hungarian government), Gerö, who had returned from Spain, and Révai; the Bulgarians Kolarov, Stepanov, and Chervenkov; the Yugoslav Viahovic; the Italians Vincenzo Bianco, Edoardo D'Onofrio, Giulio Cerreti, Ruggero Grieco; the Romanian Ana Pauker (released by the Bucharest government after an exchange of prisoners with the Soviets); the Finn Kuusinen — to mention only the leading personalities. The history of this apparatus, one of its members wrote, 'was the history of proletarian defeats'.[20]

Palmiro Togliatti took up his former post alongside Dimitrov and Manuilski. He had witnessed the last days of the Spanish tragedy and was later arrested in Paris, but managed, possibly with the aid of the Soviet secret service,[21] to avoid condemnation by a French court in February 1940. He reached the USSR in April or May 1940 (he reported that he left from Amsterdam on 10 May, 'making the sea voyage through the Baltic just as Hitler's divisions were invading Belgium and Holland',[22] but a letter of his, written on Comintern stationery to Giuseppe Berti, who had taken refuge in the United States, was dated 17 April).[23]

Togliatti was now forty-seven. His proverbial lucidity and prudence, his cool-headedness, already sorely tested by so much hardship, were now tried yet again. He found the International tottering on its last legs. Togliatti later claimed that Dimitrov was already predicting and planning its dissolution.[24] But that decision was postponed, and for the moment the views more or less freely expressed in the Comintern Executive reflected not only a certain sense of nervous expectancy, but also the most diverse and conflicting hopes. It would be an exaggeration to speak of 'pro-German' and 'pro-English' factions in the Comintern, but Ernst Fischer's memoirs suggest that something of the sort took shape in 1940. This brilliant memorialist recalls that he had bitter exchanges with the German Communist leaders, who actually seemed glad that Hitler's troops had arrived in Paris. Togliatti, he says, intervened to point out that there was no guarantee that the Nazis would respect the pact with the USSR in the long run. 'Let us not lose our heads', he advised, according to Fischer, 'but concentrate on gaining as much time as possible'.[25]

Whatever the turmoil in the apparatus, there is no doubt that the sense of uncertainty and confusion — held in check by discipline, by adherence to every tactical wrinkle of Soviet foreign policy, and by confidence in Stalin's wisdom — was accompanied by hope for a gradual disintegration of all the imperialist 'bandits', of the colonial system, of one or another of the warring parties, whether German, British, or both. Among the battered and disorganized rank-and-file militants in prison, underground, or in isolation, however, the common conviction was that only the defeat of Nazism could open new prospects. The Italian Communists, the German Communists languishing in Nazi concentration camps, the imprisoned Greek Communists, and the Spaniards exiled or imprisoned and condemned by Franco could hope for little else than an extension of the conflict, which would finally free them from their chains. More generally, all the defeats, disappointments, and grudges of the twenties and thirties had aroused a widespread spirit of revenge, stimulating hope for a revolutionary upturn that would re-open the interrupted road of the Russian October.

Resentment against Social Democracy was undoubtedly genuine and extensive, although the German Communist leaders who were toning down the anti-Nazi polemic, like Wilhelm Pieck,[26] were probably trying to recover the primordial role they had lost within the International during the time of the Popular Fronts and also thirsted to recover some contact with the German popular masses. But the Communist cadres of the various countries yearned for a new revolutionary opportunity that would enable the USSR and Communism to leap to centre stage on the ruins of war. Typical in this respect were the slogans that French Communist leaders urged their militants to paint on the walls: 'Long live the Red Army! The rich must pay! Thorez to power! Long live Stalin! Communism is freedom!'[27]

No slogans against the German occupation. The PCF —ravaged by the storm, its initial underground structure extremely fragile — was the party that manifested the greatest insincerity, betraying an almost incredible thoughtlessness. Paris had just been occupied when three leaders of the PCF asked the Nazi authorities for permission to republish *L'Humanité* legally — a serious gesture the reality of which is incontestable, although the PCF sought to evade responsibility for it after the war.[28] Although the *Kommendatur* was inclined to accept, the French police blocked the 'negotiations', arresting some of the Communist emissaries (who were later released by the Germans). The Vichy government finally succeeded in convincing the German authorities not to let this 'legalization' go any further. *L'Humanité* thus continued to appear underground. These early clandestine issues were still inspired by the 'peace campaign', by the revolutionary extravagance we have already mentioned, and by vehement denunciation of the reactionary nature of the policy of the French Vichy government in the 'free' zone, especially its social policy. Communist propaganda also declaimed against Blum, the Socialists, and the Radicals, who were held to be responsible for the country's entry into the war and its defeat. De Gaulle was accused of being in the pay of the City of London. The PCF proclaimed:

> In their struggle against the Vichy government, the Communists must show that its policy is a continuation of the policy of betrayal that led France to disaster and that the only solution for the forces of social and national liberation in France is to unite around the working class and its Communist Party, to oust the government of betrayal and to impose a true people's government of the freedom and independence of France.[29]

So violent was the polemic against the Socialists that some Communist leaders imprisoned by Pétain — Florimond Bonte and François Billoux among others — asked to testify at the trial of Blum and Daladier, who had also been arrested and were in confinement. The contradictions in which the PCF became entangled as it sought to mobilize the masses against the Vichy government while failing to mention the minor detail of the Nazi occupation were exactly the contradictions in which Moscow's foreign policy was also entangled. But there seems no doubt that PCF policy was truly a 'line', mirroring precise Comintern directives that were applied in other countries as well. The Belgian Communists, for example, requested and were granted permission to republish their newspaper *La Voix du Peuple* legally, under German occupation (although the experiment lasted for only eight issues). They then went even further, managing to win permanent legalization of one of their official newspapers published in Antwerp, *Ulenspiegel*. Looking back on this 'aberration' after the war, the Belgian CP admitted that it did great damage, above all arousing 'the hostility of the underground apparatus of Belgian Socialists towards the Communists, which has never disappeared.'[30]

The price paid for this attitude was far higher in the future French Resistance. We shall have occasion to speak of this again, but for the moment it is worth citing a comment made by a small underground newspaper distributed by a group of Socialists in northern France about a Communist leaflet that obviously reflected the position of the equally clandestine PCF:

> Anyone reading the Communist leaflet will be struck even more strongly by what it does not say than by the lies and criticism it contains. One is amazed to find that there is not a single reference to Hitler or Mussolini, as if the two dictators representing Nazism and fascism were wholly blameless in the disasters now striking the French people and the enslaved peoples of Europe.
>
> This incredible omission, the shame of the Communists, is quite understandable and explicable, since in the leaflet they still dare to assert that Stalin personifies the policy of peace. This tragic joke compels us to recall the events of the recent past.[31]

It is an indication of how far apart these forces were, though in a matter of months they would be fighting against the same enemy. A more sober but no less acute criticism of the 'incredible omission' came in the comment of the Italian Socialist leader Pietro Nenni, who resigned as secretary of his party when the German–Soviet pact was signed but did not lose hope of rediscovering the road to unity with the Communists. Nenni wrote to the Italian Communists from the small village in the Pyrenees where he had taken refuge (and where he was later arrested by the French police on German orders, and then handed over to Mussolini). His letter is dated 10 October 1940 and is of special interest because in substance it shares an outlook that was typical of the Communist mentality at the time; it even endorses the Communist judgement of the war's character. What, then, was Nenni's disagreement with the Communists?

> The disagreement does not concern the nature of the war — an imperialist war in which Britain is defending its traditional European and world hegemony, while Hitlerism, fascism, and Japanese militarism are fighting to replace Britain and France in Europe, Africa, and Asia. . . . The disagreement does not relate to the ultimate objectives and tasks that history has set for the conscious revolutionary vanguard of the proletariat: to take advantage of the circumstances to bring about a new leap forward for proletarian revolution. The disagreement concerns the tactics

to be applied in realizing our common objectives. For me it remains true today, as it was for everyone until September 1939, that Hitlerism and fascism are the main enemies both of the working class and of the USSR, despite the fact that, for reasons of state, they have had to solicit or accept a compromise with the USSR. I would gladly repeat today what your Comrade Ercoli said at the Seventh Congress [of the Comintern] in Moscow: that whoever fails to understand that the defeat of Hitler and Mussolini is a matter of life and death for the workers movement understands nothing of the laws of proletarian revolution. All varieties of imperialism are our enemies, but what Marx said of the bourgeoisie is equally true of imperialism: it does not constitute an undifferentiated reactionary mass. There are more reactionary and less reactionary imperialisms. And the Rome–Berlin Axis is the most reactionary.[32]

This is just what the leaders of the Communist parties refused to say, or could not say if they wanted. The Czechoslovak CP was the extreme case. Around the same time, its Central Committee passed a resolution that said:

Against Beneš and his agents, the party must defend the independence of the Czechoslovak struggle for liberation from the imperialists, must crush Beneš's chauvinist propaganda and denounce the service he is rendering the Anglo-American imperialists and the interests of the selfish classes of Czechoslovak capital. . . .Obeying directives from abroad, Beneš's partisans are acting on behalf of the victory of the Anglo-American bloc as if this were an opportunity for our liberation; they persist in their insane chauvinist demagogy, they sow hatred of the Czechoslovak people among the German workers in uniform, and they arouse mistrust of the policy of the USSR . . .[33]

One may well wonder how the workers of Prague and Bratislava were supposed to be convinced that the 'German workers in uniform' — in other words, the oppressor Nazi soldiers — could liberate them. And yet this document maintained that a 'Germany liberated from capitalism will also assure peace for Czechoslovakia'. Even when tension between the USSR and Germany mounted at the end of 1940 and early in 1941, the Communist International seemed determined to hold rearguard positions that might have to be abandoned overnight. In February–March 1941 a 'programme-manifesto of the Central Committee' of the PCF reaffirmed a stance of strict neutrality among the warring parties: 'The people of France, imbued with profound contempt for the clique of petty politicians of Vichy and Paris, have no desire to play soldier for Britain or Germany, for Churchill or Hitler; they have no desire to play soldier for the plutocracy, in whatever guise.'[34]

The unofficial Comintern journal *World News and Views* —
published in London while the city was being paid regular visits by
German bombers and the civilian population, alongside the fliers of
the RAF, were writing perhaps the first page of European resistance — makes chilling reading. In its editorials by Palme Dutt,
Richard Goodman, and D.N. Pritt, this newspaper demanded that
the existing 'Labour–Tory' government be replaced by a 'people's
government' that would impose peace on the unwilling British
'lords'. It attacked the Polish and Czech governments-in-exile, and
urged Greece to seek peace with the Italian invaders.[35] But the
confidential directives are equally disturbing. Let me mention one of
the few cases I have been able to authenticate. When the Italian
Communist journal *Lo Stato Operaio*, which had begun republishing
in New York, dared to print an article arguing that the war would not
end soon (since Britain was by no means defeated), hailing the
military strength of the USSR, and suggesting that a Russian–German
conflict could erupt,[36] the editorial board was rebuked by the PCI's
'ideological centre' in Moscow, led by Togliatti:

> The entire article is constructed so as to give the impression that the
> enormous military might of the USSR is a potential reserve for war against
> Germany, in other words, a potential reserve for British–French im-
> perialism. . . . The position of the journal can only confuse its readers
> and demobilize the masses of workers in their struggle against the
> imperialist war by making them believe that all problems will be resolved,
> sooner or later, by the entry of the 'Russian steamroller' into action
> against Germany. This incorrect interpretation of the peace policy of the
> USSR is politically inadmissible and dangerous. It plays into the hands of
> American imperialism.[37]

In other words, even those parties that were least uncomfortable with
the schema of imperialist war, like the Italian, were forced to fall into
line. Togliatti's submission to this line, however, was shrewd. A
careful reading of a resolution drafted by him and released in the
name of the PCI after Italy entered the war shows that while he did
invoke the 'struggle from below', he also refrained from attacking the
Socialists. Togliatti even went so far as to use the forbidden term
'fascist', denouncing Italian imperialism's aims of conquest and
raising the demand for national independence for the countries
oppressed by invaders. The statement said: 'Today the fascist rulers
want to sell our people to German imperialism. They propose to turn
the people of Italy into the jailer and executioner of nations already
groaning under the yoke of their oppressors and which have never
attacked our lives and patrimony.'[38]

This was an obvious and unusual reference to France. When Mussolini invaded Greece in October 1940, the tiny PCI foreign office that still remained in Paris issued a declaration which, while stridently equating the aggressor and the victim, also stated:

> At a time when the Italian and Greek peoples are being drawn into the ruinous maelstrom of the Second World War, victims of the insatiable lust for conquest of the plutocratic fascist gang that now rules Italy and the corrupt dictatorial Metaxas gang, slave to British imperialism, the PCI sends its warm and fraternal solidarity to the Greek toilers. [39]

In parties like the Greek and Italian, the contradiction between the anti-fascist impulse and the necessity of 'not going too far' was more clearly understood. The nucleus of the PCI's foreign office called upon militants working underground in Italy to fight for the fall of the Mussolini government and to demand democratic rights, but at the same time it explained that 'our defeatist action has nothing in common — and can have nothing in common — with the interests of the British imperialists, who are oppressors of peoples just like the Italian imperialists.' The PCI repeated that peace and freedom would be won only 'through the revolutionary action of the working class'.

The situation of the Greek CP, which was also urged to struggle against British imperialism, was more dramatic. In October 1940, from the depths of his prison cell in Athens, the party secretary Zachariades (who was deported to Dachau by the Germans in May 1941) called upon his comrades to defend national independence against the Italian invaders; but in November, when the fascists were driven back into Albania, he urged them to demand an immediate peace. In another letter, dated 15 January 1941, he called upon the party to overthrow Metaxas and the soldiers of the Greek army to fraternize with Italian soldiers on the front. These positions were endorsed in an article in *Communist International* published a month later. [40]

The last phase of Soviet 'neutrality' presented a panorama of dazzling colours tinged with sombre hues. There was now probably more desperation than anything else in the propaganda stunts of the Moscow headquarters. In January 1941 the British Communists convened a 'People's Convention' reportedly attended by 2,334 factory delegates representing more than a million British workers. The figures were bizarre, but the conference became a battle-cry of Comintern propaganda (the American author Theodore Dreiser and singer Paul Robeson were even present). The position of the British

CP was that a new government was needed to convince the German workers that there was no further need to fight — by offering Hitler peace.[41] The American Communists, who formally withdrew from the Comintern because of the Voorhis Act,[42] denounced this act as the work of an administration 'dominated by imperialist warmongers', and bent on stampeding the American people into 'submission to US entry into the imperialist war'.

Only one element sheds a somewhat less gloomy light on this conduct: organizational measures were taken by all the parties that still had some freedom of action or sought to regain it in their countries. These measures reflected a desire to prepare for a future policy that would not be merely 'defeatist' but would permit more decisive action. For the moment, however, let us return to the greatest 'worry' of all, Stalin's. Had the USSR really become 'a satellite of Berlin and Rome', as Trotsky wrote shortly before his death?[43]

Notes

1. From the report of William C. Bullitt to the secretary of state, 15 January 1940, in *Foreign Relations of the United States 1940*, Washington, D.C. 1960, vol. 1, pp. 590-91.

2. Shirer, *The Collapse of the Third Republic*, p. 507.

3. Robrieux, *Histoire intérieure du PCF*, vol. 1, p. 502.

4. Jacques Duclos, *Mémoires*, Paris 1970, vol. 3, p. 72.

5. Léon Blum, 'La tâche nécessaire', *Le Populaire*, 23 November 1939.

6. Jane Degras, ed., *The Communist International: Documents*, vol. 3, p. 441.

7. De Felice, *Mussolini, il Duce*, vol. 2, p. 751.

8. Boffa, *Storia dell'Unione Sovietica*, vol. 1, p. 640.

9. Deutscher, *The Prophet Outcast*, p. 460.

10. From the reports of party emissaries, quoted in Spriano, *Storia del Pci*, vol. 4, pp. 18-19.

11. Boffa, *Storia dell'Unione Sovietica*, vol. 1, p. 642.

12. 'Llamamiento del Cc del Pc de Finlandia', *La Internacional Comunista* (Spanish edition), vol. 8, no. 2, February 1940, pp. 30-31.

13. The complete text of the speech is in *Lo Stato Operaio*, vol. 14, no. 2, 1 May 1940, pp. 38-45.

14. 'Pane, pace e libertà', ibid., pp. 47-48.

15. Rolf Steininger, 'L'Internazionale socialista dopo la seconda guerra mondiale', in *La sinistra europea*, p. 138.

16. V. Molotov, 'La politica estera dell'Urss', *Lo Stato Operaio*, vol. 14, no. 5-6, August-September 1940, p. 81.

17. Shirer, *Rise and Fall*, p. 798.

18. Ulam, *Expansion and Coexistence*, p. 305.

19. Ibid., p. 286.

20. Giulio Cerreti, *Con Togliatti e con Thorez*, Milan 1973, p. 252.

21. See the testimony of Giulio Cerreti in Spriano, *Il compagno Ercoli*, pp. 183-84. On the question of Soviet interest, see also Giorgio Bocca, *Palmiro Togliatti*, Bari 1973, pp. 333-38.

22. Maurizio and Marcella Ferrara, *Conversando con Togliatti*, Rome 1953, p. 293.

23. Spriano, *Il compagno Ercoli*, p. 188.

24. Palmiro Togliatti, 'Diversità e unità nel movimento comunista internazionale', *Rinascita*, vol. 18, no. 12, p 909.

25. Fischer, *An Opposing Man*, p. 358.

26. See the article, signed by him, entitled *?Porqué hay guerra?* (in the Spanish edition of Communist International, no. 2, February 1940). See also the observations of Amendola, *Storia del Pci*, p. 447.

27. From the underground bulletin *La Vie du Parti*, no. 1, September 1940.

28. The contacts made toward this end by three Communist leaders—the ex-deputy Jean Catelas, Maurice Tréant, and Robert Foissin—are documented in a report to Berlin dated 10 July 1940 by Otto Abetz, the representative of the German Ministry of Foreign Affairs in France. See also 'Documents on German Foreign Policy', in *The War Years*, 10, June-August 1940, Washington, D.C. 1957, pp. 215 ff. See also Courtois, *Le PCF dans la guerre*, pp. 133-34. Finally, for the minimization of the incident, see Duclos, *Mémoires*, vol. 3, p. 55.

29. *La Vie du Parti*, no. 1, September 1940.

30. See José Gotovitch, 'Guerre et libération, jalons pour une étude', in *Le parti communiste belge (1921–1944)*, p. 67.

31. From *L'Homme Libre*, March 1941, cited in Giorgio Caredda, *L'occupazione nazista in Francia*, manuscript.

32. 'Una lettera di Pietro Nenni', *Lo Stato Operaio*, vol. 14, no. 7–8, October-November 1940, p. 11.

33. Vladimir Kraina, 'La Résistance Tchécoslovaque', *Cahiers d'Histoire de la Guerre*, no. 3, Paris 1950, p. 70.

34. *Les Cahiers du Bolchévisme*, first quarter 1941, p.11.

35. See, in particular, Richard Goodman, 'What Is Socialist Neutrality', no. 47, 23 November 1940; 'The People's Convention and Friendship With the Soviet Union' (no. 48, 30 November 1940); D.N. Pritt, 'For a People's Peace' (no. 50, 14 December 1940); R. Palme Dutt, 'The Outlook for May Day' (no. 17, 26 April 1941); as well as the 'Editorial Notes' in each issue.

36. 'I rapporti di forza in Europa dopo un anno di guerra', *Lo Stato Operaio*, vol. 14, no. 5-6, August-September 1940, pp. 88-95.

37. From the document, drafted in French, entitled 'Information sur la revue *Stato Operaio*', signed by Ercoli and Vincenzo Bianco and sent to the International's Secretariat and also to the journal's editorial board. There is a photocopy in the archives of the Italian Communist Party, 1528/67-73.

38. The full document is in 'Trent'anni di vita e di lotte del Pci', Quaderno no. 2 of *Rinascita*, 1952, pp. 191-92.

39. 'Dichiarazione dell'Ufficio estero del Pci contro l'estensione della guerra imperialista nei Balcani', *Lettere di Spartaco*, no. 19, October 1940.

40. From the testimony of Angelos Tsalkanis, cited in Courtois, *Le Pcf dans la Guerre*, pp. 200-01.

41. Jane Degras, ed., p. 464.

42. This law stipulated the immediate dissolution (and the arrest of the leaders) of organizations with international affiliations considered, at the discretion of the Justice Department, to represent a danger to national security. The formal withdrawal of the CPUSA from the Communist International occurred with the agreement of the Comintern Executive. See Starobin, *American Communism in Crisis*, p. 45.

43. 'Stalin Still Hitler's Satellite', 2 August 1940, in Leon Trotsky, *Writings of Leon Trotsky (1939–1940)*, New York 1969, p. 327.

12
Trotsky's Last Battle

Reading Trotsky's last writings, and recalling that his voice would be stilled on 20 August 1940 by the assassin sent to Mexico by Stalin, one has the sense of a tragedy of symbolic proportions. The tyrant had long since resolved to liquidate his adversary, the last and greatest of his opponents. Ramón Mercader, the young Spanish-born NKVD agent posing as a Belgian, who executed the sentence, managed to infiltrate Trotsky's entourage in 1938. But one detail of the 'execution' is extraordinary: Mercader's excuse for his session in his victim's office on that August evening was furnished by a sharp dispute among American Trotskyists about whether or not the Soviet Union could still be considered a workers state. Mercader, who had become the lover of one of Trotsky's secretaries, was supposed to be showing the leader a manuscript he had written on the subject. When Trotsky bent over the pages of his sham disciple, the assassin's pick struck savagely at the base of his skull. The wounded Trotsky fought back against his attacker, and even managed to murmur a few affectionate words to his wife. The assassin allowed himself to be captured by the guards without resistance.[1] Trotsky died in a Mexico City hospital the next day.

Stalin seemed in somewhat of a hurry to liquidate Trotsky. In May of that same year there had been an armed assault on the exile's house by Stalinist agents dressed in Mexican army and police uniforms, but they missed their target. Was it all purely a vendetta on Stalin's part? Isaac Deutscher offered a wider political and psychological explanation, related to the activity of the exile, who continued to intervene, through his articles, in all the events of the day.

> The fact remains that Stalin was not reassured. He could not bring himself to believe that his violence and terror had indeed accomplished all that he wanted, that the old Bolshevik Atlantis had really vanished. He scrutinized the faces of the multitudes that acclaimed him, and he guessed what

terrible hatred might be hidden in their adulation. With so many exis-
tences destroyed or broken up, and with so much discontent and despair
all around him, who could say what the unforeseeable shocks of war
might not bring? Might not Atlantis somehow re-emerge, with new
denizens, but with the old defiance?[2]

In substance, if the war spread and the USSR was drawn into it,
Trotsky's very existence could prove dangerous. Trotsky

> remained the mouthpiece of Atlantis, still uttering all its undying passions
> and all its battle cries. At every critical turn, when the inglorious Finnish
> campaign came to an end, when Hitler occupied Norway and Denmark,
> and when France collapsed, his voice rose from beyond the ocean to
> thunder on the consequences of these disasters, on Stalin's blunders that
> had helped to bring them about, and on the mortal perils threatening the
> Soviet Union.

It is here that we must begin in relating the reasons for the assassination to the general dispute about the turn of Soviet 'neutrality'
and about the nature of the regime that took root in the USSR in the
late thirties. It is not merely a matter of keeping the connection in
mind. Trotsky's analyses, his last political battle, and the positions he
upheld against many of his own followers are themselves a far from
inconsequential component of a broader theme: the question of
whether the prospect of world revolution, the theoretical and
methodological criteria that had inspired the Bolshevik Old Guard
(that Atlantis of which Deutscher spoke), could withstand the
terrible test of the war. The writings of the late Trotsky, even more
than his early efforts, present a blend of extreme lucidity on the one
hand and hoary ideological paradigms on the other. He felt sure that
the conflict would spread and that the United States would be forced
to intervene, and he did not believe that the German war machine was
invincible. But who would win in the end? In February 1940 Trotsky
wrote:

> Hitler cannot stop. Consequently the Allies cannot stop either if they do
> not wish to commit voluntary suicide. The humanitarian lamentations
> and references to reason will not help. The war will last until it exhausts all
> the resources of civilization or until it breaks its head on the revolution.[3]

A rather nebulous alternative. In June Trotsky affirmed that Hitler's
'victories in the West are only preparation for a gigantic move
towards the East',[4] that the Führer would 'very soon' march against
the USSR. Should an alliance, a front, be made with the 'democracies'?

Trotsky denied it passionately. Right from the fall of France he affirmed that the war was the product of rivalry between the old, wealthy colonial empires and 'belated imperialist plunderers'.[5] The workers should support neither side. The proletariat could not fight for democracy, since the war 'has not halted the process of the transformation of democracies into reactionary dictatorships.' 'Only the hopelessly blind are capable of believing that the British and French generals and admirals are waging a war against fascism.'[6]

This consonance with the themes of Soviet and Comintern propaganda recalls our earlier observation: aversion to designating political democracy as a value to be defended in its own right, against sham democrats among others, is deeply rooted in a Communist tradition that goes back to Marx and Lenin. The Trotskyists remained the staunchest opponents of the 'Stalinists' (and vice versa), but now far more than before, both were united in a wholly ideological contempt for political forms that they considered mystifications by their very nature. Whenever they spoke of the democracies, they felt compelled to prefix the noun with the adjective 'so-called' or 'imperialist'. Trotsky never would have endorsed the Short Course even if it had not ignored or completely falsified his own role. But he employed the same conceptual apparatus in defining 'the others'. Indeed, as always he was more eloquent in his invective, more tribunitial, than the icy Molotov or the sarcastic Stalin. Lev Davidovich wrote:

> The democratic governments, who in their day hailed Hitler as a crusader against Bolshevism, now make him out to be some kind of Satan unexpectedly loosed from the depths of hell, who violates the sanctity of treaties, boundary lines, rules and regulations. If it were not for Hitler the capitalist world would blossom like a garden. What a miserable lie! This German epileptic with a calculating machine in his skull and unlimited power in his hands did not fall from the sky or rise up out of hell: he is nothing but the personification of all the destructive forces of imperialism. . . . Hitler, rocking the old colonial powers to their foundations, does nothing but give a more finished expression to the imperialist will to power. Through Hitler, world capitalism, driven to desperation by its own impasse, has begun to press a razor-sharp dagger into its own bowels.
>
> The butchers of the second imperialist war will not succeed in transforming Hitler into a scapegoat for their own sins.
>
> Before the judgement bar of the proletariat all the present rulers will answer. Hitler will do no more than occupy first place among the criminals in the dock.[7]

Trotsky was not content with these ringing phrases alone. He also ventured into terrain never trodden by the Soviet press, and still less by the infrequent and evanescent publications of the Comintern: he actually evaluated the conflict between the warring imperialisms and predicted the war's outcome, or at least its possible outcomes. Trotsky was unencumbered by diplomatic impediments. Whereas the USSR, gagged by its wary neutrality and its feigned but loudly proclaimed friendship with Germany, could not openly speculate, and whereas the Comintern preferred to talk about Anglo-Saxon imperialism (so much so that readers of *World News and Views* might well have come away with the impression that the major issue was British colonialism in India or US oppression of Latin America — both undeniable realities but hardly the focus of international attention during the Second World War), Trotsky suggested two intriguing scenarios in May 1940. One projected a German, the other an Anglo-French victory.

In the former case, Trotsky wrote, *pax germanica* would inaugurate a phase of bloody conflict on a world scale. Germany, which would be the world's leading power after its victory over France and Britain, would allow Japan to expand in Asia. The Soviet Union would find itself hemmed in by a German-dominated Europe and a Japanese-dominated Asia. But things would not stop there.

> All three Americas, as well as Australia and New Zealand, would fall to the United States. If we take into account the provincial Italian empire in addition, the world would be temporarily divided into five 'living rooms'. But imperialism by its very nature abhors any division of power. In order to free his hands against America, Hitler would have to settle bloody accounts with his friends of yesterday, Stalin and Mussolini. Japan and the United States would not remain disinterested observers of the new struggle. The third imperialist war would be waged not by national states and not by empires of the old type but by whole continents. Hitler's victory in the present war would thus not signify a thousand years of 'German peace' but bloody chaos for many decades if not centuries. [8]

This last hypothesis has a curious ring to it today. For nearly forty years now, humanity has lived with the nightmare of a thermonuclear apocalypse that would annihilate all civilization in a matter of hours. The prospect of centuries of chaos seems almost comforting by contrast. But Trotsky died before the onset of the atomic age. His intuition that a new historical phase was opening during which continental powers would contend on a vast scale was acute. The outline of a German victory is naturally somewhat more confused, although it does contain another of Trotsky's incisive insights of the early thirties, which he now extended to cover every form of imperialism: because of its totalitarian character, fascism would not tolerate any sharing of power with other political and social forces.

The hypothesis of a German victory was only the first of the two scenarios. The other ran as follows. If the Allies win, France will seek to dismember Germany, restore the Hapsburgs to the throne, and 'Balkanize Europe', while Britain will resume its traditional manoeuvres to exploit the contradictions between France and Germany. In other words, a new and worse Versailles was in the offing. But the weight of the United States would be felt, too: '. . . an Allied victory without American aid is improbable, while the United States this time would demand a much higher price for its assistance than in the last war. The debased and exhausted Europe . . . would become the bankrupt debtor of its transatlantic saviour.'

This last prediction was not far from the truth. But Trotsky did not assimilate Stalin to Hitler and Mussolini — or rather, he did not mix up the USSR with Nazi-fascist Germany and Italy. For him there was still a fundamental contradiction between the USSR and world imperialism, which was far more profound than the antagonisms among the various imperialist countries. And the USSR had to be defended. Against whom? In late September 1939, with the war already under way, Trotsky asked this question and gave his answer: 'But let us suppose that Hitler turns his weapons against the east and invades the territories occupied by the Red Army. Under these conditions, partisans of the Fourth International, without changing in any way their attitude towards the Kremlin oligarchy, will advance to the forefront, as the most urgent task of the hour, the military resistance against Hitler.'[9]

This was his unwavering position, and it followed from Trotsky's analysis of the USSR. If the Soviet Union was invaded and defeated, it would mean the destruction not only of the Stalin bureaucracy, but also of the planned state economy. Russia would be 'colossal booty' for the imperialists. But how could one defend the USSR while simultaneously preparing the overthrow of Stalin's 'Bonapartist clique'? Trotsky escaped from the dilemma with one of his classic *fuites en avant*: 'The defence of the USSR coincides in principle with the preparation of the world proletarian revolution.'[10]

For the moment, even the great oppositionist remained anchored to a position of neutrality that paradoxically brought him closer to his antagonist and persecutor: no aid, he said, should be given to the

Western democracies against German fascism. He wrote:

> The victory of the imperialists of Great Britain and France would be not less frightful for the ultimate fate of mankind than that of Hitler and Mussolini. Bourgeois democracy cannot be saved. By helping their bourgeoisie against foreign fascism, the workers would only accelerate the victory of fascism in their own country. The task posed by history is not to support one part of the imperialist system against another but to make an end of the system as a whole. [11]

And if the revolutionary workers did not succeed in that task? The question repelled him, but Trotsky did ask it. With his usual frankness, he replied:

> If contrary to all probabilities the October Revolution fails during the course of the present war or immediately thereafter to find its continuation in any of the advanced countries; and if, on the contrary, the proletariat is thrown back everywhere and on all fronts — then we should doubtlessly have to pose the question of revising our conception of the present epoch and its driving forces. [12]

History's imagination proved greater than both Trotsky's 'probabilities' and his most pessimistic hypothesis. The revolution developed in the more backward rather than in the more advanced countries. Moreover, the very fact that the popular masses took part in a war one of whose objectives was democracy profoundly altered the schematic picture offered by Bolshevik-Leninist orthodoxy. The USSR not only won the war, but also remained Stalinist, as did the entire Communist movement and much of the world revolutionary movement. But that does not make the question about driving forces, about the 'conception of the present epoch', otiose. It is still an 'ongoing' story, full of unknowns and contradictions, of diverse and unpredictable processes.

The old revolutionary has been justly complimented for his 'intellectual honesty' in 'daring' to ask such radical questions. [13] Trotsky's isolation in the last years of his life aroused tension of formidable dimensions. This is one of the reasons why he braved a genuine revolt within the American Trotskyist group against his intransigent 'defence of the USSR'. Some of his supporters — James Burnham and Max Schachtman among others — maintained that the Soviet Union was no longer a workers state, that it had become a counter-revolutionary power like the others, ruled by a new class, the bureaucracy, which used state ownership of the means of production to tighten its totalitarian grip on all of society, especially the working class. The theoretical controversy had an important political corollary. The oppositionists, unlike Trotsky, did not believe in defending the USSR in the event of a Nazi attack. 'No, Comrade Trotsky, . . . we will not fight alongside the GPU for the salvation of the counter-revolution in the Kremlin.'[14]

The polemic flared up in the American section of the infant Fourth International and led to a split. This was another aspect of the tragedy of Trotsky's last battle. He died assassinated by Stalinists at a time when he was in bitter conflict with many of his own followers because of his manifest desire to defend the Soviet Union. Despite everything, he continued to believe that the USSR was capable of building a socialist society in conjunction with a new wave of world revolution.

The murder in Mexico did not arouse great turmoil in the world. The attention of masses and statesmen alike was focused elsewhere. Neither, however, did the Comintern leaders' ritual expression of hatred for Trotsky subside after his death. In an article dated January 1941 Togliatti wrote that 'the little Judas Trotsky belongs to the race of apologists and servants of capital'. Yet Ercoli's arguments sounded very much like Trotsky's: 'From the very first days of the war in every country there has been a vanguard that has explained to the people that this is an unjust imperialist war on both sides, a war of plunder, whose roots must be sought in the development of the catastrophic contradictions of imperialism.'[15]

The storm was approaching, and this particular orchestra would soon be playing a different tune. The spectre of Trotsky disappeared in the new climate of the Grand Anti-Fascist Alliance, and by the end of the Second World War, his predictions seemed wholly unreal. But his 'defeat' also posed a great question. His biographer wrote:

> It must be emphasized again that to the end Trotsky's strength and weakness alike were rooted in classical Marxism. His defeats epitomized the basic predicament by which classical Marxism was beset as doctrine and movement — the discrepancy and the divorce between the Marxist vision of revolutionary development and the actual course of class struggle and revolution.[16]

Notes

1. 'The murderer was caught and was sentenced by a Mexican court to twenty years in prison, which he served. On Stalin's order, he was awarded the title Hero of the Soviet Union, and his mother, who helped set up the murder, was given the Order of Lenin. The manager of the whole "operation", the NKVD executive Eitingen, was also

given the Order of Lenin.' (Medvedev, *Let History Judge*, p. 179.)

2. Deutscher, *The Prophet Outcast*, p. 480.

3. 'The World Situation and Perspectives', interview with the St Louis *Post-Dispatch*, 14 February 1940, in *Writings of Leon Trotsky (1939–1940)*, p. 151.

4. 'The Kremlin's Role in the European Catastrophe' (17 June 1940), ibid., p. 291.

5. 'Manifesto of the Fourth International on the Imperialist War and the Proletarian World Revolution' (26 May 1940), ibid., p. 185.

6. Ibid., p.192.

7. Ibid., pp. 193-94

8. Ibid., pp. 195-96.

9. 'The USSR in War', in Leon Trotsky, *In Defense of Marxism*, New York 1965, p. 20.

10. 'Imperialist War and Proletarian World Revolution', p. 199.

11. Ibid., p. 221.

12. 'The USSR in War', p. 14.

13. Salvadori, *La critica marxista allo stalinismo*, pp. 114-15.

14. From an article by James Burnham in the internal discussion bulletin of the Socialist Workers Party, cited by Deutscher, *The Prophet Outcast*, p. 473.

15. 'La lotta di Lenin contro il socialsciovinismo durante la prima guerra imperialistica mondiale', in Togliatte, *Opere*, vol. 4, II, p. 60.

16. Deutscher, *The Prophet Outcast*, p. 514.

13
The Surprising Surprise of 22 June

During the Khrushchev period bitter discussions were held in the USSR about Stalin's conduct of the war and his virtues as a military commander, but in the past twenty years the controversy has died down, no common conclusions ever having been reached. Amid all the conflicting assessments, however, one fact has been taken as evident, or virtually so: Stalin was surprised and disconcerted (there has even been talk of obnubilation) when German troops attacked all along the Soviet border at dawn on 22 June 1941. The first time Stalin met Churchill, in Moscow in August 1942, he told him that he had been expecting the Nazi attack. When? According to Churchill's report, it happened this way:

> In the course of one of my later talks with Stalin I said, 'Lord Beaverbrook has told me that when he was on his mission to Moscow in October 1941 you asked him, "What did Churchill mean by saying in parliament that he had given me warnings of the impending German attack?" 'I was of course,' said I, 'referring to the telegram I sent you in April '41', and I produced the telegram which Sir Stafford Cripps had tardily delivered. When it was read and translated to him Stalin shrugged his shoulders. 'I remember it. I did not need any warnings. I knew war would come, but I thought I might gain another six months or so.'[1]

The warnings, however, were particularly numerous and reliable. In late 1940 the Soviet secret service submitted a detailed report on Hitler's attack plans. Many other reports followed in the spring of 1941, not to mention the most obvious evidence, which could not be concealed: the transfer of more and more German troops from west to east in preparation for the aggression. Diplomatic warnings that an attack was near flowed in one after another from March onwards, first from the American government and then from the British. In May 1941 Soviet military attachés in Berlin and Paris reported that the border zones between the USSR and Germany were packed with men and matériel. Hitler was amassing as many as 190 fully equipped divisions there, plus about four thousand workers. According to another report from the Soviet secret service, dated 6 June, four million German soldiers were already stationed on the eastern borders.² The Soviet Union's most famous spy, Richard Sorge, a courageous German Communist militant who had infiltrated the German embassy in Tokyo, was able to report, several days in advance, not only the exact date of the attack, but also the operative plans and the major lines of march.³ When Zhukov was first named chief of the General Staff, Stalin told him, 'You can't believe everything in intelligence reports.'⁴ In the meantime, Stalin preferred to read 'dubious' reports that fuelled his illusions,⁵ and he was so openly sceptical about the reliability of all others that his closest associates, whether out of servility or fear, themselves finally presented them in a minimizing tone or even concealed them from him.

In substance, 'to the very end Stalin refused to believe that Germany was preparing to attack the USSR without first settling accounts with Britain.'⁶ Molotov, the minister of foreign affairs, uttered this almost pathetic comment about the declaration of war brought to him by Schulenburg on the morning of 22 June itself: 'Do you believe that we deserved that?'⁷ For his part, Hitler wrote in a letter to Mussolini, who was informed only one day in advance: 'I have decided under these circumstances to put an end to the hypocritical performance of the Kremlin.'⁸ The die, it seems, had long been cast: at least as far back as the end of 1940.

The atmosphere surrounding Stalin just before the attack was certainly not conducive to any dissent. He had sown terror in the high command, now barely reconstituted after the purges in the Red Army, had accustomed his collaborators to obey his orders blindly, and kept them in the dark about the general situation. There was no genuine consultation with the military commanders. The one-man monopoly of decision-making, and of the confidential information on which decisions were based, increased Stalin's responsibility for what Medvedev called his worst mistake ever, his failure to understand 'the military situation in the spring and summer of 1941'.⁹ What we know of Molotov's attitude and reactions during these difficult times would suggest that Churchill was right when he said that the Soviet foreign minister was incurably obtuse. In February 1941 Molotov brusquely interrupted Zhukov to ask him: 'So you think we'll have to fight the Germans?'¹⁰ Just a few days before the invasion he claimed, 'Only a fool could attack us.'¹¹

Many memorialists have offered astonishing details about the lack of adequate military preparation despite the growing danger signals, including confirmation from deserting German soldiers and Luftwaffe pilots landing in Soviet zones that an attack was coming. Agricultural leaves were not even cancelled. A leader of the rank of Zhdanov was on vacation at the Black Sea coast.

The military cost of the surprise was particularly high, which is why there has been so much controversy about it. It weighed upon Soviet conduct of the war for months to come. The attack caught the Red Army unprepared, disrupted the communications system, and created confusion among the various commands. After three weeks of fighting, the Wehrmacht had advanced some four to five hundred kilometres and destroyed twenty-eight Soviet divisions, while more than seventy had been reduced to half-strength. Apart from the enormous losses of equipment and resources, the planes shot down and the tanks fallen into enemy hands, three million Russian soldiers were killed or captured in the initial military disaster (while the Germans lost 550,000 men). [12]

But it is the underlying reason for the surprise, itself an element in evaluating Stalin and Stalinism, that is of greatest interest to us here. It seems highly unlikely that all that was involved was a mistaken estimate of the date of the Nazi attack, and questionable that Stalin's astonishment can be considered as no more than the puzzlement of a reasonable man who failed to foresee that his potential adversary, who had been so lucid in 1939–40, would suddenly succumb to madness and throw himself into the wild adventure of trying to liquidate Russia in the space of a few months. Let us therefore begin our probe by looking at Stalin's mentality, and at the tangle of detached pragmatism, suspicion, and ideological schematism that shaped it. These were the factors about which political leaders, generals, admirals, journalists, and historians expressed themselves most freely once the flood of revelations was opened (between 1956 and 1965 for the most part) and Soviet press sources were able to provide a glimpse, psychological more than political or theoretical, of the contradictions and limitations of the hitherto unassailable leader of the USSR.

Nearly all observers have made much of the great significance Stalin attached to the mysterious episode of the flight of the Nazi leader Rudolf Hess to Britain in May 1941. Perhaps he feared that the trip was part of some provocation hatched by Britain in league with German military circles. The account of the Soviet historian A.M. Nekrich is invaluable in this regard:

Grand Marshal of Artillery N.N. Voronov confirms that Stalin maintained that war between Nazi Germany and the Soviet Union could break out only as the result of a provocation by Nazi military cliques, and that such provocations were to be feared above all else. If Voronov not accidentally used the expression 'Nazi military cliques', this can be understood in only one way, as confirmation that Stalin still hoped that the non-aggression treaty would hold. In other words, he believed in Hitler but did not trust the German generals, intoxicated as they were with military victories. This explains the successive orders to units of the Red Army not to respond to Nazi provocations.

Stalin always reacted with particular suspicion to information from American and British sources, seeing it as confirmation of his political analysis of 'non-interference': the Western powers wanted to drag the Soviet Union and Germany into a war and thus to warm themselves at a fire that would not consume them. [13]

We know how important this mentality had been throughout the preceding period, and particularly in 1939. Since Stalin was concerned primarily about plots and provocations (possibly even directed against Hitler), he now pursued a course of action so circumspect as to avoid any action that might facilitate them. He refused to place the Red Army on alert and sought contact with Hitler to the bitter end. [14] At bottom this was the deeply rooted idea, dating back to Lenin's time, that the USSR's mortal enemy was still Britain. The most suggestive, and perhaps most decisive, observation came from Nekrich:

The aggressive nature of Germany was minimized [by Stalin]. In the meantime, the international situation was changing rapidly, becoming more complex. The course of events shattered the artificial schema of international relations created by Stalin, a schema to which he obstinately continued to adhere. As always, he believed that Britain and only Britain was looking for a chance to provoke conflict between Germany and the USSR. [15]

Even Zhukov, whose memoirs generally tend to justify Stalin's conduct, offers singular testimony of this mentality (which he shared, at bottom). He writes:

The spring of 1941 was marked by a new wave of false rumours in the Western countries about large scale Soviet war preparation against Germany. The German press raised a great outcry over these rumours and complained that such information clouded German–Soviet relations.

'You see,' Stalin would say, 'they are trying to frighten us with the Germans and the Germans with us, setting us one against the other.' [16]

Zhukov seems to have shared Stalin's distrust of anything he was told by the 'anti-Communist and anti-Soviet' Churchill, of any 'information transmitted from imperialist circles'. The extent of Stalin's suspicion is indicated by the most striking case of all: the press release of the official Soviet news agency, dated 13 June 1941, in which Tass attacked the British press for spreading rumours that war between the USSR and Germany was imminent. Tass commented: 'Despite the obvious absurdity of these rumours, responsible circles in Moscow have thought it necessary to state that they are a clumsy propaganda manoeuvre of the forces arrayed against the Soviet Union and Germany, which are interested in a spread and intensification of the war.'[17]

One may well imagine how psychologically disarming such a statement was (it was published prominently in the Soviet press and ignored in the German). No less obvious is the reasoning on which it was based: Germany and the USSR were facing the 'aligned forces' of British imperialism, which were conspiring against both. But it is rather less easy to understand why Stalin supposed that the German generals were acting independently of Hitler, and even that they were more aggressive than the dictator himself. McNeal, an American scholar very familiar with Stalin's life and works, has made the point:

> What is most surprising about Stalin's assessment of the situation in Germany is his conviction that some generals might have been tempted to invade Russia even against Hitler's will. The Führer's control over his generals in the spring of 1941, however, seemed only too obvious, and Stalin, especially in view of the purges he had conducted in his own army, should have been able to understand the moves a dictator might make in his relations with professional officers. And yet this error of judgement seems to have been one of Stalin's most stubbornly held convictions during this crucial period.[18]

If Churchill and Roosevelt warned him that the German attack was imminent, Stalin took it as one more reason to mistrust them and to suspect that a plot was afoot, hatched primarily by Britain, at the Soviet Union's expense. From the Comintern we have additional confirmation of the anti-British obsession. Togliatti and Thorez were in Moscow at the time. In May 1941 the former drafted an appeal to the Italian workers in which he wrote: 'The war against Britain is not a war for our freedom; it is not a conflict between plutocrats and proletarians, as the fascists claim. It is a war among imperialist brigands for world hegemony, for the division of the colonies and riches of the entire world.'[19] This appeal was meant to respond to fascism's demagogic propaganda, but it also hailed the initiative of the British Communists, the People's Convention, in these terms: 'Not long ago, representatives of hundreds of thousands of British workers met in London and declared that they would fight to bring down British imperialism and to end the war through a people's peace, in the interest of the peoples.'[20]

As for the French Communists, although they now began to speak clearly against the 'occupiers', Thorez and Duclos affirmed: 'If the German occupation of France amply demonstrates that Hitler's "new European order" would mean scandalous slavery for France, it is equally certain that the movement of De Gaulle and Larminat, profoundly reactionary and anti-democratic as it is, itself aims only at depriving our country of any freedom in the event of a British victory.'[21]

The anti-British obsession did not prevent Stalin from making a number of shrewd diplomatic moves before the German attack, and he did score one undeniable success. In April he signed an invaluable neutrality pact with Japan, which wanted a free hand against the British colonies of South-East Asia and was also preparing its direct attack on the United States in the Pacific. Japanese neutrality, like the coming attack on Pearl Harbour, would of course be of no help to Hitler, who let Japanese Foreign Minister Matsuoka leave Berlin for Moscow without telling him that he planned to go to war against the USSR.[22] The 'concurrent' war the fascist and militarist powers of the Tripartite Pact had to fight was one of the factors in their defeat. Soviet foreign policy, aimed at securing the USSR's influence throughout the area of most immediate interest to it — from Finland to Bulgaria, Romania to Yugoslavia to Turkey — exploited these contradictions. But Stalin nevertheless remained blind to the fundamental point: Hitler's aggressive intent.

The March-April events in Yugoslavia were instructive as well. Here a coup by army officers with popular support overthrew the Nazi vassal government and placed King Peter, the young heir to the throne, in power. The USSR signed a friendship treaty with the new government, but just one day later — on 6 April — Germany invaded Yugoslavia without even declaring war. The German troops, aided by Italians, Hungarians, and Bulgarians, easily overwhelmed the Yugoslav army (occupying Belgrade on 13 April) and continued their march into Greece, arriving in Athens on 17 April and occupying Crete in May.

The Balkan blitzkrieg, though victorious, caused a month-long postponement of Operation Barbarossa, the invasion of the Soviet

Union, which had been scheduled for mid-May. Many believe that the delay proved fatal, because it prevented Germany from conquering the European territories of the USSR before the onset of the severe Russian winter, one of the factors that halted the Wehrmacht on the outskirts of Moscow in November. But the invasion and occupation of Yugoslavia and Greece were yet another indication of Germany's intention to smooth the road to the east, and Soviet reaction was not only cautious, but almost accommodating. News of the German invasion of Yugoslavia was reported with no special prominence, on the back page of *Pravda*. The Soviet party newspaper carried no condemnation of the aggression against a country that had become a friend of the USSR.

The official history of the Yugoslav Communist Party notes, after describing the events of April 1941 in great detail, that 'the Soviet government was convinced that there was no immediate danger of a German attack'.[23] But among the many signs that such an attack was in fact imminent was the transfer of German troops into the Balkan sector: 'Between April and June 1941 most of the German operational divisions that had taken part in the attack on Yugoslavia were transferred east, and the country was occupied by the remaining German garrison divisions, along with Italian, Bulgarian, and Hungarian troops.'[24]

In the Yugoslav view, then, the policy of the Soviet government remained within the confines of the Hitler-Stalin pact. This was also the opinion of Nekrich, who says that 'Stalin was sure that Hitler's Germany would not dare to violate the non-aggression pact and attack the Soviet Union'. But not everyone agrees. As evidence, some have cited a speech Stalin made in the Kremlin on 5 May to hundreds of young officers who had just graduated from the military academies, in which he reportedly said that a German attack 'in the near future' could not be ruled out (the text of the speech, however, has never been published).[25] But the fact remains that in May and June Stalin accelerated delivery of supplies provided for in the agreement with Germany, and he continued to minimize the danger of an imminent attack. N.G. Kuznetzov, former Soviet Navy commissar, emphasized this point, arguing that it was part of Stalin's mistrust of his own associates:

> Stalin had ideas on how to wage war, but, with his usual pathological mistrust, he kept them secret from the future executors of his ideas. Mistaken about the probable date of the conflict, he thought there was still enough time. And when the course of history speeded up, the ideas, the thoughts about a future war, could not be transformed into clear strategic and concrete plans.[26]

How could such a suspicious man have trusted Hitler? And why? Was he blinded by fear? All the various conjectures of historians revolve around these questions, to which no firm answers are possible. Ulam says that it is frankly difficult to understand why in the world Stalin ordered publication of the 13 June Tass press release, which seemed tailor-made to lull the vigilance of the army and people despite the hundreds of secret service reports then pouring in.[27] The French historian Stéphane Courtois notes that the USSR even broke diplomatic relations with the governments-in-exile of the countries Germany had invaded — not only Belgium, Holland, and Norway, but Yugoslavia and Greece as well. He then goes on to ask a number of questions to which definite answers are impossible:

> Did Stalin think that Hitler's escalation was intended merely to raise the stakes before seeking a negotiated settlement in the Balkans? Was he again obsessed by Anglophobic demons after Hess's flight to Britain? Did he see this as preparation for a secret Anglo–German accord against the USSR? Did he hope to offer fresh concessions to deprive Hitler of any excuse for an attack in the summer of 1941 and thus to gain a year for Soviet military preparation?'[28]

All Courtois is sure of is what struck André Fontaine as well: that Stalin had trusted Hitler and was terribly disappointed. The one and only time he had given credence to the leader of a capitalist state he was 'very badly rewarded'.[29]

Three scholars with considerable experience in the Third International, and whose viewpoint therefore differs from that of more detached observers, have written works that go beyond the purely psychological domain: the Italian Angelo Tasca, the Swiss Jules Humbert-Droz, and the Spaniard Fernando Claudín. Each maintains, although with varying emphases, that the most important point is that in his relations with Germany Stalin clearly manifested a propensity to reason in terms of power alone, contemplating the partition of territories, countries, and regions in a manner not unlike the 'imperialists'.

Angelo Tasca holds that 'the break between Hitler's Germany and Soviet Russia was a rupture between imperialist programmes'. It occurred because of the very same conflict of interest that had brought about the break between Kaiser Wilhelm's Germany and Tsarist Russia in 1914, namely the conflict over 'the Balkans and the Straits'.[30] Humbert-Droz has drawn attention to the seriousness of the division of the world contemplated in the German–Soviet talks of November 1940. The USSR agreed to discuss a long-term agreement with the fascist states, one that not only left most of Europe under

Nazi-fascist control, but also recognized German aspirations in central Africa, Italian designs in north and north-east Africa, Japanese claims in the Far East 'south of the imperial island of Japan', and Soviet aspirations 'in the direction of the Indian Ocean'. The USSR, however, also added detailed demands for its own sphere of influence in Bulgaria and Finland and for a military base 'within range of the Bosporus and the Dardanelles'. This brought about the rupture. 'It was', Humbert-Droz writes, 'the exorbitant claims of Stalin, who wanted to enjoy all the potential advantages without firing a shot, that led Hitler to attack him.'[31]

Fernando Claudín emphasized the same factors in his even more radical criticism, which focused on permanent features of the Stalin system:

> If we consider these two pointers in the light of what has happened since, namely, the *de facto* partition of the world into 'spheres of influence' between the USSR and American imperialism which took place after the Second World War, and the pursuit of this policy by the USSR down to the present time, why should we not suppose that something like this was also the cornerstone of Stalin's policy towards that imperialism which seemed in 1939–41 to be the premier military power in the world? This hypothesis, if it should be confirmed, would furnish the key to the 'surprise' of which the Soviet army was victim when the Germans attacked. If this was indeed Stalin's plan, the idea that he held of the way history would go, then reality for him, of course, would have had to conform to this idea, and all the information supplied by the secret services of his future allies, together with all the glaring evidence of Germany's hostile preparations, would have had to be brushed aside, since they were in contradiction to Stalin's infallibility.[32]

Here Claudín broaches a different, thought closely interrelated, order of problem: Stalin's absolute predominance and his general view of relations with the imperialist world and of the search for a compromise with it, which he always considered necessary. This last problem will arise again when we consider Stalin's post-war policy. The former looms large throughout the era of the war from which Stalin finally emerged victorious.

But let us conclude this anthology of hypotheses by recalling that Fabry, a German historian whose inspiration differed completely from that of the Marxist critics, also maintained that the German–Soviet conflict was born of heated controversy about the extent and guarantees of the possible compromise. Although he makes no comment on the principled impact of an accord of such great scope between the USSR and the coalition of the most aggressive imperialist states and does not deny that such an agreement was in the offing, Fabry tends to emphasize Stalin's unwillingness to accept the notion of 'a tight-knit Euroasiatic continental bloc including Japan and directed against the Anglo-Saxon powers'.[33] Fabry argues that it was this reluctance, revealed in Stalin's obsession with guaranteeing his own sphere of influence in the Balkans, that definitively convinced Hitler that he had to settle accounts with the USSR by an invasion.

These hypotheses, supported by German diplomatic sources, further widen the gamut of conjectures, of possible scenarios. In them Stalin appears as so realistic and cautious in his aspiration for a detailed and guaranteed agreement that he finally tried Hitler's patience. Only after the collapse of his own idea of a more general division of the world did Hitler return to the Nazi vocation of liquidating Bolshevism.

In any event, the outbreak of the German–Soviet war completely transformed the Communists' view of the world conflict. It was no longer an 'alien war' or a simple inter-imperialist struggle: now it became a mortal confrontation between the Nazi-fascist powers (soon including the entire Tripartite Alliance) and the 'land of socialism', in alliance with the Western democracies, with 'Anglo-Saxon imperialism'. Stalin's error continued to have its consequences. But as it turned out, the man who really made the fatal mistake on 22 June 1941 was not Stalin but his biennial ally the Führer, who underestimated the capacity of the Soviet Army and peoples to resist. Nevertheless, the 1939–41 revelations about Stalin's mentality and intentions cannot be effaced, for they would emerge again. For this reason among others, Stalin's surprising surprise remains a litmus test.

Notes

1. Winston Churchill, *The Second World War,* vol. 4, *The Hinge of Fate,* London 1951, p. 443.
2. See the details collected by Medvedev, *Let History Judge,* pp. 447-48.
3. F.W. Deakin and G.R. Storry, *The Case of Richard Sorge,* London 1966.
4. G.K. Zhukov, *The Memoirs of Marshal Zhukov,* London 1971, p.230.
5. J. Erickson, *The Road to Stalingrad. Stalin's War With Germany,* London 1975, vol. 1, p. 89.
6. Boffa, *Storia dell'Unione Sovietica,* vol. 2, p. 20.
7. Shirer, *Rise and Fall,* p. 848.
8. Ibid., p. 850.
9. Medvedev, *Let History Judge,* p. 446.
10. Zhukov, p. 208.
11. Ibid., p. 211.
12. Medvedev, *Let History Judge,* pp. 461-62.

13. A.M. Nekrich, *Stalin nella seconda guerra mondiale aprí le porte a Hitler?*, Rome 1968, p. 150.

14. Boffa, *Storia dell'Unione Sovietica*, vol. 2, p. 22.

15. Nekrich, *Stalin nella seconda guerra mondiale*, p. 149.

16. Zhukov, p. 224.

17. Fontaine, *History of the Cold War*, p. 153.

18. McNeal, *Stalin*, p. 987.

19. 'Per mettere fine alla guerra! Per salvare l'Italia da una catastrofe!', in *Il comunismo italiano nella seconda guerra mondiale*, introduction by Giorgio Amendola, Rome 1963, p. 133.

20. Ibid., p. 136.

21. Maurice Thorez and Jacques Duclos, 'Les capitalistes d'aujourd'hui sont les dignes héritiers des Versaillais', reprinted in Maurice Thorez, *Oeuvres*, Paris 1959, vol. 19, p. 85.

22. Shirer, *Rise and Fall*. pp. 891-92.

23. *Storia della Lega dei comunisti della Jugoslavia*, a collective work edited by the Belgrade Institute of Social Sciences, Milan 1965, p. 350.

24. Ibid., p. 351.

25. For a reconstruction of the text of the speech, see Alexander Werth, *Russia at War 1941–1945*, London 1964.

26. Medvedev, *Let History Judge*, p. 450.

27. Ulam, *Expansion and Coexistence*, p. 310.

28. Courtois, *Le PCF dans la Guerre*, p. 189.

29. Fontaine, *History of the Cold War*, p. 154.

30. Angelo Tasca, *Due anni di alleanza germano-sovietica*, Florence 1951, p. 181.

31. Humbert-Droz, *Dix ans de lutte antifasciste*, p. 390.

32. Claudín, *The Communist Movement*, p. 298.

33. Fabry, *Il patto Hitler-Stalin*, p. 651.

14

Two Camps in an Ideological War

An Italian anti-fascist has written: 'It must not be forgotten that the Second World War much more than the First, and in sharp contrast to the wars of past centuries, had an overwhelmingly ideological significance. There were two sharply counterposed camps, with no room for third positions.'[1]

This became most obvious after 22 June 1941, not because the war's character changed, becoming 'just' only when the USSR was drawn into it, but because the sweep of the conflict now really did involve just two opposing camps. The choice was between the fascist powers, seeking to establish their 'new European order', and all the other nations, whose national independence[2] and liberty depended on the outcome of the struggle, for the moment raging on the eastern front and in North Africa. Nazi-fascism, against which the Soviet Union and Britain had been unable to unite in 1938–39, now made allies of the two countries.

All other ideological differences faded into the background. The European working class had an interest in the war, for an anti-fascist victory was a precondition for its very survival as an autonomous force, even though the anti-fascist alignment crossed class boundaries, not only within each nation, but in the alliance of states as well.

We shall seek to grasp the full import of this new turn, imposed, even more than the previous ones, by the force of circumstance. This does not mean that no account should be taken of the heterogeneity of what Churchill called the Grand Anti-Fascist Alliance. With the Japanese attack on Pearl Harbour, it became an alliance between two social systems as thoroughly antithetical as those of the Soviet Union and the United States. Nevertheless, the spread of the conflict further underscored the ideological significance of the Second World War, the need for an intellectual common denominator. The Allies had to speak to all the world's peoples, to bring them into the alliance in the name of great common ideals expressing fundamental sentiments and interests. This was not easy; even the terms employed did not have the same meaning everywhere. Democracy and freedom did not mean the same thing to Mao Zedong and Chiang Kai-shek, both of whom were fighting the Japanese, or to Churchill and the Egyptian and Indian peoples, De Gaulle and the Indo-Chinese patriots, the ruling classes of many countries of Latin America and the workers and peasants exploited by tyrannical cliques and juntas. But of all the various political forces and representatives of the Grand Alliance, it was the Communist component, and especially its international headquarters, the Comintern, which, after 22 June 1941, made the most of the necessity for a joint struggle and for the broadest possible national front.

For Moscow unity was a necessary objective, primarily for the war effort. The broad masses had to be directed against Hitler, those minorities prepared to fight mobilized as rapidly as possible. To win the 'ideological war' would be to arouse a conscious and voluntary commitment among the masses, to organize resistance to the enemy occupation, and to hold out the prospect of liberation. The more Hitler and Mussolini portrayed Bolshevism as the enemy of civilization itself, the more that same accusation had to be hurled back against them: a line of demarcation was now drawn between patriots on the one side and servants of the inhuman barbarian fascist invaders on the other.

As before, Stalin's words and deeds are our starting point in examining the Communist alignment. On the other flank of the new alliance, after the German attack on the USSR Churchill did not wait twenty-four hours to express British solidarity with the Russian people 'defending their own land'[3] and to assure them that Britain would never stoop to making pacts with Hitler. Although Stalin waited twelve days before taking to the airwaves to address the Soviet people, he spoke passionately in his first speech. He was now the leader who called the fighters of his own country 'my friends'. And he pointed immediately to the international and ideological dimension of the conflict between fascism and anti-fascism, between tyranny and freedom. Stalin said on 3 July 1941:

> The war with fascist Germany cannot be considered an ordinary war. It is not only a war between two armies, it is also a great war of the entire Soviet people against the German-fascist armies. The aim of this national patriotic war in defence of our country against the fascist oppressors is not only to eliminate the danger hanging over our country, but also to aid all

the European peoples groaning under the yoke of German fascism. In this war of liberation, we shall not be alone. In this great war we shall have true allies in the peoples of Europe and America, including the German people which is enslaved by the Hitlerite misrulers. Our war for the freedom of our country will merge with the struggle of the peoples of Europe and America for their independence, for democratic liberties. It will be a united front of the peoples standing for freedom and against enslavement and threats of enslavement by Hitler's fascist armies. In this connection the historic utterance of the British prime minister, Mr Churchill, regarding aid to the Soviet Union, and the declaration of the United States government signifying readiness to render aid to our country, which can only evoke a feeling of gratitude in the hearts of the peoples of the Soviet Union, are fully comprehensible and symptomatic.[4]

These remarks contain the essential elements of subsequent Soviet and Comintern propaganda: insistence on the term 'fascist', always flanked by 'German' (and also the distinction — later effaced as the war grew increasingly bitter and illusions in the possibility of a German popular rebellion against Hitler faded — between 'misrulers' and toiling classes); glorification of the value of democratic rights; gratitude toward the Anglo-Saxons (immediately extended from Britain to the United States because of Roosevelt's promise to aid the Russians). On 6 November of that same year, at a no less dramatic moment, when the Germans had nearly reached the outskirts of Moscow, Stalin — who had not abandoned the capital and was celebrating the anniversary of the October Revolution in a station of the Moscow underground — spoke in new and even sensational terms. Mention has already been made of the ease with which Stalin bent theoretical concepts to his tactical designs. But the point bears reiteration. He now described the Hitler regime as a duplicate of the reactionary system in Russia under the Tsar, the Nazi party as 'a party of enemies of democratic rights, a party of medieval reaction and ultra-reactionary pogroms'. He denied that the Anglo-American system could be called 'plutocratic'. On the contrary, it would be 'German fascist chatter' to call plutocratic a system in which there were trade unions, democratic rights, a parliament, and political parties of the toilers.

Stalin went so far in his exaltation of the Western democracies because of his evident political concern to counterpose to Nazi-fascism a 'united front' not only of states and peoples but also of principles. He resorted to revealing arguments to justify his own previous attitude, offering a new version of Hess's flight to Britain in May of that year:

They [the German-fascist strategists] calculated in the first place on creating a general coalition against the USSR, on enlisting Great Britain and the USA in this coalition, first having frightened the ruling circles of these countries with the spectre of revolution, and thus completely isolating our country from the other powers. The Germans knew that their policy of playing on the contradictions between the classes of individual states, and between these states and the Soviet country, had already produced results in France, the rulers of which, having let themselves be frightened by the spectre of revolution, in their fright laid their country at the feet of Hitler and renounced all resistance. The German-fascist strategists thought that the same would occur in Great Britain and the United States. The notorious Hess was in fact sent to England by the German-fascists precisely in order to persuade the English politicians to join in the general crusade against the USSR. But the Germans gravely miscalculated. Great Britain and the United States, despite the efforts of Hess, not only did not join in the campaign of the German-fascist invaders against the USSR but, on the contrary, proved to be in one camp with the USSR against Hitlerite Germany. The USSR not only was not isolated, but, on the contrary, it acquired new allies in the shape of Great Britain, the United States, and other countries occupied by the Germans.[5]

Once again there is little point in asking whether Stalin was consistent with what he had maintained previously (or would maintain later). What must be understood is that this new approach was a response to the stringent necessities and opportunities of the moment. German troops stood at the gates of Moscow. Aggression had to be checked and repulsed, the Hitlerite hordes had to be forced to pass through scorched earth, guerrilla war had to be waged behind enemy lines, patriotism had to be aroused among the Soviet people, the Russian people in the first place. 'Our army is defending the motherland against invaders.' It was the socialist motherland, the land of Lenin, but it was also Mother Russia, age-old Russia, the 'great nation', the nation — and these are Stalin's words — 'of Plekhanov and Lenin, Belinski and Chernyshevski, Pushkin and Tolstoy, Glinka and Tchaikovsky, Gorky and Chekov, Siechenov and Pavlov, Repin and Surikov, Suvorov and Kutusov'.

The great minds of Mother Russia — from poets to musicians, from scientists to philosophers, from painters to the generals who defeated Napoleon — were invoked as representing the historic continuity of the motherland, the source of a civilization that had to be defended as home and hearth. Religious faith could be as useful as Bolshevik resolution. The urgent anti-fascist motivation and the solidarity demanded of and offered to other peoples and countries engaged in this life-or-death struggle were linked inextricably with patriotism. Both the Soviet fighters and the civilian population, which continued to resist and produce, making indescribable sacrifices and preparing to defend Leningrad and Moscow house by house, had to be imbued with the conviction that they were not alone, that they could rely on faithful allies then and subsequently: the United States, Britain, and the peoples of the European continent, 'from France', said Stalin, 'to the Soviet Baltic regions.'

Stalin sought to concentrate moral indignation against an enemy that had 'lost any human features' (and was therefore 'inevitably doomed' in the civilized consciousness of the oppressed), in the hope that the tide would soon turn. Hence his praise for Anglo-American aid, for the billion-dollar loan the United States had granted the USSR, as well as his assurance that the German 'rear' was not secure, and even his stated belief that the German workers would rebel against Hitler, who was now the only real imperialist. There was an air of obscure self-criticism, with a pinch of *arrière-pensée*, in Stalin's mention in his 6 November speech of the failed manoeuvre of 'the notorious Hess', as well as in his praise of Britain, the traditional enemy still considered as such only a short time ago.

Churchill employed a different style, but proved no less accommodating than Stalin. He was actually the first to seek an alliance that would go beyond *de facto* military co-operation. Churchill took to the airwaves to announce that he remained as anti-Communist as ever, that he would not take back a word of the negative statements he had so often pronounced about Communism; but he paid tribute to the Russian people, and assured them that Britain would stand at their side 'to exterminate the Nazi scoundrels'. What he really thought of the Soviet government emerges more clearly in his memoirs. Mutual mistrust, a mixture of resentment and suspicion, would persist throughout the war, for both Stalin and Churchill. The former confided to Djilas that Churchill 'is the kind of man who will pick your pocket of a kopeck',[6] while the latter recalled that the Russians did not hesitate to ask for help as soon as they 'came under the blows of the blazing German sword'. He said of the behaviour of the Soviet authorities after 22 June:

> Their first impulse and lasting policy was to demand all possible succour from Great Britain and her Empire, the possible partition of which between Stalin and Hitler had for the last eight months beguiled Soviet minds from the progress of German concentration in the East. They did not hesitate to appeal in urgent and strident terms to harassed and struggling Britain to send them the munitions of which her armies were so

short. They urged the United States to divert to them the largest quantities of the supplies on which we were counting, and, above all, even in the summer of 1941 they clamoured for British landings in Europe, regardless of risk and cost, to establish a second front. The British Communists, who had hitherto done their worst, which was not much, in our factories, and had denounced 'the capitalist and imperialist war', turned about again overnight and began to scrawl the slogan 'Second Front Now' upon the walls and hoardings.

We did not allow these somewhat sorry and ignominious facts to disturb our thought, and fixed our gaze upon the heroic sacrifices of the Russian people under the calamities which their government had brought upon them, and their passionate defence of their native soil. This, while the struggle lasted, made amends for all. [7]

Whatever the positions and actions of the European Communists, the effects of the 'ideological war' were felt primarily in shifts in public opinion, and in alliances, that were closely connected to events on the battlefields of Ukraine, Smolensk, and Leningrad, where the Second World War's longest siege had begun. 'The criticism of arms' guided the criticism of the masses. The mounting resistance by the Red Army in the autumn of 1941, as the Nazi blitzkrieg began to sputter after the anxious summer months, when the avalanche had seemed irresistible, won admiration even from those most completely devoid of sympathy with the USSR. They, like Churchill, willingly forgot the lack of military preparation revealed by the German attack, and in their hearts they began to question the widespread bitter criticism made in 1939–41 of a regime whose home front now seemed to be withstanding the ultimate test: war.

It was felt that the war effort of the land of the soviets, like its battle to produce, resist, and counter-attack, was under the direction of the leader's firm hand, a man of steel, just as his party name said. A new cult of Stalin sprang up, more deeply felt than the one based on his earlier image as a great politician and important theorist. Now it was a cult of the patriot, the strategist standing up to the Germans, the courageous general who refused to abandon Moscow. Pro-Soviet sentiments were blossoming, or arising anew, among the ordinary people, workers, intellectuals, and statesmen in the Allied countries. Among Communist militants, 'the reflex of unconditional solidarity with the USSR was triggered immediately.'[8] The new turn was accepted enthusiastically and applied with determination.

The problem was to arouse action, the objective armed struggle. This was something completely new for many parties (from the French to the Czechoslovak, the Yugoslav to the Greek), which although they had been underground for months if not years, had little or no 'military' experience or even guerrilla training and had been educated in a tradition of the workers movement that repudiated terrorism ideologically and in some cases was even rooted in Second International pacifism. For each of these forces, the attack on the USSR marked a sudden and unprecedented engagement.

After the war, the leaders of the various Communist parties made a determined effort to point out that they had initiated resistance to the occupation even before 22 June 1941, that they had issued the anti-fascist call. And it is true that the parties which fought best in the liberation war were those which had shown some signs of recovery and vitality between the end of 1940 and the spring of 1941. Despite being targeted by Pétain's police (Vichy held eighteen thousand political prisoners in March 1941, the majority of whom were Communists), the PCF, under the leadership of Jacques Duclos, Benoît Frachon, and Pierre Sémard, had begun to reorganize its membership underground, creating an effective network of agitators, especially among the working class in the north (an impressive strike, lasting ten days, was held in Pas-de-Calais in May), and had formed the first armed nuclei, which often helped to support impromptu workers struggles. They were the militants of the Organisation Spéciale, the base of the courageous groups of Francs-Tireurs et Partisans (FTP), who were the first (and for quite a while the only) resistance fighters in both occupied and 'free' France.[9] On 15 May 1941 the PCF issued a call for the formation of a 'National Front of Struggle for French Independence' directed primarily against the collaborationist government, although the theme of 'national oppression' would henceforth be an element of French Communist propaganda. Proclaiming itself the essential force of national liberation, the PCF declared that France could not resign itself to becoming a 'Nazi colony'.[10]

The Yugoslav Communist Party had also been very active in the demonstrations that brought down the pro-Nazi government at the end of March 1941. It now had some eight thousand members (about three thousand of whom were still in prison), including many daring and militant young cadres, and was actively carrying on propaganda among the Yugoslav soldiers, urging them not to let themselves be taken prisoner by the German invaders but to go underground instead. The party formed its own secret war committee under the leadership of its general secretary, Tito. In short, the party was preparing for military resistance and was fast making new recruits (membership rose to twelve thousand in just a few weeks).[11]

Neither had the Greek Communist Party remained inactive. It had found a basis for collaboration with other political groups in the heat of the war against the Italians, and did not resign itself to Italo–German occupation either. As in Yugoslavia, new leading cadres were coming forward, waves of new recruits flowed in, arms were collected, and the first 'orientation' groups were formed. It has been correctly noted that the new elements, some of whom came into the Central Committee itself,

> had not been able to absorb all the implications of the Russo–German pact, either because they had remained in concentration camps on the islands, or because they had to wage a clandestine struggle against the Greek police. Although the pact did arouse some confusion in their minds, they were far more concerned with internal problems, primarily the occupation of the country, than with international affairs and debates about the 'imperialist war'. Hence the position they took in the spring of 1941 and the early signs of agitation which, as in Yugoslavia, spread rapidly with the outbreak of hostilities between Germany and the Soviet Union. [12]

In other words, there was already a noticeable trend, fuelled by the pressure of events: wherever the CPs still commanded a minimum of underground organizational resources in the occupied countries, the impetus to struggle against the occupation and to defend the workers and peasants, whose living conditions were threatened and whose possibilities of action were proscribed by the servitude to which they were subjected, tended to shatter the schema of 'neutrality' and to shift the 1939–40 axis of propaganda and agitation. But it was not until 22 June 1941 that there was a real qualitative change (first in intentions, then in action as soon as it became possible). The various national situations were and remained quite diverse. At the same time, it should be kept in mind that since the Communists were now immersed in clandestine liberation struggles in each country, they were relatively independent of the international centre; the severe circumstances of the struggle, and the alliances they managed or failed to forge, led them to interpret general directives in their own way.

Directives there were, and they began arriving straightaway. We have direct evidence of them in the relations between Moscow and the Yugoslav CP (which alone, incidentally, remained stable and documented throughout the war). On 22 June itself, just a few hours after the Nazi attack on the USSR, Dimitrov sent a secret message to Tito: 'Keep in mind that in the present stage the issue is liberation

from fascist oppression and not socialist revolution.'[13]
The political and military line was explained in two successive communications between 22 June and 1 July. The first said:

The defence of the USSR is simultaneously the defence of the peoples occupied by Germany. An opportunity is offered to the peoples of Yugoslavia to develop a comprehensive liberating struggle against the German invader. It is vitally necessary to undertake all measures to support and facilitate the just struggle of the Soviet people. It is vitally necessary to develop a movement under the slogan of a united national front and the earlier united international front of struggle against the German and Italian fascist brigands . . .[14]

The second said:

The hour has struck when Communists must launch an open fight against the invader. Organize, without wasting a single minute, partisan detachments and stir up in the enemy's rear a partisan war. Set fire to war factories, stores of inflammable material (petroleum, gasoline, and others), airports; destroy and demolish the railway, telegraph, and telephone network; do not allow the transportation of troops and munitions (or war material in general). Organize the peasantry to hide their grain and drive the livestock into the woods. It is indispensable to use all means to terrorize the enemy, to make him feel as if he were within a besieged fortress.[15]

Notes

1. Vittorio Foa, 'La ricostruzione capitalistica nel secondo dopoguerra', in *Rivista di storia contemporanea*, vol. 2, fasc. 4, October 1973, p. 541.
2. That the question of national independence was the decisive issue in assessing the nature of the Second World War is acknowledged by Soviet historians too, although with notable variations. See *Lineamenti di storia del Pcus*, Moscow 1962, p. 52.
3. Winston Churchill, *The Second World War*, vol. 3, *The Grand Alliance*, London 1950, p. 340.
4. From his speech of 3 July 1941, in Stalin, *War Speeches, Orders of the Day and Answers to Foreign Press Correspondents During the Great Patriotic War July 3rd 1941—June 22nd 1945*, London, Hutchinson and Co., n.d., p.11.
5. 'Speech at Celebration Meeting of the Moscow Soviet', 6 November 1941, ibid., p. 14.
6. Milovan Djilas, *Conversations With Stalin*, London 1962, p. 70.
7. Churchill, *The Second World War*, vol. 3, *The Grand Alliance*, p. 338-39.
8. Agosti, *La Terza Internazionale*, vol. 3, II, p. 1179.
9. See Charles Tillon, *Les FTP* Paris 1962, pp. 72-126.
10. Duclos, *Mémoires*, vol. 3, pp. 122-46.
11. *Storia della lega dei comunisti della Jugoslavia*, p. 363.
12. Levy, *Il socialismo nell'Europa di Hitler durante la seconda guerra mondiale*, p. 588.

13. See Stephen Clissold, *Yugoslavia and the Soviet Union, 1939–73. A Documentary Survey.* Oxford 1975, p. 318.

14. See Milorad M. Drachkovitch, 'The Comintern and the Insurrectional Activity of the Communist Party of Yugoslavia in 1941–1942', in *The Comintern. Historical Highlights,* p. 192.

15. Ibid., p. 193.

15

Under the Banner of National Unity

Even before the Western allies set up their famous Psychological Warfare Branch, the Comintern had been turned into a kind of giant agency for wartime radio propaganda. The whole apparatus was committed to this project, initiated by a meeting of the Secretariat that voted to establish a committee, composed of Dimitrov, Togliatti, and Manuilski, 'charged with the day-to-day direction of all the work'.[1] But this troika soon broke up. Manuilski was transferred to the Soviet army's political leadership group, and Dimitrov left the heaviest organizational tasks of the radio work to Togliatti. News, commentary, and general information was broadcast twenty-four hours a day in eighteen languages, including German, Polish, Czech, Slovakian, Bulgarian, Serbian, Slovenian, Spanish, French, Italian, and Hungarian. In October 1941 the apparatus was moved to Ufa (a city of half a million inhabitants in the foothills of the Urals), capital of the Bashkir autonomous republic, where a powerful transmitter had been erected. According to one of Togliatti's trusted Italian collaborators,

> Togliatti was the sole leader of the Comintern, which was now reduced to a propaganda army inundating the airwaves with slogans, polemical arguments, and reports designed to demolish Nazi-fascist propaganda. Dimitrov and Manuilski had been posted to Duribyshev, closer to the state apparatus, and rarely came to the Bashkir capital. The machine now functioned almost automatically. The political line was clear and would not change; the Comintern workers took regular turns listening to enemy radio broadcasts; the early hours of the morning were almost always taken up by reading the news, then everyone would be busy writing, except for the announcers, who would only look over the texts. Togliatti would be given the final draft of the transmission before five o'clock in the morning. Sometimes he was quite satisfied, sometimes less so, but in general he was happy with our work group.[2]

This army of propagandists worked well indeed. The news bulletins and ideas that flooded the airwaves were turned into material for the leaflets and information bulletins of the underground Communist organizations, and then used as organs of agitation in the workplaces and among the people. Radio Moscow broadcasts — like those of Radio London, which were also very effective, and rather more widely heeded in the West — were directed at 'the man in the street', at the masses. The tenor of the broadcasts of the two stations was not very different. Both networks sounded patriotic appeals to the value of liberty and national independence, and extolled the alliance of 'free peoples'. Calls to partisan activity were perhaps clearer from Radio Moscow.

Defeats, however, could not be turned into victories on the airwaves. The best propagandist was therefore the Red Army. During that most difficult summer of 1942 — when the Germans resumed their advance and the war in the Pacific was going so badly that its outcome seemed in doubt, when the Japanese had conquered half of Asia and the second front seemed almost a chimera, embittering relations between Churchill and Stalin — the urgings from Ufa seemed far less distinct. Nothing could be further from the historical truth than a triumphalist view of a process which did, however, finally raise the prestige of both Stalin and the USSR in the eyes of millions and millions of people. It was precisely the vicissitudes of the war, its anxieties and doubts, the tension that preceded the opening of the second front, which created a new historic situation that changed the terms of the relation between the broad masses and 'patriotic war'.

The sharpening conflict also demolished the façade of internationalism erected at the Bolshevik Party congress of 1939, when Stalin had described the solidarity of the toilers of the capitalist countries as among the USSR's strong points. The bitter reality was otherwise, especially as concerns the German working class. It mattered little that the German Communist Party (meaning Pieck and Ulbricht) called upon the German workers to 'struggle for the overthrow of the Hitler clique' and invoked the 'noble sentiment and best traditions of our people'.[3] Rather more important was the fact that the German troops were fighting fanatically and sowing terror. In the absence of solidarity from the European workers in the early days of the war, there was a widespread sense of isolation among the Soviet people. Giuseppe Boffa wrote: 'A stream of primitively triumphalist propaganda had long proclaimed that if any country attacked the USSR, the workers would rise up. This point was made about Germany in particular. Now, on the contrary, Germans, Finns, Italians, Hungarians and Romanians were fighting in the USSR — and there were more than a few workers among them — without anyone's rebelling.'[4]

Hatred of the occupiers, of the *Germans*, became an essential component of the Soviet people's consciousness, and the newspapers reflected it. Ilya Ehrenburg, one of the most effective war correspondents, went so far as to write:

> We are remembering everything. Now we know. The Germans are not human. Now the word 'German' has become the most terrible swearword. Let us not speak. Let us not be indignant. Let us kill. If you do not kill the German, the German will kill you. He will carry away your family, and torture them in his damned Germany . . . If you have killed one German, kill another. There is nothing jollier than German corpses.[5]

The poet Surkov published these fiery verses in the Soviet army newspaper *Red Star*:

> My house has been defiled by the Prussians,
> Their drunken laughter dims my reason.
> And with these hands of mine.
> I want to strangle every one of them.[6]

Although there were no outbursts of chauvinism, and consciousness of the anti-fascist ideological dimension of the war was never lost, the Russian people's patriotic pride swelled in the crucible of the war and merged with glorification of the common destiny of the Slavic peoples (who suffered from occupation by the 'Teutons', who considered them inferior races worthy of enslavement). The sons and daughters of the USSR felt that the country was making sacrifices for indifferent allies, and the longer the opening of the promised second front was delayed, the stronger did this feeling become.

Communist militants in the other countries, of course, could not be classed among the indifferent. Their ranks had been thinned by the 1939–41 crisis, but every Communist Party in Europe and elsewhere responded with solidarity. Direct contacts between each of these parties and the Comintern headquarters in the USSR, divided between Kuibyshev and Ufa, were intermittent, difficult, and episodic, especially for militants working underground in the enemy-occupied countries. Contacts with the Yugoslav, French , and Czechoslovak parties were maintained by Dimitrov personally.[7] The star of the Seventh Congress, exponent of the Popular Fronts, was now the most ardent advocate of the search for the broadest possible alliances, admonishing the comrades of this or that party against any sectarian or ultimatist temptations. The general directive was accurately summarized by Francois Fejtö, who also considered its relation to the more complex problem of applying the line in the various countries:

> As soon as the Soviet Union entered the war, the Comintern instructed all the Communist parties subject to its authority to initiate national groupings of resistance parties and movements or to join such groupings where they had been formed without Communist participation. The Anglo–American–Soviet alliance was supposed to be matched in each European nation by an alliance of political forces ranging from the Communists to the national, anti-German right.[8]

This alliance was far broader than the Popular Fronts had been, since moderate and nationalist forces were also supposed to take part. Social differentiation, programmatic views about post-war prospects, and institutional and territorial questions were to be left aside. Fejtö had this to say about the basic motivations and sources of future contradictions, which in some cases emerged very quickly:

> The aim of the 'National Front' policy was to prevent party and class rivalries, struggles between pro-West and pro-Soviet tendencies, from upsetting and weakening the war effort against the common enemy. The USSR wanted to offer a token of its loyalty to the spirit of the alliance and to demonstrate its determination to pursue a policy of co-operation with its capitalist allies after the war, preventing the resistance from being transformed into civil war and *revolution*. In exchange, the Anglo-Americans were supposed to pressure their nationalist friends to admit Communist representatives into the resistance.
>
> It was an interesting formula. The bourgeoisie benefitted from it in France and Italy. It was applied successfully by the Czechoslovak emigration. But from the very beginning it encountered the greatest difficulties in the countries in which the Communists had been outlawed by authoritarian regimes before the war. In these countries the nationalist sentiment that motivated the resistance against Germany also had an anti-Soviet thrust. The leaders of the resistance rejected any idea of co-operation with the Communists, whom they saw as no more than Soviet agents. Moreover, the Communists felt strong enough to do without the rightist nationalists.[9]

Fejtö is considering a long time span here, and is perhaps too categorical in pointing to what was nevertheless a real dynamic. It was not only in Poland (and to some extent Greece, Romania, and Hungary) that the nationalist and monarchist formations were 'tinged', (or more than tinged) with anti-Sovietism, but also in France, and Britain too, for that matter; the gulf opened in August 1939 was never completely bridged. Yugoslavia was soon the scene of open warfare between Tito's Communist partisans and the so-called Chetniks of Colonel Mihailovich, who were linked to the exiled king's government. But let us examine the situation at certain crucial moments for the Communist movement like 22 June 1941 or the years 1942–43.

There can be no doubt whatever that the Comintern 'directive' was followed. How it was applied and whether it worked is quite another matter. The PCF implemented the new orientation most literally, proclaiming in July 1941 that 'there is no difference at all among Communists, Socialists, Radicals, Catholics, and followers of Charles De Gaulle'. 'For us', a PCF manifesto stated, 'there are only French people fighting Hitler.'[10] This solemn call was directed to all the French:

> The people of France understand the need to unite against the Hitlerite invader, and Communists and Gaullists, atheists and believers, workers and peasants, intellectuals and people of all walks of life, are now determined to liberate France and have the duty to fight side by side. Communist militants must understand this, and must set to work everywhere, in the workshops, in the cities, and in the countryside, to build committees of the National Front for French Independence. This is the only way to be good Communists at present. If any party member should express aversion to certain alliances, there is no doubt that beneath such repugnance lurks a passivity unworthy of Communist militants at a time when everything impels us to the struggle.[11]

The argument used here was later employed very frequently in both France and Italy: sectarianism, reluctance to collaborate with non-Communists, masked passive opportunism or even cowardice. French Communist appeals for unity with patriotic Catholics and Gaullists were especially fervent. The 'deserter' Maurice Thorez even tried to meet with De Gaulle in London, but the request, which Stalin seems to have backed, was greeted with frigid hostility by both Churchill and De Gaulle.[12] The latter lost no time in laying the political foundations for the Committee for Free France, and was careful to include in it the Socialist survivors of the collapse of the SFIO in 1940.

The PCF long remained politically isolated. No progress was made in the creation of the National Front during 1942, for it was not easy to find political forces in the country willing to talk to the Communists. Both in the part of France occupied by the Germans and in so-called free France, where first Laval, then Darlan, and then Laval again headed regimes that were increasingly accommodating to Nazi-fascism, the Resistance functioned as a 'shadow army' that would act only at the opportune moment. The Communists, whose Francs-Tireurs engaged in acts of sabotage, attacks on German soldiers, and urban guerrilla actions, were unable to create an atmosphere of genuine fury at the occupation. A good part of public opinion was indifferent, as people took a two-faced and wait-and-see attitude, although the living conditions for the workers were growing increasingly harsh and the PCF was well organized in the factories. 'The party fought alone. No grouping of the Resistance followed it in organizing individual attacks, and still less in its generalized armed struggle and guerrilla warfare. Relations with the Gaullists were non-existent.'[13]

The PCF had attacked De Gaulle bitterly in 1940. Now unity not only with the Gaullists but also with their chief — authoritative and authoritarian, conscious of his mission as liberator of France — was not easy, and required gestures of subordination to him. The Soviets soon established good relations with De Gaulle in London; for the French Communists, the General represented an almost insoluble problem, even apart from the question of Thorez. In his war memoirs, De Gaulle himself speaks of them in these terms:

> And I wanted them to serve. There were no forces that should not be employed to beat the enemy and I reckoned that theirs had great weight in the kind of war imposed by the occupation. But they would have to do so as part of a whole and, to be quite frank, under my control. Firmly counting on the power of national feeling and on the credit given me by the masses, I had from the first decided to assure them of their place within the French Resistance — even, one day, in its guiding body. But I was quite as decided not to let them ever gain the upper hand, by-pass me, or take the lead.[14]

There was little change in the political and military situation until the Anglo-American landing in north Africa in November 1942. The armed struggle of the French Communists was heroic: thousands of members, including some of the most prestigious leaders, among them Gabriel Péri (former editor of *L'Humanité*), fell under the enemy blows. PCF influence in the working class and among progressive intellectuals rose. But the chasm dividing them from the other components of the Resistance was not bridged. Blum asked De Gaulle a still completely unresolved question: what would be the

Communists' place in a free France under the General's leadership? And he sought to answer his own question with an assertion that became general in 1944 and 1945: 'The Communists will cease to be an alien body in France to the extent that the USSR ceases to be an alien body in Europe.'[15]

The PCI spoke differently from the very outset. In the summer of 1941 the Italian Communists managed to take an initial step of reorganization that soon yielded unexpected results. Umberto Massola, one of the party leaders in contact with Togliatti, secretly returned to Italy and put together an Internal Centre, beginning in Milan and Turin.[16] Meanwhile, in October 1941, a document was signed in Toulouse by several exiled leaders of the PCI, the PSI and Giustizia e Libertà which prefigured the platform of the National Liberation Committee. The representatives of the left parties appealed to all democratic, Catholic, and liberal currents, 'to all those who are no longer prepared to tolerate the terrible responsibility of the fascist government'.[17] But the leaders of the Italian left believed that the coalition should not be broadened at the cost of the social content of the alliance:

> The anti-fascist revolution cannot be purely political but must also be social. It must eliminate the social and political foundations of fascism, which are the permanent foundations of all varieties of reaction. The monarchy and the big bourgeoisie — industrial, agrarian, banking, and commercial — must be attacked along with fascism proper.[18]

The problem now was to initiate action within the country. Militant anti-fascism was unable to win an active base among the masses and among public opinion until the armistice of 8 September 1943. But the PCI did manage to score a sensational achievement in March 1943: the organization, primarily by Massola,[19] of powerful workers' strikes in Turin and Milan. These were the only mass strikes to occur in any fascist or occupied country during those years; they marked the first sign of the disintegration of the fascist regime, sounding the alarm for the entire Italian ruling class and bringing about a major change in the PCI's specific weight within Italian society and politics.

The British Communists, target of Churchill's sarcasm, did not limit themselves to their insistent demands for a 'second front',[20] but also sought to mobilize those workers whom they influenced to step up war production. The British CP called upon the colonial peoples, in particular the Indians, to understand the necessity of forming, 'a grand united front to defeat Hitler'.[21] The American Communist Party — which had withdrawn from the Third International at the end of 1940[22] but was deeply involved in trying to arouse a general movement of sympathy for the Soviet Union among American democrats — acted similarly to the British. In fact, the American Communists had a wider area of operation than the British. Earl Browder had Moscow's ear; he directed considerable support work and had decisive influence on Communist and left parties in Latin America, from Mexico to Cuba, Argentina to Brazil, all of which were involved in forming national fronts, doing propaganda for the Grand Anti-Fascist Alliance.[23]

The Yugoslav Communist Party was the first to engage in an effective guerrilla struggle (and was therefore often cited as an example), and was also the first to create political problems and diplomatic incidents because of its conflict with the monarchists and various nationalist movements in the country's regions. On 27 June 1941 the 'Supreme Command of the People's Liberation Partisan Detachments' was founded, with Tito as commander. Armed clashes with German and Italian occupation troops began in July in Serbia, Montenegro, Bosnia-Herzogovina, Croatia, and Slovenia. The Yugoslav partisan struggle soon became a positional war, albeit a highly mobile one, with rapid advances and retreats, fuelled by centres of insurrection in the countryside and guerrilla actions in the cities. Towards the end of 1941 the Communist partisan detachments included some eight thousand armed fighters. During 1942 a fifth of Yugoslavia was liberated by the National Liberation Army, as the number of fighters mounted from year to year despite the very high casualties: it was estimated that there were 150,000 partisans in 1942, but 300,000 in 1943 and about half a million in 1944, in a country with barely 13 million inhabitants.[24] A total of 305,000 fighters were killed, about 50,000 of whom were party members.

As the partisan war intensified, there was a concurrent political and social radicalization. When the Chetniks were defeated, the Yugoslav Communists adopted a line that went beyond the Comintern's 'diplomatic' warnings, striving to create genuine organs of revolutionary power as the basis of a new state apparatus. These were, of course, subject to the changing conditions of the struggle, and they developed powerfully only as of 1943, especially after the Italian armistice; the Anti-fascist People's Liberation Council of Yugoslavia (Avnoj), however, was formed in 1942. Its declaration of November 1942 signalled an orientation that was to have sweeping consequences:

> Our victory will be complete only when our peoples feel really free, as masters of their own liberated land; when they are themselves able to

guarantee — through their own freely elected people's liberation committees, the co-operative work of all, and the organization of all the sectors of our popular economy — the conditions necessary for a social order that makes it possible for them to achieve a real and just democracy and to build a free, independent, and fraternal community.[25]

It was by no means accidental that the partisan movements that became most powerful were those which arose at the very outset of the war and also sought to root themselves in social revolution. The first instance of this general rule, of course, was the Chinese guerrilla war, which began in the 'red bases' as early as 1931–34, but it is more appropriate to discuss China later, in the context of the subsequent development of that revolution. The rule applies directly to Greece, where spontaneous instances of guerrilla struggle erupted in Thessaly and the Peloponnese immediately after the Italian–German occupation. There were further incidents in Drama, Oxato, in September, when the National Liberation Front (EAM) was formed, in which the Communist Party, the Peasant Party, the Popular Democratic Union, and the Socialist Party took part.

The EAM gave rise to a military organ, ELAS, the Greek People's Liberation Army, which began its activities in February 1942. In Greece, as in Yugoslavia (although to a lesser extent), the guerrilla army assumed mass proportions and the political front, though formally broader, was actually a left front under Communist hegemony. Monarchist forces supporting the exiled king and other groupings under British protection obstinately opposed any genuine national alliance. By the end of 1942, there were 6,000 fighters in the ELAS ranks; in April 1943 the figure was 12,000; by the autumn of that year it was 35,000, and it rose to 75,000 by the time of the Liberation. There were also clashes with another resistance group, EDES (Greek Democratic National League).[26]

These cases indicate that the formula of national unity was not easy to apply in the form of partisan action. Moreover, the political relations of the USSR and Britain with the legitimate representatives of the countries invaded by the Germans or Italians, and the looming question of whether Western or Soviet influence would predominate in this or that region, were no less important — often more so — than the purely military aspects of partisan guerrilla warfare, which, let us not forget, never genuinely inflected the balance of forces between the two great warring blocs in the Second World War. The Polish case is instructive in this regard. There the issues were national and political more than military.

The Polish knot was intricate indeed. On the one hand the Polish people's deep and widespread aversion to Russia, a sentiment whose origins lay deep in the past, was rekindled in the twenties and further inflamed by the events of 1939 and the German–Soviet partition of the country. On the other hand, no Communist Party, clandestine or otherwise, even existed any longer, for it had been dissolved by the Comintern in the summer of 1938. Stalin now thought it useful for the party to rise again. In the meantime, he had recognized Sikorski's government-in-exile and reached a general agreement with him when he visited Moscow in December 1941. The Soviets agreed to the formation of a Polish military contingent of about seventy thousand troops recruited among prisoners taken in the 1939 war. But this contingent would not fight on the eastern front. Commanded by General Anders, it was 'sent' to the British, by way of Iran, and was used, rather effectively as it turned out, in Africa and Italy in 1943–45. Also in December 1941, some surviving Polish Communist militants from Russia (some of them interned in concentration camps) were parachuted into Poland. At the beginning of 1942 they reconstituted the Communist Party, coyly calling it the 'Workers Party'. The leaders who had so adventurously returned to the country linked up with the few remaining party activists who were then reorganizing themselves in Cracow, Lodz, and Warsaw;[27] among them was Gomulka. An armed resistance group was formed, the Gwardia Ludowa (People's Guard). The first secretary of the new party, Merceli Nowotko, was killed almost immediately, shot by the Germans. Contact with Dimitrov was made only in May 1942.[28] The Communist partisans took their place alongside others who had already formed the Armia Krajowa (Home Army), a well-organized 'cadre movement' composed of military veterans, intellectuals, and students. The Home Army maintained a cautious attitude toward any mass struggle, while the Communists and Socialists were very active among the working class and the peasant youth.[29] No one even mentioned the possibility of a joint front of the two organizations, although neither necessarily opposed it. K.S. Karol gave this description of relations between the two wings of the Polish resistance:

> . . . barely a month later [in January 1942] appeared the first appeal to the nation signed by the PRP, Polish Workers Party — for to mark their difference from the former CP the Communists had decided to adopt a new name. Their manifesto was very discreet on the subject of their ties with Russia and the international Communist movement. It stressed above all the need for an immediate armed struggle against the Germans, and declared itself ready to collaborate to this end with all the anti-fascist groups.

The leaders of the Polish underground welcomed this new-born infant of the resistance with much reserve. The Sikorski-Stalin pact had by no means made them less anti-Soviet or anti-Communist. The fact that the new party called itself 'working-class' and claimed to be a partisan of Polish independence changed nothing in their eyes. For them the Communists were agents of Moscow, and Russia was an enemy. The negotiations which started between Gomulka and the heads of the AK were doomed to failure. The Communist Party thus remained as 'illegal' in underground Poland as it had been before 1939 under Pilsudski. [30]

The only German-occupied country in which unity was rapidly achieved was Czechoslovakia, especially the Bohemian 'protectorate'. As Julius Fucik, one of the future heroes of the Czech resistance, had to admit, before 22 June 1941 the Czechoslovak CP was deep underground, hiding 'not only from the German police but also from the country'. After the Nazi invasion of the Soviet Union, 'although it still had to perfect its clandestine organization against the occupation, the party could now stand openly before the nation, establish contacts with non-Communists, address itself to the entire people, and discuss with anyone who was determined to fight for freedom'. [31] The USSR's relations with the Beneš government-in-exile were good. The situation in Slovakia, formally independent under the puppet government of Monsignor Tiso, was more complicated. Here the Communists had an autonomous organization of their own, supported by the country's militant miners. In March 1942 they created a National Revolutionary Committee, adopted a very radical class orientation, and called for the birth of a 'Soviet Slovakia'. For this Gottwald criticized them, advising them that Czechoslovakia was indivisible and that their sectarian line had to be corrected. [32]

If we attempt to disentangle more general trends from the wartime events and the different national situations, we may note that the zeal with which the Communists threw themselves into armed struggle opened margins of autonomy and also led to conflict with the state interests of the great powers. In his initial instructions to the Yugoslavs, later repeated for all 'branches' of the Communist movement, Dimitrov stipulated two distinct stages. But it was not easy to separate them so sharply in such tense and dynamic conditions. The war between national states was accompanied by civil wars, or at least by powerful social disparities and contradictions, in every country of Europe. Some forces were allied with the occupiers, while other social groups remained passive and resigned; there were also sincere fighters for liberty who had no desire to collaborate with Communists. As for the Communists, they fought for socialist revolution, even if official party documents denied that it was on the agenda. The line of national unity was therefore open to interpretations of almost unlimited variation and nuance by all the Communist parties, from the underground leaderships to the working-class and peasant base, including the middle-level cadres so decisive in organizing the armed struggle.

Even in the past, official formulas had never been considered self-evident instructions. It was an honoured tradition in the Communist International, dating back at least to the Fourth Congress, to catalogue the various 'intermediate' tasks and objectives of the movement, often with Byzantine casuistry. [33] In the case of Yugoslavia, which was the most significant in many respects, Dimitrov himself — or 'grandfather', as he was called in the coded radio broadcasts — had more than one occasion to remind Tito that it was not yet time for socialist revolution and to ask him why it was that the Yugoslav Communists were unable to find allies in the war against the Germans.

As always, it was obvious that the Comintern was primarily concerned not with ideological and 'strategic' clarity but with relations between the USSR and the other warring states, Britain in particular. The USSR had recognized the London-based government of the exiled Yugoslav king. Dimitrov noted in March 1942 — as he had in 1941 — that the English were not completely wrong when they complained that Tito's partisans were monopolizing the struggle, clearing the guerrilla field of any possible rival formations. Why was it necessary to call the partisan brigade 'proletarian'? [34] he asked. But diplomatic niceties are unlikely to prevail in the midst of an arduous and bloody popular struggle. Nor should the Kremlin's reservations be exaggerated. According to Tito, they had already been overcome by May 1942. [35] In the meantime, the Yugoslav Communists had broadened the social base of the national front by incorporating a mass peasant organization built along lines that later served as a model for other Communist parties. The CPY also helped to create the Albanian Communist Party in 1941–42. Its leader, Enver Hoxha, issued similar directives for the construction of a National Liberation Council. [36]

This tendency spread wherever the partisan struggle assumed significant dimensions. More generally, it must not be forgotten that the struggle mobilized the most genuine qualities of the Communist cadres, even where, as in France, they were engaged for the most part in armed actions, sabotage, and an extension of the urban struggle based on the active presence of the working class. The Communist

Party's cell structure was well suited to organizing armed nuclei and the sabotage of war production. In this sort of test, the characteristic features of the Communist leader educated in the school of the Third International, the 'professional revolutionary' frequently of working-class origin and tempered by so many years of struggle, were invaluable: sense of discipline, self-assurance in command, precision of execution, rigour in applying the rules of conspiracy, unquenchable faith in the justness of the cause. These cadres, indoctrinated in Moscow or in the various party 'courses' on the history of the CPSU, were prepared for any amount of tactical manoeuvring, but they were none the less convinced that the eventual 'second stage', of socialist revolution, would be hastened by the war.

The argument may have seemed more complex to the young levies newly recruited in the heat of struggle. But in no country was the party hierarchy disrupted by the partisan struggle; it was even strengthened by it. 'Promotion' came as the serious losses inflicted by the enemy created new vacancies to be filled. And the young Communist partisans were the ones most deeply motivated by confidence in the victory of the revolution. It is important to recall this background when considering the official documents, which emphasized the need for a broad front to liberate the motherland from the invaders and extended a hand to anyone prepared to fight.

This does not necessarily mean that any duplicity was involved. The Communist leaders, like the rank-and-file militants, came to the national-front line with all the prejudices and mistrust accumulated during previous attempts at collaboration with bourgeois-democratic and Social Democratic forces. There was also another factor, which soon assumed great significance. The darker sides of the Grand Anti-Fascist Alliance were most evident when it came to the European resistance, especially with the consolidation of a Communist component in the national liberation movements of 'delicate' countries and regions of Europe, from France to Italy, Yugoslavia to Greece. Churchill became increasingly concerned about Communist hegemony in some of these movements. Stalin was no less attentive, keeping an eye out primarily for the interests of Soviet security in the post war era.

It is therefore quite natural that what little we know about the various leadership debates concerns how to interpret the line of national unity and the intentions of the Western powers, whether or not to take advantage of the favourable balance of forces to tilt the coalitions and alliances in a Communist direction. An example is

Tito's April 1942 letter to the Central Committee of the Communist Party of Croatia, in which he wrote: 'In public the alliance between the Soviet Union, Britain, and the United States must continue to be stressed, and the latter two powers are to be depicted as our allies. But their agents and pawns inside our country must be opposed, just as we oppose the henchmen of the invaders and the enemies of the people who are out to crush our struggle for national liberation.'[37]

Even more interesting is a discussion between a Slovenian and Italian Communist leader in November 1942. The former held that relations between the USSR and Britain were likely to deteriorate, while the latter felt that the prediction was not only mistaken,[38] but was even inspired by fascist propaganda. In the Italian's mind, Stalin's policy was far more straightforward and less Machiavellian. A more authoritative leader, Togliatti himself, said in 1942: 'It is a mistake to consider the current alliance with sincerely anti-fascist democratic forces like England, France, and the United States as brief and transitory. We must not put fascism and the bourgeois democracies on the same footing. This alliance is not a trick, but corresponds to the most profound needs of the working class.'[39]

Communist attitudes to the 'Western' democratic forces, and to political democracy, constitute a reliable barometer of the expansion and contraction of the Communist movement. The distinction between fascism and bourgeois democracy upheld in 1936 with the success of the Popular Fronts pointed to a Communist upturn; in 1939–41, Soviet retrenchment was accompanied by denigration of 'so-called democracy'. Now the pressure was on the rise again. The above quotation from Togliatti was typical not just of his theoretical-political documents but of his private conversation. His radio speeches, too, emphasize universal values and the foundations of common civilization. In part, of course, this was 'propaganda', but it also expressed his conviction that this kind of generalized ideological war would sweep away past schemas and idiosyncrasies.

Togliatti indulged, for example, in an almost ecumenical exaltation of the 'great ideas' on which the struggle of the world-wide anti-fascist coalition was based:

> If Hitler won, there would be no place in Europe or the world for democracy, Catholicism, or the experiments in social transformation in which Russia has set and is setting such a glorious example. That is why no one should be surprised that liberal England and democratic America are helping Soviet Russia. Catholics cannot oppose such aid, but must support it and press for it. To defeat Germany and destroy Hitlerite barbarism means no less than to continue the effort to civilize humanity

that began with the glimmering dawn of Christianity in the pagan world. In substance, all of European society is founded on three great ideas. The first is the idea of law, which is Roman. The second is the idea of the equality and fraternity of men and peoples, which is the fruit of Christianity. The third is the idea of the nation and of the freedom of all nations. These ideas are the outcome of a centuries-long evolution and contain the germs of future European civilization.[40]

The discourse here is far removed not only from the language but also from the conceptual structure of Marxism-Leninism. In substance Togliatti is saying that the activists of the resistance, whether Communists or not, were motivated by the 'great ideas' of liberty and equality. The great new feature of the phase of European Communism that opened with the 1941 turn was even more than the idea of national identification, the attempt to root the parties among their own people, as a fighting vanguard dependent on the fate of what was above all else an independence struggle. Here as elsewhere, various 'levels' have to be considered. The Communists felt a genuine love of country, which was linked to their love of the USSR — no other term is accurate — in a manner that none of them considered contradictory.

We will return to this theme later. But the atmosphere of the resistance is illustrated by the highest sort of testimony: the messages sent to those continuing the struggle by others condemned to death. The profession of faith of the Communists among them had a leitmotif: they hailed the Soviet Union, while expressing pride that they were about to die for the liberty and dignity of their own countries. Two examples. Pierre Sémard, a Communist leader and secretary of the French railway workers union, was shot by the Nazis on 7 March 1942, at the age of fifty-five. Before his execution he wrote:

> I await death calmly. I will show my executioners that Communists know how to die as patriots and revolutionaries. My last thoughts are of you, comrades in struggle, of all the members of our party, all the French patriots, the heroic fighters of the Red Army, and its leader, Comrade Stalin. I die certain that France will be liberated. Tell my friends on the railways not to do anything to help the Nazis. The railwaymen will understand; they will act . I am convinced of it.[41]

The Italian Communist partisan Walter Fillak wrote to his mother just before his death in February 1945 at the age of twenty-five: 'Very soon now I will be shot. I have fought for the liberation of my

country and to affirm the right of the Communists to the recognition
and respect of all Italians. I die at peace, for I do not fear death.'[42]

These sentiments flourished in every country, including the USSR
where patriotism and the socialist ideal seemed to acquire a new
dimension, a freshness far removed from the triumphalist stereo-
types of the official style.

Notes

1. *Storia dell'Internazionale comunista*, published by the Central Committee of the
CPSU, p. 486.

2. Cerreti, *Con Togliatti e con Thorez*, p. 276.

3. The text of the appeal, dated 24 June 1941, is in *World News and Views*, 26 June
1941.

4. Boffa, *Storia dell'Unione Sovietica*.

5. See Alexander Werth, *Russia at War 1941–1945*, London 1964. p. 414.

6. Ibid., p. 413.

7. Boffa, *Storia dell'Unione Sovietica*, vol. 2, p. 175.

8. Fejtö, *Histoire des Démocraties Populaires*, p. 53.

9. Ibid., pp. 53-54.

10. From the 14 July 1941 manifesto, reproduced in *World News and Views*, 16
July 1941.

11. 'Notre Politique', *Les Cahiers du Bolchévisme*. second-third quarters 1941, p.
8.

12. Cerreti, *Con Togliatti e con Thorez*, p. 271.

13. Courtois, *Le PCF dans la Guerre*, p. 261.

14. Charles De Gaulle, *War Memoirs*, vol. 1, *The Call to Honour 1940–1942*,
London 1955, p. 271.

15. Lacouture, *Léon Blum*, p. 484.

16. Umberto Massola, *Memorie 1939–41*, Rome 1972, pp. 90-93.

17. 'Unione del popolo italiano per l'indipendenza, la pace, la libertà', *Lettere di
Spartaco*, special issue, October 1941, reprinted in *Il comunismo italiano nella seconda
guerra monidale*, Rome 1963, p. 162.

18. Giorgio Amendola, 'Marsiglia 1942', *Rinascita*, vol. 22, no. 12, 20 March 1942,
now in Amendola, *Comunismo, antifascismo, resistenza*, Rome 1967, p. 221.

19. Umberto Massola, *Marzo 1943 ore 10*, Rome 1963, pp. 7-78. On the significance of the strikes, see also Paolo Spriano, 'La grande spallata del marzo 1943', in
Spriano, *Sulla rivoluzione italiana*, Turin 1978, pp. 110-19; Giorgio Vaccarino, 'Gli
scioperi del marzo 1943', *Problemi della Resistenza italiana*, Modena 1966, pp.
148-64.

20. 'Can We Invade Europe?', *World News and Views*, 1 November 1941.

21. 'The Common Defence of the British and Soviet People', *World News and
Views*, 25 June 1941.

22. See Starobin, *American Communism in Crisis*, p. 45.

23. See Saverio Tutino, *L'ottobre cubano*, Turin 1968, pp. 153-83. More generally,
see R.J. Alexander, *Communism in Latin America*, New Brunswick 1957; and M.
Löwy, *Le marxisme en Amérique latine*, Paris 1980.

24. J. Marianovic, *Guerra popolare e rivoluzione in Jugoslavia*, Milan 1962, pp.
33-99.

25. *Storia della Lega dei comunisti della Jugoslavisa*, p. 444.

26. See Antonio Solaro, *Storia del Partito comunista greco*, Milan 1973, p. 115. See also André Kedros, *Storia della Resistenza greca*, Padua 1968, pp. 96-141; and David Philips, 'La guerra civile in Grecia', in *Storia del mondo contemporaneo*, Milan 1971, vol. 5, pp. 239 ff.

27. Vaccarino, *Storia della Resistenza in Europa*, vol. 1, pp. 351-53.

28. From the documents in *Il movimento operaio polacco negli anni della guerra e dell'occupazione hitleriana*, published in *Novaja i novejsaia istorija*, no. 5, 1964, pp. 109-25.

29. Eugene Duraczynski, 'La structure sociale et politique de la résistance anti-hitlérienne en Pologne (1939-1944)', *Revue d'Histoire de la Deuxième Guerre Mondiale*, vol. 20, no. 78, April 1970, pp. 53-56.

30. K.S. Karol, *Visa for Poland*, London 1959, p. 63.

31. See also 'La Résistance et la Révolution. Esquisse d' Histoire de la Résistance Tchécoslovaque de 1938 à 1945', in Vaccarino, *Storia della Resistenza in Europa*, vol. 1, p. 247.

32. See Ibid., pp. 253-65.

33. See Paolo Spriano, 'La tattica del fronte unico (1921-25)', in *Problemi di storia dell'Internazionale comunista*, pp. 59-78.

34. The text of the message is in Milorad M. Drachkovitch, 'The Comintern and the Insurrectional Activity', in *The Comintern. Historical Highlights*, pp. 206-07.

35. See Kruno Meneghello Dincic, 'Tito et Mihailovic', *Revue d'Histoire de la Deuxième Guerre Mondiale*, vol. 8, no. 29, January 1958, p. 21.

36. Enver Hoxha, *Resistenza e Rivoluzione*, introduction by Luciano Menegatti, Milan 1977, p. 17.

37. Quoted in F.W.D. Deakin, *The Embattled Mountain*, London 1971, pp. 170-71.

38. See the correspondence in Umberto Massola, 'Una polemica tra comunisti italiani e sloveni durante l'ultimo conflitto mondiale', *Critica Marxista*, vol. 8, no. 5, September-October 1970, pp. 214-19.

39. From the account of a class given by Togliatti in October 1942 at a school for communist youth, quoted in Anna Galiussi, *I figli del partito*, Florence 1966, pp. 152-53.

40. 'Missiroli e i cattolici d'America', in Togliatti, *Opere*, vol. 4, II, p. 156.

41. Duclos, *Mémoires*, vol. 3, I, pp. 225-26.

42. Walter Fillak, *Lettere dal carcere*, Cuorgnè (Turin) 1975, p. 99.

16
The Dissolution of the Comintern

Milovan Djilas, one of Tito's closest associates, visited Stalin in Moscow in June 1944. A year had passed since the dissolution of the Comintern, and Stalin touched on the subject briefly: 'Most important of all, there was something abnormal, something unnatural, about the very existence of a general Communist forum at a time when the Communist parties should have been searching for a national language and fighting under the conditions prevailing in their own countries.'[1]

Stalin also suggested that the Comintern had been an impediment to Soviet foreign policy. But he did not go beyond these generic remarks. He expressed his solidarity with the Yugoslav comrades and his admiration for their struggle and for the sacrifices they had made; he declared that he was prepared to support them against the British on the question of relations with the government of King Peter in London.

Measured against the great wartime unpheavals on various fronts at the time (between April and June 1943), the decision to dissolve the Communist International was a relatively minor event. But because of the importance of the Soviet Union in the post-war period, the evolution of the Communist movement in subsequent decades, and the general revision of judgements about the Stalin era, the subject has been of constant interest to historians since then. The most recent historiography presents two divergent, if not outright antithetical, interpretations of the reasons for the dissolution of the Comintern, founded by Lenin twenty-four years before, in 1919. The first explanation is primarily diplomatic: by dissolving the Comintern Stalin meant to show his allies that he no longer intended to interfere in the internal life of other countries. The elimination of the international organization of the Communists, closely linked to Moscow, was therefore a gesture — or more accurately, a concrete step — in that direction. The second interpretation, while it does not ignore the diplomatic dimension, places greater emphasis on the endogenous factors: the Comintern had become an anachronism ('unnatural', Djilas reports Stalin as saying); each party ought now to be able to act 'within the framework of its own state', in the words of the official resolution signed by the Presidium on 15 May 1943. This meant acting autonomously, no longer through a centralized organization now rendered superfluous by the development of the movement itself. The Communist parties would now be able to prepare for the war's decisive phase by striving for closer unity among the patriotic forces of each individual country in their active struggle against Nazism and fascism.

The only non-controversial point in the various interpretations is that it was Stalin himself who made the decision, who chose the moment and the reasons. The Yugoslav Vlahovic insisted that Stalin had been considering the decision for some time, but it was only after the Stalingrad victory that he felt sure that the Comintern's dissolution would not be taken as a sign of weakness or capitulation[2] (although it would then remain to explain why in the world he considered the organization dispensable just when prospects of expansion were opening up for the international Communist movement). The problem was admittedly posed in terms of 'prospects', but it was the prospect of the hegemony of the Soviet Union and its Western allies that prevailed.

It is here that we must focus our attention in understanding the meaning of the Comintern's dissolution. The situation was more or less this: the three great powers had scheduled a meeting to examine the most pressing military questions and immediate post-war prospects. Victory was not yet at hand, but it seemed certain. Stalin was urging the Anglo-Americans to open the long-awaited second front (news that it would be postponed again, to 1944, reached him only in June, and he made no secret of his disappointment with Roosevelt and Churchill).[3] Suspicion and worry still plagued him (would the West perhaps sign a separate peace with the Germans in the end?). But there was still broad agreement among the victorious powers, and this was of greatest concern to the Soviet Union in safeguarding its future security.

The prudence and rigidity of Soviet foreign policy were determined by this view of matters. In April 1943 Stalin broke with the London-based Polish government-in-exile. The reason (or pretext) was the scandal that followed the discovery of the infamous Katyn graves. The Nazis accused the Soviets of having massacred thousands of Polish officers in 1939 and of having buried the bodies in mass graves (a murky event that aroused an interminable polemic, but Soviet sources never managed to dispel the suspicion that the worst sort of atrocities had been committed). [4] The Sikorski government, far from convinced that the story was a German fabrication, asked for an immediate International Red Cross inquiry. Stalin replied indignantly, and took the opportunity of the 'offence' to make what proved to be a definitive choice. He now wanted a Polish government friendly to the USSR, and decided to press for it, even it it meant a serious battle with the British (Roosevelt was far more accommodating).

The Polish question was a sore point, then, and not the only one. But this was a further reason for the Soviet line of seeking a long-term agreement with the Western allies, as was apparent in the amicable conversations held in Tehran in November 1943. The dissolution of the Comintern was a signal, a message, within this general approach. It was not a mere diplomatic expediency, but symbolized a policy that consciously rejected the promotion of a revolutionary sequel to the war by Communist parties in Europe or elsewhere.

A number of circumstances help to clarify the scope of the episode, a ratification of accomplished fact more than an event itself. As I have already pointed out, the Communist International was mortally wounded by the 1936–38 repression; any last remnant of potential autonomy was extinguished by the Ribbentrop–Molotov pact of 23 August 1939. Once the smokescreen of the revolutionary phraseology of 1939–41 had been dissipated, the Communist propaganda coming from headquarters in Ufa and Kuibyshev harped on national unity and defence of the fatherland, extolling the common ideals of liberty and democracy. Anyone who attentively examines Comintern periodicals during this period is struck by the fact that between the middle of 1941 and the middle of 1943 (when publication ceased), the magazine *Kommunisticheskii Internatsional* completely ignored the problems of the colonial revolution, failing to publish even a single article on China, for example.

> The theoretical level of the other Comintern periodical, *World News and Views*, was also quite low during these years. In all of 1942, for example, the weekly never discussed the subject of world revolution, barely mentioned the Comintern's existence, and did not publish the customary Executive Committee message on the anniversary of the Bolshevik revolution. [5]

As we shall see, the national outlook of each Communist party, the fact that they were virtually buried in patriotic coalitions, was an even more important factor in the dissolution. But the way the decision was made was quite significant in itself. A meeting was held in Kuibyshev on 13 May, attended by Dimitrov, Manuilski, Pieck, Thorez, Marty, Koplernig, and Kolarov as members of the Presidium, as well as Rákosi, Ibarruri, Ulbricht, Vlahovic representing the International youth, and a few others. Togliatti seems not to have been present, nor is there any mention of representatives from the Chinese, Indian or Latin American CPs; the North American Earl Browder, on the other hand, seems to have attended and even to have acted as reporter.[6] According to the official account, however, the report was given by Georgi Dimitrov. The meeting concluded with the 'proposal' to dissolve the International, to be submitted to the various national sections. The document is dated 15 May; it was published in *Pravda* on 22 May, and on 8 June it was announced that the proposal had already been approved by thirty-one national sections.[7] On 10 June the International was dissolved, along with its appendage, the youth International.

The circumstances point to a somewhat unseemly haste. The Seventh Congress, the organization's last, had recognized sixty-five affiliated parties, together with a few collateral 'mass' institutions. This means that at least a sizeable majority of the Communist parties could not possibly have had time to express their opinion but were none the less forced to accept the Executive's decision. Moreover, it is not difficult to imagine how the leading bodies of each party were consulted. The Yugoslav Communist party seems to have been the only case in which a collective leadership organ was actually contacted, having been sent a radio message laconically soliciting the Central Committee's view of the proposal.[8] For the most part, assent was given by party functionaries living in the USSR. In the case of the Spanish CP, although Ibarruri was present and supported the proposal, Jesús Hernández states that he learned the news from *Pravda*.[9] But the most eloquent and detailed testimony was given by the Italian representative to the Comintern Executive, Vincenzo Bianco, a courageous militant who had already fought in Spain and would soon be parachuted into Yugoslavia. He was summoned by Dimitrov, who showed him a draft of the Presidium document. Bianco, somewhat taken aback, wanted to consult Togliatti before signing and expressed some objections: 'Georgi Dimitrov listened until I had finished. Then he looked at me and answered: "Bianco, do you agree with the Presidium proposal or not?" Yes, I did agree, but it was the dissolution of the Comintern! I did not answer his question immediately, but after a few moments of silence, I took a pen and signed.'[10]

That signature was required is proven by an incident that is significant in more than one respect. On 28 May, without waiting for the Presidium to announce approval of the proposal on 8 June, Stalin received the Reuters correspondent in Moscow and granted an interview in which he said that he expected dissolution, calling it 'proper', and explained it by reference to the political and propagandistic opportunities of the war, in the context of the Grand Alliance. Stalin said:

> The dissolution of the Communist International is proper because:
>
> (a) It exposes the lie of the Hitlerites to the effect that 'Moscow' allegedly intends to intervene in the life of other nations and to 'Bolshevize' them. From now on an end is put to this lie.
>
> (b) It exposes the calumny of the adversaries of Communism within the labour movement to the effect that Communist parties in various countries are allegedly acting not in the interests of their people but on orders from outside. From now on an end is also put to this calumny.
>
> (c) It facilitates the work of patriots of all countries for uniting the progressive forces of their respective countries, regardless of party or religious faith, into a single camp of national liberation — for unfolding the struggle against fascism.
>
> (d) It facilitates the work of patriots of all countries for uniting all freedom-loving peoples into a single international camp for the fight against the menace of world domination by Hitlerism, thus clearing the way for the future organization of a companionship of nations based upon their equality.
>
> I think that all these circumstances taken together will result in a further strengthening of the United Front of the allies and other united nations in their fight for victory over Hitlerite tyranny. I feel that dissolution of the Communist International is perfectly timely — because it is exactly now, when the Fascist beast is exerting its last strength, that it is necessary to organize the common onslaught of freedom-loving countries to finish off this beast and to deliver the people from Fascist oppression. [11]

Stalin's interview makes it absolutely transparent who the Soviet Message was aimed at: Moscow's American and British allies, Anglo-American public opinion, and the political forces that could be attracted to the national resistance movements. The argument was equally clear: let us put aside the encumbrance of a Communist International that has served its purpose in any event; let us unite more closely, country by country and 'internationally', to win the war. No less evident was his insistence that the dissolution was real, that it was not a trick but a strategic option, harbinger of the future establishment of the United Nations on the basis of equality (a theme that was later discussed in Tehran). Could the reference to forces 'within the labour movement' that considered the Communists agents of Moscow also have signified something new? Was this a hint that an obstacle to the unity of the workers movement in each country had now been removed? This question arose again in a more developed form between 1944 and 1946. In the meantime, the gesture, the political signal to the two great powers, was unmistakable. And it was received as such — and rather positively, too — by Anglo-American diplomats, especially the Americans. Although it has never been proven that Roosevelt had asked Stalin for such a demonstration of good will,[12] it is documented that in the autumn of 1942 Litvinov, the Soviet ambassador to Washington, told Joseph Davies, who had been US ambassador to Moscow, and returned there on a private mission in May 1943, not to be too concerned about the Comintern, since the organization was not all that dear to Soviet hearts. The American replied by suggesting that Litvinov convince Stalin to dissolve the organization.[13]

But the State Department was holding more diplomatic cards than that. On 18 May 1942, shortly before the official announcement, Cordell Hull, the American secretary of state, was informed by Czechoslovak President Beneš, who was notoriously friendly with the USSR that Russia intended to do away with the Comintern. Hull expressed satisfaction, commenting that such a gesture would be regarded by the American and British governments as a significant symbol of Soviet intentions to cease fomenting subversive agitation in other countries. He then asked Beneš to pass on his remark.[14] On 25 May, having just received news of the dissolution (or of the 'proposal', which amounted to the same thing), Standley, the American ambassador to Moscow, sent his government a message in which he made no secret of his satisfaction. It was his view that the Soviets were trying to respond to Western requests for the dissolution of an organization that constituted 'one of the greatest problems' in Soviet–American relations.[15]

Standley was not unaware of another, no less real, aspect of the measure: at the time the USSR enjoyed 'unprecedented' popularity in Britain and America, not only because of the 'heroic resistance of the Soviet people and the Red Army', but also because of the impressive showing of a 'system' that had demonstrated surprising industrial and productive capacity and organizational strength. Now, the American ambassador wondered, why should Russia, which had grown and consolidated its power in this way, continue to identify with the Communist parties of the most disparate countries? Why should the Soviet Union limit its own freedom of action and subordinate its own state interests to the cause of revolutionary efforts of uncertain outcome all around the world?

Communist memorialists and observers who closely followed the events of May 1943 are also in no doubt that the dissolution of the International was a response to the exigencies of Stalin's foreign policy. All interpretations agree on this point. The sharpest was Ernest Fischer: 'The dissolution of the Comintern on 22 May 1943 was a concession made by Stalin to his Western allies.'[16] Giulio Cerreti, who was also in Ufa at the time, says the same thing in more detail:

> There were two sides to the coin, the second being Roosevelt's insistence that Stalin offer the capitalist nations effective guarantees about the future of the Alliance. Roosevelt maintained, for instance, that his people would not understand how a lasting alliance could be formed with a great country that offered asylum and resources to an instrument of world subversion like the Communist International. Now that obstacle was being removed. Stalin, a practical and consistent man, was certainly prepared to pay a price for the post-war alliance, and he kept his word to Roosevelt, eliminating an obstacle that was by now more symbolic than anything else.[17]

Alexander Werth, then a war correspondent in Moscow, also considered dissolution a 'gesture to impress Britain and America', and he, too, holds that 'it was well known that both Churchill and Roosevelt had pressed for this step'.[18] Nor did Isaac Deutscher have any doubt: the sacrifice of the Comintern was Stalin's 'political contribution to the coherence of the Grand Alliance'.[19] Even more significant is the comment of Vlahovic, who was on the scene: 'The reasons for Stalin's decision to dissolve the Comintern must be sought in the international situation, characterized by the formation of the anti-Hitler coalition, and not in the analysis of the workers movement or the needs and prospects of that movement.'[20]

Other commentators of the Communist world join the same chorus. Fernando Claudín notes the urgency of Stalin's decision and argues that it was a 'politico-military necessity'.[21] Even the orthodox American Communist leader William Z. Foster explicitly mentions the relation between the conduct of the war and the 'historic' measure. He writes:

> It is significant that the historical decision was taken right at the most crucial moment of the fight to establish the second front. This front was very greatly needed for a quick and decisive victory; but the Western

reactionaries (who also believed Goebbels' lies about the Comintern) were blocking it. Undoubtedly the favourable impression all over the bourgeois world made by the dissolution of the Comintern helped very decisively to break this deadly log-jam. It was only a few months later (in November-December 1943) that there was held the famous Tehran conference, at which the date for the second front was finally decided.[22]

Joseph Starobin, a former member of the American Communist Party, states that 'Stalin gave Churchill and Roosevelt to understand that he saw Soviet post-war interests in exclusively Russian terms'.[23] Even more significant is Togliatti's satisfaction, expressed in a radio talk broadcast to his Italian listeners: 'the English and American press in particular are emphasizing that thanks to this decision, every reason for mistrust among the great democratic nations has been removed and their bloc has been consolitated and is now unshakeable.'[24]

It would thus seem that even an 'endogenous' interpretation of the Comintern's dissolution makes sense only in connection with Moscow's general view of the prospects for post-war peaceful co-existence. But could the dissolution actually have been a mere manoeuvre, a 'trick'? The enigma can be unravelled by paying close attention to the official motivation, which exhibits a number of oddities. Let us look at the 15 May resolution on the assumption that it reflects some degree of independent analysis and judgement. The resolution observes that 'long before' the Second World War, 'it became more and more clear that, with the increasing complications in the internal and international relations of the various countries, any sort of international centre would encounter insuperable obstacles in solving the problems facing the movement in each separate country.'[25]

Does 'long before' refer to the early thirties and the policy of 'class against class' or to the Seventh Congress and the policy of the Popular Fronts? In either case, the intent seems to be to emphasize the mounting inability of the international centre to deal with 'differences'. The text then presents this list of them:

The deep differences of the historic paths of development of various countries, the differences in their character and even contradictions in their social orders, the differences in the level and tempo of their economic and political development, the differences, finally, in the degree of consciousness and organization of the workers, conditioned the different problems facing the working class of the various countries. The whole development of events in the last quarter of a century, and the experience accumulated by the Communist International convincingly showed that the organizational form of uniting the workers chosen by the first congress of the Communist International answered the conditions of the first stage of the revival of the working-class movement but has been outgrown by the growth of this movement and by the complications of its problems in separate countries, and has even become a drag on the further strengthening of the national working-class parties.[26]

In other words, the resolution of the Comintern Presidium celebrates the third-class funeral of the organization it had led for a quarter of a century (even admitting that it had become an obstacle to the growth of those parties whose development it was supposed to foster). But beyond this attempt to offer historical background for its current actions, the resolution also overturned the original theory of the International born under Lenin's impetus in 1919–20. Its purpose was not only to wage a struggle against 'opportunism' (which task was reiterated even in the 1943 resolution), but also to endow the international proletariat with a united, cohesive, and disciplined instrument that could act world-wide, that could deal with the interrelation of specific national situations and the more general dynamic of the contemporary epoch — not only in the capitalist countries but also in the colonies, in the industrialized and backward countries alike, leading the workers, poor peasants, and even the bourgeoisie in struggle against the oppressors (even the emir of Afghanistan was listed among the potential allies of the revolutionary working class).

Leninism's starting point was exactly the unevenness of capitalist development, the nature of imperialism as the export of finance capital, and inter-imperialist contradictions. From these it deduced the necessity for an international organization of toilers that would exploit these contradictions by striking the enemy at its weakest point. But far more than a shift of emphasis was now at issue. 'Each country taken in itself' became not only the object but also the circumscribed field of action of the Communist parties. International prospects were dominated by the interests of the great powers and the possibility of arriving at a balance that would bring lasting peace, guaranteed by an accord among these powers. Although this was not a strict partition of the world into spheres of influence — this was not the substance of the Tehran and Yalta agreements, as we shall see — it did entail a general supervision of the fate of the world's countries, for the moment primarily in Europe. So great was the contrast with the theory of 1919 that one left critic of Stalinist Communism, Fernando Claudín, wrote: 'For this was the irony of history . . . Born with a programme of world revolution in the near future, it [the Communist International] died twenty-five years later postulating a prospect of brotherly collaboration between the Soviet state and the capitalist states.'[27]

We have followed the demise of the Third International at great enough length not to be astonished at this epilogue, at the extinction of its original reason for existence. With the turn in the war marked by the battle of Stalingrad, the development of the resistance in the countries occupied by the Nazi-fascist powers, and the beginning of the collapse of Germany's European satellites, a new relationship between 'headquarters' (Moscow) and the Communist parties took shape. It is true that the dissolution of the Comintern widened the freedom of manoeuvre of the various CPs and enhanced their ability to sink roots in their respective national realities; to some extent, it also encouraged them to apply independent policies, so long as these fell within the limits of the accords of the Grand Alliance. But the real novelty lay elsewhere: the strength and predominance of the USSR and the prestige of Stalin, who was now becoming a mythical symbol of victory and justice, resulted in an even more rigid hierarchical relationship.

This may be seen in various respects. All the leading political personnel of the Communist parties were Stalin's trusted men, trained in his school and ready to take up posts of responsibility in their countries, East and West. In fact, they derived a good part of their authority precisely from Stalin's trust in them. The expansion of the Communist parties, of the 'vanguard' that was fighting so courageously, was closely linked to the proletarian masses and poor peasants' messianic image of the victorious USSR as the land of trumphant socialism. In other words, it was the party of Stalin rather than the party of Togliatti, Thorez, Dimitrov, Gottwald, Rákosi, Gomulka, Tito, and so on, that aroused their sympathy and enthusiastic allegiance. In substance, the hierarchical relationship was now more direct even though it was no longer internationally institutionalized — or rather, just *because* of that lack.

Organizationally, a part of the Comintern apparatus, with Dimitrov in charge, remained intact, attached to the Bolshevik Party Central Committee and charged with dealing with 'foreign' Communist parties. More than one militant had occasion to recall this.[28] Apart from this organizational fact, political and ideological subordination was reflected in innumerable ways. Luigi Longo, who with the 8 September 1943 armistice became head of the partisan groups organized by the Italian Communist Party in the war of national liberation, offered an assessment of this phenomenon that is well worth quoting in full:

> The dissolution of the CI had a liberating function, since it encouraged the Communist parties to develop a line that conformed to the political, economic, historical, and cultural features of their respective countries. I do not believe, however, that the turn was considered the inauguration of a new epoch and of new methods as far as relations within the international Communist movement were concerned. I maintain on the contrary that the end of the Comintern was seen substantially as a wide-ranging tactical adjustment and as the elimination of an organizational conception that no longer corresponded to the exigencies of the struggle. The CP of the USSR remained the reference point, the 'hierarchy' that had to be respected under the new dynamic of the workers movement. From this point of view, the logic of the Third International survived (and acquired a new form in 1948, with the founding of the Cominform), and determined the behaviour of all, or almost all, the Communist parties. Clearly, this was a gross contradiction, which became increasingly acute with the further development of the process of expansion and diversification that began at the Seventh Congress and continued through the dissolution of the CI.[29]

This historical comment is supported by what Léon Blum had to say in *Le Populaire* upon his release from Mauthausen prison in 1945. He emphasized the psychological element:

> Stalin was perfectly sincere in his elimination of the Comintern, and the dissolution of the Third International is real. The PCF is no longer organically dependent on and hierarchically controlled by the Russian state, whether directly or indirectly. . . . But what we failed to foresee — and what the Communist leaders themselves failed to foresee — is that although it has recovered its freedom to make decisions, French Communism has not recovered its freedom of judgement. The relation of hierarchical dependence has been broken; the relation of material dependence, to the extent that it existed, has also been broken. But a psychic, emotional dependence subsists, anchored in habit and passion. Its motor force is not obedience, nor material interest, but the persistence in the very being of the Communists, of something like love. If you think I am exaggerating, you have only to leaf through any issue of *L'Humanité*, or, more simply, to read the draft of the 'unity charter'. After the dissolution of the Comintern, just as before, French Communism's gaze is fixed on Russia: Soviet Russia remains the permanent pole of attraction and the infallible yardstick.[30]

In this article Blum refers specifically to the projects of Socialist–

Communist reunification, whose stormy fate we will examine shortly. But he puts his finger on a permanent factor that operated with special force just when the USSR was emerging as a great power and when patriotic and anti-fascist sentiments were fused in the minds of Communists, with their love for the land of victorious socialism. The figure of Stalin loomed large: his image was gigantic. We could well conclude, as Jacques Droz did, that Moscow's decision to dissolve the Comintern was not just a consequence of Stalin's assumption that it would be useful in negotiations with the Allies, nor was it merely a response to the requests of the Americans, 'anxious to efface the revolutionary mission of Communism'. There were other, deeper motivations.

> The Soviet government's decision was also related to the fact that the Communist International had changed definitively and was now in absolute accord with the thought and action of Soviet Marxism: the national Communist parties, like the USSR itself, had become nationally based and therefore estranged from the idealization of existing socialism, that is, from communism as it was being applied in the land of socialism, and therefore from the glorification of the Soviet motherland . . . In substance, a formal structure became superfluous, since the organic centralization of the Communist Party continued to dictate dependence, and unity around the USSR and the person of Stalin was by now an irreversible fact. The war marked the ultimate outlet of the process of consolidation of Stalinism, internal and external alike. Stalin was president of the council, grand marshal, party general secretary, strategic and ideological genius, father of the Fatherland, and sole leader of the international Communist movement.[31]

Notes

1. Djilas, *Conversations With Stalin*, p 77.

2. Velijko Vlahovic, 'La dissolution du Komintern', *Est-Ouest*, no. 216, 16-31 May 1959, pp. 7-8.

3. See the 'personal and secret message' to Churchill of 24 June 1943 and the earlier message of 11 June to Roosevelt, in Stalin-Churchill-Roosevelt-Attlee-Truman, *Carteggio 1941-1945*, Rome 1965, pp. 155-58 and 503-04.

4. See the observations and biographical information in Boffa, *Storia dell'Unione Sovietica*, vol. 2, pp. 181-82 and note.

5. MacKenzie, *Comintern e rivoluzione mondiale*, p. 193.

6. Cerreti, *Con Togliatti e con Thorez*, p. 280.

7. They were the parties of: Australia, Austria, Argentina, Belgium, Bulgaria, Britain, Hungary, Germany, Ireland, Spain, Italy, Canada, Catalonia (the PSUC),

China, Colombia, Mexico, Cuba (the Revolutionary Communist Union), Poland, Romania, Syria, the Soviet Union, Uruguay, Finland, France, Czechoslovakia, Chile, Switzerland, Sweden, Yugoslavia, and South Africa, as well as the youth International. See 'Statement of the Presidium of the ECCI on the Dissolution of the Communist International (9 June 1943)', in Claudín, *The Communist Movement*, p. 44.

8. Dedijer, *Tito Speaks*, p. 197.

9. Jesús Hernández, *La grande trahison*, Paris 1953, p. 248.

10. From the testimony published in Guerra, *Gli anni del Cominform*, p. 31.

11. Claudín, *The Communist Movement*, p. 45.

12. McNeal, *Stalin*, p. 1093.

13. See the memorandum of a conversation with Joseph E. Davies drafted by Elbridge Durbrow on 3 February 1943, in *Foreign Relations of the United States, 1943* (III), Washington D.C. 1963, pp. 500-05.

14. From the memorandum drafted by Cordell Hull, 18 May 1943, ibid., pp. 529-30.

15. From the 25 May dispatch from Moscow, ibid., pp. 534-35.

16. Fischer, p. 400.

17. Cerreti, *Con Togliatti e con Thorez*, p. 280.

18. Alexander Werth, *Russia at War*, pp. 671-72.

19. Deutscher, *Stalin*, p. 464.

20. 'La dissolution du Komintern', p. 8.

21. Claudín, *The Communist Movement*, p. 22.

22. William Z. Foster, *History of the Three Internationals*, New York 1955, p. 439. Quoted by Claudín, p. 23.

23. Joseph R. Starobin, 'Origins of the Cold War', *Foreign Affairs*, vol. 4, no. 47, July 1969, p. 685.

24. 'Sullo scioglimento della Internazionale comunista', 25 May 1943, in Togliatti, *Opere*, vol. 4, II, p. 455.

25. 'Text of the Resolution of the Presidium of the ECCI (15 May 1943)', in Claudín, *The Communist Movement*, p. 40.

26. Ibid., pp. 40-41.

27. Claudín, *The Communist Movement*, pp. 32-33.

28. See Djilas, *Conversations with Stalin*, p. 35; and Cerreti, *Con Togliatti e con Thorez*, p. 282.

29. Luigi Longo, *Opinione sulla Cina*, Milan 1977, pp. 196-97.

30. See Lacouture, *Léon Blum*, p. 521.

31. Jacques Droz, 'Il comunismo sovietico ed europeo', in *Storia del socialismo*, Rome 1981, vol. 4, p. 465.

17

Spheres of Influence and the Peoples of Europe

However paradoxical it might seem, one of the effects of the Comintern's dissolution was a burst of internationalism — or rather, a resurgence of internationalist ideas and utopias. These emerged mainly from the dispersed and often enfeebled ranks of the Socialist and Social Democratic parties. The Communist parties, on the other hand, had moved squarely into a phase of that 'double-sided patriotism' we mentioned earlier. For its part, the USSR was more than ever sustained by the spirit of the 'great patriotic war', by awareness of its own emergence as a victorious power.

It was surely not accidental that on 1 January 1944 the traditional *Internationale* was replaced as the Soviet national anthem by a new song whose lyrics reflected what were now the two dominant images: great Russia and Stalin. 'Nationalism', it has been noted, 'was the conspicuous feature of Stalinism as an ideology and mode of political practice during the final phase of the conflict.'[1] And yet the paradox did have its effects, from below and above, to use the Third International's terminology. Otherwise it would be impossible to understand the powerful pressures for unity that arose in the workers movement of each country, or the proposals and programmes that made unity a major issue in nearly all the countries of Europe. A few examples will illustrate the atmosphere. Speaking of France, René Girault wrote:

> Among the Socialists — and I have in mind those who fundamentally shared the ideals of the Resistance, like Blum in his prison writings — there are people motivated by an ideal that may be defined as internationalist, or at least Europeanist. They believe that in the not too distant future, after the Liberation, there will be no living in a Europe divided into nation states, and that we must work towards a real United States of Europe [the expression was then beginning to gain currency], to which it may be added, and this is fundamental, the 'Socialist United States of Europe.'[2]

In France, Socialists like Daniel Mayer and Vincent Auriol (who later became president of the Republic) emphasized this slogan in an effort to satisfy two of the most sharply felt needs of the peoples of Europe: to prevent Germany from becoming a threat to peace in the future, and to promote general conditions of cross-border political and social reform. Auriol favoured the creation of unions based on 'European regions'. He had in mind a Balkan union (an idea also considered by Tito and Dimitrov in 1946, but angrily rejected by Stalin); a union of Belgium, the Netherlands, and Luxemburg (later realized as Benelux); an Iberian union between Spain and Portugal (which never happened: the dictators Franco and Salazar remained in power under American protection, though in 1944-45 everyone thought their days were numbered). Vincent Auriol also believed in 1944 that the creation of the Socialist United States of Europe would resolve the German problem. 'In this manner,' he wrote, 'that fortress can be dismantled, first by socializing it and then by internationalizing it, entrusting all its heavy industry to international people's organization.'[3]

There were new internationalist impulses among the Italian Socialists too, which led in August 1943 to the formation of a new party, the Italian Socialist Party of Proletarian Unity (PSIUP). PSIUP supporters raised the slogan of a 'new and free International' to be built on the ruins of the Second and Third Internationals. The newspaper of the left socialist movement, which coalesced in this new party, unreservedly declared what it did *not* want: 'If being Socialists means repeating the reformist practice of the Second International, then we are not Socialists. If being Communists means absorbing the authoritarian, centralist, and rigidly schematic tradition of the Third International, defending its mistakes and deficiencies, then we are not Communists.'[4]

Anxious desire for something different, a yearning to turn over a new leaf, were characteristics of Socialist-minded and liberal-Socialist groups in particular, as well as of individual intellectuals in various countries. This sentiment prevailed over a wide spectrum of political tendencies, from far-left to liberal, from revolutionary, Jacobin, and Trotskyist radicals to supporters of federalism who made no secret of their admiration for the US model.[5] Groups within the Czechoslovak resistance called for the 'reconstruction' of their state (which Germany had dismembered) 'in accordance with the principles of progressive modern socialism'.[6] German political refugees in London invoked 'a new Europe as an organization of co-operation among equal peoples'.[7] The Labour Party's Harold

Laski held that 'this is the time' for a revolution, 'with the consent of all', to bring about a socialist economy while safeguarding the values of democracy and liberty 'within our civilization'.[8]

These positions were articulated in 1943 and 1944. The war was not yet over, and the contours and features of the emerging political phase were still vague: it was by no means certain that the great powers would have everything their own way. The idea of a common socialist future was widespread indeed, partly because of its very vagueness. It was to be a triumphant socialism, in the words of Blum in his famous pamphlet *À L'échelle humaine*: 'the culminating point of all the great currents that have flowed through human history since the dawn of civilization, currents of mind and conscience, aspirations to human justice and charity.'[9]

Hope for the unification of the European workers movement burned even more brightly in 1944 and 1945. Although the aspiration rapidly collapsed, for the second time since the era of the Popular Fronts, it nevertheless expressed genuinely felt needs, an expectant state of mind that was linked to awareness of the daunting tasks of reconstruction out of the ruins of war, a universal desire for peace, and a weariness after all the horrors. On 15 April 1945, the German Social Democratic survivors of the Buchenwald extermination camp issued a manifesto calling for the 'foundation of an active and militant trade-union and political organization including all the socialist parties'.[10] Trade-union unification had already been achieved in Italy, and to some extent in France, during the resistance. In Italy there was even a Catholic component of the movement. In France there were forces among Catholic public opinion — in particular militant minorities of great intellectual vigour and moral stature, like the *Esprit* group — who were receptive to a socialist perspective not dissimilar to that evoked by Blum.

This yearning for something new, for a just and free world, this rediscovery of the original values of the socialist ideal, was especially powerful and spontaneous since the nations of Europe, and indeed of the whole world, were emerging from the tragedy brought about by Nazism and fascism, by racial hatred, and by the politics of violence and power that had accompanied the advent, triumph, and ultimate catastrophe of fascism. The world had seen the holocaust of more than 5 million Jews (perhaps as many as 6 million), most of them exterminated in the Nazi camps. The victims of the madness of Hitler's 'final solution' had been put to death in the most barbaric manner, either gassed or condemned by starvation and disease. The Nazis had 'liquidated' millions of other prisoners (more than 2 million of them Soviet soldiers) and had massacred entire populations in the occupied territories, especially in the East, from Yugoslavia to Poland, Ukraine to Belorussia, and on into the Urals. The figures on total losses of life are chilling:

> More than 50 million people lost their lives in the war, about 30 million of them in Europe alone. It was the Soviet Union that suffered the greatest losses in absolute terms, with about 20 million dead,[11] 13.6 million of whom were soldiers and about 7 million civilians (about 10 per cent of the population of the European and Asian regions); Poland lost more than 6 million (about 22 per cent of the population, proportionally the highest of any country); Germany suffered about 5 million dead, Yugoslavia 1,690,000, France 810,000, the British Commonwealth 544,596, Italy 300,000 dead and wounded, Japan about 1,800,000 dead, the United States 292,000 dead (all of them soldiers). China was the worst hit after the USSR, for more than 15 million died, counting from the beginning of the conflict with Japan. [12]

Conditions were not disastrous in all the countries of Europe at the end of the war, but there were ruins and grief everywhere. The USSR was bled dry: more than 25 million people were homeless, 2 million were forced to live in primitive refuges built of earth. The situation was particularly serious in the countryside, where agricultural production had fallen by half. A total of 31,850 factories had been destroyed, 65,000 kilometres of railways ripped up. It took the Soviet people ten years to recover their pre-war living standards. Germany, too, was a heap of ruins, entire cities completely razed. Poland had lost nearly three-fourths of its industrial capacity, while Yugoslavia suffered enormous devastation. Even countries whose industrial apparatus had been less severely damaged like France, Italy, Czechoslvakia, Belgium, and Holland, had grave wounds to heal.

Before a shift of the electorate to the left could be registered, projects and programmes were drafted by popular parties and governments in every country calling for sweeping changes in property relations, especially in the countryside, and massive state intervention in reconstruction. In some cases (like Czechoslovakia) Communists, Socialists, and Social Democrats called for nationalizations in the industrial and credit sectors even before Liberation. From his London exile President Beneš stated that he favoured a combination of elements of socialism and 'a democratic society in motion'. Advances had to be made gradually and without violence, he said, for a slow process 'is sometimes more revolutionary than unreasonable violence.'[13]

No less significant was a minor incident that occurred in Germany in 'the year zero': the first workers to speak freely after the war talked of socialization, for they felt that the end of Nazism should also mark the end of capitalism:

> Characteristic in this regard was Bockler's observation at the first meeting of trade unionists in the British Zone. He said: 'Capitalism is now at an end. . . . The old class enemy no longer stands before us. . . . What economic system should be applied? Is it better to opt for total nationalization or to rely primarily on co-operative-type enterprises?'[14]

The need for socialism, of course, is nowhere to be found in the documents and formulas of the victorious powers. They spoke instead of the restoration of democratic rights, of self-determination, of the organization of the United Nations in order to guarantee peace by ascribing special functions and responsibilities to the great powers, of punishment of Nazi-fascist war criminals. Neither did the Communist parties argue that socialism was on the agenda: the themes of patriotism, democracy, and the demand for social reforms remained predominant. Some have wondered whether this moderation was accepted by the increasingly numerous masses of members and sympathizers. Eric Hobsbawm has suggested an answer, writing:

> The Italian and French Communist parties have been bitterly criticized for not having pursued a more radical policy in 1943–45, or even for not having tried to take power. But the bulk of members and sympathizers, most of them recruited during the resistance and the Liberation, seem to have accepted their line without serious question. As for the USSR, the very idea that it might not favour socialism in other countries seemed absurd to Communists whose political analyses were based on the assumption that independent of the shifts in Soviet international policy, the interests of the world's first and only socialist state and of those who desired to build socialism along the same lines elsewhere could only be fundamentally identical.[15]

In reality, however, this connection was far from proven. The logic of the policy of dividing the world into spheres of influence became increasingly evident in the last days of the war. This is admittedly more obvious with hindsight than it could have been at the time. The European peoples as a whole, the great popular masses East and West, and more particularly the minorities actively engaged in the resistance movements, were only imperfectly aware of this pressing reality. Many of the plans and agreements of the great powers were secret, and it was thought in any event that once the war was over and the temporary occupation authorities had departed, there would be more room for real autonomy. The solemn public commitments of the three great powers themselves seemed to encourage such illusions. In fact, however, the grip of the victors would get steadily stronger.

Some trends were already manifest by late 1944 and the beginnings of 1945. First of all, for the first time in its own or Europe's history, Russia (now *Soviet* Russia) was the sole major military power of the continent. In the prevailing conditions of misery and economic bankruptcy, Russia needed peace, but its military power was incomparably superior to that of the other European nations. The Red Army had reached Warsaw and Belgrade, Budapest, Prague, and Vienna, and soon the red flag would fly over Berlin itself, in the heart of Germany. Bulgaria and Romania were well within the Soviet occupation zone.

In substance, the negotiations about respective spheres of influence at the Tehran meeting of 1943 and in the Moscow discussions with Churchill in October 1944, were conducted in traditional balance-of-power terms, although the nature of the government that would rule Poland and the fate of defeated Germany were by no means resolved questions. The Allies were beginning to realize that Russia had to be guaranteed a predominant position in the Balkans and in central-eastern Europe[16] (although tension and resistance soon developed to the way in which the USSR went about assuring that security politically and socially). The international alignment of Yugoslavia and Hungary was yet to be decided. In Moscow Churchill and Stalin had agreed that they would each maintain a 50 per cent influence over these countries.[17]

Before the war's end, an attempt was made to deal with the major contentious issues and great territorial problems in a spirit of negotiation and collaboration. In November 1944 Stalin hailed the alliance of the three great powers as a patrimony that should be defended in years to come, observing that their co-operation was ultimately based 'not on transitory factors but on vital and lasting interests'.[18] Among the vital and lasting interests of the USSR was its concern to ensure that it would be ringed by a belt of friendly states. By 1944 the compensation had become equally clear: in the West, or at least in Western Europe, there would be British 'tutelage' (without much opposition from the United States, which was not dominated by the Eurocentric mentality of the other two great powers). Britain asserted its own hegemony and its own conservative political inspiration in Italy, which had been liberated by British armies;

London was suspicious of the anti-fascist parties of the CLN and sustained and protected the Savoy monarchy. In Greece at the end of 1944 British troops conducted an armed repression against the resistance (in which pro-Communist formations predominated), which had liberated Athens. Churchill wanted the ELAS forces dissolved; when they refused, he had his paratroops open fire. On 7 November 1944 he wrote to Eden: 'Having paid Russia a price for freedom of action in Greece, we must not hesitate to use our troops.' The 'price' was the free hand given to Stalin in Romania and Bulgaria. It has been recalled by an American historian that 'Greece was the first of the liberated states to be openly and forcibly compelled to accept the political system of the occupying Great Power. It was Churchill who acted first, and Stalin who followed his example, in Bulgaria and then in Romania, though with less bloodshed.'[19]

In any event, when ELAS was forced into a sort of armistice in February 1945, Churchill encountered no Soviet protest. Stalin did not oppose the repression. With his usual frankness, Churchill wrote in his memoirs that one month later, in March 1945, when the USSR set up a government in Romania in which Communists held decisive positions (after a sharp intervention by the Soviet representative, Vyshinski, before the young King Michael), he had no choice but to resign himself to it, although some formal remonstration was made:

> We were hampered in our protests because Eden and I during our October visit to Moscow had recognized that Russia should have a largely predominant voice in Romania and Bulgaria while we took the lead in Greece. Stalin had kept very strictly to this understanding during the six weeks' fighting against the Communists and ELAS in the city of Athens, in spite of the fact that all this was most disagreeable to him and those around him.[20]

The year before, in June 1944, Churchill had opposed the replacement of Marshal Badoglio by Ivanoe Bonomi, the man designated by the Liberation Committee, as head of the Italian government. Stalin responded: 'If circumstances suggest to you and the Americans that a government other than the Bonomi government is required in Italy, you may rest assured that there will be no objection from the Soviet side.'[21]

The spirit of spheres of influence was thus already rife. In fact, Italy had been a precedent in this respect as early as the Tehran conference. It has been pointed out:

> At the time of the first conference of the three great powers, one of the

countries of the fascist coalition, Italy, had already been liberated, at least partially. Not for a moment did the Western powers contemplate the possibility of joint control or administration with the USSR; instead they began to impose their own men and their own choices. . . . What happened in Italy in the autumn of 1943 was in some respects a paradigm for what happened in the other half of Europe in the months and years ahead. . . . Although with methods far less brutal than those the Soviet Union later employed in Eastern Europe, the Western powers demanded their right to total control of the 'liberated countries'. Their occupation had an openly political character, and even when planning military operations, they never overlooked the objective of weakening those forces which, though fighting against the common enemy, had a different political orientation.[22]

Churchill was obsessed by the nightmare of the spread of Communism in Europe, and he was not alone. South African Field Marshal Smuts wrote to him on 14 December 1944 that 'we may, I fear, find, if private partisan armies and underground movements are kept alive, the peace degenerating in civil convulsions and anarchy not only in Greece but also elsewhere in Europe.' Churchill answered on 22 December that indeed, 'this may spread to Italy.'[23] When a militant partisan movement arose in northern Italy and the Apennines in the summer of 1944, with nearly a hundred thousand armed men and a working class that waged its own war through powerful political strikes, the Allied High Command viewed the matter with mounting irritation, partly because about half the Italian partisans were organized in the Communists' 'Garibaldi' detachments.

In mid-November 1944 Marshall Alexander issued instructions that effectively asked the partisans to return home for the winter. When representatives of the Liberation Committee for northern Italy visited the Allied High Command in December 1944, they agreed to a sort of *diktat*: upon the liberation of the northern regions, the partisans would have to dissolve their organisations and turn in their arms; all power and authority would pass to the Allied military governor. The resistance pledged to execute 'any order' issued by the Allies; even the military commander of the resistance detachments had to be 'an officer acceptable to the commander-in-chief of the Allied Armies in Italy'.[24]

The Italian resistance was balanced on a razor's edge. That it managed to maintain its unity, to strengthen the partisan movement while 'disobeying' Alexander's proclamation,[25] and to organize and lead a national insurrection in the major northern cities was a political more than a military master stroke. The Allied attitude did arouse tension and suspicion, of course. As early as the autumn of 1944 there was great bitterness in the ranks of the fighters of the Garibaldi brigades, especially among the Communist cadres, who were most concerned about the ultimate fate of the battle they were waging.[26] On this there is abundant documentary proof. What is less widely known but no less significant is that this atmosphere had effects on the line recommended by Togliatti.

I refer here to the results of a meeting held in Apulia in southern Italy between Togliatti and Kardelj, a top Yugoslav Communist leader whom we have already encountered. On 19 October 1944, after the meeting, the PCI leader sent a directive to the Communist partisan commanders of the armed struggle in the eastern border zones, who had contact with the Yugoslav Liberation Army, urging them to help Marshal Tito's troops occupy the Giuliana regions. These directives were confidential, and especially significant for that very reason. They instructed the Communist commanders not to engage in any discussion about how the problem of Trieste and the eastern border regions with mixed Slavic and Italian populations would be resolved after the war. But of greatest interest for our investigation is Togliatti's reasoning in justifying his instruction to facilitate a Yugoslav occupation of Venezia–Giulia:

> This means that in this region there will be no English occupation and no restoration of the reactionary Italian administration; in other words, a profoundly different situation will be created from that which exists in the part of Italy liberated so far, a democratic situation in which it will be possible to destroy fascism completely and to organize the people both to continue the war against the German invaders and to resolve all their vital problems.[27]

It may well be wondered whether this directive — issued in October 1944, while the PCI was participating in the Bonomi government (Togliatti himself was a minister without portfolio and was fighting day by day to augment liberated Italy's contribution to the common struggle — did not exaggerate the more sombre features of the Italian situation the better to justify Yugoslav and perhaps Soviet pressure in the eyes of fighters who had more than a few good reasons to regret the claims to hegemony and the nationalist spirit of their Slovenian comrades-in-arms. But the episode nevertheless indicates that Togliatti too was already eyeing future tensions, in particular the new contest between the victors in Europe, each of which was aiding the political and social forces that were closest to its own conceptions and system of government. Togliatti's directive was issued ten days after the Churchill–Stalin talks in Moscow, which were dominated by the logic of a 'European balance of forces' based on the definition, albeit not yet rigid, of spheres of influence. Part of this procedure was a Soviet attempt to initiate a Balkan agreement, since it was quite obvious that Anglo-Saxon predominance and interests in the West were beyond challenge.

One Italian historian has argued that it is difficult to explain why Stalin 'agreed so rapidly to an arrangement that ruled out any broader and fresher visions of the international order than the mere consolidation of the USSR's influence as one of the victors in the Second World War.'[28] He sought a possible explanation in one 'of the deeper contradictions of the personality of that eminent statesman and international political leader'. But things may well have been far less complicated. Stalin acted in accordance with his own view of Soviet interests and security. He was an internationalist only in so far as he felt that these interests automatically coincided with the cause of world socialism. Take, for example, his famous 'confidential comment' to Djilas in April 1945, in a conversation that included Tito as well. Stalin was not the sort of man to indulge in confidences, even with interlocutors like these, whom he admired but whose national pride he also feared. Nevertheless, the following account of the conversation, written years later by Djilas, has often justly been cited as revealing:

> Stalin presented his views on the distinctive nature of the war that was being waged: 'This war is not as in the past; whoever occupies a territory also imposes on it his own social system. Everyone imposes his own system as far as his army has power to do so. It cannot be otherwise.'
>
> He also pointed out, without going into long explanations, the meaning of his pan-Slavic policy. 'If the Slavs keep united and maintain solidarity, no one in the future will be able to move a finger. Not even a finger!' he repeated, emphasizing his thought by cleaving the air with his forefinger.
>
> Someone expressed doubt that the Germans would be able to recuperate within fifty years. But Stalin was of a different opinion. 'No, they will recover, and very quickly. It is a highly developed industrial country with an extremely skilled and numerous working class and technical intelligentsia. Give them twelve to fifteen years and they'll be on their feet again. And this is why the unity of the Slavs is important. But even apart from this, if the unity of the Slavs exists, no one will dare move a finger.'
>
> At one point he got up, hitched up his trousers as though he was about to wrestle or to box, and cried out emotionally, 'The war will soon be over. We shall recover in fifteen or twenty years, and then we'll have another go at it.'[29]

Some of the features of Stalin's political personality come through here: detached realism, exaltation of Slavic solidarity, a summary identification of social system and political institutions, concern about possible future German threats (and mistrust of a working class that had shown no sign of rebellion against Hitler, even in the final years). As we shall have occasion to see, Stalin did not rule out the formation of transitional societies, of regimes and states that could not be defined as capitalist or socialist. He referred to De Gaulle's France and, more significantly, to Yugoslavia, denying something that Djilas and Tito considered a foregone conclusion: that Yugoslavia was a soviet-type state and not 'something in between'.

Stalin had a keen sense of his own manoeuvring room. He showed no hesitation in taking advantage of his newly acquired positions of strength to create a *glacis* of loyal countries and governments along the Soviet borders. This design was by no means clear to the broad masses, or even to many politicians. Beneš, for instance, hoped that Czechoslovakia could be 'both in the East and in the West' (although it must be recalled that the country was occupied partly by Americans and partly by Russians, and that both armies did ultimately withdraw).[30] But the term *glacis*, which later gained such wide currency, was used by Léon Blum as early as 1945 in discussing Soviet policy:

> One of its obvious objectives is to establish, on the western border of the USSR, a 'glacis' of states beholden to the USSR, or at least subject to Soviet influence. . . .
> It looks very much as though Stalin intends to base the security of his country, and simultaneously the security of his own efforts, solely on the consolidation and extension of the military and industrial might of the USSR. . . .
> He is acting as the representative not of the international proletariat but of one of the world's greatest national powers.[31]

Much historiography of the USSR, primarily but not exclusively Anglo-American, has followed the line traced in that initial assessment by the French Socialist leader. With varying nuances, nearly all historians maintain that Stalin did not contemplate promoting, and still less supporting, a wave of socialist and communist revolution in Europe at the end of the war.

The 'Soviet Union', Ulam wrote, 'was bent upon expanding her sphere of power and influence but without incurring the risk of war.'[32] Brzezinski too holds that Stalin counted on a long period of peaceful coexistence with the West and urged caution and flexibility on the Communist leaders in power in the East European countries precisely for that reason.[33] According to D.F. Fleming: 'No people in the world who had first suffered as the Soviet peoples have and then won a tremendous military victory would go into Eastern Europe merely for the ride. They would be bound to make sure that the invasion gate was closed, and by the methods which seemed sound to them, not those recommended by others living at a great distance.'[34]

Fred Warner Neal is of the same view. He writes, in addition:

> Stalin's policy itself showed no sign of expansionist designs outside Eastern Europe. On the contrary, in general his foreign policy was increasingly oriented to the interior, which now meant the Soviet Union and Eastern Europe. It became ever more isolationist, ever more concentrated on that geographical area without regard to the rest of the world.[35]

That is perhaps going too far. But it is difficult to gainsay another American scholar, Robert Strauss-Hupe, who wrote in 1947: 'The western borders of the Soviet sphere of influence coincide so closely with those that Tsarist Russia sought to assure after the defeat of the Central Powers that the policy of the Tsars and of the Soviet Union seem to differ only in methods.'[36]

'Revisionist' American historiography has emphasized another, not unimportant point. From the spring of 1945, after the death of Roosevelt, some influential and authoritative American politicians argued that Soviet foreign policy was guided by an intricate and insidious design that was anything but 'isolationist'. Averell Harriman, for example, the US ambassador to Moscow, said that the Soviet Union was acting along three parallel lines. The first was in collaboration with the United States and Britain in world organization; the second sought to create an external security zone by establishing Soviet domination of neighbouring countries (which Harriman described as 'a barbaric invasion'); the third aspired to the penetration of other capitalist countries through the expanding Communist parties.[37]

Western suspicion and inclination to resist were apparent immediately, but they had to face the harsh reality of Soviet battlefield victories, more extensive and rapid than those of the Allies. Recalling the situation at the time of Yalta, Edward Stettinius, Roosevelt's last secretary of state, had this to say about Poland, the 'thorniest' problem of February 1945: 'As a result of this military situation, it was not a question of what Great Britain and the United States would permit Russia to do in Poland and in the rest of Eastern Europe , but what the two countries could persuade the Soviet Union to accept.'[38]

Indeed, if we examine the results of the famous Yalta conference of February 1945 — without being led astray by the subsequent myth that it was the site of a genuine division of the world, and still less of Roosevelt's alleged surrender to Stalin — we find that in substance there was no contradiction between Yalta and the conclusions reached in the previous October's meeting between Churchill and Stalin. But the conference did mark a great effort at peaceful coexistence, and was not meant to sharpen controversy about disputed issues. On the problem of whether or not a defeated Germany should be dismembered, the conference was deliberately imprecise; a no less unstable solution was found for Poland: elements of the exile government in London entered the government formed by the 'friends' of the USSR, the Lublin Committee. The USSR put forward rather moderate territorial demands in the Far East and pledged to enter the war against Japan within three months of the end of hostilities in Europe. It was agreed that China (Chiang Kai-shek's Nationalist China, that is) and De Gaulle's France would be recognized as first-class powers in the United Nations, where the five great powers would have veto rights as permanent members of the Security Council.[39]

The criteria and basic inspiration of the policy of spheres of influence were confirmed. And the USSR insisted that they be applied first of all in Poland, which country it wanted to be not merely friendly, but subject to the USSR. Perhaps the most balanced comment on the results of Yalta was that of D. F. Fleming, the best-known 'revisionist' American historian:

> At the time the Yalta conference adjourned there can hardly be any serious doubt that both sides wanted to cooperate, not only to win the two wars which still raged, but to live together in the post-war world. But this did not extinguish the intention of each side to restore or establish in the areas coming under its control its own kind of government.[40]

It seems equally certain that the Soviets and the British were in closer agreement than the Americans about dividing Europe into spheres of influence. After Roosevelt's death, American foreign policy became inflamed over this question, and Truman and Harriman, Forrestal and Stimson, sought to contest the pure and simple acquisition of the countries of Eastern Europe by the Soviet Union. Knowing what we do about the past behaviour and orientation of Stalin and Churchill, it is difficult to see how Yalta could have yielded any other results, however serious the consequences may have been. Giuseppe Boffa has written:

> The division of Europe into spheres of influence has often been deplored in the post-war period, and even today any other assessment may well seem cynical. Yet it is difficult to see how the historical analyst could conclude that any other solution was practicable at the end of the war. It was inevitable that the victorious great powers would retain an influence in Europe once the continent was liberated from Hitler and occupied by their armies. In any event, this was not an absolutely negative phenomenon, for the prime feature of that influence was anti-fascism. The three Allies could not exercise joint influence because their unity was not sufficiently profound. Each had to be predominant in their respective regions. This did not necessarily rule out the possibility of a high degree of collaboration, so long as each respected the legitimate interests of its interlocutor. The real problem was (and remains) how that influence would be manifested and with what results.[41]

Notes

1. Boffa, *Storia dell'Unione Sovietica,* vol. 2, p. 205.

2. René Girault, 'La sinistra di fronte alla crisi del dopoguerra: il caso francese', in *La sinistra europea,* p. 248.

3. Vincent Auriol, 'Hier-demain', in ibid., p. 249.

4. 'Unità proletaria', in *Avanti!,* 'newspaper of the movement of proletarian unity for the socialist republic', 1 August 1943.

5. See Noberto Bobbio, 'Il federalismo nel dibattito politico e culturale della Resistanza', in *L'idea dell'unificazione europea dalla prima alla seconda guerra mondiale,* S. Pistone, ed., Turin 1975, pp. 221-36.

6. Vaccarino, *Storia della Resistenza in Europa,* vol. 1, p. 249.

7. Ibid., pp. 72-73.

8. Harold Laski, *Reflexions sur la révolution de notre temps,* Paris 1946, pp. 261-63. The original English edition was published in 1943.

9. Blum, *À l'échelle humaine,* p. 170.

10. Wolfgang Abendroth, *La Socialdemocrazia in Germania,* Rome 1980, p. 167.

11. According to Soviet authors, more than 20 million were killed. Jean Elleinstein (*Storia dell'Urss,* Rome 1973, vol. 2, p. 172) speaks of 25 million dead.

12. Massimo L. Salvadori, *Storia dell'età contemporanea,* Turin 1976, p. 924.

13. See *Memoirs of Dr Edward Beneš: From Munich to New War and New Victory,* London 1954, pp. 240, 282, 284.

14. E. Schmidt, *Die Verhinderte Neuordnung,* Frankfurt-am-Main 1971, p. 68.

15. Eric J. Hobsbawm, 'Gli intellettuali e l'antifascismo', in *Storia del marxismo,* vol. 3, II, pp. 485-86.

16. See Antonio Gambino, *Le conseguenze della seconda guerra mondiale,* Bari 1972, p. 38.

17. Churchill, *The Second World War,* vol. 6, *Triumph and Tragedy,* London 1954, p. 198.

18. Boffa, *Storia dell'Unione Sovietica*, vol. 2, p. 253.
19. D.F. Fleming, *The Cold War*, vol. 1, p. 182.
20. Winston Churchill, *The Second World War*, vol. 6, *Triumph and Tragedy*, p. 369.
21. 'Segreto e personale dal primo ministro I.V. Stalin al primo ministro signor Winston Churchill', 11 June 1944, in Stalin, Churchill, Roosevelt, Attlee, Truman, *Carteggio 1941–45*, p. 258.
22. Gambino, *Le conseguenze della seconda guerra mondiale*, p. 39.
23. Churchill, *The Second World War*, vol. 6, *Triumph and Tragedy*, pp. 263 and 270.
24. See Spriano, *Storia del Pci*, vol. 5, pp. 444-46.
25. See 'istruzioni del generale Alexander per la campagna invernale', circular drafted by Luigi Longo, vice-commander of the Corpo Volontari della Libertà, 2 December 1944, now in Giorgio Rochat, ed., *Atti del Comando generale del Cnl*, Milan 1972, pp. 265-72.
26. See Spriano, *Storia del Pci*, vol. 5, pp. 449-50.
27. For the full text, see ibid., pp. 437-38.
28. Ernesto Ragionieri, preface to Churchill, Roosevelt, Stalin, *Da Teheran a Yalta*, Rome 1965, pp. xxxiv–xxxv.
29. Djilas, *Conversations With Stalin*, pp. 105-06.
30. See Vaccarino, *Storia della Resistenza in Europa*, vol. 1, p. 269.
31. Extracts from articles in *Le Populaire*, 21 and 22 July and 1 August 1945, quoted in other essays in *L'URSS vue de gauche*, p. 149.
32. Adam Ulam, *Expansion and Containment*, p. 404.
33. Zbigniew K. Brzezinski, *The Soviet Bloc: Unity and Conflict*, New York 1961, pp. 53, 56-58.
34. D.K. Fleming, *The Cold War*, vol. 1, pp. 253-54.
35. Fred Warner Neal, 'La politica di Stalin sall'Est europeo', in McNeal, *Stalin*, p. 1072.
36. Robert Strauss-Hupe, 'The Western Frontiers of Russia', in *The Review of Politics*, New York, July 1947.
37. For an analysis of the documents published in *Foreign Relations of the United States* for 1945 and of the testimony of Harriman and Stettinius, see Fejtö, *Histoires des Démocraties Populaires*, pp. 51-52, and Gar Alperovitz, *Un asso nella manica*, Turin 1966, pp. 24-28.
38. Edward Stettinius, *Roosevelt and the Russians*, London 1950, p. 266.
39. See D. Shaver Clemens, *Yalta*, Turin 1975.
40. Fleming, *The Cold War*, vol. 1, p. 208.
41. Boffa, *Storia dell'Unione Sovietica*, vol. 2, p. 257.

18

Revolution Blocked
in the West?

The partisans of the Garibaldi brigades used to sing:

> A strange soldier is on the march,
> Out of the East, with no horses tall.
> With roughened hands and sunburnt face
> He's still the most glorious knight of all.

And he was one of them, this strange soldier:

> No waving plumes or brassy medals
> But on his cap and deep in his heart
> He wears the hammer-and-sickle crossed:
> The symbol of all work and craft.

Throughout the resistance and after the Liberation, Communists clung to a triumphant image of the USSR, and to the messianic expectation on which it was based. This state of mind could perfectly well coexist with the democratic policy and perspective of the various parties, and indeed did so. As Eric Hobsbawn has noted, the national emphasis of Communist propaganda and its insistence on a harmony of efforts transcending class boundaries corresponded to genuine necessities and commitments of the struggle. Although Togliatti and Thorez missed no opportunity to pay homage to Stalin, they always added that it was not their intention to copy Russia, that their parties were independent, that they were essentially concerned to follow every wrinkle of their own societies, to seek immediate and concrete solutions. The leadership's policy was seen as a temporary necessity, a tactical ploy, especially in the working-class ranks most thoroughly imbued with radicalism and maximalism.

Officially, the Italian partisans, like the French FTP, laid down their arms and demobilized with the Liberation. In reality, many rifles and revolvers, home-made bombs and machine-guns, were hidden away with some connivance of the party organizations. At first, there were frequent instances of rebellion, episodes of summary justice meted out to individual fascists and collaborators, landowners, and industrialists; but the real sharpening of class tension came in subsequent years. In 1945 and 1946 the mass mood was a mixture of confidence and expectation. Organized proletarian forces that believed in the unity of the workers parties gained massive presence in the social arena; many were convinced that a fresh general crisis of capitalism was inevitable, that sooner or later socialist revolution would unfailingly spread from east to west.

The defeat of Nazi-fascism was a genuine liberation for everyone. The thirst for newly rediscovered freedom was reflected in open political and programmatic debates, in electoral meetings large and small, and in the flowering of newspapers produced by parties and movements that had emerged from the resistance. Moderate, middle-of-the-road, and reformist forces were organizing too. In Italy and France, West Germany and Belgium, Austria and Hungary, Chrisian Democratic and Christian-Social parties coalesced around the Catholic church; they enjoyed a powerful peasant base, strong support from bourgeois and petty-bourgeois classes, and had a working-class component too. These groupings sought to become mass parties and to fight the Communists on their own ground. Socialists and Social Democrats also emerged from their long years of crisis. Although they were uncertain whether to found a new international organization, they did have a base among the current of left reformist opinion which remained distinct from, and resisted being absorbed by, the Communists.

This multicoloured panorama is often obscured by adherents of a revisionist historical tendency which, on the basis of political and ideological entreaties and recriminations, insists that revolutionary opportunities were missed in the two major countries of the Western European continent. This theory holds that the radical development of the 'red' resistance movements was blocked by the Communist parties, or by their Stalinist leaderships. But there is also a parallel argument, based more strongly on 'ifs', which targets Stalin directly. The victorious USSR it is said, failed to fulfil its proper task as the first socialist country: to hold aloft the banner of socialist revolution in Western Europe.

This is an old Trotskyist thesis, presented anew in 1944 and 1945 almost exactly as it had been argued in 1935–37. It must immediately be added, however, that the most authoritative scholar of Trotskyist inspiration, Isaac Deutscher, was far more cautious. On the one hand, he noted that Stalin may have feared a spread of revolution in the west, which would have endangered the political and ideological foundations of his system of bureaucratic and dictatorial power. On the other hand, Deutscher nevertheless presented Stalin's intentions as double-edged, calling them simultaneously conservative and revolutionary. In the view of the Polish historian, Stalin remained convinced that the Western working classes would not make a real socialist revolution. (As far as the German workers were concerned, he is said to have admitted to a visitor that 'Communism suits Germany like a saddle suits a cow'.) But Stalin also held that the process of world revolution was ultimately irrepressible. Deutscher summed up as follows the difference between Stalin on the one hand and Lenin and Trotsky on the other: the latter fixed their attention on the French, German, and British working classes, whereas Stalin looked primarily to revolutions in Warsaw, Bucharest, Belgrade, and Prague. In other words, he had shifted from socialism in one country to socialism in one region. [1]

Far more adamant in accusing Stalin of a counter-revolutionary policy is Fernando Claudín, who argues that his supreme objective was to reach a lasting compromise with American imperialism in order 'to assume world leadership in partnership'. In Europe the intent was to 'give up the West' (diplomatically and politically speaking) 'in order to guarantee the East'. Claudin bases his argument on the thesis that France and Italy in particular were ripe for revolution in 1945, and he adds a consideration about China too:

One of the main aims of Washington in the Pacific war was to consolidate the Chiang Kai-shek regime, thanks to which American capitalism could be assured of economic penetration and political control in China. Success in this enterprise would be made considerably easier if the Chinese Communists continued their collaboration with the Kuomintang bourgeoisie in the same spirit of loyalty and moderation which had been shown by the Italian and French Communists in collaborating with their own bourgoisies. To achieve this purpose Washington needed the good offices of Stalin. . . . The same factors which forced Washington into a policy of conciliation towards Moscow, in spite of the instinctive anti-Communism of Truman and his team, make it even clearer to what extent the overall relation of forces in Europe in the spring and summer of 1945 was swinging in favour of a bold revolutionary policy in the countries where internal conditions were also favourable. In the event of an Anglo-American military intervention against the revolutionary movement, the

Soviet Union was in an exceptionally favourable military and strategic position to give decisive military help.[2]

Since Stalin actually had not intention of furnishing such help — and we shall see that the question was posed retrospectively when the Cominform was created in 1947, the Yugoslav Communists openly accusing their Italian and French comrades of opportunism and virtual cowardice for not having taken power in 1945 — the problem can be reformulated this way: did the USSR generally underestimate the new features of the world situation or not? This is the criticism made by the Italian Communist scholar Adriano Guerra:

> Adequate reflection about the role of the Soviet state in the new phase of history was completely lacking in the Communist movement (and most of all in Moscow, on Stalin's part). The fact that the problem of security was posed in the same terms as in the thirties clearly betrays not only a fundamentally Eurocentric view of the international situation but also a deep-rooted pessimism about the possibilities of new and significant steps forward for socialism beyond the borders of the USSR through the development of the democratic struggle.[3]

Post-war vistas were not limited to the logic of spheres of influence. Neither Stalin nor the Anglo-Americans foresaw the course and outcome of the Chinese revolution, the seizure of power by Mao's Communists in 1948–49. No less surprising was the fight for emancipation of the colonial peoples in Africa and Asia. But to return to the question posed above, let us examine to what extent Stalin can justly be accused of myopia. Was his supposed desire to curb revolutionary developments in 1945 the decisive 'subjective' factor, or were there far more substantial objective limits?

On the whole, if we compare the European situation at the end of the two world wars, it is undeniable that the first post-war revolutionary upsurge was far more sweeping and tempestuous, investing Germany and Poland, Italy and Hungary. The military power of the victors in the Second World War was wholly intact in the late forties. Most of the countries of Europe — with the exception of Yugoslavia, and of Greece to some extent — had been liberated not by the resistance but by the offensive of the Allied armies. In Germany there had been no mass opposition to Hitlerism even in the war's final year, and in the other countries popular insurrections had not broken out universally. Would the situation have been different if Stalin had pressed for socialist revolution in Western Europe? It would have been inconceivable to break the Alliance before Japan was defeated.

The USSR had already lost twenty million dead in the 'great patriotic war'. Could the Red Army have been committed to a revolutionary war in the West? It is not simply a matter of gauging the Kremlin's intentions. The question concerns the nature and limits of the liberation movement in Europe.

It may be that Stalin underestimated the potential of independent mass movements and popular shifts to the left, of 'democratic development'. It is probable, for example, that he had ruled out the possibility of a Labour victory in Britain. Indeed, it seems certain that at Yalta he expressed assurance that Churchill would win the July 1945 elections, 'since the people would understand that they needed a leader, and who could be a better leader than he who had won the victory?'[4] But the liberation movement that culminated in national insurrections in France in the summer of 1944 and in northern Italy in the spring of 1945 inevitably remained no more than a national, anti-fascist, and democratic upheaval (for various reasons, primarily because it occurred in the context of the advance of the Anglo-American armies, which were determined to keep the situation well in hand).

The real problem facing the Communist parties of these countries was to bring the broad popular masses, primarily the workers, into the movement and to bring their weight to bear politically and socially; it was certainly not to take power. The limits of this movement were quite clear to the top leaders of the PCI and the PCF from Togliatti to Longo and Secchia, from Thorez to Duclos and Frachon. Neither the external nor the internal conditions for socialist revolution were at hand. Pietro Secchia, the Italian Communist leader who has always evinced greatest dissatisfaction with what the resistance 'failed to achieve', was none the less quite explicit both in detailing its real limits and in denying that any more advanced prospects were possible:

> The resistance was limited not because there were no socialist perspectives or slogans, not because the programme of post-liberation structural reforms was not sufficiently detailed, and not because the wrong sort of unity was achieved. Nor was it because the tricolour was stuck in the gun barrels instead of the red flag. The fundamental reason is that we did not manage to make the resistance a broader and more robust movement, with more numerous, better trained, and more powerfully armed partisan detachments capable of liberating entire regions so that upon their arrival the Anglo-Americans would have faced an organic army and a solidly rooted people's power.[5]

These observations express an obvious bitterness at not having managed to duplicate the Yugoslav experience (primarily as regards the breadth of the partisan struggle and its component of social revolution), which strongly influenced the Italian Communists during the liberation war in the North. But Togliatti too was well aware of the limits of the resistance, although he considered the national insurrection a great act of democratic revolution. In the directives sent to his comrades in the North, he wrote: 'Always remember that the insurrection we want is aimed not at imposing socialist and communist political and social transformations, but at national liberation and the destruction of fascism. All other problems will be resolved by the people later, once all of Italy is liberated, through a free popular consultation and the election of a Constituent Assembly.'[6]

Togliatti's reasoning was based on two considerations. First: 'there has been no revolution in this country to destroy an entire social order violently and lay the basis for a new one'.[7] Second: a 'Greek development' had to be avoided at all costs. In other words, the Italian partisans could not allow themselves to be drawn into a civil war against the Allied armies and the Italian conservative and reactionary forces (who were not only present, but on the offensive in parts of liberated Italy). Togliatti was almost obsessed with this danger. As early as 1944 he warned his party comrades not to fall into any provocation that could usher in a civil war, which would inevitably lead to 'a definitive catastrophe for the country'.[8] At a PCI National Council meeting held in Rome on the eve of the liberation of the North, he indicated as among the party's fundamental objectives: 'To prevent the liberation of the North from being accompanied by clashes and conflicts that could create serious misunderstandings and disagreements between the people and the liberating Allied forces. To maintain the most fraternal unity and collaboration with the Allied forces.'[9]

On this occasion, Togliatti again spoke of a 'Greek perspective':

The tendency that seeks a gradual sharpening of political and class struggles . . . during the liberation of the North would like to force upon Italy what I would call a Greek perspective: the prospect of a violent clash, of armed conflict, between the forces of the anti-fascist front and those of the police and army, commanded by anti-democratic elements. The goal of this tendency . . . backed by obscure and well-organized forces, is to avert any popular consultation, to prolong the occupation of Italy by the liberating Allied armies indefinitely, and thus to erect a virtually insuperable obstacle to the advance of the democratic forces.'[10]

Allied military administration in the liberated North continued throughout 1945. Two years later, Togliatti told Luigi Longo and Eugenio Reale, who were on their way to Poland as delgates to the conference that founded the Cominform: 'If they chide you for our inability to take power or for having been thrown out of the government, tell them that we could not turn Italy into another Greece. Not only in our own interest, but also in the Soviet interest.'[11]

It is worth noting that this reasoning guided Togliatti's political leadership and thought for twenty years, and was often intertwined with his insistence on a strategy based on the development of political democracy and on structural reforms. Different emphases emerged at different times, for this too is a discussion about 'ifs'. In 1945–47 Togliatti stressed that a democratic revolution had only just *begun*[12] (and with the onset of the Cold War he felt that all the freedoms won would be under fresh attack).[13] In 1957, speaking to a very special audience (the representatives of sixty-four Communist parties meeting in Moscow, where Togliatti found himself somewhat isolated), he played down the endogenous factors and said;

> When the war ended it would not have been difficult to take power and inaugurate the construction of a socialist society in Italy. The majority of the people would have followed us. But the country was occupied by the American and British armies, and this road could not have been taken, because an insurrection against these armies would have been a political absurdity condemned to certain defeat.[14]

In 1962 he reiterated the point when speaking to the delegates of the Tenth Congress of the PCI, but now the emphasis had once more shifted to the claim that the 'main road' that had been travelled had been the only possible one:

> It is often said that the foreign occupation of national territory, which made the victory of a popular insurrection impossible, was the decisive factor in Communist policy after the liberation. In reality, our policy was inspired and dictated by far more profound motives. A union of democratic forces had been forged in the resistance which included, socially, groupings of the progressive middle bourgeoisie and politically a good part of the Catholic mass movement. We were among the leading promoters, organizers, and directors of this unity, which had its own programme for the reform of the whole life of the country. . . . Our policy was to struggle openly and consistently for this solution, which entailed a democratic development and social reform oriented in the direction of socialism.[15]

The creation of a regime of advanced political democracy, the welding together of a new bloc of social forces, was the touchstone of several Communist parties immediately after the war. The often rather problematical relation between this orientation and the logic of the spheres-of-influence policy generated fresh contradictions for the Communist movement. Was the realism of the Italian Communists (and of the French, of whom we will have occasion to speak later) the product of specific advice from Moscow? Scant documentation is available. It is known that Stalin tried to dissuade the Greek Communists from opposing the British head on.[16] For France we have a hint from one of the resistance leaders, Charles Tillon, the main organizer of the FTP (he was later expelled from the party). Tillon states in his memoirs that in the autumn of 1944 the Soviets advised the French Communists 'not to mount the slightest opposition to the demands of De Gaulle or the Allies.[17] For the PCI there is an elusive remark in the discussion of this subject by Emilio Sereni, one of the Milan organizers of the April 1945 national insurrection.

Sereni maintains that it is by no means certain that an attempted seizure of power by Italian Communists in the surgent North at the end of April 1945 would have been repressed by Anglo-American troops. He says that there were other reasons why the party was loath to attempt such a feat. One of them had to do with internal factors: fear of creating a schism in the country between the advanced North and the Centre-South, 'the less industrialized and economically, socially, and politically more backward region, which would have remained permanently subject to occupation by the Western Allies (as happened to Germany)'. The second basic reason was this:

> The establishment of a Communist regime in northern Italy would have automatically and inevitably caused a very serious crisis in the Allied coalition, just when the Allies were still deeply involved in the final phase of the war against Hitler's Germany and Japanese militarism. . . . If I am not mistaken, it was not impossible to get the opinion of our Soviet comrades on this matter, albeit in a most indirect form. From their vantage point, which offered a much broader view of the situation than ours, their appreciation of the dangers, of the difficulties and of the incipient fracturing of the Allied coalition, seemed little different from ours.[18]

Whatever their motivation in rejecting a revolutionary solution, there is no doubt that the leaders of the PCI, without any appreciable resistance from the rank and file, strove to avert it both in April 1945 and in the subsequent period. It is equally certain that the French Communists made a similar choice the year before, between June and autumn 1944. The objective situation was different, of course. The role of France in the concert of great powers had been recognized, with Stalin's aid; the resistance had a charismatic leader in De Gaulle. But the French resistance had never attained the degree of unity of the Italian, nor its numerical weight. The PCF's tactic had been to form small groups of sappers and saboteurs rather than to organize large-scale partisan contingents. The figures cited by Communist sources are significant: in April 1944, a scant two months before the Allied landing in Normandy, the FFI (Forces Françaises de l'Intérieur) had a grand total of barely 4,200 fighters, 'including unarmed or poorly armed men'.[19] Even the summer insurrection, though it achieved great glory for which the PCF was centrally responsible revealed deficiencies in various zones.

The PCF line, forcefully reaffirmed by Thorez when he was pardoned by De Gaulle and allowed to return to the country in November 1944, was no different from Togliatti's after the 'Salerno turn' of March of the same year. After uniting, at least formally, with the other components of the resistance in the CNR in May 1943, the French Communist Party did its utmost in 1943 and 1944 to fight for an insurrection aimed at national independence in which the popular forces grouped around De Gaulle would take the initiative. It is significant that in the interests of achieving this objective, the PCF rejected an offer from the French Socialist Party in November 1943 to form a left union. The rejection came in a confidential letter of the PCF Central Committee addressed to the 'Clandestine Socialist Party'. This letter, while recalling that 'the unity of the working class is and has always been our objective', obstinately reiterated all the PCF positions of 1939–40. Its political message was clear: at the moment we shall not seek closer unity of the workers parties through the creation of joint Socialist–Communist Committees. 'What is important today is sincerity in relations and in action, and the will to struggle, of the various elements of the resistance, their will to unite all the French people in the battle to liberate France, to assure its absolute independence, both political and economic, and to restore its grandeur.'[20]

The PCF letter professed complete agreement with General De Gaulle and concluded by rejecting the Socialist offer in these terms:

> We believe that we have demonstrated that working-class unity can be realized only through the resistance movements. The PCF-SP Action Committee that you propose, far from representing progress or contributing to fortifying the unity of the resistance, would lead to a division of the patriotic forces. As far as relations with us are concerned, such an Action

Committee is redundant, since we meet already in the various resistance organs.

It is an eloquent document. We shall have to take due note of it when examining the turbulent course of a fresh attempt to fuse the two parties. But the PCF letter is unambiguous testimony to the essential concerns of the French Communists: not to isolate themselves, to seek the broadest possible national unity, loyally to acknowledge De Gaulle's leadership. One of the basic articles of the 'Charter' of the National Resistance Committee (CNR), drafted by PCF representative Pierre Villon, reads: 'It shall be our task to defend the nation's political and economic independence, to restore the power, greatness, and universal mission of France.'[21]

Such watchwords tallied perfectly with the deep commitment of the French Communists — who could proudly call themselves the *parti des fusillés* — to the resistance: they had been among the first to initiate it, and their heroic sacrifices, including the loss of tens of thousands of militants, showed how genuine was the patriotism that now earned them not only new sympathy but also unanimous recognition from the other political forces. The party image of Popular Front days was emerging anew; with Thorez's return to France, the emphasis was increasingly on the restoration of French 'grandeur'. Unite and work to rebuild the fatherland: that was now the party motto. Since Nazi Germany was not yet defeated definitively, this slogan was joined to another, issued by Thorez in his triumphant first meeting at the Vel d'Hiv on 30 November 1944: 'A single state, a single police force, a single army!'[22] It is time, he said, addressing his own reluctant comrades most of all, to dissolve the armed groups of 'snipers and partisans' and to strengthen the Liberation Army.

Although this line was opposed by some of the Communist leaders who had emerged in the resistance, it was none the less applied without hesitation, as the PCF collaborated with the De Gaulle government and awaited a new rise of party strength under the reformed parliamentary democracy that Thorez sought to establish through a Constituent Assembly. De Gaulle had certainly not turned pro-Communist. He knew that collaboration with the PCF entailed risks, but he accepted their arduous cohabitation. The description in his memoirs of Thorez's role 'upon his return from the USSR' amounts to a certificate of merit issued in the name of France:

> As for Thorez, although he sought to act in the interest of Communism, on many occasions he served the general interest. Immediately upon his return to France, he endeavoured to halt the outbursts of the 'patriotic

militias' that some of his comrades persisted in maintaining in a new underground. To the extent that the bleak and stern rigidity of his party allowed him, he opposed attempts to have the liberation committees endorse the acts of violence that fanatical groups sought to carry out. He never neglected to urge the many workers (especially miners) who attended his meetings to work as hard as they could and to produce at all costs. Was this merely for tactical reasons? It is not my business to judge. For me it was sufficient that the interests of France were served.[23]

Thorez, like Togliatti before him, joined the government. The similarities in the policies the two leaders recommended for their respective parties are significant: both extended a hand to Catholic public opinion; both conceived of national unity and solidarity going well beyond mere working-class unity. Thorez, too, waged an internal struggle against revolutionary impatience. After telling the Central Committee quite clearly in January 1945 that 'at present we do not formulate any demands of a socialist or communist character',[24] he rejected recurrent temptations of the sort even more explicitly at the Tenth Congress in June of that same year, calling them 'provocations of reaction' designed to drive 'the most advanced elements of democracy and the working class into adventures, so as to divide the people'. He warned party members and workers against lingering instances of armed rebellion, against 'supposed *maquis* now reorganizing, against fresh incitement of attacks, against summary executions'.[25]

The causes of these phenomena were complex. In part they were a more or less inevitable after-effect of the war, but they also reflected dissatisfaction, general disappointment in a political and social situation in which the conservative forces soon raised their heads again (the purge of collaborators, cautious enough in France, was a resounding failure in Italy). But these instances of rebellion never burgeoned into a mass movement, nor did they induce party leaders to break off collaboration with other political forces in the government. The initiative for the expulsion of the Communists from the government in 1947, in fact, came from these Catholic and Social Democratic forces.

Subsequent party historiography has tried to emphasize the issues that divided the PCF from De Gaulle from 1944–45 onwards. But it also polemicizes against the claim that an opportunity for proletarian revolution was missed:

The thesis that the working class missed the boat is both absurd and hypocritical, because the Anglo-American armies controlled the national territory and its supply, while French and international reaction hoped that the French proletariat would make precisely that capital error. The workers would have been isolated from the rest of the population, which would not have supported or followed what would have been nothing more than a Blanquist *putsch*. It would have brought repression and caused a sharp reduction of the democratic forces in France.[26]

In September 1947 (long before the radicalization of the 1960s), when the Yugoslav Communists, apparently with Soviet support, raised the ill-founded thesis that a revolutionary opportunity had been missed, they were rebutted with extreme timidity by Jacques Duclos, who had led the PCF in the resistance. But before that bitter month arrived, the French and Italian Communists enjoyed some further time in the sun.

Notes

1. Deutscher, *Stalin*, pp. 534-55.
2. Claudín, *The Communist Movement*, pp. 427-28.
3. Guerra, *Gli anni del Cominform*, p. 22.
4. See Churchill, *The Second World War*, vol. 6, *Triumph and Tragedy*, p. 344. For a subsequent erroneous prediction by Stalin that the Conservatives would win with a majority of eighty seats, see Fontaine, *History of the Cold War*, p. 255.
5. Pietro Secchia, 'Perché la Resistenza non ha dato di piú, *Città Futura*, no. 9, April 1965.
6. See the text of the directives sent by Togliatti to the PCI's northern headquarters in April 1945, *Rinascita—Il contemporaneo*, no. 8, August 1965.
7. 'La nostra politica nazionale', in Palmiro Togliatti, *Discorsi alla Costituente*, Rome 1973, p. 36.
8. From a speech delivered in Pergola, Florence, 3 October 1944, collected with other speeches in Palmiro Togliatti, *Politica comunista*, Rome 1945, p. 89.
9. 'Il Pci nella lotta contro il fascismo e per la democrazia', in ibid., p. 259.
10. Ibid., p. 249.
11. Eugenio Reale, *Nascita del Cominform*, Milan 1958, p. 17.
12. On 2 June 1945 he said, 'A profound process of renovation, which we do not hesitate to call a democratic revolution, has now begun and is under way.' From 'Discorso alle donne' in Togliatti, *Politica comunista*, p. 303.
13. See Togliatti, 'Il nostro congresso', *Rinascita*, vol. 4, no. 11-12, November-December 1947, pp. 313-15.
14. Togliatti, 'Sugli orientamenti politici del nostro partito', *Rinascita*, vol. 16, no. 11, November 1959, p. 757.
15. From the report to the Tenth Congress of the PCI (Rome, December 1962), in Togliatti, *Nella democrazia e nella pace verso il socialismo*, Rome 1963, p. 186.
16. See Solaro, *Storia del Partito comunista greco*, p. 122.
17. Charles Tillon, *On Chantait Rouge*, Paris 1965, p. 504.
18. Emilio Sereni, 'La scelta del 1943–45', *Rinascita*, vol. 28. no. 5, 29 January 1971.
19. See 'Annexe no. 1', published in 'La libération de France', *Cahiers d'Histoire de*

l'Institut Maurice Thorez, no. 8-9, Paris 1974.

20. The letter is one of a number of documents that may be consulted in the Musée de la Résistance in Ivry-sur-Seine; there is no further specific classification.

21. See Girault, 'La sinistra di fronte alla crisi del dopoguerra: il caso francese', p. 248.

22. See Jacques Fauvet, *Histoire du Parti communiste français*, Paris 1965, vol. 2, p. 158.

23. Charles De Gaulle, *Mémoires de guerre*, vol. 3, *Le salut*, Paris 1959, p. 101.

24. 'S'unir, combattre, travailler', report presented in Ivry on 21 January 1945, in Maurice Thorez, *Oeuvres*, Paris 1960, vol. 20, p. 183.

25. 'Une politique française', report to the Tenth Congress of the PCF 26 June 1945, in Thorez, *Oeuvres*, Paris 1963, vol. 21, p. 127.

26. Jean Gacon, 'Première expérience De Gaulle', *Recherches Internationales*, no. 44-45, July-December 1964, p. 244.

19
Communists Proliferate

The famous opening sentence of Marx and Engels's *Communist Manifesto* would have been equally applicable almost exactly a century after it was written between 1945 and 1948. Once again Communism was a spectre haunting Europe, in at least one sense. For entire peoples it was still an unknown quantity; for the poor it meant hope; for the privileged classes, who felt that they were on the point of being disposed, it was a nightmare. Bertaolt Brecht put it this way in 1945, setting the *Manifesto* itself to verse:

> It speaks in many tongues: in all. And in many still is silent.
> A guest in poor abodes, an bogey in the palaces,
> It has come to stay for ever more: Communism is its name.[1]

But in the languages of Europe, Communism now spoke as a government party: from Iceland to Denmark, Belgium to Holland and Luxemburg, from France to Italy, Sweden to Norway and Finland, Austria to Czechoslovakia, not to mention the obvious cases of Poland, Hungary, Albania, Romania, Yugoslavia, and Bulgaria. Even in Germany divided into four occupation zones (British, French, American and Soviet), an organized workers movement was rising from the ashes, and a Communist component was present in it from the very outset, not only where it 'climbed aboard giant tanks' in the Red Army's wake (to use Brecht's imagery again) but also in Hamburg and Hesse.

It was an exceptional moment in many respects, destined to fade rapidly once the profound division of Europe set in. To assess this novel shift to the left by masses of people and political forces, we must begin from this time of fears and hopes, messianic expectations and concrete projects of reform and reconstruction. Let us take an example that is both an exception and a confirmation of the rule: Britain. Here the Communists enjoyed no electoral success, and in

1946 appealed in vain, for the nth time, to be admitted to the Labour Party.[2] But Labour's triumph in the July 1945 elections (393 seats in parliament against 163 for the Conservatives) was unprecedented. For the first time, there was a government of left forces which, while not Communist, earned their leftist credentials with a great programme of social services and nationalization in the credit and industrial sectors, with a perspective not merely of the Welfare State but of a socialist society. A grand idea of the European left was realized: an attempt was made 'to govern the economy'. Reformists saw this as a corpus of specific programmatic objectives, revolutionaries as a period of preparation for transforming the relations of production.[3]

British Labourism had an international vitality that made it a pole of attraction for European Socialists. In March 1945 a meeting was held in London to resuscitate the Second International, but the road proved long and rocky. Prejudice against Communists was still strong in the Labour ranks, but for the moment the anti-fascist and anti-capitalist spirit was even stronger, and to many this suggested the hope that British Labourism might serve as a bridge between Russian Bolshevism and great American democracy.[4]

No less symptomatic was the rebirth — once again in London, and even before the war's end: in February 1945, as the three great powers were meeting in Yalta — of a united trade-union movement whose aim was to form a world association of workers. The London conference, at which American trade unionists played a major role, led to the birth of the World Federation of Trade Unions (WFTU) at a Paris conference in October of the same year. When the Cold War broke out the WFTU was unable to maintain its unity (the atmosphere was already somewhat gloomy at the Paris conference). Nevertheless, it is significant that it was thought necessary to form an organization to represent the workers' interests, an independent trade union openly antithetical to the forces of capital and imperialist colonialism, in an effort to bring these interests to bear on the fate of the post-war world through international labour unity. All three great powers sent messages to the London conference, which heard the harmonious voices of the large American affiliates of the CIO, official Soviet union representatives, British trade unionists, the reborn French CGT, and even — though not without discord and suspicion — the Italian CGIL, in which the Communist component was already predominant, represented by one of its top leaders, Giuseppe Di Vittorio. Trade-union militants from the colonial countries brought to the conference the full force of their denunciation of inhuman conditions of exploitation and the desire of their peoples for national emancipation.[5] The British trade unionists themselves offered an inspiring model: they boasted of six million active and militant members.[6]

No less interesting were events in Germany in the 'year zero'. Here as elsewhere, the anti-Communist pressure of the Western occupying powers was felt very soon. But Germany was not immune to the general shift to the left. A trade-union federation was formed in the Soviet occupation zone in June 1945 (and in the French zone too), and the factory elections held in the British and American zones in 1945 yielded interesting results, Communist representatives scoring well.[7]

We may therefore begin with this observation: immediately after the war, before Europe was visibly split into two counterposed camps, the 'left' was clearly on the rise. And the growth of the Communist parties was part and parcel of this wider process.

In chapter one I presented a brief group portrait of the Communist parties on the eve of the Second World War: almost all of them were persecuted and underground. Outside the Soviet Union, they had slightly more than a million members, while the Soviet Communist Party alone had 1.6 million. Now the figures had multiplied many fold. First there was the phenomenal growth of the Chinese Communist Party, which took in huge levies of peasant-soldiers during the war, recruiting 800,000 members in 1940. In 1945 there were 1,211,128 members.[8] In the USSR too a new levy had come into the party, mostly soldiers: by 1945 there were 5.7 million party members (of whom 1.8 million were candidate members). According to a Soviet source, there were 20 million Communists world-wide by the end of the war.[9] The total given by Western sources was not very different: about 14 million Communists outside the USSR in 1948, in Europe, Africa, Asia, and the two Americas.[10]

About 10 million of these 14 million were in Europe. But other nerve centres of the world Communist movement were beginning to arise, especially in the Far East. The bitter war between Nationalists and Communists in China resumed in 1946,[11] and Communist strength rose to 2.7 million by 1947. In Vietnam the Communists were leading a national revolution. The Democratic Republic of Vietnam was born in Hanoi on 2 September 1945, after the anti-Japanese August insurrection. Ho Chi Minh judged the 'moment favourable': the objective was to win democratic rights and national independence.[12] Revolution had broken out in Indonesia too, and the Communists — who became a powerful mass party some ten years later — were active in it. In India and Japan the Communist movement experienced notable political and numerical growth. In August 1946 'after a series of peasant revolts, a people's republic based on rural councils formed on Communist initiative to implement and control an agrarian reform arose over a vast territory of south-eastern India.'[13] The Japanese CP won 2 million votes in the first post-war elections, in 1946.[14]

In Latin American there was a robust trade-union movement, with a union federation, headed by the Mexican Lombardo Toledano, representing workers of fifteen countries. The Cuban CP was the largest, with 200,000 members; the Argentinian CP had about 40,000, the Brazilian 20,000, the Mexican 30,000. There may have been as many as 400,000 Communists in Latin America as a whole, though the figure is somewhat doubtful.[15] In the United States the Communist Party reached 100,000 members, before the entire movement was affected by an event that we will consider shortly.

The Communists had an undoubted presence in the Middle East and North Africa, though it is difficult to gauge the actual membership figures. In Europe, however, the statistics are less uncertain, if not always crystal clear. It was on the old continent, East and West alike, that the Communist expansion was greatest. The East-West division was not hard and fast at first. The Czechoslovak party, for instance, developed under a democratic political system and was not dissimilar to the French and Italian parties; in fact, it enjoyed somewhat greater success in free elections. Numerical growth was nothing less than sensational in the states that were turned into 'people's democracies' in the Soviet sphere of influence; here membership was undoubtedly encouraged by state pressure, though there was some degree of spontaneous mass adherence.

The figures speak eloquently. Between 1945 and 1948 the membership of the Romanian and Hungarian Communist parties rose from several thousand to half a million and more each. The Polish Workers Party, which fused with the left Socialists, reached almost a million and a half members in 1948. In the Soviet occupation zone in Germany, the Communist Party — which also fused with the Socialist Party in a new formation, the Socialist Unity Party of Germany, SED — had more than a million members. The Albanian party, founded in 1941, had 45,000 members in 1947. The Czechoslovak Communist Party, with more than half a million members in 1945, had doubled its strength by 1948. In Yugoslavia the number of Communists rose from 141,000 in 1945 to half a million in 1948. The Bulgarian Communist Party — the party of Dimitrov and Kolarov

— also expanded powerfully, from 15,000 members in 1945 to 495,000 in 1948. In total, then, the Communist parties of the 'people's democracies' had a good 7 million members, a million more than the CPSU.[16]

Shifting to the West, we find that the rise of the left parties (including the Communists), although halted around 1948, was as rapid as in Eastern Europe during the first two years after the war. The Iberian peninsula — where the dictators Salazar in Portugal and Franco in Spain stayed out of the war and held onto power — was a painful exception. The Cold War later turned these countries into Anglo-American satellites, and the fate of the militants of the workers movement, Socialists and Communists alike, was tragic. The Portuguese Communist Party, in which Alvaro Cunhal's star was rising (he was later arrested, in 1949), remained illegal. Violent repression resumed in Spain, as the Republican government-in-exile (joined by the young Santiago Carrillo as a representative of the Communists) waited in vain for some concrete measure to follow the condemnation of the Francoist regime at the Potsdam Conference and the United Nations General Assembly. The PCE had placed its hopes on a popular uprising, on partisan action organized from the Pyrenees, but without success.[17]

In France the situation was completely different. At its Tenth Congress the PCF boasted 906,727 members. Growth had been tumultuous indeed, for there were only half a million members at the beginning of 1945. The electoral leap forward was even greater: the PCF became the country's largest party in the elections of October 1945, garnering 5 million votes, more than three and a half times the 1936 figure (although the electorate was much larger), 500,000 more than the Socialists. One-fourth of the electorate voted Communist. In the two elections of 1946 the Communists gained a further 200,000 votes on 2 June and 300,000 on 10 November. Socialists and Communists commanded a large majority in the Constituent Assembly.

In Italy the PCI became a mass party even faster. At its Fifth Congress, at the end of 1945, the party had 1,770,896 members; the figure rose to two and a quarter million by the end of 1947. If parties are organized democracy, as Togliatti once said, then Italy surely exhibited unusual democratic vitality. Apart from the Communists, there were the Socialists PSI); the new Catholic party, Christian Democracy; and the mass organizations of the united union federation, the CGIL, which had 5,735,000 members at the time of its First Congress in June 1947. In the 1948 elections to the Constituent Assembly the Socialists overtook the Communists (21 per cent of the vote for the former, 19 per cent for the latter), while DC won 35 per cent. But the strength of the left parties was decisive in the republican victory in the referendum on the monarchy held concurrently with the elections.

If the presence of a strong Communist component became a permanent feature of Italian and French political life throughout the post-war period, the same cannot be said of the nations of central-western and northern Europe. Between 1945 and 1947, however, the Communists made palpable gains everywhere. The Belgian CP peaked in 1945, with 100,000 members. In that year the Danish party had 75,000, the Dutch 53,000, the Swedish 40,000, and the Norwegian 45,000. Most surprising of all, given Finland's role in the war, was the success of the Finnish CP, which had 150,000 members and became the biggest Communist party of northern Europe. That figure was equalled by the CP in Austria (a country occupied by the four victorious powers). There were fewer than 50,000 British Communists, while the Greek CP had more than 70,000 in 1945. In Italy, France, and Finland, the Communist vote was close to or just above 20 per cent, while it was more than 10 per cent in Belgium, Denmark, Luxemburg, Norway, Holland, and Sweden in 1945 and 1946. Even in neutral Switzerland, where the CP called itself the 'Labour Party' and had 13,500 members, the Communists won 5 per cent of the vote in 1947. In Germany's Western occupation zones Communist influence proved significant in the first elections to regional assemblies in 1946 and 1947: despite efforts by the Allied Command to counter them, the Communists secured more than 10 per cent of the vote.[18]

It is not easy to enumerate all the various factors in this success, although popular revolt was certainly among them. Communist expansion was undoubtedly part and parcel of the general leftist surge. Had not the Communists stood in the front ranks of the struggle in many countries during the war? Now they were also upholding a reasonable programme for reconstruction, offering positive solutions to the most urgent problems of the day, advocating a package of reforms that seemed not only sensible but also designed to make sure that there could be no return to fascist barbarism in social institutions. A utopian 'ideal' of total messianic emancipation was put forward.

In the eyes of the new generations who had grown up in the war, Marxism and Leninism seemed to offer the certainty of a correct interpretation of history, delineating the tortuous pathways through which it moved. Intellectual elites arose who were determined to spread Marxism, to 'restore' it before its dogmatic aspect was revealed. Works poured out of the London School of Economics and the colleges of Cambridge, where youth were educated with a Marxist bent. The biologist J.B.S. Haldane was a Communist. Christopher Hill, historian of the English revolution, wrote an enthusiastic portrait of Lenin and the Russian revolution, noting that 'the influence of the USSR and of Communism is far greater today than at the time of Lenin's death: they have acquired the prestige of demonstrated success.'[19] Hill went further: ' . . . the USSR has demonstrated in practice that socialism is a system which can work even under the most unpromising conditions.' The great historian of Bolshevism E.H. Carr was clearly pro-Soviet.[20] Joseph Needham and J.D. Bernal were strongly influenced by dialectical materialism.

In France philosophers, scientists, artists, and writers were active in the Communist Party: Frédéric Joliot-Curie, Paul Langevin, Pablo Picasso, Fernand Léger, Louis Aragon, Paul Éluard, and a host of economists and scientific researchers. Among the new levies of Communist historians were Emmanuel Le Roy Ladurie and Albert Soboul. Pierre George and Henri Lefebvre, Jean Paulhan and Georges Lefebvre contributed articles to the new series of the journal *La Pensée*, which resumed publication with an issue devoted to Georges Politzer, who had died a hero of the resistance.

In the United States the world of literature and cinema was peopled by 'fellow travellers'. Likewise in Italy. Vittorini, Pavese, Pratolini, and Bilenchi were Communist authors who wrote of Communist workers themselves. The historian Delio Cantimori and the archaeologist Ranuccio Bianchi Bandinelli were Communists, as were humanist philosophers like Concetto Marchesi, Antonio Banfi, and Ludovico Geymonat. Poets like Umberto Saba, Salvatore Quasimodo, and Alfonso Gatto sang of the Garibaldian heroes of the second Risorgimento. As is always the case with intellectuals, these people were Communists each in their own way, but moral fervour and a desire to strive for the birth of a new humanity had not yet been stifled by aesthetic dogmas or ideological censorship. The 'new man', Louis Aragon lyrically affirmed already exists: he is *communist man:*

> Communist man, the man towards whom humanity is on the march, was revealed with great clarity in these years by exceptional circumstances. Not as an exception, though. It was a time when heroism was no longer exceptional but a mass phenomenon. . . .From the trials there emerged above all, this image of communist man. In whom are fused the features of workers, peasants, intellectuals, as different as the clouds in the sky, but coming together in courage and sacrifice, in that morality common to all men against the enemy of man, labour.[21]

Intellectuals, like young people, were moved to join the Communist movement by two sorts, or two levels, of inspiration. One Italian writer, speaking of his own initiation into Communism during the resistance, recalled his experience (which was far from unique) in this way:

> Two sentiments coexisted both in my own mind and in the world around me: in one sense, Resistance was a legitimate and constructive response to fascist subversion and violence; in another, it was a revolutionary and destructive act, born of a passionate identification with the rebellion of the oppressed and the eternally outlawed. . . . Communism, too, combined both these sentiments. Depending on my psychological mood at the time, Togliatti's constitutionalist line and pleas for unity, which I happened upon in mimeographed leaflets, sometimes seemed the only world of untroubled wisdom amid the general extremism, and sometimes incomprehensible and remote, far removed from the reality of blood and fury in which we were immersed. [22]

When peace came, millions upon millions of ordinary people viewed Communism with a mixture of subversive and legitimist sentiments: jobless deportees returning home, landless peasants, workers who wanted to be master in their own factories. Recruitment among workers was massive in France, Belgium, and Italy, but also in Poland. [23] For them, behind the Communist parties stood the victorious Soviet Union; such was its image and role. Stalin too toasted the 'average man' and presented Communism as open to democratic liberties. [24] In central and eastern Europe no less than in the West, writers and artists were drawn to Marxism in a passionate quest to rediscover theoretical traditions and to begin a conscientious investigation of the origins and roots of Nazism (the typical case here was Germany). Other founts of revolutionary thought better able to speak to youth were also sought, from Luxemburg by György Lukács. 'There prevailed at the time . . . an atmosphere of lively discussion in which Marxism had many opportunities to assert its authority.' [25] The decision of many émigré intellectuals and artists to return to live in East Germany —not only Anna Seghers, Erich Weinert, Friedrich Wolf, and Bertolt Brecht, who were already Communists, but also democratic-progressive writers like Heinrich Mann and Arnold Zweig — was in part a spiritual option. [26] Lukács who had returned to Budapest, exercised great influence in both Hungary and Germany. In many cases it was impossible to distinguish Socialists from Communists. The left Socialist economist Oskar Lange was an advocate of fusion with the Communists in Poland.

Nor could the Russian and Soviet world isolate itself from this general phenomenon. The moment was fleeting, for the brakes of state ideology and police repression were soon applied in this society that dreamed of finally breathing free after the terrible trials it had suffered. But it was also real. Some of the giants of Russian poetry and art experienced and helped to create the climate of anti-fascist struggle, from Pasternak to Akhmatova, Shostakovich to Eisenstein. In the summer of 1944 a Soviet writer made a speech to the 'society for cultural relations abroad' in which he articulated the sentiments of many of his country's intellectuals.

> When the war is over, life will become very pleasant. A great literature will be produced as a result of our experiences. There will be much coming and going, and a lot of contacts with the West. Everybody will be allowed to read whatever he likes. There will be exchanges of students, and foreign travel for Soviet citizens will be made easy.[27]

The lives of entire nations and peoples were turned upside down by the rapidly frustrated hopes and aspirations of the post-war era. There was ample room for a plurality of voices and opinions, so long as they were not fascist. There was little talk of following the Soviet system. The shadows of the tragedy of Stalin's 1936–38 repression had lifted. Most of the Communist parties declared their acceptance of political democracy. But where society had already been marked by social revolution, things began to change. National and political differences were generating tensions and inviting one-sided solutions.

Elections-plebiscites were held in Yugoslavia and Albania. If there was any such thing as a Soviet model (the elections to the Supreme Soviet in the USSR in February 1946 produced a 98 per cent vote for the single joint list of party and 'non-party' candidates!), the Yugoslavs applied it to the letter. The Federated People's Republic of Yugoslavia was born at the end of 1945. In the elections to the Constituent Assembly, held in November, 97 per cent of the 8 million voters supported the People's Front. A few weeks later, Albania, which in those years was 'just like Yugoslavia, only smaller',[28] organized elections that yielded more or less equally satisfactory results: 93 per cent support for the 'Democratic Front', a copy of the Yugoslav 'People's Front'. The two constitutions were also similar; they anticipated a version of 'people's democracy' that was no more or less than a variant of the Soviet 'dictatorship of the proletariat' — as was proudly pointed out by their authors when the character of the new regime became a subject of discussion among Eastern governments and theoreticians.

The pattern differed elsewhere, depending on the balance of forces among parties and social groups. In Bulgaria a political crisis erupted at the very origin of the new regime. The Communists formed an alliance with part of the Agrarian Party, but another, larger wing of that party, led by Nikolai Petkov, rejected the election-plebiscite around the lists of the 'Patriotic Front', challenged the validity of the results, and protested to the Western powers. In fresh elections held in October 1946, the 'Front' nevertheless obtained 78 per cent of the vote (and 364 seats, 277 of which went to the Communist). The Petkov opposition got 22 per cent of the vote and 101 seats.[29]

In Czechoslovakia the return of freedom brought the return of political parties — genuine parties, in accordance with the democratic tradition of the only highly industrialized state in Eastern Europe. Four of them — Communist, Social Democratic, the People's Party, and Beneš's National Socialists — were grouped into a single Front, but the political dynamic was wide open.[30] The Communists scored an impressive success in the April 1946 elections, taking 38 per cent of the vote (41 per cent in Bohemia-Moravia, 31 per cent in Slovakia), while the Social Democrats got 14 per cent. The two workers parties therefore had a majority. Of the 300 members of parliament, 115 were Communists, 55 were Social Democrats, and 47 were from the People's Party. In Slovakia, however, the Democratic Party outstripped the Communists, winning 62 per cent of the vote).

In Hungary and Romania, where the Communist parties' roots had been feeble, if not wholly eradicated by the long years of fascist dictatorship, election results reflected the mistrust of broad layers of the peasantry, as well as widespread anti-Russian sentiments. In Hungary the party of the small landowners won an overwhelming majority in the November 1945 elections, taking 246 seats against 67 for the Communists and 23 for a 'national peasant' party. In the November elections of the following year in Romania the national-peasant and liberal parties were overtaken, even swamped, by a coalition under Communist hegemony (which won 348 seats out of 414), but these elections were far from free.

The Polish case was even more serious. The 'premature' Warsaw insurrection against the Germans in August 1944, when the Soviet army stood virtually at the gates of the city and did nothing to help, had been tragic. Part of the Home Army went underground and waged a full-fledged guerrilla war against the new regime for two years. As we shall see, there were many changes in this country too, social transformations in particular. Yet it soon became obvious that

Stalin was disinclined to allow Polish political developments to take their free course. The 'government of enemies' formed in June 1945 with Mikolajczyk, the representative of the Peasant Party who returned from London and took up the post of vice-president of the council, was mired in increasingly bitter internal conflict.

> . . . his [Mikolajczyk's] political power was almost nothing from the day of his arrival in Poland (as vice-rpremier of the newly constituted government), to his departure two years later. True, he enjoyed great popularity among the peasantry, and most democratic and even conservative forces considered him their only source of salvation from Soviet and Communist domination. In a free election he most certainly would have won a sweeping victory. . . . [31]

But free elections were never held in Poland. In January 1947 the 'anti-fascist bloc' won a ballot victory over the Peasant Party, by 9 million to 1.5 million. Oppressive and illegal methods were abundantly used.

Notes

1. Bertolt Brecht, '*The Communist Manifesto* in Verse', translated here from *Poesie e Canzioni*, Turin 1959, p. 433.

2. H.M. Pelling, *The British Communist Party. A Historical Profile* London 1958, p. 123.

3. From the interview with Luciano Cafagna reproduced in *La sinistra europea*, p. 26.

4. This was in particular the hope of the Italian Socialists. See especially the articles from spring 1945 collected in Pietro Nenni, *Vento del Nord*, Turin 1978, pp. 255-405.

5. On the conference sessions and the various speeches, see Oreste Lizzardi, *L'internazionale del lavoro*, Milan 1976.

6. H.M. Pelling, *A History of British Trade Unionism*, Harmondsworth 1969, p. 218.

7. Sophie G. Alf, 'Repubblica federale tedesca: sindacato e democrazia economica (1919–1976)', *Quaderni di Rassegna sindacale*, vol. 15, no. 66-67, May-August 1977, pp. 83-84.

8. Guillermaz, *Storia del partito comunista cinese*, p. 413.

9. *Storia dell'Internazionale comunista*, p. 524.

10. See Martin Eban, *World Communism Today*, New York-Toronto 1948; Branko Latich, *Les partis communistes d'Europe: 1919–1955*, Paris 1956; *Storia del socialismo*, J. Droz, ed., vol. 4.

11. Enrica Collotti Pischel, *Storia dell rivoluzione cinese*, Rome 1972, pp. 413-18.

12. Francesco Montessoro, 'Rivoluzione nazionale a sociale in Indocina', in *Storia dell'Asia*, Enrica Collotti Pischel, ed., Florence 1980, p. 163.

13. Guerra, *Gli anni del Cominform*, p. 52.

14. *Fifty Years of the Communist Party of Japan*, edited by the Central Committee of the Japanese CP, Tokyo 1973, pp. 86-102.

15. See Boris Goldenberg, *Kommunismus in Lateinamerika*, Stuttgart 1971, and the criticism of it in *Storia del socialismo*, vol. 4, p. 229.

16. Fejtö, *Histoire des Démocraties Populaires*, p. 195.

17. See Santiago Carrillo, *La Spagna domani*, Bari 1945, pp. 132-36; and Cesare Colombo, *Storia del Partito comunista spagnolo*, Milan 1972, pp. 164-66.

18. Enzo Collotti, *Storia delle due Germanie*, Turin 1968, pp. 194-95.

19. Christopher Hill, *Lenin and the Russian Revolution*, London 1947, p. 235.

20. On Carr's political evolution, see Marco Palla, 'La via alla storia di Edward Hallett Carr', *Passato e Presente*, vol. 1, no. 1, Florence, January-June 1982, pp. 115-44.

21. Louis Aragon, *L'homme communiste*, Paris 1946, pp. 49-50.

22. From Italo Calvino's response to a questionnaire on the 'generation of the difficult years', published in *Paradosso*, a youth cultural review, vol. 5, no. 23-24, September-December 1960, p. 17.

23. The social composition of the Polish Workers Party in December 1945 was 62.2 per cent workers and 28.2 per cent peasants. See W. Zaleski, *The Pattern of Life in Poland*, Paris 1952, p. 56.

24. From a speech of 9 February 1946, in *Stalin and Molotov Address their Constituents*, published by *Soviet News*, London 1946, p. 4.

25. Cesare Cases, 'Alcune vicende e problemi della cultura nella RDT', *Nuovi Argomenti*, no. 34, September 1958, p. 2.

26. Collotti, *Storia delle due Germanie*, pp. 883-85.

27. See Alexander Werth, *Russia: The Post-War Years*, London 1971, p. 99.

28. Fejtö, *Histoire des Démocraties Populaires*, p. 88.

29. On these events, and on the political evolution of the People's Democracies in general, see Franco Gaeta, *La seconda guerra mondiale e i nuovi problemi del mondo (1939–60)*, Turin 1969, pp. 321-52.

30. Josef Belda, 'Alcuni problemi della via cecoslovacca al socialismo', in *La crisi del modello sovietico in Cecoslovacchia*, Carlo Boffito and Lisa Foa, eds., Turin 1970, pp. 73-75.

31. Brzezinski, *The Soviet Bloc*, pp. 11-12.

20

A Party Old and New

Numerical expansion was not the only significant feature of the Communist parties' activity immediately after the war. They were slow to respond to some challenges, and contradictions were soon evident. In the meantime, new factors were emerging. Centres of Communism were taking shape in the Far East, while the development of the movement in Europe was halted in 1947, conventionally considered the first year of the Cold War.

Here it will suffice to note the contrast between the dynamic situation in Asia and the static division of Europe, from Szczecin to Trieste, along what Churchill called the 'iron curtain' in his famous Fulton, Missouri, speech of March 1946. China still seemed distant in 1945–47. The revolution in that immense country was undoubtedly helped by the USSR's victory in the Second World War. Without the existence and power of the USSR, the Chinese revolution would not have succeeded, and Communist China would not have entered the 'socialist camp', the international bloc headed by the Soviet Union, in 1949. Nevertheless, the Chinese revolution followed an independent line of march, both in 1934–1945 and in subsequent years, going far beyond Stalin's plan for post-war reconstruction under the leadership of Chiang Kai-shek.[1] That genuine independence, along with the national and social peculiarities of the revolutionary process experienced by the Chinese Communists, ultimately led to a divergence from the 'first socialist country' which evolved into dissent, detachment, and finally rupture.

In Europe negative factors transpired and had their effects even before the outbreak of the Cold War. It is not easy to separate periods sharply. The trend toward the formation of two counterposed camps was evident, though not yet dominant, as early as the summer of 1945, with the Potsdam conference and the new political and military role of Truman's America after the first atomic bombs were dropped on Hiroshima and Nagasaki. Divergent pressures from the two great powers, for example, clearly contributed to the failure of the attempt to reunify the European labour movement, both in individual countries and internationally. The critical observer, however, cannot avoid pausing to note one limitation of the Communist movement that was not primarily a result of the gathering clouds darkening relations between the war's victors, but was inherent in the movement itself.

Palmiro Togliatti himself raised this issue in 1962, as a historical question. He asked whether a real opportunity had not been lost, going so far as to speak of the 'straitjacket' in which Communism was trapped at the end of the war. Togliatti said:

> We must not be afraid to criticize past errors. They should be corrected, and both the circumstances in which they were committed and their content carefully studied. The mistaken political trends inspired by Stalin, the erroneous doctrine that our enemies augmented as a consequence of our very success, the violations of legality and other consequent sectarian conclusions were a sort of straitjacket that prevented the Communist movement, just when so many gains were being made after the war, from bringing its full strength to bear, from developing all its creative capacities, from proving to everyone that the socialist system for which we are fighting is a one of genuine democracy in all fields of social life.[2]

Togliatti thus began from the limitations (in 1956 he had spoken of 'degeneration') of a system of power and mode of political behaviour whose effects were evident even before the war. Moreover, in this case, far from indulging in delusions of retrospective justification, Togliatti alluded to the 'mistaken political trends inspired by Stalin', which had negative effects in an otherwise favourable situation — in other words before the outbreak of the Cold War; after that the Communist movement presented Stalin's every move as a 'response' to 'Truman's containment offensive'.

Togliatti died two years later, in 1964, and never clarified just which political errors he had in mind in the extract quoted above. One may nevertheless attempt to enumerate them on the basis of his two accompanying comments. First, the conflict between old and new, the inadequacy in the face of the great task of combining democracy and socialism, occurred just when 'so many gains were being made'. Second, the 'straitjacket' was placed on the movement by Stalin (by Stalinism, let us add, using a term Togliatti rejected).

It seems clear that if we accept this approach to the criticism of Communist errors and limitations, then the question of the causes of the Cold War must also be posed differently. It is at least possible, though not certain, that the mistaken political course, the curbing of the 'creative capacities' of the Communist movement, also contributed to generating international tensions, to encouraging suspicion and inflexible opposition in the other camp. In the European countries in which they held power, for example, how did the Communists pursue their efforts to establish 'a system of genuine democracy in all fields of social life'? The plebiscites and rigged elections must be counted substantial departures from a democratic road to socialism. Later we shall return to the process of formation of the 'People's Democracies'. For the moment, let us consider the Communist movement as a whole.

The movement was sailing uncharted seas. Each ship, not being part of a convoy or flotilla, had to plot its own course in the national context in which it had to operate. Local leadership groups continued to concentrate on their specific tasks, nation by nation. And the various situations were quite diverse. Some countries, having been part of the Nazi-fascist camp, were awaiting peace treaties; there were thorny problems of national minorities, especially in the Balkans. The Communist parties produced no common resolutions in 1945 and 1946, nor even any bilateral resolutions. It was not even clear what sort of instructions and suggestions were coming from Moscow, whether from the rump headquarters over which Dimitrov presided, or more directly from Stalin. There were few contacts even between French and Italian Communists. The historian must therefore make do with the rare hints, the few surprising episodes, that permit at least some conjectures.

The first of these episodes concerns the American Communist Party (CPUSA). At a special convention held in May 1944 this party, headed by Earl Browder, decided to transform itself into a 'political association'. The party as such was dissolved. This move was based on a considered analysis of the function of Communists in North American society as a whole. The motivation was more or less this: as an association, the Communists could act as a left reformist force within the American political and economic system, actively supporting Roosevelt's progressive orientation against conservative resistance. It seems well established that Browder was acting with Dimitrov's consent,[3] which would certainly not be surprising. The initiative, like the measured support it received, reflected the 'spirit of Tehran', the prospect of peaceful coexistence (it must be remembered that this was on the eve of the long-awaited opening of the 'second front'), and sincere admiration for Roosevelt's commitments and for his friendship with the USSR. But it transformed the American party, a small one on the margins of national political life, and was an intriguing symptom of a potentially broader development. Autonomy was pressed to its outer limits, and the possibility arose of the integration of a Communist minority into a modern system, country by country, in a manner completely different from the past. But no comparable case would occur anywhere else. Browder himself was careful not to generalize. His argument was based on American conditions: 'It is my considered judgement that the American people are so ill-prepared, subjectively, for any deep-going change in the direction of socialism that post-war plans with such an aim would not unite the nation but would further divide it. And they would divide and weaken precisely the democratic and progressive camp, at the same time uniting and strengthening the most reactionary forces in the country.'[4]

The North American example may have influenced the parties of Latin America, encouraging already existing tendencies toward liquidationism under the banner of anti-fascist national unity. Regimes that were anything but democratic consolidated power under this line — Batista in Cuba, for instance.[5] But when criticism of the latent opportunism of Browder's proposal came, it was from an unlikely source. In April 1945, a year after the event, the authoritative and crafty Jacques Duclos, number two in the French Communist Party, wrote an article that unleashed a flood of outraged criticism denouncing Browder as a revisionist and right deviationist. Why would a man like Duclos feel it necessary to issue a call to orthodoxy just when the war was drawing to a close in Europe, with Soviet and American troops joining hands across the Elbe? The article was placid in tone. In substance, Duclos chided Browder for the decision to dissolve the party and warned that certain of his ideas took him dangerously far from the 'victorious doctrine of Marxism-Leninism'. Duclos also reminded Browder that 'the natural basis of fascism lies in the monopolies'.[6] A short time later, in the summer of 1945 — when, according to one witness, Togliatti harboured some sympathy for the positions expressed by Browder[7] — the journal edited by the PCI secretary published a harsh and contemptuous attack written by an Italian Communist leader then living in Mexico. The author, Mario Montagnana, used language unusual for the post-Liberation period. He spoke of aberrations and of the collapse and destruction of Marxism. He also raised the spectre of an 'enemy' that was to be cited repeatedly during 1947 and 1948:

When, in the final analysis, the political line of a party serves not the interests of the proletariat but those of its class enemies, when a party lacks ideological and political vigilance, it is absolutely inevitable that that same party will also lack vigilance against the enemy's political and police infiltration. It would be childish and criminal to believe that the class enemy has not done its best to make maximum use of such a situation.[8]

It is hard to believe that Mario Montagnana was expressing anything more than the opinions of European Communist exiles then living in North and Central America, especially the Italians. But Duclos's sally may well have been encouraged, if not ordered, by Soviet advisers,[9] even if it is by no means obvious that he was speaking on Stalin's behalf. At the end of the war, Stalin refrained from pronouncing on the political options and organizational decisions of the various Communist parties. He seemed prepared to tolerate their autonomy so long as no general foreign-policy imperatives or basic interests in the Soviet Union's sphere of influence were at stake. Duclos may have received encouragement from some other high-ranking leader in Moscow or elsewhere. There was no dearth of conservative pressures; and in the absence of a leadership centre, there was also greater scope for internal dissent. But the American incident was soon closed. Browder was expelled, severely condemned by Foster, the new party leader (for Browder, he said, 'American imperialism virtually disappeared, no sign of the class struggle remained . . . '[10]). The association became a party again, and turned in on itself.

Resistance to the new was inevitable and natural to some extent. And it was often expressed in other ways than open debate. For some time the Communist press had ceased to carry any discussion of the nature and internal regime of the party or on the subject of transition to a new society. Conditioned reflexes continued to function — such as the automatic attempt to mask Communist hegemony in mass front organizations. Once the war ended, parties like the Italian and French helped to draft democratic constitutions in their countries. There were some initial, albeit timid, attempts to develop a theory of transition in the East European countries. In May 1945 the Hungarian Rákosi predicted that socialist transformation would be preceded by a long transitional phase, possibly lasting ten years.[11] In February 1946 Dimitrov affirmed: 'The fact is — and we Marxists should be well aware of it — that not every people will follow exactly the same road to socialism: they will not all follow a particular road, they will not all follow the Soviet model exactly, but will act in their own way, in accordance with their own historical, national, social, cultural, and other conditions.'[12]

When their party was legally reconstituted in June 1945, the German Communists went further, using an argument familiar to the Italian Communists as well, based on the need to complete the bourgeois-democratic revolution, which had been blocked by reaction and Nazism in Germany.

> Simultaneous with the destruction of Hitlerism, we must complete the democratization of Germany, the cause of bourgeois democratic transformation begun in 1848. Feudal remnants must be completely liquidated, Prussian militarism and all its political and social props annihilated. It is our opinion that the decisive interests of the German people in the present situation require something else, namely the construction of an anti-fascist, democratic regime, a democratic-parliamentary republic, with full democratic rights and freedoms for the people.[13]

In other words, in various quarters there was talk of 'new roads', national particularities, and 'diversity'. By late 1946 this became a common, though soon proscribed, theme. In the meantime, there was a repetition and extension of a phenomenon that had also occurred back at the time of the Popular Fronts: every 'opening', every new initiative, was carefully tailored so as not to alter the doctrinal concept whose triumph and historical vindication was now celebrated: 'Marxism-Leninism'. These were the years when the Short Course was widely distributed in countries in which it had barely circulated underground. And the Short Course represented exactly the Soviet model, the Stalin version of historical and dialectical materialism, and contempt for political democracy and democratic rights, which were nonetheless then being championed. In other words, every attempt was made to render the period of expansion compatible with an ideological rigidity tempered by the glorification of progressive national traditions, and of the specific contributions to Marxism and Leninism they were making or had made.

So it was for the rather tougher nut of party continuity. Even Dimitrov, who said that it was necessary to follow the Soviet model, added: 'The party must have an *iron* discipline — conscious and voluntary, but *iron* — which must be based on our unanimity of thought, on our tasks, on our united aims as a party, and on our Marxist science, which is leading us to victory.'[14]

The triumphalist tone was constant. Thorez said at the Tenth Congress of the PCF:

Marxism-Leninism is the unity of theory and practice, of thought and action. No work can be done in any branch of militant activity without an effort to master Marxist-Leninist science. The greatest scientists, like our friend Langevin, say that they gained knowledge in their own particular sciences only in the light of dialectical materialism. [15]

Togliatti, too, shared this concept of 'doctrine' as a science that had to be correctly applied, re-integrated into the culture of each country, and spread. He told university students in Pisa:

Marxism is a great movement of men and ideas, a reality of our social life, a reality of the modern world, which may suffer periods of crisis and reversal, but has always triumphantly continued its development. . . . It inspired the first great revolution of modern times, a revolution from which has issued the first great attempt to create a society of free and equal people. In fact, the word 'attempt' is no longer appropriate, for the fundamental hopes of all social reformers have been realized. [16]

The speeches of Communist leaders in 1945 and 1946 also contain more than a few proud references to the 1936–38 Moscow Trials, as if history had endorsed them too. Immediately after Liberation, the danger of the penetration of the movement by Trotskyist agents was raised anew. Dimitrov warned against the 'mask of left slogans' behind which the Trotskyists hid, and urged that this mask be penetrated. Thorez said simply that 'freedom of opinion in the party does not mean freedom to introduce alien opinions', such as those of the party's 'Hitlerite-Trotskyite'[17] enemies. Felice Platone, one of Togliatti's closest associates and the editor of Antonio Gramsci's *Prison Notebooks*, devoted a long article to the dangers of renewed Trotskyist provocation and called on party members not to tolerate it: 'To nip any reprise of Trotskyite sabotage and disintegration in the bud is now a vital task not only for our party and for the working class, but for the entire anti-fascist, democratic movement of national liberation.'[18]

The genuine Trotskyist groups in Europe were as fragmented as ever after the war; their main field of activity now shifted to Latin America. But the point of denouncing the Trotskyists as insidious enemies and of equating them with fascists was to brand any left opposition as provocation and to reconfirm obedience to the Stalin tradition of 'Bolshevik' purity. The leaders of the Communist movement in the various countries may have begun to stir, but they had not forgotten the bleak days of the purges. In fact, many of them were survivors of those years. A brief glance at the composition of the leadership groups shows a combination of varied experiences and continuity of tradition.

The Communist leaders had until recently been secretaries or functionaries in the apparatus. Most were little known to the party ranks, either because they had been forced into long periods of exile or because they had been imprisoned by the fascists or by military dictatorships. These revolutionary leaders — unlike those who came to prominence after the First World War — were not generally young: the majority were in their forties or fifties, and some were quite old. The fusion in leading bodies of national cadres with experience in different places and militias was not easy. The most homogeneous, newest, and least 'Cominternist' leadership group was perhaps the Yugoslav, almost all of whose members had come out of the partisan struggle: Tito of course, but also Kardelj, Ranković, Djilas, Vukmanović, Tempo, Moša Pijade, and Vlaho Vlahović, who had fought with the International Brigades in Spain. The Albanians Enver Hoxha and Mehmet Shehu were also partisans.

The French Communist leaders had long been well known in their country: first of all Thorez; then Duclos, the great parliamentary orator; the trade-unionist Benoît Frachon; the former editor of *L'Humanité* Marcel Cachin; and even Etienne Fajon, Raymond Guyot, François Billoux, and the crusty and irascible André Marty, who had been an officer in the International Brigades in Spain and had now returned from Moscow. The famous resistance leaders — like Charles Tillon, Léon Mauvais, Auguste Lecoeur, and Waldeck Rochet — were assimilated by the 'old guard', who had consolidated their influence during the stormy years of the war. Thorez boasted of the continuity of the Communist leaders compared with those of other political forces: 'Only our party comes before the country with its pre-war leadership.'[19]

The PCI emerged from the long dark night of fascism with a distinct personality of its own. In fact, the Italian party is one of the most typical cases of a combination of new elements and continuity. Ercoli, already enveloped in the mysterious aura of having been the leader of the Communist International, became known to the public under his real name, Palmiro Togliatti, and put himself forward as the inheritor of Gramsci's political tradition. At the head of the unions was another man esteemed by the masses, the ex-labourer Giuseppe Di Vittorio. The top leaders of the PCI — from the oldest, like Mauro Scoccimarro, Giovanni Roveda, and Umberto Terracini, who had spent almost twenty years in prison or in internal exile, to Girolamo Li Causi, Velio Spano, Antonio Roasio, Arturo Colombi, to the youngest, like Eugenio Reale, Giorgio Amendola, Celeste Negarville, and Gian Carlo Pajetta — were all veterans of a long armed struggle, as were the men who now returned from Moscow: Ruggero Grieco and Edoardo D'Onofrio, and Luigi Longo and Pietro Secchia, who served as Togliatti's vice-secretaries. They had led the party and the 'Garibaldi' partisan brigades during the resistance.

In the Communist parties of northern Europe, from Finland (where Kuusinen and his daughter Hertta Elina returned), to Denmark, Norway, Holland, and Belgium, the leadership groups were unable to make effective use of the new situation, and in Britain the previous leadership re-formed (Pollitt, Palme Dutt, Gallacher, who was re-elected to parliament). The Greek Communist Party became a special case after the dramatic upheavals of late 1944. Zachariades returned from the Dachau extermination camp in 1945 and resumed his post as secretary. He favoured a line of conciliation with the British 'protectors',[20] but the conservative government, headed by Admiral Petros Voulgaras, launched a fresh anti-Communist repression: tens of thousands of militants and former partisans were arrested, and it soon became impossible for the Greek CP to take its place under a system that was parliamentary in form but reactionary and military-dominated in reality, even under the new Sophoulis government. In 1946 the Truman administration, not bothering with the guarantees of free elections insistently demanded for Eastern Europe, supplanted the British in imposing the most rigid tutelage. The internally divided Greek CP was forced into a line of renewed armed resistance, as were the Spanish Communists Carrillo, Lister, Francisco Anton, and Ibarruri.

But Spain, like Greece, suffered a tragedy that represented a black page for the liberal West: protracted exile was the bitter fate of Spanish anti-fascism. The Communist leadership group, headquartered in Moscow, wandered from country to country in Eastern Europe, seeking aid for a dead-end guerrilla struggle within the country. Stalin himself told Carrillo to abandon it[21] (but only in 1948) and to work within the organizations of the Francoist regime, trying to infiltrate them as the Bolsheviks had done in Tsarist Russia.

Among the German Communists the only outstanding figure to remain in the Western occupation zones was Max Reimann, liberated from a Nazi concentration camp. The others, almost all of whom had been living in Moscow, went to the eastern zone. They included the prestigious Wilhelm Pieck, an old Spartacist and former member of the International Executive; Walter Ulbricht, the future party secretary; Heinrich Rau, Willi Stoph, and Hermann Matern. The Polish

Communists were led by Gomulka, who had been secretary of the underground organization during the Nazi occupation; Boleslaw Bierut and Alexander Zadawski returned from the USSR. Gomulka was the 'strong man of the new regime'.[22] Some intellectuals also held important party posts, like the economist Hilary Minc and Jakub Berman.

Among the Czechoslovak and Hungarian Communists there were many political personalities of considerable prominence. Gottwald held the prime position in Czechoslovakia, flanked by Antonin Novotny, Antonin Zapotocky, Siroky, Slánský, Clementis, and Husak; the Hungarians, led by the (temporarily) uncontested Rákosi, also included experienced cadres like Gerö, Farkas, Révai Rajk, Kádar, and Imre Nagy. Bulgaria saw the return of Dimitrov, an already legendary figure who continued to play a major role despite serious illness. With him were Chervenkov, T. Kostov, and Raiko Damianov.

Apart from the Spanish, the Romanian Communists were the only ones to have a woman in their top leadership group. She was Ana Pauker, whom we have already encountered (the party secretary was Gheorghiu-Dej). And although Dolores Ibarruri (La Pasionaria), whose son had died fighting in the Red Army, spent another thirty years in exile before being able to return home, Ana Pauker was a victim of the tragedy that befell the Communist cadres of the 'People's Democracies' during the 1949–52 waves of repression, which closely paralleled the 1936–38 terror in Russia. Kostov, Rajk, Slánský, and Clementis were all shot, while Gomulka and Kadar were imprisoned. Imre Nagy was summarily executed after the 1956 workers revolt in Budapest.

Because of this tragedy — and also because the party gradually demonstrated its determination to occupy the entire state apparatus, to monopolize the key positions of power, from the Ministry of the Interior to the Ministry of Defence — it is often forgotten that at first the left parties of the West had great hopes in and sympathy for Eastern Europe, where the situation seemed ripe for sweeping reforms and the workers movement faced new tasks, with many Socialists working side by side with the Communists. It was felt that in this region where reaction and feudalism had always triumphed, new societies might now arise with popular consent, without having to face the isolation and capitalist encirclement with which the Russian Bolsheviks had had to deal. Czechoslovakia, with its advanced social, political, and economic features, was already being spoken of as the country closest to a socialist breakthrough. The

Czechoslovak industrial and banking systems were soon nationalized, but the Communists also pressed forward in the other East European countries, in a manner that was particularly important since the region lay in ruins. Bridges and railways had been destroyed, and food and shelter were lacking. The role of the Communists had been acknowledged by historians of the most varied orientations. Joyce and Gabriel Kolko, noted 'revisionists', wrote that 'wherever the Communists had responsbility for a phase of reconstruction they goaded the workers, traded welfare for production, and demonstrated greater patriotic fervour than ministers from the other parties.'[23] Another American historian who has dealt with these matters (and is anything but revisionist), Z.K. Brzezinski, noted that the seriousness, concreteness, and reformist content of the Communists' programmes won them the support of politically active progressive and liberal-democratic groups in Eastern Europe.[24] Most important was the achievement of a great agrarian reform that distributed land to millions of peasants. About 20 million hectares were expropriated in all, and 12 million of these were distributed to more than 3 million peasants.[25] An entire landlord class, often composed of foreigners (in Poland and Czechoslovakia it was German) was eliminated. Isaac Deutscher spoke of the 'strange revolution', the revolution from above, undertaken by the Soviet occupation troops but generally supported by the popular masses:

> Yet, by sponsoring that strange revolution, Stalin rendered the peoples of Eastern Europe 'services of which it is difficult to overrate either the wickedness or the utility', to paraphrase Macaulay's verdict on an English statesman. Between the two wars nearly all those peoples had been stranded in an impasse; their life had been bogged down in savage poverty and darkness; their politics had been dominated by archaic cliques who had not minded the material and cultural retrogression of their subjects as long as their own privileges had been safe. . . . It may well be that for its peoples the only chance of breaking out of their impasse lay in a *coup de force* such as that to which Stalin goaded them. In Poland and Hungary, the Communist-inspired land reform fulfilled, perhaps imperfectly, a dream of many generations of peasants and intellectuals.[26]

At the end of September 1944 a decree was issued in Poland expropriating landed estates of more than 100 hectares in total area, and more than 50 hectares if the estate was purely agricultural. Tens of thousands of small farms were formed. The ex-German territories of Pomerania and Silesia were incorporated into western Poland. About 6 million Germans left, and 4.5 million hectares of their land were distributed to four hundred thousand Polish peasant families. In Bulgaria, which had no big landlords of the Polish type, a post-war decree limited the apportionment of land to 20 hectares and affected no more than 3 per cent of total land-area. The agrarian reform was impressive in Romania, Hungary, Czechoslovakia, Yugoslavia, Albania, and East Germany. In Romania more than eight hundred thousand families benefitted from a distribution of about 1.6 million hectares after a decree of the Groza government in March 1945. In Hungary about 33 per cent of the cultivated land was affected by an agrarian reform at the end of 1944. In Czechoslovakia about 2.6 million hectares that had been owned by Germans, and another 900,000 owned by big landlords were distributed to about a quarter of a million families. In Yugoslavia the agrarian reform soon distributed 392,000 hectares and established an upper limit of 20 or 30 hectares for private plots, depending on the fertility of the soil. In Albania the reform followed the same standards. Tens of thousands of agricultural wage-workers benefited. In the Soviet occupation zone in Germany the large estates were confiscated immediately, more than 2 million hectares in all, and distributed to half a million peasants. Estates larger than 100 hectares were subdivided.

All these measures of course gave rise to serious problems, as did industrial development, which would not be easy in these semi-feudal countries. There was not yet a socialist transformation, and still less was industrial development inspired by the Soviet model. Stalin's reason for promoting communization has been much discussed. It may be that one of the basic reasons had to do with the USSR's security policy itself; socialization destroyed the economic power and social weight of those groups of landowners who were the principal supporters of reactionary internal policies and an anti-Russian foreign policy subordinated to Germany. The priveleged position of German landowners in Slavic territories was also destroyed immediately. Was there also a political design: to enable the Communist parties to win hegemony over the peasantry, supplanting the various groupings and parties of the small proprietors? Was it an attempt to draw the Social Democratic and independent peasant parties into the front, and thus to absorb them? There can be no doubt that an agrarian reform of such depth, accompanied by economic reconstruction in which the state played the prime, if not the exclusive, role, both augmented the Communists' responsibilities in the general direction of society and created new conditions of political struggle. (In Poland and Hungary this included the paradox of the ouster of peasant parties in favour of new smallholders who feared that in the not too distant future the Communists would deprive them of the land they had only just obtained.)

But let us now return to the general discussion. The dominant feature of the situation was that the various European Communist parties seemed to have been summoned to social prominence. Given the dimensions assumed by the movement, a new relation had to be established between the mass of members and the leaders and intermediary cadres. It was here that the old and the new so often coexisted, and not always happily. The traditional structure was imposed even before the question of fusion with Socialist or Social Democratic parties arose, and sometimes contemporaneously with it. The time-honoured Stalin version of 'democratic centralism', rigid and bureaucratic, was strongly reaffirmed. Political decision-making, control of the party, and debate over the line remained the exclusive province of a very small group of leaders within which the general secretary stood far above the others. The secretary was the party *boss*, and around him arose a cult much like the cult of Stalin that was reaching its apogée in every Communist party, including the French and Italian, Yugoslav and Bulgarian).

This does not mean that the various Communist parties appeared before the mass of workers with the same image as during the inter-war period. The intense participation in party life by the working-class and peasant rank-and-file (a party acquires features of a turbulent mass movement when there are so many new members) and the influx of fresh generations of militants turned them into new organizations that were not only lively but also proud of their discipline and of their open confrontation with other political forces. Here too there were trends toward differentiation: parties like the Yugoslav and French remained essentially cadre parties, as did the Bulgarian, Hungarian, and Romanian. The Czechoslovak, Polish, and Italian parties were more easily transformed into mass organizations.

In the case of the Italian party, a number of innovations suggested a more pronounced desire for change. Article 2 of the statutes approved at the Fifth Congress granted all Italian citizens the right to join the party, 'regardless of race, religious faith, or philosophical conviction'. This gave a secular aspect to party membership, and allowed Catholic believers to join the party on the same basis as atheists, convinced 'materialists'. Caution and lack of dogmatism were also apparent in party eduction. Article 5 stated that militants simply had to 'acquire ever greater awareness of the classics of Marxism–Leninism'.

These innovations were summed up in Togliatti's 1944 call for the birth of a 'new party': not only a mass, popular, national party, but also an instrument 'capable of expressing — in its policy, organization, and daily activity — the profound change that has occurred in the position of the working class with respect to the problems of national life'.[27] This change was reflected in the 'leading' position and positive function of the working class in the construction of a democratic system. It was now a real 'political subject'.[28]

Togliatti was convinced that this kind of party could furnish the broadest platform for the political unification of the working class. But not even Togliatti's post-Liberation PCI shed the fundamental features of a Leninist, indeed Stalinist, party. The prohibition of internal factions was maintained; the development and primacy of a layer of 'professional revolutionaries', was encouraged; decision-making powers remained in the hands of the group closest to the party secretary; the promotion of cadres was cautious indeed. It may be of some interest to note that when a turn to increased centralism was made with the advent of the Cold War and the birth of the Cominform, the PCI statutes were also amended: the existence of a Communist current in the trade-union federation was codified, for example, and Article 5 of the 1948 Fifth Congress was altered; it now stipulated the obligation 'to deepen knowledge of Marxism-Leninism', the consolidated doctrine.[29]

Let us now return to the 'creative' capacities of the Communist movement, stifled by Stalin's 'mistaken political trends'. Did the error consist purely in the maintenance of the party's traditional character? Or was the role of the movement as a 'political subject', and therefore enjoying its own autonomy, contricted and undervalued? This problem arises in considering the possible fusion, at least in some countries, of Communists and Socialists just after the war.

Notes

1. See Aldo Natoli, 'Comunisti e rivoluzione in Cina', in *Storia dell'Asia*, p. 119. See also H.E. Salisbury, *The Coming War Between Russia and China*, London 1969.

2. From the report to the Tenth Congress of the PCI, December 1962, in Palmiro Togliatti, *Nella democrazia e nella pace verso il socialismo*, Rome 1963, p. 213.

3. Starobin, *American Communism in Crisis*, p. 72.

4. Earl Browder, *Tehran and America*, New York 1944, p.19.

5. See Tutino, *L'ottobre cubano*, pp. 153-83. More generally, Alexander, *Communism in Latin America*.

6. J. Duclos, 'A propos de la dissolution du PCA', *Cahiers du Communisme*, new series, no. 6, April 1945, pp. 21-38.

7. I. De Feo, *Diario politico (1943–48)*, Milan 1973, pp. 114-26.

8. Mario Montagnana, 'Sul "nuovo corso" dei comunisti americani', *Rinascita*, vol. 2, no. 7–8, July-August 1945, p. 187.

9. See the testimony of Ambrogio Donini and Giuseppe Berti, as described in Sergio Bertelli, *Il gruppo*, Milan 1980, p. 208. See also Lilly Marcou, 'La problematique d'un rapport difficile: URSS et mouvement communiste', in *L'URSS vue de gauche*, pp. 158-63.

10. William Z. Foster, 'Letter to the National Committee of the Communist Party', in *On the Struggle Against Revisionism*, New York 1946, p. 5.

11. See Brzezinski, *The Soviet Bloc*, p. 50.

12. 'La missione storica del Partito operaio bulgaro', in Gheorghi Dimitrov, *Opere scelte*, Rome 1977, vol. 2, p. 228.

13. From the text of the appeal of the KPD, 11 June 1945, in Collotti, *Storia delle due Germanie*, pp. 474-75.

14. 'La missione storica del Partito operaio bulgaro', p. 222.

15. Thorez, *Oeuvres*, vol. 21, p. 115.

16. From the text of the opening address, 10 March 1946, published posthumously on the basis of a stenographic report and entitled 'Il marxismo di Togliatti', *Rinascita*, vol. 24, no. 33, 25 August 1967.

17. The expression was used in the report to the Tenth Congress itself. See *Oeuvres*, vol. 21, p. 119.

18. Felice Platone, 'Vecchie e nuove vie delle provocazione trotzkista', *Rinascita*, vol. 2, no. 3, March 1945, p. 99.

19. Fauvet, *Histoire du PCF*, vol. 2, p. 155.

20. See Solaro, *Storia del Partito comunista greco*, pp. 129-31, and Joyce and Gabriel Kolko, *The Limits of Power. The World and United States Foreign Policy, 1945–1954*. New York 1972, pp. 219-226.

21. Carrillo, *La Spagna domani*, pp. 136-37.

22. Karol, *Visa for Poland*, p. 90.

23. Kolko, *The Limits of Power*, p.181.

24. Brzezinski, *The Soviet Bloc*, p. 6.

25. See Fejtö, *Histoire des Démocraties Populaires*, p. 150.

26. Deutscher, *Stalin*, pp. 521-22.

27. Palmiro Togliatti, 'Che cosa è il "partito nuovo" ', *Rinascita*, vol. 1, no. 4, November-December 1944, p. 25.

28. See Alessandro Natta, 'Togliatti e il "partito nuovo" ', *Rinascita*, vol. 23, no. 34, 29 August 1969.

29. See Giuliano Procacci, 'Appunti sugli statuti del Pci dopo la Liberazione', *Critica Marxista*, vol. 16, no 6, November-December 1978, pp. 69-77.

21

The Chimera of Organic Unity

The plans and projects for the political unification of Communists and Socialists in various European countries faded so rapidly that it is reasonable to wonder whether the much-vaunted 'organic unity' was sincere or whether it was ever much more than a projection of the atmosphere of unity that prevailed in the resistance. I have already mentioned the aspiration for unity that came mainly from the Socialist ranks in the last days of the war. There were similar impulses in the Communist camp too. But things turned bad in short order. In 1945 and 1946 unification failed in France, West Germany, and Italy, the countries in which it had been most widely sought; in Eastern Europe it turned into the gradual absorption of the Socialists by the Communists during 1946 and 1947, such that by 1948, when the process ended, the Socialist wing had been virtually liquidated.

The international panorama was even more discouraging. The *European* workers movement soon disappeared as a political subject with a voice of its own. The prime cause of the failure must be sought in the logic of spheres-of-influence politics. The seeds of the Cold War, with its counterposition of enemy camps, stifled any attempt at organic unity. The interference of the great powers was not the sole factor. In the resistance movements neither side produced a drive toward fusion powerful enough to establish new organs, or to generate sufficient pressure from the rank and file to place the leaders in a new situation. When the time came to opt for fusion or reject it, the Western Communist and Socialist parties rediscovered sufficient ideological differences and divisions, and enough diversity in their respective internal regimes, to halt, suspend, and finally abandon the project.

By 'the logic of spheres-of-influence politics' I do not mean only the conscious obstruction, even sabotage, of unification by the victorious great powers, although such action was indeed taken, especially by the British and Americans, who brought pressure to bear on the European Socialist and Social Democratic parties. I refer also to a widening schism between those (the Communists, or perhaps only some of them) who saw organic unity as a confirmation of the primacy of the USSR as the fount of actual socialism, at least in the ideological field, and those (some of the leaders of Social Democracy and Labourism, from Blum to Saragat, Bevin to Schumacher) who rejected unity exactly because they felt that it would mean subordination to Soviet foreign policy and the transformation of the united party into a Marxist–Leninist organization. The picture was complicated both by the genuine yearning for united action, which was widespread in both wings, and by the fact that sympathy for the USSR was common among European Socialists after the war, among the Poles and Czechs, Italians and French, and even British and Scandinavians. But the weight of suspicion and impediments, which now also meant the weight of the counterposed state authorities, prevailed in the end.

The most symptomatic case was Germany, partly because this country, divided among four occupying armies and lacking a state or well-defined borders, had no political independence. The action taken by the Allied powers to block the unification of the working-class left, or to turn unification into the dominance of one wing over the other, was therefore decisive. Wolfgang Abendroth, perhaps exaggerating somewhat but nonetheless capturing the underlying reality, wrote:

> When the German workers movement sought to reconstitute itself after the collapse of Nazism — initially in semi-legal conditions, without authorization from the occupying powers — almost everywhere there was a tendency to abandon the old parties and to build a united socialist party. But all four occupying powers opposed this trend toward socialist unity, as did those members of the Social Democratic emigration who had been driven to an excessively rigid anti-Bolshevik attitude by the bitter experiences of the Stalin terror against the best cadres of Russian Bolshevism and the Communist exiles in the USSR [1].

Another German scholar, Peter Brandt (son of the current president of the Social Democratic Party in West Germany), drew similar conclusions. He noted that at the end of the war united labour parties were formed spontaneously at local and regional levels. But the early reconstitution of the Communist Party (on 11 June 1945) brought a sudden halt to the further development of such parties, even though many continued to favour unification. Some pioneer groups of left

Socialists championed unity from below. Hermann Brill, for example, urged the formation of soviet-type people's committees which would later hold a constituent congress. Wilhelm Pieck, however, upon his return from Moscow, sought the immediate reconstitution of the Communist Party, and got it. His aim was not to impose the Soviet political system in the Russian occupation zone, but to guarantee a policy of friendship toward the USSR by ensuring that Communists would occupy key positions in society. On the other hand, there was a patriotic front, a 'bloc of working people' headed by the CP[2] and including Socialists, liberal democrats, and Christian Democrats in the Eastern zone, which preferred the formation of a new workers party.

It should be added that the anti-fusion tendency was also dominant among German Social Democrats, like Kurt Schumacher (the most prominent political figure, a powerful personality and popular leader), who made no secret of their aversion to Soviet Communism and their basic pro-Western stance. But the decision to reconstitute the CP gave enormous encouragement to Schumacher's 'separatism' and created a difficult situation for those Socialists who favoured fusion, like Otto Grotewohl, former Reichstag deputy. This caused them to temporize. Grotewohl soon found himself in a minority in the Central Committee of the reborn Social Democratic Party of Germany (SPD).

Schumacher's tenacity, his courageous past (he had spent more than ten years in Nazi concentration camps), and the aid he received from many Anglo-American political and trade-union forces helped him to reorganize the SPD ranks and to orient them not only against organic unity but even against united action with the Communists. As early as October 1945 Schumacher argued that 'the line of demarcation between Social Democrats and Communists exists because the Communists are closely linked to just one of the Allied powers, namely the Russian state, and to its foreign policy objectives'.[3] The American trade-union federation AFL exerted strong pressure in West Germany against trade-union unification. In April 1946 the American military governor in Germany opposed the formation of a united labour federation.[4] By then Schumacher had already broken off relations with the fusionist Socialists in the eastern zone, had blocked the fusion process in Berlin, and had blunted the trend toward united parties in the Western Zone.

Germany is therefore the most obvious case of pressure against unity from the Allied powers. Not only Truman's America, but also Attlee's Britain and De Gaulle's France, wanted no part of a united

Socialist–Communist German left. Stalin's only objective was to make sure of a loyal political leadership in his own occupation zone. And here he lost no time. Ths Socialist Unity Party (SED) was founded in April 1946. In the months ahead it became, in principle, the fused party of the Communists and Socialists of the eastern zone, and it did enjoy the support of many workers and peasants, for an economic and social transformation was then under way. But the fusion in the east nevertheless implied the abandonment of any similar prospect beyond the borders of the Soviet occupation zone. The foundation of the SED naturally had immediate effects in the western zones, where the KPD's fusion proposals were rejected by the SPD. Meanwhile, the process of absorption of the Socialists in the east continued apace. At first the united party had an equally apportioned leadership, with two presidents, Pieck and Grotewohl. Then, in 1948, as the international crisis sharpened, the SED was transformed into a 'party of a new type', with a clearly Stalinist stamp and of mounting ideological rigidity. The unification in Poland, Hungary, and Czechoslovakia was similar. I will have more to say about the foundation of the People's Democracies later. For the moment, let us return to the situation immediately after the war, where similar situations prevailed in Italy and France.

Although there were differences, there was one essential similarity: protestations to the contrary, genuine belief in the possibility of achieving unity in the near future was so feeble that unification was finally postponed indefinitely. Each of the two partners placed such great emphasis on their respective fusion proposals that the healing of the historic split of 1920–21 often seemed just around the corner. But no one ever turned up to the historic rendezvous — or at least both partners never turned up at the same time. In France the story begins in 1944. The SFIO made the first advance, in November. A standing liaison committee was formed, but it never produced anything concrete. At their Tenth Congress in June 1945 the Communists adopted an organic unity proposal of their own, calling for close collaboration between the local federations of the two parties, regular joint meetings of the national leadership bodies, and common lists in the upcoming elections. Although they favoured united action, the Socialists rejected the Communist unity proposal at their own congress two months later. In 1946 the prospect of unity vanished. The SFIO congress in August rejected even united action.

Many factors in France weighted against unification: the lacerations of 1939–41; the lack of unity during the resistance; the mounting concern of the SFIO that it would be a small minority in any new party, since the more numerous PCF had overtaken the Socialists in the last elections. The Communists, led by Frachon, had also consolidated their supremacy over Léon Jouhaux's Socialists in the 5-million-member CGT, the labour federation. Theoretical irreconcilability was also more evident in France than elsewhere. There was more Manichaeanism than bullying in the Communist claim (in a proposed 'unity charter') that the doctrinal basis of the united workers party should be 'dialectical materialism as enriched by Lenin and Stalin'.[5] The Social Democratic and humanist tradition of French Socialism, dominated by the intellectual personality of Léon Blum, certainly could never accept dissolution into Marxism–Leninism. Nor could the Socialists, already newly divided into various political and cultural currents, accept 'democratic centralism'.

And yet even here the greatest obstacle to unity was the vexed question of relations with Moscow. As we know, Blum opened the wound when he returned from deportation in the summer of 1945, citing the PCF's 'double patriotism' as the reason why the Communists could not possibly be independent of the USSR. 'Let us suppose', he wrote, 'that there is a crisis — or worse, a conflict — in which Soviet Russia is involved. What would happen in the united party?' Blum cited Stalin's unpredictability as the insoluble unknown of unification: 'Although united action is indispensable, the success of unification does not depend on us Socialists and Communists alone; it depends on the pace and course of events, or rather on one man, whose name is Stalin.'[6]

In Italy, unlike France, there was a solid political and social basis for united action by the two parties. In fact, co-operation was not only not halted, but even cemented, by the outbreak of the Cold War, as Communists and Socialists lined up against the social and ideological bloc forged by Christian Democracy and the Catholic Church. Neverthelesss, there were two great similarities with France. In Italy, too, a Social Democratic component was determined to extract the Socialists from the Communist embrace; its battle-cry was independence from Moscow. This Social Democratic wing split from the PSIUP and, at the beginning of 1947, formed a new party that later co-operated with Christian Democracy.

But this does not mean that the majority of the Socialist leaders — like Rodolfo Morandi, Lelio Basso, Pietro Nenni, and Sando Pertini — actually supported outright fusion in 1945 and 1946, although they did speak in favour of unity. The reservations had appeared during the resistance, when the Communist leaders in the North, particularly Longo and Secchia, proposed the immediate formation of a united party on the strength of the insurrectional struggles.[7] At the end of the war, when the left parties were recruiting so rapidly (even the PSIUP boasted some seven hundred thousand members) and the mass rank-and-file of both parties saw no good reason for continued separation (not only sympathy, but even enthusiasm for the USSR was common to both parties), the Socialist leaders seemed to favour a rapid unification process. In October 1945, however, speaking to the Central Committee, Nenni began to take some distance from the impatient fusionist forces, which were now vehemently opposed by an 'autonomist' minority: 'The solution to the question of the new united party does not depend on us alone, but on national and international factors that we will be able to modify with time and patience. Right now, when we face the prospect of the struggle for a Constituent Assembly, is there any point in sharpening the polemic, or is it rather time for us to look loyally and frankly into our conscience?'[8]

The answer to Nenni's question was to postpone, if not definitively renounce, the fusion proposal. The struggle within the PSIUP on this issue was bitter indeed, and led to a split.[9] December 1945 was the last time the objective of organic unity was on the agenda in Italy. Luigi Longo made a report to the Fifth Congress of the PCI (as Duclos had done at the Tenth Congress of the PCF in June) in which he invoked the birth of the united party. Longo referred to the various forms of unity of the labour movements, which possessed, he said, a singular 'organizational variety and elasticity' that should be taken as exemplary. He therefore proposed to initiate a phase of 'federation' of the two workers parties, each of which would enjoy the strongest possible guarantees against any prevarication by the other and could 'maintain its own political and organizational physiognomy' while at the same time forming permanent party organs at the leadership and rank-and-file levels.[10]

This proposal was not dissimilar to Duclos's to the SFIO. But nothing came of it; even in the ranks of the PCI it got no great response. It was probably formulated in an effort to aid, and simultaneously to avoid embarrassing, the pro-unity currents of the PSI. In any event, the Communist congress did not concentrate on unity, which it considered premature. The Socialist congress of April 1946 in turn shunned the fusion perspective, and the two parties contested the Constituent Assembly elections with separate lists. The success scored by the Socialists showed that a good part of the electorate was not only wedded to the old banners, but also favoured a clear differentiation from the Communists.

The Italian case is especially interesting because of its international repercussions. Both Nenni and Togliatti, though luke-warm if not averse to immediate fusion, had resolved to foster united action on a European scale. Their common view was that the 'grand anti-fascist alliance' should continue, or at least that there should be peaceful coexistence between the victorious powers. Nenni still had ties to his friends of the Second International, which had vanished in 1940. Accompanied by Giuseppe Saragat, he had gone to London in March 1945 to attend the first post-war meeting of European Socialists, organized by the Labour Party. The conference was attended by representatives of the Socialist parties of France, Sweden, Belgium, Holland, Norway, Czechoslovakia, Spain, and Poland (emigrés in the latter three cases). Nenni hoped that the meeting would form a 'United Workers International' beginning with all the Socialists.[11] Little came of the London meeting: a committee was named to draft a plan to resuscitate the Second International. Fusion with the Communists was not even discussed. Back in Italy, Togliatti criticized the Socialist proposal to reconstitute their International, but he also went further:

> The task facing the working class and democrats in Europe today is to consolidate unity between the most advanced part of the proletariat, whose gaze and hopes are fixed on the great conquests of the October revolution and the triumphant victories of the Soviet Union, and that part of the Socialist proletariat which, while remaining in the old organizations, is nevertheless more conscious of the international duty of the workers and of the fact that unity serves the cause of democracy and socialism.[12]

It was as if Togliatti wanted to remind the Socialists that differentiation not only subsisted but had grown more pronounced with the rise of the USSR's attractive power for 'the most advanced part of the proletariat'. Were not Soviet triumphs now the lodestar for all? But although fusion was impossible, that was no reason to forsake closer unity, on a platform of the development of democracy. Hence a possibility, or rather a desire, which Togliatti formulated this way: 'What was and still remains necessary is a great European conference of all the workers parties to lay the basis for stable united action among them — united action that can subsequently be developed and strengthened in every sense. The Communist and Socialist workers of our country would all support such a proposal enthusiastically.'

There is no reason to believe that Togliatti's proposal was advanced on anyone else's suggestion. In fact, it rather seems that neither Moscow nor the other Communist parties were at all interested, and Togliatti himself let the matter drop when he saw the lack of response. Each national political party was wholly absorbed by conditions in its own country, and the non-socialist democratic and moderate forces were also organizing themselves, East and West alike, for the movement. In West Germany, for example, the Christian Democratic movement, co-operating with the already powerful French and Italian Catholic parties, was on the rise. The Socialists' silence also indicates that on the whole the European workers parties lacked any independent political initiative; nor did they manifest an international aspiration corresponding to the proposals of the most ardent exponents of union.

The reasons for this weakness were related to the state of the Socialist parties at the time. In May 1946 a sort of international Socialist conference was held at Clacton-on-Sea, near London. There were two major points on the agenda: the reconstitution of the Socialist International and the healing of splits in the workers movement. The conference results were disappointing on both counts. But the discussion showed the depth of the crisis of a perspective that had seemed realistic at the war's end: a reunification made possible by the close collaboration of the victorious powers, the British Labour Party acting as a bridge between the Americans and the Soviets. The tension of the Clacton conference was the product of the chill wind now blowing, of the incipient though not yet consolidated counter-position of international camps. The Socialist parties of East and West alike were caught in this pincer, the Labour Party no less than the others. Attlee and Bevin's foreign policy was by now decidedly Western-oriented, based on a close alliance with Washington. The idea of a 'third force', so warmly supported by the Labour left (including Laski, Richard Crossman, and Michael Foot), was fast being abandoned.

Laski refused to give up hope that a reformed International could play a positive role vis-à-vis the Soviet Union. At Clacton he affirmed:

> If Russia and the Social International reach an agreement, Europe will be a socialist continent in twenty years; on the other hand, if collaboration with Russia fails, most of Europe will fall prey to monopoly capitalism, which implies the danger of a Third World War. The new International will have to strive to win the friendship of the Soviet Union in order to avoid this catastrophe: that is its principal task. [13]

The political and ideological conflicts among the European democratic Socialists in Clacton inevitably split them along geographic lines. The Eastern parties insisted that their Western comrades had to understand that the Polish and Czechoslovak Socialists, for example, had no choice but to collaborate with the USSR in order to assure even their political survival. One author, who used archive sources to analyse the confidential debate closely, offered this particularly astute account:

> The first attempt to reconstruct the International failed in Clacton. Only the French, Belgians, Swiss, and Austrians supported reconstruction without reservation. All the others were against it. Moreover, the East European parties made it quite clear that they would never be able formally to join an international organization that would inevitably fall under the hegemony of the Western parties. They therefore fought for a workers International which, like the World Federation of Trade Unions founded in autumn 1945, would include both Socialist and Communist parties. Although this project was also supported by Nenni, De Brouckère, and some representatives of the French party, it was rejected by the majority of the delegates and was never discussed again. [14]

Although the Clacton delegates may not have realized it, the vote marked the end of a project, and the end of a period too. Fusion, having failed on a national scale, was now unthinkable internationally. Another six years passed before the Socialist International was finally reconstituted. For the moment, the conference formed the 'Comisco', a committee assigned to convoke the reconstruction congress, which was held only in 1951. The new International was thoroughly anti-Communist, aligned behind American foreign policy. In the meantime, there had been one last spurt of hope for the possibility of a 'third force'. In July 1946, the British Labour Party decided to send a delegation to the USSR to confer with Stalin directly. The 'goodwill mission', as it was called, included the party secretary, Morgan Phillips, as well as Alice Bacon, Harold Clay, and Harold Laski. Steininger writes:

> After a two-and-a-half-hour conversation, the British Labour leaders were convinced that Stalin harboured friendly feelings for Britain. Stalin expressed the 'fullest understanding' on international issues and said that he favoured the British road to socialism, although he remained convinced that the Russian road was the shortest, even though he recognized that it was accompanied by 'bloodshed'. But he avoided the question of healing the division in the international workers movement and its repercussions for possible collaboration among workers parties in Europe. [15]

Here we have another feature of the broader picture. The Americans, acting at first through their unions and then more and more decisively through the State Department itself, sought to isolate the Communists of Western Europe, primarily by using Christian Democratic forces, but without neglecting the Social Democrats either. Meanwhile, the Soviet Union, and Stalin personally, carefully refrained from countering this attempt by pressing for the unification of the European working class. He allowed the French and Italian Communist parties, and temporarily even those of Eastern Europe, a considerable degree of independence in seeking political alliances and delineating their own perspectives. But he demanded his own independence too, and he was interested mainly in the pursuit of his own foreign policy objectives. The years 1946 and early 1947 mark the final interlude in the evolution, or involution, if you will, of the Cold War.

Notes

1. Abendroth, *La socialdemocrazia in Germania*, pp. 79-80.

2. Peter Brandt, *Dopo Hitler: antinazismo e movimento operaio 1945-46*, Rome 1981, pp. 193-205.

3. From the programmatic declarations cited in Collotti, *Storia delle due Germani*, pp. 435-36.

4. Horst Lademacher, 'Possibilità e limiti d'azione del movimento operaio europeo nel primo dopoguerra', in *La sinistra europea*, pp. 51-52.

5. From the PCF's 'unity charter', *L'Humanité*, 12 June 1945.

6. See Fauvet, *Histoire du PCF*, vol. 2, pp. 162-63.

7. See 'Ipotesi di fusione tra comunisti e socialisti', letter sent from Milan to Togliatti, 26 March 1945, in Luigi Longo, *I centri dirigenti del Pci nella Resistenza*, Rome 1973, pp. 482-91.

9. For a documented reconstruction of this phase in the internal life of the PSI, see Stefano Merli, *Il 'partito nuovo' di Lelio Basso*, Padua 1981.

10. Luigi Longo, 'Per il partito unico della classe operaia', in *Documenti del V congresso del Pci*, Rome 1946.

11. 'Le riunioni di Londra', *Avanti!*, 4 March 1945, reprinted in Nenni, *Il vento del Nord*, pp. 306-08.

12. 'La costituzione della Seconda Internazionale', *l'Unità*, 11 March 1945, reprinted in Palmiro Togliatti, *Per la salvezza del nostro paese*, Rome 1946, p. 375.

13. From the memorandum presented to the conference, preserved in the Labour Party archives and quoted in R. Steininger, 'L'Internazionale socialista dopo la seconda guerra mondiale', in *La sinistra europea*, p. 143.

14. Ibid., p. 145.

15. Ibid., p. 146.

22

'New Roads' to Socialism

Sometimes even jokes leak out of the most tightly sealed archives — and the ones that concern our investigation are almost all hermetic. One, related by Khrushchev, was recounted by a Czechoslovak historian who was fortunate enough to get a look at documents stored in the Central Committee archive of that country's Communist Party. It seems that at the 1960 international conference of eighty-one Communist parties Khrushchev was boasting of Soviet conduct in the East European countries just after the war. 'We helped the Communists take power', he said, and continued: 'Some of you must remember the joke that was going around in Poland at the time of the elections in January 1947. A Pole says, looking at a ballot-box, "What kind of box is this? You put in Mikolajczyk and it comes out Gomulka." Who was in power in the People's Democracies at first, comrades? It wasn't the Communists. The Communists came to power later.'[1]

The joke concerns one of the most controversial problems, and in considering it one has no choice but to rely on inferences and conjectures. The issue, closely related to the course of the Cold War, is this: what were Stalin's intentions with regard to the 'Communization' of Eastern Europe? Was there a master plan from the very outset, or were retaliatory measures taken as American policy stiffened? Was Stalin simply reacting to Truman's policy, which was aimed not only at 'containing' Soviet expansion, but at rolling it back, in Greece and Turkey, Iran and China? There is no sign of any such plan at the beginning. The Communists of Eastern Europe were simply supposed to ensure control, stabilization, and friendship.[2] The date of the turn is important: exactly when was the 'later' to which Stalin's successor referred? And can this question be separated from the controversy about who began the 'new course' that unleashed the Cold War? Historians are divided on the more general theme. Most

American revisionist historians, from Kolko to Alperovitz, ascribe great importance to the differences between Truman's political orientation and Roosevelt's policy of collaboration with Moscow. It was, they argue, Truman's preconceived hostility that triggered a matching Soviet response. In recent years, with the turbulent waters of ideological Manichaeanism stilled, the British scholar A.J.P. Taylor has affirmed that 'the Cold War was started and pursued by the Americans. All Stalin wanted was to guarantee Russian security'.[3] On the other hand, another American historian, D.F.Fleming, also a revisionist, sees the issue differently, particularly as regards events in Eastern Europe:

> The advance of Russian influence and control to the Stettin-Prague-Trieste line was the greatest result of the Second World War. It was Russian control of Eastern Europe which alarmed the West and precipitated the Cold War. If the Russians had been willing to fight the war without any permanent power gains in this region there would have been no plunge toward a third world war after 1945.
>
>   Russian-Communist control of East Europe was the basis of the belief in the West that Russia was out to conquer the world. Vice versa it was the Western oppositions to Soviet organization of Eastern Europe which convinced the Red leaders that the West was fundamentally as hostile as ever.[4]

There was thus a sort of 'vicious circle'[5] It is perhaps not even possible to say which side initiated the escalation, since the Soviet Communists could not have avoided establishing a social and political organization corresponding to their own tradition and conviction, and to their own system of rule, in the zones in which they had special influence. But — and here is the key question — was it inevitable that the East European countries would follow that road? And were they not motivated by the obsession with security that dominated Stalin's policy rather than by his aspirations for world conquest?

It seems completely out of the question that Stalin had the will to conquer all of Europe in the politically foreseeable future, or even that he nurtured the hope. We have already made this point, and it is by no means difficult to confirm it for 1947 and the birth of the Cominform. Probably less far from the truth are those observers who have argued that the 'Communization' of Eastern Europe was part and parcel of Stalin's need to protect the USSR from penetration by excessively 'democratic' political and cultural ideas and experiences.[6] Avoiding Western contamination was a prime concern right from the end of the war: it sparked not only a new police crackdown internally, with the rebirth of coercive measures in the reconstruction effort, but also Stalin's almost unbelievable decision to intern in concentration camps perhaps as many as half the Soviet prisoners returning home from German camps. It has been estimated that more than half a million ex-soldiers suffered this 'punishment'. [7]

According to Giuseppe Boffa, Stalin's determination to 'stand firm' against the Western powers, convinced that they would not go to war against him, at least for the moment, took root 'very quickly'. [8] Perhaps as early as 1945, certainly by the spring of 1946. Nor did Truman waste any time. Immediately upon his assumption of the presidency, he began manifesting intransigence on various questions. He wanted to 'stop coddling' the Russians — or so he said, both to Molotov and to his own associates. [9]

The psychological element is a recurring theme in the enormous literature on the causes of the Cold War. The USSR and the US were always suspicious of each other's intentions, and each consistently placed the worst possible interpretation on every initiative or demand of the other — for their mentality, historic memory, political traditions, and ideological schemas were directly counterposed. Not everything, of course, was a result of a failure to communicate. More weighty factors were at issue too: antithetical economic systems and interests, intricate territorial questions that often aroused dissension at peace talks, in the Balkans, on the Italian–Yugoslav border, the Yugoslav–Austrian border. The temperature was also raised by sharpening social conflicts in many countries, in the course of which the contending classes sought support from, and even pressured, the leading nation of one or the other international camp. The lack of 'strategic equilibrium' was perhaps the prime reason for tension. On a world scale, the US was militarily stronger than the USSR. Washington's intransigence stimulated Soviet desire to close the gap with its potential enemy, which held a monopoly on atomic weapons.

While no agreement was reached on the problem of Germany — which led to a freezing of positions in the occupation zones and to serious crises like the Berlin blockade of 1948–49 — Stalin unilaterally resolved the question of Poland in the manner he had long desired, turning it not simply into a friendly state, but into a satellite. Between 1945 and 1947, the USSR faced an outright guerrilla war on its Western borders, with thousands of dead, not only in Poland, but also in Lithuania and Ukraine.

In Europe as a whole, however, the balance of forces was favourable to the USSR in 1945–46. The *glacis* of which Blum had spoken was a reality, and Communist and pro-Communist left parties had great weight in Western societies and governments. Allied troops stationed in Europe were demobilized fairly rapidly. The first American cries of alarm date from 1945. Pope Pius XII and the Vatican were increasingly worried about the threat of Communist predominance and what it could mean for the Catholic Church. In the East — Poland, Yugoslavia, and Hungary — the Church had been directly affected by the socio-economic changes under way and was already complaining, especially in Yugoslavia, about persecution of clerics and the ecclesiastical hierarchy, if not of religion itself. In Italy even more than in France, the Pope was so concerned that he took the lead in a general struggle against the Communist Party. The gathering clouds were soon evident in the words of political leaders.

Symptomatic was the reaction to two speeches, one by Stalin in Moscow in February 1946 and one by Churchill the following month in Fulton, Missouri. In his programmatic address, the Soviet leader resuscitated the concept, traditional in Marxist-Leninist culture, that 'the capitalist system of world economy conceals in itself elements of general crisis and military clashes'.[10] Stalin recalled that the Second World War had broken out as an inevitable result of the development of world economic and political forces on the basis of modern monopoly capitalism'. This contention stirred American political circles, which took it — or pretended to do so — as a return to ideological rigidity and as an indication that Stalin believed that future wars were inevitable too, since monopolist imperialism was now stronger than before. Yet it was in this same speech that Stalin acknowledged that 'from the very outset' the Second World War 'assumed the nature of an anti-fascist war, a war of liberation'.

Churchill's speech in Missouri the following month also aroused great apprehension and genuine alarm in Moscow. Fleming pointed out its psychological effect. The Soviet leaders were alarmed, while depression and indignation spread among public opinion:

> They would therefore be slow to believe in the possibility of war again, without a bombshell such as Churchill's speech. It 'had the effect of electrifying and depressing everyone' and it fell squarely into the familiar pattern of Soviet beliefs — capitalist hostility, encirclement, and the violent imperialism of a dying capitalist economy leading to war — this time against the Soviet Union.[11]

Alexander Werth, a British journalist then in the USSR, also called attention to the great impression made by Churchill's denunciation of 'the unlimited expansion of Soviet power and of its doctrine'. People began anxiously talking about 'the next war'. In an interview published in *Pravda* that same month Stalin rejected Churchill's accusations, denied that the Soviet Union had 'expansionist tendencies', and said that the 'neighbouring' states of Eastern Europe were governed by 'a bloc of several parties, ranging from four to six, and the more or less legal opposition parties can take part in the government'. They were, he said, far from the 'totalitarian police states' that Churchill claimed. [12]

The great efforts at reconstruction in these countries scored significant successes in 1946. The process of transformation of economic structures began in the industrial sector (especially in Czechoslovakia and Poland), but despite strong social tension, there were no sharp breaks pointing to immediate 'Communization'. Many observers have spoken of this period as an 'interlude'. [13] The same might well be said of the international situation, for although there were points of tension, there were also instances of relaxation, and even of Soviet retreat, such as on the question of a naval base in the Dardanelles, or Iran, from which country Soviet troops were withdrawn. The first peace treaties with defeated countries were also signed. The future People's Democracies had the most diverse constitutional regimes, ranging from monarchies to parliamentary republics to the 'people's republic' of Yugoslavia. Fejtö resurrected the term 'dual power' [14] to describe the mounting superimposition of a 'secret power' exercised by the local Communists and the Soviet occupation authorities over the legal regime and the institutional and political system, which were still pluralist.

Were democracy and national sovereignty in these countries no more than tactical cover, or could their evolution have really diverged from the Soviet model? There was undoubtedly great uncertainty, as the Soviets manifested day-to-day pragmatism and caution. It is difficult to detect any definite plan of gradual Communization. This is also the opinion of an American observer, Fred Warner Neal: ·

The original concept of 'people's democracy' foresaw a mixed political system in which the Communists would play an important, but not necessarily dominant, part. The assumption was that Soviet military strength would be used to guarantee the 'security' of these regimes. Only in Yugoslavia, which was not under direct Soviet control, was a Communist dictatorship established immediately after the war. In the other East European countries Communization began only when Stalin concluded that Western interference in his East European policy constituted a threat in this area of vital interest to the Soviets. In fact, the complete Communization of the region began only after the proclamation of the two-blocs doctrine, in 1947, and in Hungary it was deferred to the following year. [15]

Since there was a clear tendency of assimilation to the Soviet system of rule in 1947 and 1948, many historians have naturally suspected that all the talk in late 1946 about new roads to socialism, and even the dispute about the nature of the People's Democracies, was nothing but a 'well-devised trick' — the expression is Brzezinski's. But according to Kaplan, the Czechoslovak historian quoted above, Stalin himself encouraged a campaign to popularize the so-called new roads. During the 'goodwill mission' of the British Labour Party members led by Morgan Phillips in July 1946, Stalin held a private and confidential conversation with Laski, one of his British guests. Stalin abandoned himself to curious confidences, telling Laski, for example, that there were people in the Kremlin like Molotov who believed that no rapprochement with Britain was possible and who wanted a tougher Soviet policy against the Anglo-Saxons, and others, like himself, who disagreed. He encouraged Laski to pursue the building of socialism in Britain, which would also 'contribute to the realization of socialism throughout Europe'. [16]

There is no mention of such overtures, promises, and conjectures in the account of the official conversations between Stalin and the Labour delegation. [17] Instead we find only academic discussion about two different roads to socialism, British and Soviet. The latter, according to Stalin, was 'shorter', though also more painful. The indiscretion about dissension in the Kremlin may have been no more than a clever ruse, quite typical of the leader's behaviour. Stalin was adept at drawing his interlocutors into relations of confidence, at hinting to them that he personally was always ready for compromises to overcome internal obstacles. It was a kind of foretaste of the designation of 'hawks' and 'doves', or 'hard' and 'soft' wings that later became so common in distinguishing between conservatives and reformists in leadership groups, whether American or Soviet.

But the Czechoslovak archives contain a less debatable item: a report by the secretary of the Czechoslovak Communist Party to the Central Committee, dated September 1946. In it Gottwald says:

You have certainly read the news in the papers about Comrade Stalin's discussion with the delegation from the British Labour Party. In that discussion Comrade Stalin mentioned, or referred to, the possibility of various paths to socialism. I do not know how accurately the discussion was reported in our press, but as proof that the subject certainly came up, I can assure you that during my last visit to Moscow I too spoke to Stalin about this problem. Comrade Stalin told me that experience has demonstrated and the classics of Marxism–Leninism teach that there is not just the one path, through soviets and the dictatorship of the proletariat, but that there can also be other roads to socialism in particular circumstances. [18]

If the quoted document is authentic — and it appears to be — then it sheds new light on a singular phenomenon: in subsequent months, a veritable chorus of Communist leaders began singing the praises of the 'new roads', of paths to socialism different from the Russian way. This chorus included not only the Polish, Czech, Hungarian, and Bulgarian Communists, but also the French and Italians. In September Dimitrov promised that 'Bulgaria will not be a Soviet republic'. Soon after, Rákosi added that 'there is not just one single road to socialism'. Gottwald repeated that 'experience and Marxist–Leninist teachings alike demonstrate that the dictatorship of the proletariat and the construction of a Soviet regime is not the only path leading to socialism'. Gomulka openly polemicized against those who claimed that the Polish Workers Party wanted to follow the 'same path' as the USSR explaining: 'We have chosen a Polish road of development of our own, a road of people's democracy, and we think that under these conditions, along this road, the dictatorship of the working class, and still more of a single party, would be neither useful nor necessary.' [19]

In November 1946 it was Thorez's turn to declare, in an interview with the London *Times*, that 'the advance of democracy everywhere, throughout the world (with rare exceptions which only confirm the rule), offers socialism the choice of other paths different from that of Russian Communism.' [20] Togliatti spoke in similar terms in Florence in January 1947:

International experience tells us that, in the present conditions of class struggle throughout the world, the working class and the vanguard toiling masses can find new paths to socialism — that is, to the development of democracy to its ultimate limits, which is precisely what socialism is — which differ, for example, from those followed by the working class and the toilers in the Soviet Union. [21]

Togliatti went into the various 'roads' at great length, singling out Yugoslavia for special praise: there 'new forms of the organization of power' had arisen and the liberation front was 'a mass organization'. There was no dictatorship of the proletariat in Yugoslavia, Togliatti said, and there were no soviets. It was one of the many paradoxes of the time that while the Soviets and the Italian Communists were talking about how different 'Yugoslav people's democracy' was from the Soviet model, Yugoslav speakers on the matter always insisted that the opposite was the case, that their 'people's democracy'[22] was no more or less than a form of the dictatorship of the proletariat, precisely of the *Soviet type*. When the break with the other Communist parties came in 1948, the Yugoslavs retaliated against this distinction with vehement polemics. Kardelj, for instance, said that the theory of 'new paths' lacked all foundation, and he recalled that in September 1947, at the founding conference of the Cominform, the Yugoslavs had vigorously expressed their view of the matter:

> We owe the victory of our people's revolution precisely to the fact that we nurtured no illusions as to the 'new paths in principle' which lead to socialism. We were the only ones to set out this attitude clearly at the first session of the Informbureau [Cominform]. Contrary to it, the leaders of the Communist parties of the other People's Democracies constantly made some kind of 'discoveries, about their own — in principle — 'new path' to socialism, about various 'specific harmonies' between socialist and capitalist elements, and about the especial worth of some vestiges of bourgeois democracy, which they glorified as a singular aspect of a People's Democracy. And all of them were unendingly claiming patents for these 'discoveries' of theirs. Then the Soviet professors repeated these phrases in countless variations. That is why the Soviet press always gave more prominence to various opportunistic absurdities from the other People's Democracies than to facts about the new Yugoslavia, which stood far ahead of the others. And we, who contended that we had won our socialist revolution, that our People's Democracy was of the Soviet type, we were told that we were narrow-minded sectarians and entirely incapable of inventing something new, despite the fact that practically everything that is really new in our present People's Democracies had been created in our country.[23]

A very significant passage. It also confirms that there was a genuine press campaign about the 'new roads' at the end of 1946, that the possibility of maintaining forms of parliamentary democracy, of avoiding institutional upheavals, and of not embarking on the road of the dictatorship of the proletariat was still being upheld. Was this a mere propagandistic smokescreen to parry accusations from Western powers that the Communists held power 'secretly' in Eastern Europe? There was undeniably an element of this, given the simultaneity and exact concordance of the statements of Gomulka, Rákosi, Gottwald, and the others. But it was more than that, for these overtures genuinely corresponded to each country's and each leadership group's need for autonomy, to the desire of the Communist leaders to experiment with gradual evolution without losing the required political allies. The same goes for the French and Italian Communists, who joined the chorus by trumpeting their own democratic perspective, the constitutional road to socialism. The Yugoslav polemic — which reflected the pride of a party and country which, unlike the others, had made a socialist revolution with its own forces — also indicates that the irritation of the Soviets and the other People's Democracies does not date from the beginning of 1948 but actually goes back to 1945–47.

The subject of the possibility of and the right to attempt 'new roads' to socialism was at first closely related to another subject of controversy: the nature of the People's Democracies. In 1946-47 the expression commonly used to characterize the regimes taking shape in Eastern Europe was 'new democracy' rather than 'people's democracy'. But the terminological shift is secondary. The more delicate and interesting point is that in some of these countries forms of genuine political pluralism really existed and seemed possible even in the future. This was especially true in Czechoslovakia, a classical parliamentary democracy that was moving rapidly toward a socialist social transformation. Recent Czechoslovak historiography — although prevented from expressing itself fully because of the intervention of the Warsaw Pact countries in 1968 — had begun to suggest that in 1945–47 there was a real possibility of pioneering an original, democratic road to socialism. It has been noted:

> Some Czechoslovak historiography is of the opinion that after the nationalizations of October 1945, when an economic model was created based on various sectors (small private production, middle-sized private entrepreneurial activity, and large-scale nationalized industry, including the mines, energy sources, banks, insurance companies, etc.), and when the two-year plan was hinged on the active participation of all these sectors, the preconditions existed for the continuation of pluralism in the political domain as well. Had favourable international circumstances prevailed, a new model of socialism could have gradually arisen, significantly different from the Stalin model.[24]

The first economist to attempt a systematic theory of the new reality was Eugene Varga, in a book published in 1946 whose main ideas were summarized in a widely noted article in early 1947.[25] In this article, the Hungarian economist, who commanded great scientific and political authority in the Soviet world, took a series of important steps. First of all he argued that the states that he defined as 'absolutely new in the history of humanity', both economically and politically: economically because although private property in the means of production persisted, 'the great industrial enterprises, transport, and the credit system are in the hands of the state'; politically because the Communist parties played an essential part in the ruling fronts or blocs. But no less important was a factor reminiscent of the point made by Fred Warner Neal: these countries, to quote Varga, 'have received moral, political, and economic support from the Soviet Union, without which the new democratic states would probably have been unable to resist the attacks of reaction, external and internal alike. The fate of Greece is quite instructive in this regard.'[26]

In the second half of 1946 Greece had already become one of the theatres of Cold War. King George II had returned to the country, and despite the monarch's reservations, the Tsaldaris government had embarked upon an increasingly right-wing policy. The shift from British to American 'tutelage' was fast approaching, while the Communists were organizing partisan bands in the north, under the command of Markos Vaphiadis, the ELAS leader. The Soviet attitude to Greece was more than prudent, while considerable aid for the partisans came from the Yugoslavs, Bulgarians, and Albanians. Varga's essay concluded, not without reason, by noting the bleak international outlook. A year later, this would be a Communist leitmotif, Varga recalled that the USSR had every interest in ensuring that the new states were strong enough economically, politically, and militarily to withstand a foreign attack, 'at least until Soviet armies could come to their aid and thereby prevent their transformation into the anti-Soviet military bases that they were during the Second World War'. He then sketched out the terms of the broader conflict that had now opened up: 'The new democratic states are the crucial front of struggle between the two systems that survived the war.'

It was, indeed, a time of transition. On the twenty-ninth anniversary of the October Revolution (November 1946), Zhdanov hailed 'the new, genuine democracy' of the East European states, calling them 'fraternal Slavic countries'. A good part of his speech was devoted to the threat from 'reactionary Anglo-American circles'.[27] There was no explicit and direct denunciation of Truman's orientation yet, but that would come soon. The American president himself was about to add fuel to the fire.

Notes

1. 'Karel Kaplan, 'Il piano di Stalin', *Panorama*, vol. 15, no. 575, 26 April 1977.
2. See Starobin, *Origins of the Cold War*, p. 686.
3. From an interview with Laura Lilli, *La Repubblica*, 26 August 1976.
4. Fleming, *The Cold War*, vol. 1, p. 249.
5. See Gambino, *Le conseguenze della seconda guerra mondiale*, p. 87.
6. See especially, Claudín, *The Communist Movement*, pp. 465-66.
7. Boffa, *Storia dell'Unione Sovietica*, vol. 2, p. 311.
8. Ibid., p. 316.
9. On the major instances of Truman's intransigence, see Alperovitz, *Un asso nella manica*, pp. 19-41, drawn mainly from American memoirs.
10. From the text in *Stalin and Molotov Address their Constituents*, p. 3.
11. Fleming, *The Cold War*, vol. 1, p. 354.
12. Werth, *Russia: the Post-War Years*, pp. 112-13.
13. See especially Brzezinski, *The Soviet Bloc*, pp. 45-46, and Droz, *Storia del socialismo* pp. 520 ff.
14. Fejtö, *Histoire des Démocraties Populaires*, p. 125.
15. Neal, 'La politica di Stalin', p. 1072.
16. Kaplan, 'Il piano di Stalin'.
17. See 'Goodwill Mission to the USSR', in the archives of the Labour Party: account of the Moscow meetings signed by all the members of the delegation (photocopy in possession of the author).
18. Kaplan, 'Il piano di Stalin'.
19. This, like the statements quoted previously, was published in *Rinascita*, vol. 4, no. 7, July 1947, pp. 193-95, and no. 8, August 1947, pp. 225-29. This also indicates that Togliatti wanted to emphasize that the statements were meant as a general pronouncement.
20. Ibid., July 1947.
21. The text of Togliatti's speech was reproduced in *Critica Marxista*, vol. 2, no. 4-5, July-October 1964, p. 191.
22. At the end of November 1943 the Yugoslav Communists declared the creation of a revolutionary state, a 'people's democracy'. See Droz, *Storia del socialismo*, p. 491. On the lack of clarity of many of the claims and comments about people's democracy, see Hobsbawm, 'Gli intellettuali e l'antifascismo', p. 487.
23. A. Kardelj, 'On People's Democracy in Yugoslavia', *Komunist* (Belgrade), September 1949. The extract above is quoted in Brzezinski, *The Soviet Bloc*, p. 38.
24. Josef Belda, 'Alcuni problemi della via cecoslovacca al socialismo', in *La crisi del modello sovietico*, p. 62.
25. E. Varga, 'Democracy of a New Type', in *Mirovoe Khoziaistvo i Mirovaia Politika*, no. 3, 1947. Earlier statements of the same sort appeared in his book *Izmeneniia v Ekonomike Kapitalizma v itoge mirovoi voiny*, chapter 15, Moscow 1946. On the development of the theory of people's democracy, see H. Gordon Skilling, 'People's Democracy in Soviet Theory', *Soviet Studies*, vol. 3, nos. 1 and 2, July 1951 (pp. 16-33) and October 1951 (pp. 131-49).
26. I am quoting from the Italian translation of the article, published in *Rinascita*, vol. 4, no. 6, June 1947, p. 141.
27. 'The Twenty-Ninth Anniversary of the Great October Socialist Revolution', in Zhdanov, *Politica e ideologia*, pp. 3-24.

23

The Cold War Arrives

Eugene Varga can be considered the emblematic figure of a turn, to some extent even its scapegoat. In 1948–49 his theory that the People's Democracies were a historic novelty was confuted by events, as they became dictatorships of the proletariat forced to conform to the Soviet model. Varga had also argued that capitalism would be able to ward off, or at least to postpone, a general crisis. By May 1947 he was being subject to harsh criticism for this. He was soon relieved of many of his duties, and the Institute of World Economy and Politics, of which he had been director, was closed down.[1] The official line was that the capitalist system was poised on the brink of a catastrophic crisis. Indeed, the virulence and imperialist aggressivity of capitalism were said to result precisely from desperate attempts to avert this crisis by provoking tension, conflict, and war. Propagandistic use of this thesis became common in subsequent years.

The Yugoslav Communists, who stood in the front ranks of the People's Democracies, were struck by a kind of law of retaliation. Their conception of the new regime as revolutionary, as a national adaptation of the Soviet model, had triumphed, but this coincided with their excommunication by the Kremlin in 1948. Soviet ideological fury, whether genuine or artificial, gave a heavy hint of things to come, now as in the past. Whether he really believed in an imminent crisis of capitalism or not, Stalin was facing mounting difficulties. Once again Manichaeanism was his response to these difficulties, both foreign and domestic. The Soviet countryside was under pressure again. The winter of 1946–47 had been tragic, with a serious famine. 'There was literal starvation.'[2] The individual kolkhozes were severely tested. Cherished hopes that there would be some relief, some degree of well-being after the war, vanished. Reconstruction did score successes too, but once again at the cost of grave sacrifices and fresh restrictions. Not only was the standard of living driven down, but the areas of relative freedom in civil and cultural life that had arisen at the end of the war were narrowed.

It was not by accident that in September 1946 Zhdanov began thundering against instances of laxity in literature, singling out the journal *Zvezda* and particularly Zoshchenko and Akhmatova, the former the author of 'revolting' short stories, the latter of 'mystically reactionary' poetry, and pornographic to boot. The cultural ideologue Zhdanov called Akhamtova a typical representative 'of this idea-less reactionary morass'.[3] In 1947 there were no less bitter attacks on philosophers who 'lagged behind'.[4] The 'ideological front' was heating up, and the new intolerance outstripped even that of the early Stalin era.

In many respects, 1947 was the year of the turn. It began in January with the fraudulent election results in Poland that Khrushchev found so amusing. The ruling bloc, led by the Communists, got an overwhelming majority of 327 seats, while Mikolajczyk was left with only 24 and wiped off the political map. In October he fled to the West, never to return.

The other events that marked the opening of the Cold War are well known. In March Truman announced the doctrine of 'containment', according to which the security of the United States was said to be in danger wherever peace was threatened by direct or indirect aggression. America became the leader of what was called the 'Free World'. In March and April the international conference of foreign ministers in Moscow failed. It proved impossible to reach a joint solution to the problem of Germany. In fact, the designation 'defeated countries' now practically disappeared. Each of the two Cold War protagonists tightened its grip on the zones controlled by its armed forces. Truman sought to secure political and military control not only of Greece, but also of fascist countries like Spain and Portugal, not to mention Japan. He also still hoped to shore up Chiang Kai-shek against the Chinese Communists. In April the Communists were expelled from government in France and Italy (along with the pro-unity Socialists in the latter country). Events followed swiftly, one after another. Alexander Werth noted:

> In 1947, after the breakdown of the Moscow conference, there appeared the very striking phenomenon of the 'parallel advance' of East and West. It was as if every American move to eliminate Communists from West European governments and make these countries benefit under the Truman doctrine was followed by a parallel Russian move to strengthen the Soviet hold on the countries of Eastern Europe.[5]

At the end of May a plot by the smallholders party was discovered in Hungary and Ferenc Nagy, president of the Council, left permanently for Switzerland. Rákosi already had control of the situation, although he was in no hurry to act. That same month, Truman initiated the first measures to vet government employees for loyalty. In June special measures were enacted in the USSR against those who revealed 'state secrets'; the atmosphere for Western correspondents in Moscow grew sombre. Soon came the most important factor of all, the launching of the Marshall Plan, named after the American secretary of state who proposed it on 5 June 1947 at a conference at Harvard University. It was a vast project of American aid to Europe, West and East, apparently with no political strings atteached. But Truman himself said in his memoirs that with this massive economic aid, the United States 'helped save Europe from economic disaster and lifted it from the shadow of enslavement by Russian Communism.'[6]

Events then took their course. At a conference organized by Bidault in Paris in June–July 1947 to discuss the project, Molotov rejected the American plan, which officially was also addressed to the USSR. But it was warmly received by the French and British governments. The Soviet minister of foreign affairs replied that nothing good could come of a plan that was in substance an instrument for the political subjugation and blackmail of the European countries in the interests of American supremacy. The Polish and Czechoslovak governments, which had decided to accept the plan because of their industries' great need for dollars, were compelled to renounce this decision after an ultimatum from Stalin at the beginning of July. Hubert Ripka, Czechoslovak minister of foreign trade and a Socialist leader, commented: 'Could we risk a complete break with Moscow? The Soviets might well incite the Communists, in that case, to effect a *coup d'état.* [In those circumstances] we were unfortunately unable to expect effective help from the Western powers. . . . But there was another reason, still more serious. I know that we could not win over the majority of the people for such a policy.'[7]

The Czechs, like the Poles, bowed to the ultimatum. Ripka's remarks recall two features of the time that mark the decisive beginning of the Cold War. One was the counterposition of the two great powers, the other a serious radicalization of antagonistic social and political forces, East and West. The first factor was undoubtedly predominant. Stalin faced a fundamental choice: once all hope of collaboration with America had collapsed (and with it the possibility of amicably resolving the outstanding major problems, including the question of reparations from defeated Germany or even an American loan to the USSR without political strings), he felt that if he was to avoid acknowledging US international hegemony, he had to accept the risk of global conflict. It was now time to close ranks (and to tighten belts), to make up the atomic-weapons gap, and to mobilize all the energies of the Soviet camp and sphere of influence to stand up to the 'imperialists'. In any event, was not capitalism heading for a grave economic crisis?

The subsequent shifts of Soviet policy, both foreign and domestic, as well as the changes in Stalin's policy toward the Communist movement, were consequences of that basic choice made in the summer of 1947. It has been asked whether the choice was really necessary, whether Stalin could not have allowed the Czechs and Poles to accept American aid, whether he could not have responded other than through a defensive involution. These are legitimate questions, not dissimilar in spirit to Togliatti's 1962 comment about 'mistaken political trends' and the inadequate use of the creative capacities of the European Communist movement. But the fact remains that after the Second World War Stalin maintained a very rigid view of Soviet security. While he believed that Truman would not go so far as to launch a war, he sought to fortify his own camp without allowing it a political articulation whose autonomist dangers he feared more than he appreciated its 'creativity'.

Soviet policy had reason for great concern.

> During the summer of 1947 Stalin found himself trapped in a situation which the Soviet state had always tried — with success — to avoid since the time of Lenin, the formation of an anti-Soviet block made up of all the capitalist states. The situation in 1947 had the additional feature that the bloc was taking shape under the leadership of the most powerful state in history. There could be no doubt that this was disaster for the 'peace' Stalin had sought, the 'peace' which was to ratify the division of the world into 'areas of influence' on the basis of a world-wide Soviet–American agreement.[8]

The reflex was primarily one of defensive entrenchment. This did not necessarily mean complete renunciation of manoeuvring room. In an April 1947 interview with Harold Stassen, a candidate for president in the US elections of 1948, Stalin said that 'the possibility of co-operation is always present, but the same is not true for the *desire* for co-operation; and when there is no such desire, there can be war'.[9] Stalin then invoked a curious historical parallel: 'That was what happened to us with Hitler's Germany; we wanted to co-operate even with her, but she refused.' No less significant was the insistence with which Stalin asked his interlocutor whether he thought an economic crisis was possible in the United States. The Soviet leader was probably genuinely convinced that the American economy was doomed to sink into crisis and that France and Britain 'would not put up with the Truman *diktat* indefinitely'.[10] The traditional Communist thesis of a capitalist West sapped by deep internal contradictions; suspicion of, or rather hostility toward, European Social Democracy: the reprise of these ideological schemas and political convictions became increasingly prominent during the rule of the late Stalin, the Stalin of old age, when the suspicion congenital to his character assumed truly paranoid forms.

But as I mentioned, there were also reflections of international tension in the internal situations of various European countries, and these reflections often themselves contributed to an increasingly pronounced dichotomy, a bipolarism that lasted for decades. The expulsion of the French and Italian Communists from their respective governments, for example, was not primarily a response to pressure, and still less any sort of order, from Washington. Although the two events occurred in the same month, they had to do with specific *internal* developments. In France the break between Ramadier, the old Socialist president of the Council, and Thorez's party occurred over serious differences about social policy, wages and prices, militant agitation by the workers, and colonial policy (the SFIO supported open warfare against the Vietnamese liberation movement, which had begun in late 1946). And the initiative for their departure from the government, 'at least temporarily',[11] seems to have come from the Communists themselves. In Italy a long list of tensions and instances of imcompatibility, especially over economic policy, convinced De Gasperi to oust the Communists. A good part of Christian Democracy, the Church of Rome, and many big industrialists were all pressing for the removal of the Socialists and Communists from the government coalition. The break was brought about by endogenous impulses and the Communists took no strong mass action to oppose their expulsion, or *éviction*, as the French called it. It has long been established that it was Rome that was pressing Washington for economic support and firm guarantees (military ones included) to ward off the danger of internal uprisings; no offer or request came from the Truman administration.[12] It is true, however, that the rupture was made possible by the international situation, and that Truman and Marshall lost no time in rushing to the aid of their French and Italian friends, just as they had in March, handing out credits left and right. But at the time European social and political forces did not understand that the summer of 1947 marked a lasting turn. It was difficult to gauge its import, partly because not all bridges between the US and the USSR were down, and the apex of the Cold War did not come until 1949–51. Although the perception that national unity was finished was not widespread, the point did soon dawn on the most alert leaders. One of these was Togliatti, who more than most others had believed in the possibility of a long phase of collaboration among the powers of the 'grand anti-fascist alliance' and who had laboured mightily to contribute to the drafting of a democratic constitution as a 'social pact' among various popular components: Catholic, Communist, Socialist, and liberal. At the July 1947 session of the PCI Central Committee he sounded the alarm, presenting a bleak picture of the international situation: 'The characteristic fact about the world situation as far as the imperialist forces are concerned is that one great imperialist power has won a position of such strength that it stands far above the others; this power has now set itself the task of winning world domination.'[13]

Togliatti was not unaware that a military imbalance lay at the root of the existing tension, that the US monopoly of atomic weapons was its most tangible expression, and that it would continue to be until the other side acquired such a weapon or 'it was outlawed'. Had international tension reached the point that war had become 'a real and imminent prospect'? 'I maintain', Togliatti answered, 'that it cannot yet be considered imminent. But there is no doubt that the most aggressive imperialist elements, American in particular, are acting so as to bring this prospect about; it already exists, and is becoming ever more real and even imminent.'

In any event, Togliatti admonished those who felt that the PCI's explusion from the government was temporary, that the breach would soon be healed: 'I maintain that the situation in which the party is not in the government but stands outside and in opposition to it may also last for a long time.'

It turned out to be even longer than Togliatti expected, partly because the following year, 1948, the Italian left parties boldly threw themselves into an electoral test, in which they stood on common lists in a 'people's democratic front', and suffered a truly historic defeat, Christian Democracy taking the absolute majority of seats in parliament. In July 1947, however, Togliatti seemed quite concerned and perplexed. Something more than a shift to the right was at issue. Peaceful coexistence itself was at stake, and with it the entire prospect that the Communist movement in Europe had upheld after the war:

what the Italian Communists called 'progressive democracy', meaning a legal struggle for major reforms, beginning with a general
agrarian reform, to be achieved through a process of democratization
of the state and society. 'Progressive democracy' was supposed to
open the road to socialism, and that road would be travelled with
other political forces, Socialist and Catholic, so that the monopoly
capitalist groups and reactionary rubbish would be countered by a
front of reformers.

This was not supposed to be just an 'Italian road'. In his report
Togliatti recalled that it had been considered throughout Europe, but
he now began to doubt — for the first time — whether it was still
practicable. The relevant passages are carefully measured. First he
offered this assessment of post-war Europe:

> The reality is that a highly singular new situation was created in Europe
> after the war — one unprecedented in the recent history of the European
> peoples and characterized by a direct and organized popular upsurge
> under the leadership of well-qualified political forces. An attempt was
> made, on the basis of the tragic experience of the war, to bring about
> profound changes in the economic, political, and social structure. . . .
> This upsurge had the following character: in all the European countries, it
> sought to achieve, under the leadership of the most advanced democratic
> forces, the creation of democratic systems of a new type that would
> introduce something completely new into the political direction and
> economic structure of the individual countries. The general formula
> under which this upsurge occurred was anti-fascist unity.

Nowhere else did Togliatti express greater conviction in the general
validity of this experience and this prospect.

> The advent of Communist parties to power after the war in nearly all the
> countries of Europe, with the exceptions of which we are all aware, meant
> the participation of the working class in economic and political recon-
> struction, and therefore the participation of the most advanced demo-
> cratic forces, which are those of the Communist and Socialist parties.

But Togliatti noted that the situation had now changed, with the
opening of the East–West fissure.

> This situation has now changed. It still exists only in those countries in
> which the armies of the Soviet Union have guaranteed political stability,
> where the occupation forces have carefully refrained from intervening in
> the political life of the individual countries and have at the same time
> guaranteed the security of the political power won by those great popular
> blocs.

The picture Togliatti painted in the West, of course, was just the reverse: interference by the Anglo-American occupation forces; an offensive by national reactionary and capitalist forces; a rapid turn to the right by Social Democracy. But if that were the case, could a democratic, progressive perspective still be held out for the Western countries, or at least for Italy? Togliatti did not answer 'yes' or 'no'. He did not evade the question; indeed, he asked it explicity during his report. But he said that no firm answer was possible. 'It would be a mistake to answer 'yes' or 'no', he said. Mired in this uncertainty, Togliatti resorted to the classic expedient, the 'in so far as' argument. The perspective was still valid, but only 'on certain conditions' that he vaguely delineated. Among these was the success of tougher class battles and mass struggles and the abandoning of parliamentariest illusions.

This evasive response was not the least significant aspect of the political view of a man who had been one of the leaders of the Comintern and now leaned toward an attitude similar to that taken during hard times in the past, although he did not regard it as inevitable that things would again be like 1929–30 or 1938–39. The onset of the Cold War was clearly perceptible in his position (a brief summary of which was made public in *l'Unità*).[14] The 'new roads' to socialism were now in crisis East and West. In the East they were promptly abandoned, while in the West the Communist parties were already asking themselves a different question: had they made opportunist errors immediately after the war, if now, only two years later, they were forced to declare a halt to the process initiated with the anti-fascist alliances that went beyond the working class socially and beyond the Socialist–Communist united front politically? Togliatti did not evade this question, but once again his answer was highly problematic.

I do not know if we were too afraid of the danger of breaking the alliance, of civil war and foreign intervention. Nor do I know whether, at given moments, we could have brought the popular forces to bear far more decisively, even challenging the reactionary forces of our country in open struggle. . . . But when the national unity of our country was threatened at the end of the war, and the very existence of the Italian state was in doubt, we prevented that threat from becoming a reality. I believe that this is the fundamental fact that must be credited to our party. If we had accepted the challenge of civil war at certain points — in particular when that challenge could have been accepted, between July and October 1945 — what would the result have been? Perhaps part of Italy, having escaped the control of Anglo-American troops, would be more advanced economically and politically today. But the rest of the country would not be free, independent, and united. I believe that in view of the results we have obtained, we can consider any partial errors we may have made, whether nationally or in individual localities, as of secondary importance.

Togliatti's answer to the question of whether or not an opportunity had been missed, while not conclusive, neither evaded the issue nor argued from the standpoint of the interests of any particular party, class, or international camp. It was the proud response of a political force that had gained an awareness of its own national historic role. It was especially significant that Togliatti gave that answer now. In discussions with Longo and Reale, who were about to leave for the founding conference of the Cominform, Togliatti suggested another motive for the PCI behaviour to which Stalin was more sensitive: namely, that aversion of the threat of civil war was also advantageous for Soviet policy in 1945. When Secchia asked him in December 1947 whether it would not be a good idea to press the class struggle further and to intensify political opposition to the Christian Democratic government, Stalin answered in the negative: 'it is not possible today.' It would lead to an insurrection, and insurrection had to be avoided. [15]

Stalin assigned the Communist parties of the West an auxiliary role. He had no use for illegal parties, since any insurrection was doomed to failure, and the USSR was certainly in no position to rush to its aid. In the summer of 1947 Thorez was less pessimistic (and less realistic) about France than Togliatti was about Italy. He simply said that 'reaction has scored a point' by expelling the Communists from government, and he bitterly attacked not so much the Americans as French Social Democracy and the capitalist forces it protected. But Thorez too was beginning to wonder whether the prospect of new democracy, of the gradual conquest of an advanced democratic system, was still correct. He answered more or less as Togliatti did. He claimed for the PCF the merit of having begun, back at the time of the Popular Front, to seek a road to socialism 'appropriate to our own country'. What would decide how to go further? 'It is the struggle, the battle itself, that will decide: it depends on the way we conduct ourselves in uniting, organizing, and leading the people in the striving for new democracy and further toward socialism.' [16]

There was no renunciation of the previous line. In an unusual move for the PCF, Thorez now held up the Italian Communist Party as an exemplary mass party. The PCF, he acknowledged, was not sufficiently oriented to the masses, and still had too traditional a notion of the party. Thorez anticipated possible objections from the left, even on the concept of 'people's democracy'. And he parried them cleverly: in the East, he said, it was correct to create a system that, while not challenging the principle of the dictatorship of the proletariat, sought to combine the forms of parliamentary democracy with the rising power of the working class. For France he repeated that what he had said in his *Times* interview was correct, including his defence of a freely elected parliament:

> When we affirmed this for our country, we were correct, and we still are. We do not have a democracy of a new type in our country. If we had such a democracy, we would be in government, indeed in the leadership of government. But there are elements that can permit a transition to this kind of democracy. Nationalizations. The organization of the Factory Committees. The growing role of the workers organizations and of the Communist Party.[17]

Such were the tensions aroused by the turn of events in the West's two largest Communist parties. Party members wondered whether they had made mistakes, and if so, how and when. The correctness of the line was reaffirmed; there was insistence on the party's national role. At the same time, these parties were preparing for a new and open conflict with international and national reaction. There were therefore calls for greater centralism in the movement, which would soon be brusquely introduced. The leadership groups of some of the emerging People's Democracies took similar attitudes. They had accepted Moscow's veto of their use of the Marshall Plan. Did that automatically mean that they had to renounce the 'new roads'? Not all of them were yet prepared to do so, least of all the Czechs and the Poles.

Before the summer of 1947 was out, Moscow took its new initiative: the constitution of an organ called the Information Bureau of Communist and Workers Parties, better known as the 'Cominform'.

Notes

1. See Boffa, *Storia dell'Unione Sovietica*, vol. 2, pp. 355-57 and Brzezinski, *The Soviet Bloc*, p. 44n.

2. Boffa, *Storia dell'Unione Sovietica*, vol. 2, p. 313.

3. 'Report on the Journals *Zvezda* and *Leningrad*, 1947', in A.A. Zhdanov, *On Literature, Music and Philosophy*, London 1950, pp. 19-51.

4. 'Speech at a Conference of Soviet Philosophical Workers, 1947', in ibid., pp. 76–112.

5. Werth, *Russia: the Post-War Years*, p. 253.

6. *The Memoirs of Harry S. Truman*, vol. 2, *Years of Trial and Hope, 1946–1953*, London 1956, p. 121.

7. See Werth, *Russia: the Post-War Years*, p. 266.

8. Claudín, *The Communist Movement*, p. 433.

9. See Werth, *Russia: the Post-War Years*, pp. 112-13.

10. See Giuliano Procacci, 'Aspetti e problemi della politica estera sovietica', in *Momenti e problemi della storia dell'Urss*, p. 51.

11. See Vincent Auriol, *Mon septennat*, Paris 1970, p. 36. See also Fauvet, *Histoire du PCF*, vol. 2, p. 198.

12. See Giorgio Amendola, 'La rottura della coalizione tripartita', in *Gli anni della repubblica*, 1976, pp. 83-84; Enzo Collotti, 'La collocazione internazionale dell'Italia dall'armistizio alle premesse dell'aleanza atlantica', in *Italia dalla Liberazione alla repubblica*, Milan 1977, p. 99; Ennio di Nolfo, 'Problemi della politica estera italiana: 1943–50', *Storia e politica*, vol. 14, no. 1-2, January-June 1975, p. 310.

13. From the full text of Togliatti's report, which the author was able to consult in the PCI leadership's archive. There is also a copy of the text in the Secchia Archive, at the Feltrinelli Institute, Milan. Enzo Collotti called this report 'one of the most important and interesting texts by Togliatti during this period'. (From the presentation of the 'Relazione sulla situazione italiana presentata da Secchia a Mosca nel dicembre 1947', in *Archivo Pietro Secchia 1945–1973*, Milan 1979, p. 610.)

14. See the issue of 2 July 1947.

15. From the *Archivo Pietro Secchia*, p. 426.

16. 'À la conference de la Fédération de la Seine', concluding speech, 8 June 1947, in Maurice Thorez, *Oeuvres*, Paris 1965, vol. 23, p. 134.

17. Ibid., p. 136.

24

The Cominform:
a New Freeze

We have seen that throughout the succession of Communist zigzags, turns, and counter-turns of the critical decade from the eve of the Second World War to the post-war period, the primary factor was the requisites of Soviet foreign policy, to which ideological constructions and historical arguments were adapted, though these were also part and parcel of the mentality of the leadership groups and in turn influenced their judgements, attitudes, and states of mind.

The Soviet–German Pact of 1939, Molotov's 'theoretical' speeches of 1940, Stalin's glorification of democratic rights and even of the Anglo-Saxon political system in 1941–44: all these are examples. But no decision in the international Communist movement was ever more pragmatic and 'state-motivated' than the foundation of the Cominform in 1947. And never was the real motive more carefully buried in a flood of doctrinal argumentation and principled pronouncements; between 1947 and 1955–56 a thick new layer of dogmatism settled over the Communist movement, which had in the meantime become the ruling power in half of Europe.

Stalin made his decision to create a new international organ in the summer of 1947. It was his initial response to the Marshall Plan and the Truman Doctrine. All the invited parties attended the founding conference, which was held from 22 to 27 September in Poland, in Szkalarska Probea, 'a small town noted for its glass factories a few dozen kilometres from Wroclaw'.[1] The sessions were held in a large villa, 'a magnificent residence that once belonged to some German noble, surrounded by an impressive birch forest'. It was normally used as a vacation home for police officials of the new Polish state. The arriving delegates were not quite sure of the agenda. The invitations had arrived quite recently. They had been officially sent by the host party, the Polish, but it was no secret that the initiative had come from Moscow. Everyone was somewhat surprised by this, from the Yugoslav Communist leaders[2] to the Italian. When questioned about the matter twenty-five years later, Luigi Longo said: 'We had been told very generally that the aim of the conference was to establish a link among Communist parties, but we had no idea that we would be presented with such a sharp political turn, and still less that we would find ourselves under attack.'[3]

One of the most revealing indices of Stalin's intentions was the list of who was present and who was not. The Cominform was a primarily European affair, for Europe was now the epicentre of the Cold War. In his report to the conference, Zhdanov paid scant attention to Asia. In fact, the Asian component of the Communist movement was wholly absent: neither the Chinese nor the Vietnamese were invited, and there were no representatives from India. No one from the countries of Latin American and Africa attended either. In this the Cominform was profoundly different from the Comintern. Eurocentrism was also reflected in ways other than geographic: the intent was to mobilize parties and social forces around immediate foreign-policy objectives (the struggle against the Marshall Plan, the organization of Communist regimes in Eastern Europe); each was allotted specific tasks in the conflict with the United States and its allies. The conference addressed itself to European 'democratic forces'; it condemned the Social Democratic parties, or at least their leaders (especially the British Labour Party and the SFIO), as servants of imperialism, but not in the name of world revolution — now a forbidden phrase — but in the name of peace and the national independence of peoples.

Only two really important Western parties were invited: the French and the Italian. The Belgian party was not there (although it had also been expelled from its national government in 1948), nor the Spanish (whose freedom struggle had been one of the high points of the Third International), nor the British, which had played an important part during the war as the mainstay and voice of the Comintern in its last year. No less striking was the absence of the Scandinavian countries, particularly Finland where the Communist Party was strong. The USSR was manifestly content for this country to remain friendly not being drawn into the circle of states hegemonized by Washington. There was no attempt to 'Communize' Finland, in all likelihood both because of the experience of the Finnish resistance in 1940 and because political tension in Finland would give fresh impetus to Western anti-Soviet propoganda and could provoke serious incidents.

The Greek Communists were also absent. The Greek CP was now

embroiled in a new civil war: twenty-three thousand partisans had already taken up arms, and the first American aid to the government troops had arrived (a joint US–Greek General Staff was even formed in November). Greece was too much the hot spot, and Stalin had no intention of directly involving the USSR. When he received a Yugoslav delegation at the beginning of 1948, he told Kardelj: 'Is it possible that you believe in the victory of the insurrection in Greece? . . . It is a real illusion to think that the Western powers will let the Communists take Greece. You are nurturing the same illusion as the Greeks, and this is creating political difficulties for all of us.'[4]

The military and political limits of the new organization were therefore fairly clear. It was an instrument of 'positional warfare', and certainly not an offensive weapon. The core of the affiliated parties were those of ths Soviet *glacis*. But even here there were significant exceptions.

First let us list those present. Apart from the Soviets (Zhdanov and Malenkov), there were representatives from Poland (Gomulka and Minc), Bulgaria (Chervenkov and Poptomov), Yugoslavia (Kardelj and Djilas), Romania (Gheorghiu-Dej and Ana Pauker), Hungary (Farkas and Révai), Czechoslovkia (Slánský and Baštonavský). Attending for the PCI were Luigi Longo and Eugenio Reale (who was the Italian ambassador to Poland just after the war); for the French there were Étienne Fajon and Jacques Duclos. Most of these parties were not represented by their general secretaries — neither Tito nor Togliatti, Rákosi, Gottwald, Thorez, nor Dimitrov attended. But that was not because they had rejected invitations. Stalin shrewdly wanted to create the Cominform without any particular fanfare, another deliberate departure from the experience of the Comintern.[5]

As for the parties excluded from the exercise, the absence of the East German SED was not surprising: officially, this was a united Socialist party, Grotewohl's as much as Ulbricht's. In any event, at the Moscow conference of foreign ministers the USSR had argued that Germany should be united, neutral, and demilitarized. It was therefore advisable not to flaunt the close association of East Germany with the other East European states. The Albanian CP was not invited either. Some have wondered why, and have suggested that Stalin did not want a party so completely subordinate to the Yugoslav CP at the conference. That, however, would imply that from the outset he intended to reduce the Yugoslav representation — which, while not impossible, has never been proven.[6] The absence of the Albanian party therefore remains a mystery, especially since it turned out to be anything but pro-Tito. It must be remembered, however, that although the founding partners of the Cominform club did not throw open the membership books in the years to come, this did not prevent other Communist parties from joining the Cominform chorus with articles and statements of position in the new organization's press.

In 1947 the Yugoslav Communists were the star pupils, so to speak. In his report to the PCI Central Committee on 11 November 1947, Togliatti himself said that 'the Yugoslav People's Republic is the most advanced of the new democratic regimes'.[7] And this was after Longo and Reale had told him about the broadside of criticism that had been directed at the Italians from the opposite shore of the Adriatic. It may be added that in this context 'more advanced' meant 'further left'. The Yugoslav delegates hailed the struggle of the Greek partisans and considered the Greek situation better than the Italian or French: they held precisely the illusions for which Stalin chided them even before he pilloried them. But the intransigent line of the CPY, with its adventurist inclination, did not prevail at the conference. Instead it was used as a pretext for a call for common discipline in the movement, for a new 'Bolshevization'.

Were there also other hints more directly related to the internal Soviet situation? The question arises because of the strong insistence of the two Soviet delegates, Zhdanov (considered Stalin's *dauphin*) and Malenkov, on the importance of the ideological struggle. Western Europe had 'lined up' behind the Marshall Plan, one of whose aims was economic recovery. Adam Ulam observed:

> This restored prosperity in the West would in turn exert irresistible attraction on the not yet fully secured Soviet satellites. Hadn't Poland and Czechoslovakia been ready to join the Marshall Plan until pressured against it by the USSR? The defection of Russia's satellites would then present a challenge to the survival of the Communist system in the USSR. Thus into the Americans' 'containment' policy the morbidly suspicious Kremlin mind soon read the implications of what became known some years later as the 'rollback' scheme.[8]

The official purpose of the conference was to create an organ of consultation and liaison, the lack of which, it was argued, was particularly lamentable in the new situation that arose in the summer of 1947, as the Socialist and Social Democratic parties were striving, albeit slowly, to reconstruct the Second International. But why was a new organization so necessary when the 'hierarchy' of which Luigi Longo spoke[9] was more strictly respected by the various Communist parties than ever before, both in terms of their fervent acknowledgement of the historic primacy and doctrinal infallibility of the Soviet Union and in terms of complete deference to the land of socialism in all the great questions of foreign policy? All these matters remained the exclusive province of the leading country. Another Italian Communist leader, Gian Carlo Pajetta, made the point more recently:

> If one wants to understand the atmosphere of those years, as well as our assessment of the prospects and consequently our attitude on international questions, it is important to remember that at the time we were convinced that the Soviets, and only the Soviets, were capable of understanding and acting on the great international questions. . . . In the last instance, Soviet decisions had to be well founded, since we recognized that the leading role of Stalin and the USSR was based in part on their superior experience and knowledge of the international situation.[10]

The central question — why bother to found the Cominform, if the USSR could confidently exercise its supremacy without the impediment of collective organs? — can be answered by examining events after the formation of the Information Bureau. Although it had no independent decision-making powers whatever, and never became a 'political subject' (something Stalin was careful to avoid from the very outset), the Cominform was quite useful as a means of pressure, instrument of internal cohesion, and vehicle for transmitting public directives and propaganda slogans to the mass of Communists and party sympathizers. With the Cominform, the various Communist parties could be constantly influenced, both collectively and singly, without any orders appearing to come from the Kremlin. Not for nothing had Stalin already conceived the idea (which he explained to Zhdanov, who in turn passed it on to Eugenio Reale) of a common press organ which would begin as a fortnightly and later became a weekly. He even had a title in mind: *For a Stable Peace, for People's Democracy!*, a combination of the two objectives set for the Communist movement. It was an ugly enough title, and when Reale complained and suggested something shorter ('I cannot imagine an Italian worker walking up to a news-stand and asking for a copy of 'For a Stable Peace, for People's Democracy!'), Zhdanov chided him: 'There is no such thing as a short title of a long title. Titles have to express a concept, a programme. If you want to know the truth, the title was invented by Stalin, who gave it to me by telephone this morning.'[11]

The hierarchical order was mirrored in the conference sessions. First came two long reports by Zhdanov and Malenkov, which took up the entire opening day, 22 September. The basic theme of

Zhdanov's report was that the world was divided into two counter-posed camps and that the border between them was political, social, and ideological as well as military. There was the 'anti-democratic imperialist camp' on the one side and the 'democratic anti-imperialist camp' on the other. [12] Although the second adjective was familiar enough in Communist and Marxist terminology, the first now had a particular connotation. 'Democratic' was not meant to denote democratic-socialist or bourgeois-democratic; it was instead synonymous with People's Democracy, systems and movements based on people's power, on the working class, or rather on the party, acting as the people's representative. The United States was the 'major leading force' of the imperialist camp; alongside it Zhdanov listed France and Britain ('satellite' countries), Holland and Belgium (colonialist states), as well as Turkey and Greece, the countries of the Middle East and South America, and finally China (Nationalist China, of course). Zhdanov also briefly mentioned West Germany and Italy as states in which the United States was 'legally consolidating privileged positions', luring them away from Britain; this was also happening in Iran, Turkey, Greece, Japan, Afghanistan, and even China.

The 'anti-imperialist and anti-fascist' forces constituted the other camp, of which 'the USSR and the new democratic countries are the pillars'. It is of more than passing interest that when these countries were cited by name — Yugoslavia, Poland, Czechoslovakia, Bulgaria, and Albania — Romania and Hungary were missing. These were specially classed as 'countries that have broken with imperialism and have resolutely embarked upon the road of democratic development', as had Finland, though only 'partially.'

The geopolitical map drawn by the reporter for areas outside Europe was somewhat haphazard. 'Indonesia and Vietnam are part of the anti-imperialist camp, and India, Egypt, an Syria are sympathetic to it.' The fluidity of the report reflected the turbulence of the colonial and semi-colonial world. There is no such explanation for Zhdanov's silence about a phenomenon that had already assumed truly massive proprtions: the advance of the Chinese Communists. At that very moment — September 1947 — civil war was raging in China. [13] Mao's People's Army had liberated all the rural areas of Shantung as far as ths Hwang-ho, and had gained control of the Yellow River Valley. At stake was the fate of an enormous territory, as an army of more than 3 million Nationalists faced the 2-million-strong Communist army. Zhdanov's silence did not mean that the Soviets were not aiding Mao's army (and US aid to Chiang Kai-shek was massive). It may have been a sign that Stalin was sceptical about the possibility of a rapid Communist victory, or perhaps that Soviet interest was now focused primarily on Europe. In fact, when Zhdanov turned from states to peoples, he was very general in describing the role of the independence movements in the countries outside Europe, whereas he placed the Communist parties of Western Europe squarely in the anti-imperialist camp, assigning them a particular task:

> A particular task devolves upon the Communist parties of France, Italy, Britain, and the other countries. They must hold aloft the banner of defence of national independence and the sovereignty of their countries. If the Communist parties hold their positions resolutely, if they refuse to allow themselves to be intimidated and blackmailed, if they courageously uphold a stable peace and people's democracy, national sovereignty and the liberty and independence of their countries, if they are able to take the lead of all the forces prepared to defend the cause of national honour and independence in the struggle against attempts to subjugate their countries economically and politically, then no plan of subjugation of Europe can succeed.[14]

Plan of subjugation. Zhdanov's entire report was an indictment of American imperialism, whose thirst for world domination was attributed to its inherently aggressive nature, its need to avert a crisis in its own society, and a dynamic of military rearmament and expansionism that was both serious and dangerous. But there was no talk of an imminent threat of war, and Zhdanov was careful to reaffirm that Soviet foreign policy was still inspired by the possibility of peaceful coexistence between the socialist and capitalist systems. The predominant impression was of a concerned reporter, prudent in substance, who unhesitatingly assigned eminently defensive tasks to the European Communist parties, especially those of Western Europe, which were called upon to 'take up' the cause of peace and national independence. The final conference resolution, approved by all nine participants, listed only defensive tasks, insisting that the greatest danger was to underestimate their own forces and overestimate those of the adversary. They had to 'close ranks'.[15] All parties had to unite around the Soviet Union, which was advancing along the road of 'communism in one country'. It has been noted that there was no talk of socialist objectives for the new democratic countries. The platform of the 'anti-imperialist struggle for freedom and independence' applied to them as well.

The fundamental task was still the 'building of communism' in the USSR. The leap forward in Communist eschatology was the cement holding this bloc together, and its corner-stone remained defence of the Soviet state. The only concept of socialism present in the report was in relation to the consolidation of the USSR. The decisive factor in the future of the workers movement was the growth, implicitly both military and economic, of the USSR. This argumentation resulted in a doubly irrational contention: the USSR was now defined as socialist, and the putrescent world of capitalism in crisis condemned as incurable.[16]

No psychoanalytical explanation is necessary, of course. The conference delegates believed that the sharpening of political and social struggles in their countries fully justified Soviet alarm. The PCF and PCI needed no ideological guidance to see the conservative offensive under way in France and Italy. Tension was rising within the front in Czechoslovakia as well as in Poland, Hungary, and Romania, where the opposition groups, especially the peasant parties, were becoming more self-assertive and some Communists, even some left Socialists, now sought to provoke a shown-down. Soviet desire to prevent the success of the Marshall Plan (the implementation of which was instead accelerated by the foundation of the Cominform) merged with its determination to assure the cohesion and invulnerability of the *glacis*. Here the turn was to be sharp indeed. The purpose of the new organization was to provide an ideological and propagandistic cover to establish and promote the conviction and consciousness of a monolithic 'bloc' led by the USSR.

There was to be no more talk of 'new roads' to socialism. The definition of 'people's democracy', which now became the common term, was altered to conform to the Yugoslav version, which Kardelj repeated at the conference: people's democracy was a system in which the Communists held power and exercised it within the state. Polemicizing not only against the Italians and the French, but also against his East European comrades, Kardelj said, 'The opinion has been expressed that any government in which Communists participate is automatically a new people's democratic government. This view is not only false, but quite dangerous. People's democracy begins when the working class, in alliance with the other toiling masses, hold the key positions of state power.'[17]

Kardelj's concept was defended by a tactic that the other eight conference participants used against the Yugoslavs equally unscrupulously less than a year later: any interpretation of 'new democracy' that contained an element of political pluralism was denounced. Did anyone continue to defend pluralism? According to notes taken by Hungarian sources, both Slánský and Gomulka did so with resolution, even winning over the majority of delegates, except the Soviets and the Yugoslavs.[18] This contention has not been established beyond doubt, but if true it would explain the further 'turn of the screw' in subsequent months. The second Soviet reporter, Malenkov, emphasized the need to fortify what was being called with mounting insistence the 'ideological front'. What was striking was that the exhortation was directed not so much at the other parties Zhdanov had already dealt with them in his report) but at the Communist Party of the Soviet Union and at Soviet culture more generally — and quite sharply too. It was now argued that the imperialist offensive to upset the 'anti-democratic, anti-imperialist' camp was concentrated precisely on the ideological front. Culture as a Trojan Horse. Malenkov repeated Zhdanov's criticism of authors and philosophers in the USSR:

> In recent times the party has had to wage an energetic struggle against various manifestations of servility to the boureois culture of the West. This spirit of servility, which has been manifested in certain circles of our intellectuals, represents a hangover from the terrible past of Tsarist Russia. . . . The hangovers of this capitalist conception are now being used by agents of American and English imperialism, which spare no effort in their search for points of support within Soviet soceity for their espionage and anti-Soviet propaganda. The agents of the foreign spy services obstinately seek out points of weakness and vulnerability among certain wavering groups of our intellectuals . . . . They easily fall prey to the foreign spy services.[19]

The frigid atmosphere of the conference is eloquently represented by this sort of 'denunciation', which brought both the Communist movement and life in the USSR back to the climate of the years of the Great Terror. Fresh acts of repression soon followed, as mounting suspicion led to the paroxysm of Stalin's last years, culminating in the supposed plot of the 'Zionist' doctors, 'assassins in white coats'. The new wave of police repression in the USSR did not reach pre-war proportions, although forced labour in concentration camps was widely used once again. But in the People's Democracies a Lesser Terror raged against leaders and militants, and against political opponents too. It is beyond dispute that methods of torture and forced confessions were used again: this was officially admitted in the countries concerned during the period of 'de-Stalinization'. The most rigorous and dramatic testimony came from the Czechoslovak Communist Artur London.[20] In the meantime, the USSR's breathless race to close the atomic-weapons gap with the United States succeeded sooner than expected. The first Soviet atomic device was exploded in the summer of 1949. Once again productive efforts were completely dominated by militarization.

In 1947 the brakes were just beginning to be applied. And as I mentioned, the Yugoslavs were the most zealous. Zhdanov suggested to them that they launch a bitter attack on the French and Italian Communists. Both Kardelj and Djilas went at it heart and soul. They later said that they had fallen into a trap, a Soviet provocation intended to sow resentment against Tito's associates the better to be able to isolate them and put them in the dock the following year.[21]

Whether this suspicion of Machiavellianism was well founded or not, the Yugoslav attack on the Western parties had a very specific aim for Stalin and his representatives: to get the PCI and PCF to commit themselves against the Marshall Plan more strongly, through mass agitation and more energetic opposition in parliament, although without going so far as to get themselves outlawed. They too had to drop all reference to 'new roads', which were now resolutely abandoned. The Yugoslavs denounced the Italian and French Communists for opportunism during the resistance and for illusions about parliamentary democracy and dialogue with Catholocism. They were attacked for having allowed themselves to be ejected from government without resistance. According to Reale — the official texts do not mention this controversy — Longo reacted with dignity to the Yugoslav offensive, without repudiating his party's past conduct, whereas Duclos obliged with a painful self-criticism.[22] In any case, the attack had its effects. Self-criticism was evident in the official account of Longo's speech to the conference (in which he referred to the PCI's expulsion from government as 'De Gasperi's coup d'etat'): 'The Communist Party was particularly lethargic when we were expelled from the government and thrown back into opposition. Our opposition was manifested primarily in words, in our press and our meetings.'[23]

The preparations for the Sixth Congress of the PCI were affected by the accusations made at the Cominform conference. 'An element of contradiction and restraint' was introduced, and had significant effects.[24] Even in the PCI, there would be no further talks of national roads to socialism until 1956. In July 1948 Togliatti said: 'For everyone, there can be only one guide: in the field of doctrine it is Marxism – Leninism; in the field of real forces it is the country that is already socialist and in which a seasoned Marxist – Leninist party tempered by three revolutions and two victorious wars plays a leading role.'[25]

Just a few days later, Togliatti was seriously wounded in an assassination attempt, and the Italian working class responded with a genuine revolutionary tremor. Masses of people were now caught up in the atmosphere of Cold War, of global confrontation, and the 'choice of camp' was no longer open to discussion. There was great social tension in France too. While Thorez admitted in November 1947 that serious opportunistic errors had been made in the recent past, Duclos branded the Socialists in the Assembly as lackeys of American imperialism, and the Gaullists as outright 'neo-fascists'.[26]

The characteristic features of the entire 'Cominform period' (1947–55), all of which were already apparent *in nuce* at the founding conference, cannot be separated from the dramatic broader context of the Cold War, which was just then beginning. The Cominform reflected the tension of this East–West schism which in coming years spread far beyond Europe, as the 1948–49 Berlin crisis was followed by the Korean war. The conflict continued through new upheavals in Asia, from the victory of Communist China to the liberation struggle against French colonialism in Vietnam and the first workers revolt in the 'socialist camp', in East Berlin in 1953. But the new freeze in the Communist movement also marked the opening of contradictions that could not be suppressed by the monolithism of the late Stalin period.

The 1945–46 interlude was over. The process of absorption and liquidation of other political forces in Eastern Europe continued rapidly through the autumn of 1947. Indeed, it is even possible that the remnants of Czech, Polish, and Bulgarian resistance convinced the Soviets that this process had to be accelerated sharply. The East European Socialists, or those of them that resigned themselves to the inevitable, dissolved into the Communist parties, where they lost all capacity for political intervention. The peasant parties and the bourgeois-democratic, liberal, and Catholic parties either disappeared or were completely divested of all vitality. By 1948–49 there was no longer any trace of genuine pluralism in political organizations, parliaments, or trade unions behind the 'iron curtain'.

The Romanian Socialist Party fused with the Communists in January 1948. The same year saw fusion in Czechoslovakia (April), Hungary (June), Poland, and Bulgaria (December). Pressure was heavy wherever the Socialists and Social Democrats resisted absorption, as in Czechoslovakia, where in February 1948 the Communists, with the support of the USSR and the consent of the majority of the working class, organized a coup d'état that effectively smashed constitutional legality. All power passed into Gottwald's hands,

Beneš resigned shortly afterwards, and Masaryk, the minister of foreign affairs, killed himself. In Poland the Mikolajczyk opposition had been hobbled even earlier. He left the country twenty days after the founding of the Cominform. The change of regime was accompanied by a change in economic direction, along lines inspired by the Soviet experience, with some variations.

But although it was several years before this process encountered serious difficulties and rising imbalances (and although successes in industrialization were registered), the Cominform as such, and with it the rigid subordination of the Communist movement to the Soviet hierarchy, ran aground on an unexpected reef at the very beginning of the voyage, the reef of Yugoslavia. Only the essential point is of interest to us here. Tito and the great majority of the Yugoslav leadership group, which remained loyal to him, were able to resist Soviet pressure, refusing to submerge all national autonomy into the *glacis*. Stalin would no longer tolerate any real spirit of independence in his own zone of influence. At the beginning of 1948 he brusquely repudiated Dimitrov's plan for a Balkan federation, treating the Communist International's former secretary to a scolding in *Pravda*.[27] But an unexpected reaction came from Yugoslavia, the motivation and secret of which was precisely national consciousness, the pride of a revolution that had triumphed on its own strength and now had the courage to defy the omnipotent despot.

The Yugoslav schism exhibits all the traditional Comintern logic (including a thunderous 'excommunication'). But there was also a historic novelty that would have been inconceivable in the days of 'socialism in one country': one of the 'branches' of the movement proved strong enough not to yield. Comparison with the case of Trotsky and the Bolshevik oppositions of the twenties is instructive. In 1936–38 Stalin turned Trotsky into a 'demon' in order to bring about his own personal tyranny. Now, in June 1948, Tito became the devil. Just as it had been claimed that Trotsky was no longer the exponent and symbol of a deviation or error within the movement but had become the representative of an enemy class, an agent of fascism, and a tool of foreign secret services, so in 1948 the same epithets were soon being hurled at the leader of the Yugoslav Communists.

First came the list of ideological deviations: nationalistic spirit, but also an extremist policy toward the peasantry; the disguising of the Communist party within a Front, but also 'Turkish-style despotism'.[28] From this list of the most varied kinds of errors (with which the entire Communist movement went along, accepting and parroting the most improbable accusations), a leap was made: Tito became an agent of American imperialism, an executioner of his people, a traitor. Searing indictments flowed monotonously one after another in the Cominform's leaden press organ. Grotesque cartoons depicted Tito dripping with blood, his epaulets and beret sporting dollar signs. The logic of the Terror was reproduced in another respect as well. Just as the Kirov assassination in 1934 opened the road to the 1936 trials, so now the denigration of Tito was a prelude to the trials of leaders in the 'People's Democracies' in 1949 and the early 1950s. All the defendants in these trials were accused of having relations with 'Tito's clique of assassins', of plotting to overthrow the people's power.

The fundamental motive for the blow against the Yugoslav leadership was to demonstrate to everyone else that absolute submission was required. 'It was a conscious attempt by the leadership of the Soviet party and by Stalin himself, acting in the spirit of a great power, to compel the leaders of the CP of Yugoslavia to total obedience.'[29]

The lesson was meant for the others as well. Before the persecution of deviationists in each People's Democracy, the leaders indulged in merciless ideological self-criticism. Dimitrov stated in July 1948 that 'the peculiarities of the so-called Bulgarian road to socialism were exaggerated', adding that 'the transition to socialism cannot be achieved without the dictatorship of the proletariat', that the Soviet experience 'is the only instance of building socialism for us and for the other People's Democracies', and that 'whoever is not a Leninist and a Stalinist cannot be a real Marxist'.[30]

In December 1948 the Hungarians Gerö and Rákosi wrote in the Cominform organ that 'the basic features of socialist construction in the Soviet Union are universally valid', that 'there are no specific national roads to socialism'. Gomulka, who opposed Yugoslavia's expulsion from the Cominform and argued that there were national specificities in the building of socialism, was summoned to the dock in Poland. When the Polish Workers Party and the Socialist Party fused in December 1948, Bierut was named secretary, and he attacked the notion of national roads to socialism. The Albanian Party and the SED, although not part of the Cominform, also attacked the Yugoslav Communists.

According to Khrushchev's famous report to the Twentieth Congress of the CPSU in 1956, Stalin once exclaimed: 'All I have to do is lift a finger and that's the end of Tito.' But things did not work out that way. The struggle against Tito was a big defeat for Stalin in his own lifetime. Perhaps he mistakenly thought he could crush the Yugoslav secession easily because he underestimated the cohesion and courage of the 'reprobates', the effectiveness of their appeal to the country's working masses, and their ability to walk the tightrope of the Cold War without aligning themselves with either of the two camps. In the end, the Yugoslav case opened the first historic schism in the international Communist movement. The element of national autonomy later became predominant in the various new nerve centres of Communism.

Today, decades after the 1947–48 events, it is clear that this historic schism was inevitable in the long run. In Asia Chinese Communism had even greater potential for independence, and in Western Europe the entire workers movement — functioning under conditions of political democracy, with its experiences of mass struggle, its conquest of new social and cultural positions, and its genuine pluralist dynamic — could not long be held in the straitjacket of obedience to and conformity with Stalinism. It is no accident that in 1956, when the great crisis erupted, the issues of autonomy, the search for 'national roads', and refusal to accept the concept and practice of a movement guided by a particular party and state were the first to re-emerge.

In the band of satellite countries, this schism — like the expansion of autonomy, the need for democracy, and the assertion of freedom and independence — was smothered by force. But Budapest of 1956, Prague of 1968, and today's Poland have passed into historic memory as 'tragedies of socialism'. That in itself is counter-evidence of the necessity for a tendency and impulse the first expressions of which, in 1935–37, 1941–43, and 1945–47, we have tried to follow through the troubled years covered by our research.

Notes

1. Reale, *Nascita del Cominform*, p. 18.
2. Edvard Kardelj, *Memorie degli anni di ferro*, Rome 1980, p. 109.
3. Bocca, *Palmiro Togliatti*, p. 478. According to Secchia, during one of his meetings with Gomulka in Poland after the middle of August, he was informed of a 'plan to convoke a meeting of the CPs of various countries, at least the most important parties . . . for an exchange of views' (*Archivio Pietro Secchia*, p. 208).
4. Kardelj, *Memorie degli anni di ferro*, pp. 121-22.
5. See, on this thesis, Marcou, *Le Kominform*, pp. 45-46.
6. See Adam B. Ulam, *Titoism and the Cominform*, Cambridge, Mass. 1952, p. 49, in which it is argued that the Albanian absence cannot be explained solely by the fact that the country and party were under Yugoslav protection.

7. From the complete text of the report (archive of the PCI).

8. Ulam, *Expansion and Containment*, p. 436.

9. See pp. 201-2 of the present volume.

10. Gian Carlo Pajetta, *Le crisi che ho vissuto: Budapest, Prague, Warsaw*, Rome 1982, pp. 30 and 41.

11. Reale, *Nascita del Cominform*, p. 51.

12. I am quoting from the text of the speech, reprinted with other writings in Zhdanov, *Politics and Ideology*, pp. 25-54.

13. See Collotti Pischel, *Storia della rivoluzione cinese*, pp. 421-23.

14. From *Politics and Ideology*, p. 54.

15. See 'Déclaration', in *Pour une paix durable, pour une democratie populaire!*, vol. 1, no. 1, Belgrade, 10 November 1947.

16. Droz, in *Storia del socialismo*, vol. 4, p. 531.

17. From Kardelj's report, in *Pour une paix durable, pour une démocratie populaire!*.

18. See Marcou, *Le Kominform*, pp. 51-55.

19. From the text published in *Pour une paix durable, pour une démocratie populaire!*, vol. 1, no. 2, 1 December 1947.

20. Artur London, *On Trial*.

21. Kardelj, *Memorie degli anni di ferro*, pp. 111-12.

22. *Nascita del Cominform*, pp. 47-48.

23. From the report published in *Pour une paix durable, pour une démocratie populaire!*, vol. 2, no. 1, 1 January 1948.

24. Alessandro Natta, 'La resistenza e la formazione del "partito nuovo" ', in *Problemi di storia del Pci*, Rome 1971, p. 59.

25. Palmiro Togliatti, 'Considerazioni preliminari', *l'Unità*, 2 July 1948.

26. Fauvet, *Histoire du PCF*, vol. 2, pp. 201-12.

27. See Brzezinski, *The Soviet Bloc*, pp. 56-57; Kardelj, *Memorie degli anni di ferro*, pp. 99-104.

28. See 'Risoluzione dell'Ufficio d'Informazione sulla situazione esistente nel Partito comunista di Jugoslavia', *Pour une paix durable, pour une démocratie populaire!*, vol. 2, no. 16, 15 July 1948.

29. Jaroslav Opat, 'Dall'antifascismo ai "socialismi reali": le democrazie popolari', in *Storia del marxismo*, vol. 3, II, p. 758.

30. Ibid., p. 759.

Index